M. Higgins, '91.

ALCHEMY

»PRACTISING ALCHEMIST« (SO-CALLED »FAUST«)

ETCHING BY REMBRANDT

ALCHEMY

THE MEDIEVAL ALCHEMISTS AND THEIR ROYAL ART

by

Johannes Fabricius

The Aquarian Press

An Imprint of HarperCollins*Publishers*

The Aquarian Press
An Imprint of HarperCollins*Publishers*
77–85 Fulham Palace Road,
Hammersmith, London W6 8JB

First published by Rosenkilde and Bagger, Copenhagen, 1976
Revised edition published by The Aquarian Press 1989
3 5 7 9 10 8 6 4

FOR MY AUNT

GERTRUD NIELSEN

A catalogue record for this book
is available from the British Library

ISBN 0 85030 832 1

Layout and typography by
Kirsten and Johannes Fabricus, Copenhagen
Printed in Great Britain by
Woolnough Bookbinding Limited,
Irthlingborough, Northamptonshire

CONTENTS

PREFACE

Alchemy attempts to elucidate the symbolic structure of the *opus alchymicum* and, in so doing, to shed light also on the structure of the individuation process — the developmental process that goes to form the individual, or the human personality. Jung formulated the problem in *Psychology and Alchemy* (§564) thus:

'I hold the view that the alchemist's hope of conjuring out of matter the philosophical gold, or the panacea, or the wonderful stone, was only in part an illusion, an effect of projection; for the rest it corresponded to certain psychic facts that are of great importance in the psychology of the unconscious. As is shown by the texts and their symbolism, the alchemist projected what I would call the process of individuation into the phenomena of chemical change. A scientific term like "individuation" does not mean that we are dealing with something known and finally cleared up, on which there is no more to be said. It merely indicates an as yet very obscure field of research much in need of exploration: the centralizing processes in the unconscious that go to form the personality. We are dealing with life-processes which, on account of their numinous character, have from time immemorial provided the strongest incentive to the formation of symbols. These processes are steeped in mystery; they pose riddles with which the human mind will long wrestle for a solution, and perhaps in vain.'

The solution offered by the present study explains the individuation process and its alchemical reflection in terms of a sustained regression into the unconscious during which the imprints of the individual's entire psychological and biological development are uncovered in symbolic form. The psychobiological frame of reference thus established for the alchemical work and the individuation process agrees with the unity of mind and matter emphasized by the alchemists, just as it conforms to Freud's conception of the unconscious as a reality to be understood within a psychobiological framework.

The chief sources of this reconstruction of the alchemical work are the medieval *Rosarium* series of the work and its engraved variant in the *Philosophia reformata*; the *Splendor solis* series, Barchusen's *Crowne of Nature* series, the *Pandora* series, the *Mutus liber* series, and the *Twelve Keys of Basil Valentine*. The literary sources of the *opus alchymicum* are the corpus of Hermetic writings collected in *De alchemia* (1541), *Ars chemica* (1566), *Artis auriferae* (1572), *Aureum vellus* (1598), *Theatrum chemicum* (1602-1661), *Theatrum chemicum britannicum* (1652), *Musaeum hermeticum* (1678), and *Bibliotheca chemica curiosa* (1702). The origin and history of the chief sources of *Alchemy*, pictorial and literary, are presented in the notes and the appendix, where the reader may also find a description of the few pictures not analyzed in the text. The book is a revised edition of the original which appeared in 1976 in a folio format at *Rosenkilde and Bagger*, Copenhagen.

Johannes Fabricius

1.

Ancient Origins of a Medieval Subculture

About 1520 an unknown German artist called the Petrarcha Master made two of the oldest-known pictures of alchemists at work (above and below). Fig.1 shows a couple of goldmakers frustrated by an unfortunate breakage at the hearth, causing the loss of weeks of labour. Fig.2 presents a mining scene with two workers gathering lumps of gold pouring out of a rich vein just struck (background). The book-keeper, engineers and workers function as parts of a greater whole saturated with Hermetic meanings and allusions: in the alchemical cave an old master reading in a book receives the philosophers' stone at the hands of the philosophers' son; the goldmakers' work is threatened by the winged dragon against which the group in the middle seeks protection by drawing a magical circle round them while searching for guidance in a Hermetic treatise. When these pictures were produced, alchemy was at its height in Europe after a period of growth lasting approximately two thousand years.

The art of alchemy is almost as old as human civilization itself. In their quest for metallic transmutation, the European alchemists or 'goldmakers' continued a venerable tradition originating as far back as the Greek and Egyptian civilizations. The alchemists of the Middle Ages learnt their art from the Arabs in Spain and Southern Italy, who in turn had adopted it from the Greeks, who again had developed alchemy on Egyptian soil in the fourth century B.C. Thus, alchemy extends its roots into the tombs and labyrinths of Egyptian religion, and the Hellenistic figure of Hermes Trismegistus, who is the model for the medieval Mercurius, derives ultimately from the ancient Egyptian Thoth, god of mathematics and science.

During the Twelfth and Thirteenth Centuries alchemy filtered into Western Europe via Sicily and Spain. Christian students were welcomed at the universities at Palermo, Toledo, Barcelona, Segovia and Pamplona, and study was soon followed by translations. The greatest of the translators were Robert of Chester, Adelard of Bath, and Gerard of Cremona, all working in the first half of the Twelfth Century. During the next hundred years alchemy began to find European adepts who wrote original books, not merely adapting the Arabian ones. The great names among medieval alchemists were those of Albertus Magnus (1193-1280), Roger Bacon (1214-1292), Arnold of Villanova (1235-1311), and Raymond Lully (1232-1315), all of them prominent figures within the Catholic Church. They believed in the basic theory of alchemy, namely the possibility of metallic transmutation, the sulphur-mercury theory of metallic constitution, and the Aristotelian tenets of the 'prime matter' and the four elements. Still more important, they arrived at a broader view of nature by combining alchemical experiment with ancient natural philosophy and Christian theology (fig.3).

Arabian Alchemy

The first scientists of the West were philosophical and mystical types to whom practical alchemy was a branch of a comprehensive philosophical system. Their ideas rested on the Hermetic doctrines formulated by Alexandrian science and Greek alchemy and disseminated throughout the Roman Empire on the wings of syncretism. Due to this development, the Hermetic doctrines became saturated with a number of mystical teachings and myths, such as astrology and Gnosticism, Orfic speculation and Eleusinian mystery religion, the worship of Isis and Osiris, the worship of Serapis and of Sol Invictus, the teachings preserved by Nestorians, Monophysites, and Manichees in Persia, Syria and Iraq. This heritage did not pass directly to the Western alchemists, it went through an important intermediate link—the Arabs.

Historically it was the function of the Arabian philosophers to recreate the Hermetic doctrines of antiquity when large parts of the Empire succumbed to the Arabs during the miraculous conquests of Islam in the Seventh and Eighth Centuries A.D. Even if the Arabs developed new ways of rational experimentation, they retained the Hermetic doctrines with their two-fold approach of making gold and of revealing a way which could bring enlightenment to the soul. Thus, in seeking counsel with the Arabian alchemical tradition, the European alchemists resuscitated the Hellenistic syncretism of the ancient world which the Christian Church thought it had exterminated for ever.

2. Mining in a cave filled with monsters, gold, and the light of Hermetic illumination.

*3. Kneeling in his laboratory, an alchemist prays before a tabernacle inscribed: 'Happy the one who follows the advice of the Lord';
'Do not speak of God without enlightenment'; 'When we attend strictly to our work God himself will help us.' The inscription over
the doorway at the far end of the sumptuous hall reads: 'While sleeping, watch!' Engraving 1604 designed by Heinrich Khunrath.*

Because the alchemists originated in a pre-Christian cultural world, they had to establish themselves as a subculture in medieval Christianity. Here they occupied a strange position, religiously as well as scientifically. The alchemists were mystics without being orthodox Catholics, scientists without following the learning of their time, artisans unwilling to teach others what they knew. They were sectarians, the problem-children of medieval society, and their contemporaries were ever hesitant about deciding whether to regard them as pure sages or sacrilegious impostors.

Those who pursued the 'royal art' to the point of 'dropping out' found that an elaborate subculture had been constructed for them to drop into. Once inside it, they invariably adopted the apocalyptic visions of the underground which were wholly alien to the rationale of Western Christian society. This remarkable development was further accelerated by the psychological revolution that took place in the wake of the alchemists' hopeless attempts at 'transmuting the elements.' To understand this series of events, it will be necessary first to examine more closely this central idea of the goldmakers.

The Transmutation of the Elements

Alchemy is the art of transmuting base metals into silver or gold by freeing the crude materials from their 'impurities.' The strange belief that such a procedure might be undertaken derives from the natural philosophy of the Hellenistic alchemists. Basing their theory of nature on Aristotle, they assumed that the basis of the material world was a *prima materia,* or prime, chaotic matter, which might only come into actual existence if impressed by 'form.' Out of the swirling chaos of the prima materia, 'form' arose in the shape of the four elements: fire, air, water and earth. By blending these 'simple bodies' in certain proportions, God finally succeeded in creating out of the prime matter the limitless varieties of life.

According to Aristotle, the four elements are distinguished from one another by their 'qualities.' The four primary qualities are the fluid or moist, the dry, the hot, and the cold. Each element possesses two of the primary qualities, while the two absent qualities are the contraries which cannot be coupled. Therefore, the four possible combinations of the paired qualities are: hot and dry=fire; hot and fluid (or moist)=air; cold and fluid=water; cold and dry=earth. In each element, one quality predominates over the other: in earth, dryness; in water, cold; in air, fluidity; in fire, heat.

Transmutation is an obvious consequence of this theory: any element may be transformed into another through the quality which they have in common. Thus, fire can become air through the medium of heat, just as air can become water through the medium of fluidity. Also two elements may become a third element by removing one quality from each: by parting with the dry and cold qualities, fire and water can become air; by parting with the hot and fluid qualities, the same elements can give rise to earth.

Improving the Base Metals

The alchemical idea that the variety of things depends on the proportions in which the four elements are present in them may be illustrated by the process of transmutation undergone by a piece of green wood when heated. Drops of water form at the cut end of the wood, therefore wood contains water; steam and vapours are given off, therefore wood contains air; the wood burns, therefore it contains fire; and an ash is left, therefore wood contains earth. Thus, in a piece of green wood, prime matter is present in its four elements, the particular proportions of which account for the particular form and nature of a piece of green wood. In the same way a piece of metal owes its specific form of nature to *its* specific proportioning of the four elements.

From this belief it follows that any kind of substance can be transformed into any other kind by simply changing

its elemental proportions through the processes of burning, calcination, solution, evaporation, distillation, sublimation, and crystallization. If iron and gold are metals consisting of fire, air, water and earth in differing proportions, why not attempt to change the elemental proportions of iron by adjusting them to the proportions of the elements in gold? Here we have the germ of all alchemical theories of metallic transmutation, and it was based on this theoretical background that the alchemists sweated over their furnaces in their attempts to 'improve' the valueless metals.

4. Illumination by the light of nature.

The alchemists' hope of metallic transmutation was further supported by the sulphur-mercury theory of the origin of metals. A derivative of the theory of the four elements, the sulphur-mercury theory presented the two opposed, or contrary, elements, fire and water, in a new guise. Fire became 'sulphur' and water 'mercury,' the former composed of the primary qualities of hot and dry, the latter of the primary qualities of cold and moist. In general, sulphur stood for the property of combustibility or the spirit of fire, and mercury for that of fusibility or the mineral spirit of metals.

When sulphur and mercury united in different proportions and in different degrees of purity, the various metals and minerals took shape, according to the sulphur-mercury theory. If sulphur and mercury were perfectly pure, and if they

combined in the most complete equilibrium, the product would be the most perfect of metals, namely gold. Defects in purity and, particularly, in proportions, resulted in the formation of silver, lead, tin, iron, or copper. But since these inferior metals were essentially composed of the same constituents as gold, the accidents of combination might be rectified by suitable treatment and by means of elixirs.

From the theoretical structure described above evolved the two *a priori* postulates which the deductive reasoning of alchemy was based upon. These were 1) the unity of nature as expressed by the idea of the prima materia from which all bodies were formed and into which they might again be dissolved; and 2) the existence of a potent transmuting agent capable of promoting the change of one kind of material into another. This imagined agent became known as the 'philosophers' stone,' the most famous of all alchemical ideas.

As we know today, the alchemists' pursuit of elemental transmutation was on the wrong track. It was not until the Twentieth Century and the atomic age that men were enabled to change the elements into one another. Such processes of metallic transmutation consist in changing the number of protons in the atomic nucleus of the basic elements: if, for instance, iron is to be changed into gold, 53 protons must be added to its nucleus of 26 protons if it is to be transformed into the element of gold which carries 79 protons in its nucleus. This procedure requires a profound knowledge of the atomic structure of matter and a highly refined technical apparatus. The alchemists possessed none of these prerequisites and so they were dealing with a problem made insoluble by their primitive instruments and by their limited understanding of matter.

Naturally the alchemists' enthusiastic 'improvement' of the base metals had a number of secondary consequences. Centuries of refined laboratory techniques and alchemical manipulation of nearly *any* material (including urine, feces, and menstrual blood) didn't fail to produce a long list of chemical discoveries: alcohol, nitric acid, hydrochloric acid, ammonia, sugar of lead, and a number of antimony compounds. But the production of silver and gold out of the metallic species remained a blind alley which led the alchemists still deeper into a mountain from which there was no escape into the sunlight of scientific understanding. Instead, the frustrated goldmakers got entangled in a subterranean labyrinth of fantasies, hallucinations, visions, and dreams. Thus, what appeared to be the greatest mistake of the alchemists actually turned out to condition their greatest achievement: in the darkness of their blind alley the Sons of Hermes at last came to discover the *unconscious.*

I. SPIGEL DER KVNST VND NATVR.

5. A 'mirror of art and nature' (headline), the engraving shows the alchemists' pursuit of their stone in the depths of the earth and among the chemical apparatus of their laboratories. Two goldmakers present their 'prima materia' (top row); the primary qualities form the stone called Vitriol and Azoth (middle row); the second circle depicts the four elements blending in universal creation.

6. A chemical workshop reflecting the operations of the unconscious mind.

Projections of Unconscious Imagery

Alchemy is a strange blend of religious science and scientific religion; its gospel of chemical faith combines a scientific pursuit of nature's secrets with a religious quest aiming at an understanding of ultimate nature. Alchemy has thus an exoteric or 'scientific' aspect and an esoteric or 'mystic' aspect; it is the latter side of alchemy which will engage our attention in the present study.

In explaining the strange development of esoteric or 'mystic' alchemy one encounters the psychological phenomenon of *projection* and the universal law that *nature abhors a vacuum*. As the alchemists' agelong investigation of matter on the wrong track plunged them into a dark void, the darkness was finally 'illuminated' by the groping psyche of the laboratory worker which projected its contents into the smoking retorts of his laboratory. Thus, through the indirect way of projection and free association the alchemists came to activate the unconscious which allied itself to their work in the form of hallucinatory or visionary experiences (figs.7-13).

Psychologically, visions and hallucinations represent projections of unconscious contents, and frequently assert themselves in the form of *illusory sensory images*. In the 'Liber de alchemiae difficultatibus' Hoghelande recounts of the alchemists:

'They say also that different names are given to the stone on account of the wonderful variety of figures that appear in the course of the work, inasmuch as colours often come forth at the same time, just as we sometimes imagine in the clouds or in the fire strange shapes of animals, reptiles, or trees. I found similar things in a fragment of a book ascribed to Moses. When the body is dissolved, it is there written, then will appear sometimes two branches, sometimes three or more, sometimes also the shapes of reptiles; on occasion it also seems as if a man with a head and all his limbs were seated upon a cathedra.' (1)

In his 'Compendium artis alchemiae' Raymond Lully writes: 'You should know, dear son, that the course of nature is turned about, so that without spiritual exaltation you can see certain fugitive spirits condensed in the air in the shape of divers monsters, beasts and men, which move like the clouds hither and thither.' (2)

A final example may be taken from the 'Introitus apertus' in which it is asserted: 'The substance of the vessel will exhibit a great variety of forms; it will become liquid and again coagulate a

7. A rich stimulus for free association.

hundred times a day; sometimes it will present the appearance of fishes' eyes and then again of tiny silver trees, with twigs and leaves. Whenever you look at it you will have cause for astonishment, particularly when you see it all divided into beautiful but very minute grains of silver, like the rays of the sun. This is the white tincture . . . ' (3)

These and numerous other examples from the alchemical treatises indicate that the opus alchymicum is concerned with imaginary contents and thus represents an essentially *psychological* phenomenon. The truth of this statement may be appreciated even by the sceptical reader, for a cursory glance at the engravings reproduced in this study makes it clear that the alchemical figures, elements and actions have little to do with chemical procedures in a modern, scientific sense.

Imaginative Character of the Work

The two connected stills in fig.7 may serve the reader as a stimulus for free association, a method by which Freud arrived at an exploration of the unconscious psyche and its contents. In a unique way, the alchemical workshop with its strange apparatus and chemical transformation processes must have served as a stimulus for free association, thus effecting a partial elimination of conscious control. As demonstrated by the Rorschach test, the shape of an inkblot or, in fact, almost any irregular shape can spark off the associative process. Leonardo da Vinci wrote in his 'Notebooks': 'It should not be hard for you to stop sometimes and look into the stains of walls, or ashes of a fire, or clouds, or mud or like places in which . . . you may find really marvellous ideas.' (4)

Figs.8-13 give an example of the rich imaginative activity unfolded by the alchemists during their chemical work. Fig.8 renders the winding pipe used for distillation of aqua vitae and called by the adepts their 'mercurial serpent.' The adjoining figure renders the pear-shaped Hermetic vessel frequently called uterus. It is compared to the female matrix from which the homunculus or philosophers' son is to be born. According to one alchemical author, the 'visions' of the Hermetic vessel 'are more to be sought than the scripture.' (5)

In fig.9 the dangerously bulging vessel is conceived in the image of a dancing bear, a symbol of the evil mother or of the perilous aspect of the prima materia. In fig.10 the distilling apparatus is conceived in the image of the seven-headed Hydra or the dragon.

In fig.11 the alchemical basin is identified with a tortoise. The 'double pelican' used for distillation and sublimation appears in fig.12 as an image of the copu-

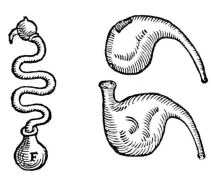

8. The mercurial serpent and uterus.

lation of the sexes. In fig.13 the vessel of circular distillation is seen as a pelican pecking open its breast to nourish its young with its blood. (The pelican is a famous medieval symbol of Christ.)

Chemistry of the Mind

The psychological nature of alchemy is proved by the way in which the trea-

9. The dangerous vessel, or the 'bear.'

tises talk about their 'chemical' stuff. Its elements are all of a 'spiritual' or imaginary character such as the philosophical son, the philosophical tree, the philosophical water, the philosophical mercury, the philosophical egg, the philosophical stone, etc. It is frequently emphasized that the work of alchemy has a philosophical side which must illuminate its material side if the true significance of the opus alchymicum is to be grasped. The divine mind operates in nature, hence

10. Numerous evidence of the projection of symbolic contents into the alchemical vessel proves the unconscious at work.

the correspondence between physical and philosophical insights.

The abundance of hallucinations, visions and dreams in Hermetic science helps to explain the paramount importance ascribed by the alchemists to man's powers of *imagination*. In the final analysis, the imaginative function appears to be the most important 'instrument' of the goldmakers, whose chemical operations seem to have served as projection-hooks for mental processes of unconscious origin. 'Imagination is the star in man, the celestial or supercelestial body' says Ruland's 'Lexicon alchemiae' (1612) in its definition of *imaginatio*. (6)

In the 'Rosarium' the alchemist is admonished to perform his opus in the following manner: 'And take care that thy door be well and firmly closed, so that he who is within cannot escape, and —God willing—thou wilt reach the goal. Nature carries out her operations gradually; and indeed I would have thee do the same: let thy imagination be guided wholly by nature. And observe according to nature, through whom the bodies regenerate themselves in the bowels of the earth. And imagine this with true and not with fantastic imagination.' (7)

In alchemy the adept comes to terms with 'true imagination' by means of the act of *meditation*. Ruland says of this: 'Meditation: The name of an internal talk of one person with another who is invisible, as in the invocation of the deity, or communion with one's self, or with one's good angel.' (8)

The meditative aspect of the opus reveals the alchemists' understanding of their 'work' as a psychic process of transformation also, unfolding *pari passu* with the chemical process of transformation. In such a manner the alchemical laboratories took on the function of psychological laboratories as well. The effect was the symbolized chemistry of alchemy which, in the last analysis, represents an alchemy of the *mind*.

The Drugged Alchemical Mind

Still another feature may have accelerated the psychological investigations of the alchemists. Since the Sons of Hermes were the leading chemists of the Middle Ages, and since they experimented with all kinds of plants and herbs, it is inconceivable that they should not have known or used themselves a number of hallucinogenic drugs. The Middle Ages knew the *Solanaceae* family of drugs—the plants Thorn Apple, belladonna, mandragora, and the henbanes. They contain the alkaloids atropine, hyoscyamine and scopolamine among others. They served as poisons, intoxicants, love potions and as sources of dreams and visions. The Solanaceae were employed as drugs by the European witches, who under the influence of Thorn Apple, henbane or

11. The maternal basin, or the 'tortoise.'

belladonna, experienced vivid hallucinations of flying to the Witches' Sabbats. In addition to projection, imaginative experiences, and dreams, we shall probably have to add hallucinogenic drugs as instrumental in producing the visionary experiences of the alchemists. This would explain the vividness and authenticity of the unconscious processes described by the opus alchimicum, processes which today are reproduced with

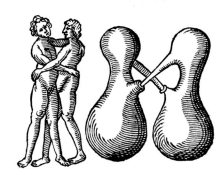

12. 'Intercourse' of two distilling vessels.

staggering correspondence by modern drugs such as LSD, psilocybin, and mescalin. What are the secrets hiding under the alchemists' cryptic allusions to their 'red elixir,' their 'elixir of life,' 'our wine' *(vinum nostrum)*, and the miraculous mandrake *Lunatica* or *Lunaria*, not to be found in any herbal because not identical with the botanical Lunaria (honesty)? (9) We do not know, but almost certainly the alchemists availed themselves of drugs in their search for the philosophers' stone.

13. Laden with unconscious reveries, the alchemical work was a product of both projection and hallucinogenic drugs.

14. Initiation into the royal art: a closed body of knowledge, sacred to the elect.

The Mystical System of Alchemy

As gradually the alchemical laboratories changed into psychological laboratories and the alchemical work into explorations of the inner universe, the purgation and transformation of metals were 'translated' into symbolic procedures concerned with the purgation and transformation of *souls*. Thus, the meeting between the alchemists and the unconscious had a revolutionary impact on the alchemical work, which at the end of the Middle Ages began to develop into a *mystical system*.

As a host of dream images and symbolic procedures invaded the goldmakers' laboratories, the alchemical treatises and recipes to an increasing degree became ambiguous in language and intent. Finally, in the Thirteenth, Fourteenth, Fifteenth and Sixteenth Centuries the psychological experiences of generations of alchemists were brought upon a common

denominator and 'distilled' into a mystical system remarkable for its theological boldness and unity of doctrine: the *opus alchymicum*.

After having produced the *rosa mystica* of the 'alchemical work,' alchemy faded and soon disappeared as a cultural feature of European civilization. The rational spirit of a dawning age of enlightenment was unpropitious to the spirit of alchemy; it further, in 1661, suffered a death-blow in the purely scientific field. In that year Robert Boyle published his 'Sceptical Chymist,' which destroyed the basic conceptions and theories of alchemy and replaced them by a rational system from which our science of chemistry has arisen.

For two and a half centuries, alchemy and its heritage virtually disappeared from the consciousness of Europe. The growing alienation between the world of alchemical experience and the world of the industrial age was furthered by the

materialistic and positivist spirit of the Nineteenth Century, which understood still less of alchemical symbolism until it was finally rejected as ravings, superstition and pure nonsense.

Significantly, it was not until the Twentieth Century and the modern trends of irrational thought that the alchemists came into focus again after their long sleep. Depth psychology paved the way by discovering the unconscious foundations of the opus alchymicum (Silberer and Jung), and when the psychedelic revolution got under way in the 1960s, the alchemists became the heroes of the day. Hallucenogenic drugs evoked a wealth of imaginative experiences which were interpreted as an alchemy of the mind very much resembling the kind of 'alchemy' engaged in by the medieval goldmakers, who probably used the same means.

Pioneers of Alchemical Research

In 1914—fourteen years after Freud's publication of 'The Interpretation of Dreams'—the Austrian depth psychologist *Herbert Silberer* published a penetrating study of alchemy called 'Problems of Mysticism and Its Symbolism.' Silberer, who drew on the scientific method of Freud and his school, quickly recognized the unconscious foundations of the opus alchymicum, whose images and motifs closely resembled those uncovered by Freud through his study of dreams. Silberer further demonstrated alchemical symbols as eruptions of repressed unconscious forces, thus discovering in the Hermetic writings the presence of the Oedipus complex and the unconscious psychodynamics of introversion, regression, parricide, incest, castration anxiety and rebirth. By applying the dream interpretation of Freud, Rank, and Stekel to the symbolic images and motifs of alchemy, Silberer succeeded in unlocking their unconscious meaning and, thus, translating them into psychodynamic terms.

This induced him to view the alchemical opus as a psychic 'work' of regressive and incestuous nature, a journey of the soul leading the adept to final death and rebirth inside an Oedipus complex of religious proportions. In addition to this insight, which was not substantiated theoretically, Silberer glimpsed the goal of the opus as that of the alchemist's attainment of a psychic totality curiously reminding Silberer of the mystic totality of the soul in Indian religion.

The Jungian X-Raying

During the Second World War *Carl Jung* published his study on 'Psychology and Alchemy' (1944), which in 1946 was followed by the 'Psychology of the

Transference Interpreted in Conjunction With a Set of Alchemical Illustrations.' Together with his 'Alchemical Studies' (1931-1954) and his last major study 'Mysterium Coniunctionis' (1956), these books furthered the understanding of alchemy considerably. First of all, Jung brought order and structure into the jungle of alchemical writings. By x-raying their pages he discovered the skeleton of the opus alchymicum: its leitmotifs, basic concepts, principal symbols and—dimly—its successive stages of transformation.

Like Herbert Silberer, Carl Jung was put on the track of alchemy by his discovery of the close resemblance between the imaginary world of the alchemists and the *dream-world of his patients.* This insight set the process going and finally led him to regard the opus alchymicum as a mental process of transformation aiming at a goal identical with the ego's total integration of its unconscious background. Jung christened this hypothetical process 'individuation,' a term implying psychological totality, individual wholeness, or, theologically, the soul's attainment of divine selfhood. Concluded Jung:

'In my book 'Psychology and Alchemy' I showed how certain archetypal motifs that are common in alchemy appear in the dreams of modern individuals who have no knowledge of alchemical literature. In that book the wealth of ideas and symbols that lie hidden in the neglected treatises of this much misunderstood 'art' was hinted at rather than described in the detail it deserved; for my primary aim was to demonstrate that the world of alchemical symbols definitely does not belong to the rubbish heap of the past, but stands in a very real and living relationship to our most recent discoveries concerning the psychology of the unconscious. Not only does this modern psychological discipline give us the key to the secrets of alchemy, but, conversely, alchemy provides the psychology of the unconscious with a meaningful historical basis . . . Most accounts of alchemy are vitiated by the erroneous assumption that it was merely the precursor of chemistry. Herbert Silberer was the first to try to penetrate its much more important psychological side as far as his somewhat limited equipment allowed him to do so.' (1)

'We no longer believe that the secret [of alchemy] lies in chemical substances, but that it is rather to be found in one of the darker and deeper layers of the psyche, although we do not know the nature of this layer. Perhaps in another century or so we shall discover a new darkness from which there will emerge something we do not understand, but whose presence we sense with the utmost certainty.' (2)

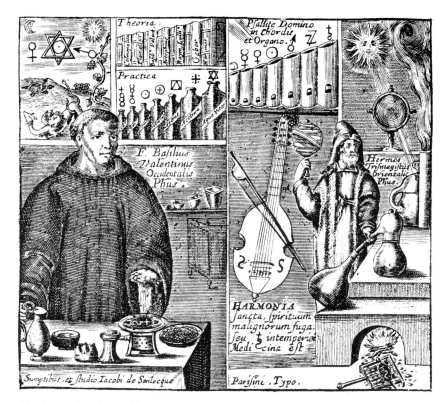

15. The mythical Benedictine Basil Valentine at work in his alchemical laboratory.

The Oath of Secrecy

Before presenting the opening of the opus alchymicum, we shall give a brief summary of the structure of the alchemical work and the conditions laid down for initiation into its mysteries. These are given in fig.14, in which an old master initiates an adept with the words: 'Accept the gift of God under the consecrated sign.' The praying adept replies:

'I promise to conceal the secrets of the alchemical science.' The dove soaring above the ceremony and suffusing it with a heavenly light symbolizes the 'royal art' which the 'Rosarium' terms 'a gift of the Holy Ghost.' (3) Two angels hovering over the rite sing: 'Because you have loved justice and hated evil, God thy Lord has anointed you with the oil of joy. Put your trust in God, act like a man, and He shall comfort your heart.'

16. Medieval monks and heretics going underground to form a psychedelic subculture.

17. Four sisters and four degrees of fire governing the 'circular work' of the Zodiac.

Protecting Christendom through Secrecy

In his popular treatise the 'Ordinal of Alchemy,' (1) written in 1477, the English alchemist Thomas Norton advances the observation: 'Nor can anyone attain to this art, unless there be some person sent by God to instruct him in it. For the matter is so glorious and wonderful that it cannot be fully delivered to any one but by word of mouth. Moreover, if any man would receive it, he must take a great and sacred oath, that as we his teachers refuse high rank and fame, so he will not be too eager for these frivolous distinctions, and that he will not be so presumptuous as to make the secret known to his own son; for propinquity of blood, or affinity, should be held of no account in this our magistery. Near-ness of blood, as such, does not entitle anyone to be let into the secret, but only virtue, whether in those near to us or in strangers. Therefore you should carefully test and examine the life, character, and mental aptitude of any person who would be initiated in this art, and then you should bind him, by a sacred oath, not to let our magistery be commonly or vulgarly known. Only when he begins to grow old and feeble, he may reveal it to one person, but not to more—and that one man must be virtuous, and generally approved by his fellows. For this magistery must always remain a secret science, and the reason that compels us to be so careful is obvious. If any wicked man should learn to practise this art, the event would be fraught with great danger to Christendom.' (2)

In Senior we are informed about the oath of secrecy taken by the adepts when initiated into the opus alchymicum: 'This is the secret which they promised on oath not to divulge in any book.' (3)

Agrippa von Nettesheim, the merciless scoffer and blasphemer of the Renaissance, says of alchemy: 'I could say much more about this art (which I do not find so disagreeable) were it not for the oath of silence usually taken by initiates into the mysteries.' (4)

An Outline of the Opus

Figs.17-19 render a gross outline of the mystical system of alchemy, protected and hidden from the public in so many ways. Figs.17-18 show the four alchemical sisters, or virgins of the sun, with their vessels, symbolizing the four regimens of fire, or the four degrees of fiery love imparted to the alchemist by his *anima,* or 'soul sister.' Fire is the fuel of the alchemical work and the main agent of its continuous process of transmutation. Once kindled, the alchemist's fire is maintained without interruption until the end of the Great Work.

Fig.18 shows the four sisters balancing on four globes marked with the signs of the four elements: earth, water, air, and fire. In addition to the four degrees of fire, the virgins' vessels contain the emblematic figures of the corresponding four stages of the opus: the earthy *nigredo,* or 'blackening' stage, represented by a little inky man; the watery *albedo,* or 'whitening' stage, represented by a white rose; the airy *citrinitas,* or 'yellowing' stage, represented by an eagle winging toward the sun; the fiery *rubedo,* or 'reddening' stage, represented by the glowing lion. This division of the process into four elements, colours, or stages is termed by the adepts the 'quartering of the philosophy.' (5)

Fig.17 shows the virgins of the sun seated at the cardinal points of the Zo-

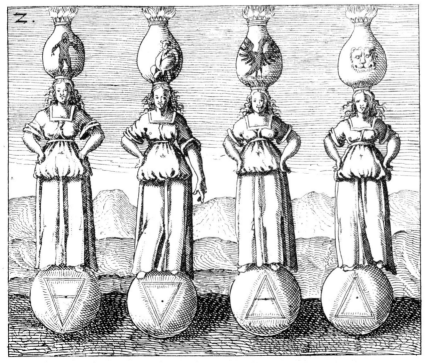

18. Four sisters, four elements, four fires, four colours, and four stages of the work.

diac, i.e., at the Ram, the Crab, the Scales, and the Capricorn. The circular table indicates the sun's yearly movement through the twelve houses of the Zodiac, also rendered by the twelve astrological signs along the ecliptic, or the band of the Zodiac. The circular path of the sun through the Zodiac is the model of the opus alchymicum, which is frequently called the *opus circulatorium*, the work beginning in the Ram and finishing in the Fishes.

Another image of the 'circular work' is the uroboros, or universal snake, which, according to the Gnostic saying, 'passes through all things' by biting its own tail and devouring itself. Speaking of the circular work and its fuel, an alchemist says: 'The fire is enkindled by an invisible sun unknown to many, that is, the sun of the philosophers . . . corrupting man back to his first essence.' (6)

The Wheeling Work

Fig.19 shows this aspect of the circular work, also called the *rota philosophica* or 'philosophical wheel.' Spiralling leftward toward a reunion with the 'divine mind' *(1: Mens; Deus)*, the wheeling soul at first ascends the elements of earth, water, air, and fire *(22-19)* that belong to the terrestrial and impure, sublunary world. Then comes the ascent through the seven planetary spheres, where the soul blots out the imprints formerly received at the hands of the seven planetary gods *(18-12)*. Having traversed the seven planetary spheres, the reborn and sublimated soul is exalted to the heavenly sphere and embedded in the 'starry sky' *(Caelum Stellatum: 11)*. This is the sphere of the heavenly children, or unborn souls. The last ascent leads the soul up through the nine choirs of angels or past through the spheres of pure spirits *(10-2)*. Finally the opus circulatorium releases the 'dry' soul by reuniting it with the 'divine mind' *(1)*—described as 'simple unity, origin, ultimate limit, essential fountain, primal act, pure being, nature of nature.' This ultimate goal of the opus is expressed by the element of fire.

The Four Degrees of Fire

Alchemy lays down four regimens, or degrees of heat, of its 'philosophical fire': 'The first, slow and mild, as of the flesh or embryo; the second, moderate and temperate, as of the sun in June; the third, great and strong, as of a calcining fire; the fourth, burning and vehement, as of fusion. Each of these is twice as great as the preceding degree.' (7)

The heightened intensity of the fire heating the alchemist's retort in the four

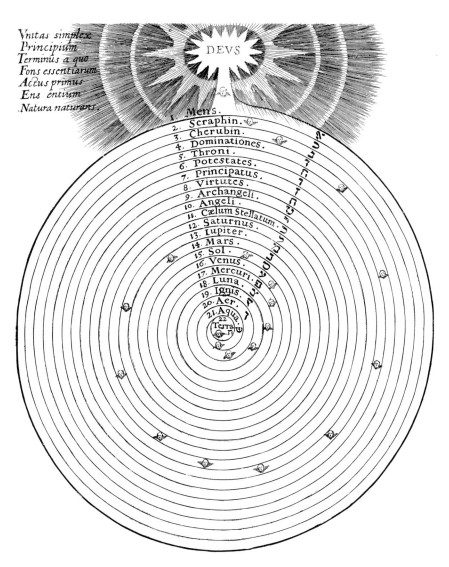

19. The divine record of the soul's fall: the 'circular work' of its Hermetic redemption.

stages of his work serves the two-fold purpose of sublimation and purification. As the alchemist's love is transformed into 'mercurial fire,' its flames gradually consume all that is earthly within him. To be loved by the four virgins of the sun means to be consumed in the flame, finally to shine with the inexhaustible light of the sun itself *(solificatio)*.

This process is expressed by an elemental symbolism in which the body *(corpus)* is represented by water and earth, the soul *(anima)* by fire, and the spirit *(spiritus)* by air. Through the interplay of fire and air, the wet and instinctual soul is freed from its bodily tomb and finally transformed into heavenly fire.

A famous alchemical formula says *solve et coagula*—'dissolve and coagulate.' This method underlies the opus alchymicum with its streaming process of cyclic transformation. The fiery wheel of the philosophers leads the alchemist into four stages of dissolution and putre-

faction and again out of them—into four stages of coagulation and conjunction.

The success of the work is therefore conditioned by the alchemist's continual surrender to the autonomous dynamics of his strange arcanum, or 'primal matter.' This means that the adept must never rest in the 'coagulating' stages of his work, but must always 'dissolve' the philosophical stone just won. Progressing in this way, the alchemist discovers the finer details of his art, just as his personality becomes a pure medium for divine transformation. Says the 'Rosarium':

'It is therefore clear that the stone is the master of the philosophers, as if [the philosopher] were to say that he does of his own nature that which he is compelled to do. Therefore the philosopher is not the master of the stone but rather its minister. Consequently, whoever tries, by means of the art and by unnatural artifice, to introduce into it anything which does not by nature exist in the arcanum, he will fall into error and repent of his error.' (8)

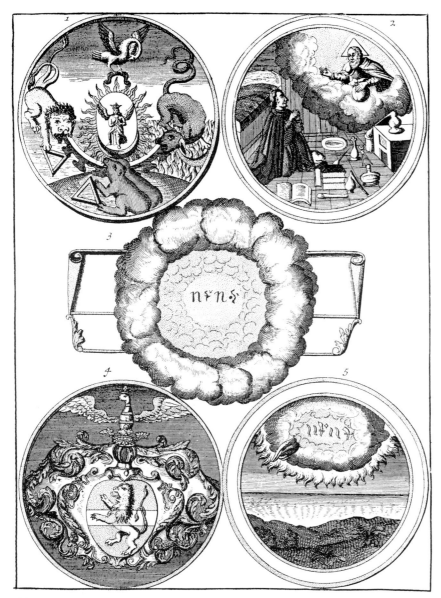

20.

Prima Materia: the Opening of the Work

Above is shown the first of 19 copperplates printed in Johann Conrad Barchusen's 'Elementa chemiae' (1718) and presenting the entire opus alchymicum. (1) The first circular plate shows the alchemist as the 'philosophers' son' reborn in the 'philosophers' egg' and illuminated by the sickle of the moon united with the sun. The winged alchemist is surrounded by the lion, the toad, the dragon, and the pelican, all elemental symbols of alchemy. Surrounded by his phials, instruments, and books, the alchemist in plate 2 is overwhelmed by visions and hallucinations. From a dream-cloud a wise old man emerges with a halo in the form of a triangle. His right hand makes the sign of the Trinity, his left rests on an orb adorned with a cross. This figure symbolizes *Mercurius philosophorum,* the god of alchemy. His Greek origin is Hermes, the god of sleep

and revelation, and the guide conducting the souls of the dead to the underworld.

The dream-cloud parting before the eyes of the kneeling alchemist reappears in plate 3, where the name of the Highest is inscribed at the centre of the foggy circle. The engraving's symbolism thus equates God with the cloud of dreams (or the unconscious). The dream-cloud is further identical with the prima materia, the original material of the opus.

The scutcheon of the royal art is shown in plate 4: a crowned bird wafts its wings in the 'nest' of a still bigger crown, while a 'double-sexed' lion with two tails performs its dance inside a heart-shaped emblem. In plate 5 the spirit of God moves upon the face of the waters at the dawn of creation: 'And God said, Let there be light: and there was light' (Gen.1:3).

Conjuring up the 'Eternal Unconscious'

Baring his head, an alchemical philosopher in the first medal of fig.21 greets the descending cloud of the 'eternal unconscious' *(sopor aeternitatis).* The circular inscription reads: 'It is the task of the wise to investigate the eternal secrets with raised eyes and a lofty mind.' In the second medal, the hand of Mercurius philosophorum emerges from the dream-cloud with the Book of Secrets adorned with Hermetic symbols. Such weird imagery constitutes the 'material' of the opus alchymicum, the dream-stuff of which is described by the inscription: 'Our material is stuff of no price or value; whoever comes across it hardly troubles to pick it up.'

The alchemical work is offered to king and beggar alike since its 'material' is present in everybody. The inscription of the first medal of fig.22 reads: 'Much money does not buy it; it is thrown in the ways of both poor and rich.' In the second medal, an alchemist brings low the crowns of the forest with his ax. The inscription explains: 'In the filth is the beginning of our putrefaction, its *sine qua non.'*

A Spring of Putrefaction

The putrefaction of the opening work is the motif of the first painting of Salomon Trismosin's 'Splendor solis' reproduced in fig.23. (2) Two hesitating philosophers debate in front of the Temple of the Wise, the portal and doorstep of which lead to a green meadow with flowers and a running brook. On the dais of the sanctuary is erected the 'coat of arms of the art,' which shows the sun hovering above a crown adorned with three moon sickles and studded with stars. At the bottom shines the moon, its cracked face adorned with three homunculi. The text explains the alchemical work as an *opus contra naturam* in which the libido is pulled back to the germinating earth for the purpose of letting it 'putrefy' there in a cruel spring: 'The philosophers' stone is produced along the course of nature when she bursts into leaf. Hali, the Philosopher, says about this, 'This stone arises from the growing things when they turn green.' When therefore the green is reduced to its former nature, whereby things sprout

21. Alchemy made on dream-stuff.

and come forth in ordained time, it must be putrefied and decocted in the way of our secret art.' (3)

The adepts' initial act of putrefaction explains why the running brook in fig.23 disappears inside the temple as a river Styx leading to the underworld and the land of the dead. The very direction of the temple's watery threshold accounts for the hesitant attitude of the two debating alchemists. Torn between fear and desire, they discuss the *descensus ad inferos* implied by an entrance into the strange sanctuary. Its season of spring is a season of sacrifice, its river of life a stream of blood, its royal rulers a violent sun and moon.

Returning to the Primal Matter

The alchemical principle of putrefaction builds on the doctrine that all nature is renewed after dying away, and that in order to grow, an organism must first die. An apple, or any other fruit, has to putrefy before its seed can take root and produce more apples. Similarly dung, which is considered to be matter in the state of putrefaction and hence close to death, is renowned for its life-giving properties as fertilizer. Further, putrefaction is one of the forms of corruption; and the 'corruption of one is the generation of another,' according to the testimony of the 'Rosarium.' (4)

In alchemy 'putrefaction' applies not only to the material but also to the spiritual world. Just as material death is necessary for the material rebirth of things, so spiritual death is necessary for the spiritual rebirth of man.

According to alchemical doctrine, the much-sought-after act of rebirth is always preceded by a return to the source of life: 'That from which a thing is naturally made, through that same thing it must return again and be dissolved and broken up into its own nature . . . Everything must be resolved and reduced into that from which it sprang.' (5)

A variation of this principle is the doctrine that regeneration depends on a 'reduction to the primal matter.' Metals can only be transmuted into gold after having been reduced to a formless, indeterminate mass; that is, after having been melted down. In this state (which the adepts compare to primeval chaos) they can be worked into any form the

22. 'Filthy' dream-material of alchemy.

23. Hesitating before a palace of putrefaction and regeneration, death and rebirth.

alchemist may choose. In so far as metals lose their unique characteristics in the melting process, in a certain sense they putrefy and 'die.'

There are two methods of reducing the metals to a formless mass: melting the ingredients down to a fluid state or by placing them in a bath of mercury, which can dissolve most other metals. Mercury is therefore referred to by the adepts as the 'universal solvent.' As we shall see on the following pages, achieving the fluid state, or applying the universal solvent, is synonymous with the release of the Flood, the dramatic and fearful beginning of the opus.

In our introductory section we mentioned most of the fundamental ideas of alchemy. All-important is the dualistic view of the universe as the battleground of opposing forces. The alchemists' intention is to resolve this conflict harmoniously 1) by a 'putrefying' movement of death and rebirth 2) by a return to the primal matter; and 3) by a rotary movement turning the wheel of creation backward in an *opus contra naturam* aimed at a return to the source of all creation, or 'God.' This is the famed opus circulatorium, in which the subject of regeneration consumes himself in the manner of the uroboric serpent.

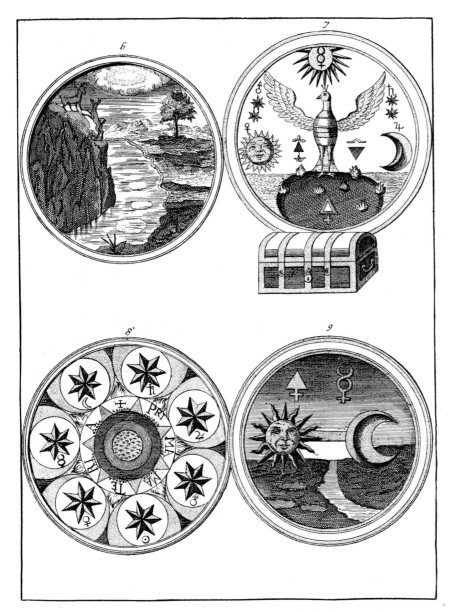

24. *Producing the primal matter by putrefaction, or a reversal of the creation process.*

Fearful Opening of the Opus

Barchusen's plates 6-9 (above) depict the terrifying beginning of the opus while explaining the meaning of the divine hand stuck through the fiery dream-cloud in the previous plate. As the Creator's hand withdraws from the receding cloud in plate 6, the divine command is carried out: the calm sea suddenly breaks upon the land, flooding everything. Alchemically this means the turning on of Mercurius philosophorum and the beginning of the work. *Psychologically the event means the eruption of the unconscious into the sphere of consciousness.*

The opening work is compared by the alchemists to the biblical Flood, or second Deluge, depicted in fig.27: 'In the same day were all the fountains of the great deep broken up, and the windows of heaven were opened. And the rain was upon the earth forty days and forty nights . . . And every living substance was destroyed which was upon the face of the ground, both man, and cattle, and the creeping things, and the fowl of the heaven; and they were destroyed from the earth: and Noah only remained alive, and they that were with him in the ark. And the waters prevailed upon the earth an hundred and fifty days' (Gen. 7: 11-24).

Fertile Chaos of a Disruptive Creation

In Barchusen's plate 7 the deluge leaves only a small patch of land, on which the Hermes bird descends. The chaotic situation is emphasized by the emergence of the seven planets on the horizon, a symbol of universal disorder. As indicated by the sign of sulphur, the sinking island is set on fire by sulphurous flames from the hellish interior of the earth. Yet the alchemist's sinking island is 'supported' by a sealed chest of drawers emerging from the sea and containing immense riches of silver and gold. Although the adept's world has become a sinking island, it has been simultaneously transformed into a *treasure island.*

The disruption of the earth by flood and fire, and the heavens by planets shooting from their orbits illustrates the alchemist's encounter with the prima materia, further depicted in plate 8. As the seven planets perform a retrograde circling movement, the world of creation splits up into the four elements. This *divisio elementorum* is shown inside the centre of the 'prima materia,' which consists of the earth surrounded by water, air, and fire. Says an alchemical author about this movement:

'The stone is separated into the four elements mingled together, which is brought about by the retrograde movement of the stars . . . The production of the stone takes place on the model of the creation of the world. For it is necessary that it has its own chaos and its own primary material, in which the elements are to fluctuate, confused, until they are separated by the fiery spirit. The waters congregate into one place and the dry land appears.' (1)

Barchusen's plate 9 depicts the darkening alchemical landscape soaked by the deluge but illuminated by the power of love awakening with all the magic of its first eruption. Sol (identified with sulphur) falls in love with Luna (identified with mercury). The two lovers reach for each other across the barrier of a brook or river. Even if thwarted, the act of solar and lunar love brings the terror of the prima materia to an end: the Flood appears to have receded with the planetary chaos and to have left the earth soaked and sodden—as compared with its rocky features in plates 5 and 6.

25. *The sorcerer's apprentice at work.*

The Killing and Vivifying Wine

The cosmic inundation of the opening work is depicted in an interesting way by the first woodcut of the 'Rosarium philosophorum' (fig.25), the model of Barchusen's opening plates. (2) (The 'Rosarium' series of the work represents the most complete version of the opus and forms the backbone of the present study.)

In the woodcut, the mercurial fountain with its base of lion-claws overflows with the mercurial waters of the prima materia. These appear as the 'virgin's milk' *(lac virginis),* the 'fountain's vinegar' *(acetum fontis),* and the 'water of life' *(aqua vitae),* all spouting from the mercurial fountain inscribed with the 'three names' *(triplex nomine)* of Mercurius philosophorum. These refer to his three manifestations in the fountain as 'mineral,' 'vegetable,' and 'animal' matter. Yet the inscription on the rim of the basin admonishes that *unus est mercurius mineralis, mercurius vegetabilis, mercurius animalis.* These manifestations of the triune earth-god of alchemy reappear in the two-headed *serpens mercurialis* which is also *triplex nomine,* as its inscriptions *animalis, mineralis,* and *vegetabilis* bear out. The mercurial serpent or dragon spews the poisonous fumes of the prima materia which contain the seven planets or metals in evil mixture and disorder. The woodcut is accompanied by the following verse:

*We are the metals' first nature and only
    source,
The highest tincture of the art is made
    through us.
No fountain and no water has my like
I make both rich and poor men whole
    or sick
For deadly can I be and poisonous. (3)*

Descent into the Bowels of the Earth

Fig.26 shows the engraved variant in which a small party of alchemists eagerly drink the fountain's vinegar, the virgin's milk and the water of life. After having intoxicated themselves with this remarkable cocktail termed 'our wine' *(vinum nostrum),* (4) the alchemists walk into the dark crevices of the mountain in order to begin their arduous mining. In the depths of the earth they will wrest the primal matter from the rock and later refine its impure metals into silver and gold.

A Recipe for the Magic Potion

The 'Rosarium' gives the following recipe for the mercurial wine which intoxicates the alchemists while 'dissolving their bodies': 'Sap of the moon plant, water of life, quintessence, ardent wine, *mercurius vegetabilis:* all these things are

26. *'The chosen one who drinks of this water will soon experience his rebirth.' (7)*

one thing. The sap of the moon plant is made of our wine which is known to few of our sons. With it is effected our solution and by means of it our potable gold is produced and without it nothing can be made. For the imperfect body is converted into the primal matter, and when these waters are conjoined with our water they produce a pure and clear water which purifies all things. Yet this water contains within itself all that is necessary, and that same water is precious and cheap out of which and by means of which our magistery is brought to perfection. For it does not dissolve the bodies by means of a vulgar solution as the ignorant think who convert the body into cloudy water; but it takes place by means of a true philosophical solution in which the body is converted into the primal water out of which it has existed since the beginning (5) . . . The corporeal must be rendered incorporeal and the incorporeal must be rendered corporeal. Therefore . . . the water is that which kills and vivifies.' (6)

27. *The biblical waters of destruction and salvation inundating the laboratory.*

CHAOS

28.

Confusion and Poisoning of the Mind

The alchemist's initial encounter with the prima materia is characterized by feelings of frustration, bewilderment, dissociation, and disintegration. The Petrarcha Master's woodcut (fig.1) with its exploding laboratory experiment and confused scientists gives the outer manifestations of the prima materia, while the pictures on these and the following pages give the symbolic or inner manifestations of the same experience. The failures and dangers of alchemical experimentation as initiating factors of alchemical symbolism may be taken for granted even if one should also include the existence of some unknown hallucinogenic drug ('our wine known to few of our sons,' for instance). Chemical intoxication and poisoning sustained by prolonged experimental frustrations, or vice versa, would be suffi-

cient for stirring up the unconscious psyche and producing fantasies, hallucinations, and visions.

In this connection it is interesting to see the majority of alchemical treatises emphasizing the dangers and hazards of chemical experimentation. Thus the 'Aurora consurgens' mentions the 'evil odours and vapours that infect the mind of the laborant' (1) at the outset of his work. In another treatise the prima materia acquires human voice and says of itself: 'I give them a blow in the face, that is a wound, which makes them toothless, and brings about many infirmities through the smoke.' (2) In the 'Theatrum chemicum' it is stated that 'because of the fires and sulphurous exhalations it brings with it, the opus is highly dangerous.' (3) Ventura in his 'De ratione conficiendi lapidis' confirms the hazards of the opening opus: 'From the beginning the opus

is like a death-dealing poison.' (4) Such statements reveal the real dangers of the alchemical art while explaining the intoxicating effects of the alchemists' fuming laboratories.

Ignition of the Art

The mental dangers of the royal art are illustrated by the two medals of fig. 29. The falling figure of the first medal is inscribed: 'This science requires a philosopher and not a madman.' The second medal shows an alchemist ascending the Jacob's ladder assisted by two angels. From the top of the ladder a colleague ends on the ground in a scorched and blackened state. The inscription explains: 'It depends not only on man's industry: the ability and the urge are all in all in God's hand.'

The perils of the royal art are expressed by a much quoted saying from Alphidius which runs: 'This stone proceeds from a sublime and most glorious place of great terror, which has given over many sages to death.' (5) Also the 'Turba' admonishes the adepts: 'Know ye, who seek after wisdom, that the foundation of this art, on account of which many have perished, is a thing stronger and more sublime than all other things.' (6)

In the first medal of fig.30 the fiery waters of the prima materia surge into the alchemical landscape while opening the opus along this line: 'The magistery proceeds from one root, expands into several, and reverts into the one.' In the 'Rosarium' the prima materia is called *radix ipsius* (root of itself) (7): because it roots in itself, it is autonomous and dependent on nothing. In the second medal the fiery and sulphurous vapours of the 'ignited art' arise from the dispensing scales of three magical hands. The inscription explains: 'By the ignited art the shadow is bereft of a thick body.'

For all its horror and confusion, the experience of the prima materia is hailed by the alchemists as a fruitful event: the relationships of the personality to itself and to its environment are felt in a new way. The customary viewpoint is shattered; the 'salt of wisdom' enables the adept to view his old problems with new eyes. He has 'broken up' into an organized and revealing experience comparable to baptism or a bath of renewal. Still, there is always the possibility that

29. Schizophrenic dangers of the art.

experiencing the prima materia may become an infernal chaos; hence Hoghelande, citing Hali, says: 'Our stone is life to him who knows it and how it is made, and he who knows not and has not made it and to whom no assurance is given when it will be born, or who thinks it another stone, has already prepared himself for death.' (8)

Repulsive Matter of the Discovered Stone

Fig.28 shows the opening-up of the earth to its very centre and the parallel development of the 'chaos' of the prima materia. The sinister layers of the subterranean continent are illuminated by the rays of a golden stone at the bottom of the bottomless chasm: the philosophers' stone, which at first appears in a shoddy and despicable form. Filth or dung are some of the many synonyms of the prima materia, which the adepts frequently compare to secretions and excrement such as feces, urine, milk, and menstrual blood.

It is repeatedly stressed that the stone is to be found 'in filth,' and that it is so cheap and despicable that it is thrown out into the streets and trodden upon by people. An alchemical poem reads: 'There is a secret stone, hidden in a deep well, worthless and rejected, concealed in dung or filth.' (9) In the 'Tractatus aureus' the philosophers' stone is described as follows: 'Our most precious stone, cast forth upon the dunghill, being most dear, is made the vilest of the vile.' (10) The paradox of the stone being simultaneously vile and precious occurs already in the Greek texts. Zosimos says that the stone is 'contemned and much esteemed, not given yet given by God.' (11) Similar paradoxes appear in the 'Turba,' which describes the lapis as 'a thing . . . which is found everywhere, which is a stone and no stone, contemptible and precious, hidden, concealed, and yet known to everyone.' (12)

The repulsiveness of the stone and the primal matter is also compared to the 'shadow.' In the 'Novum lumen' the 'ignition of the art' is explained as follows: 'To cause things hidden in the shadow to appear, and to take away the shadow from them, this is permitted to the intelligent philosopher by God through nature . . . All these things happen, and the

30. Opening-up of the dark continent.

31. The cosmic chaos unloosened by the initial procedures of the alchemical work.

eyes of the common men do not see them, but the eyes of the mind and of the imagination perceive them with true and truest vision.' (13)

The advice given in the 'Aquarium sapientum' concerning the opening stage follows the same lines and reads as a commentary on the dark scenery of fig. 28: 'Let it be your first object to dissolve this prima materia or first entity which the sages have also called the highest natural good. Then it must be purified of its watery and earthy nature (for at first it appears an earthy, heavy, thick, slimy and misty body), and all that is thick, nebulous, opaque and shadowy in it must be removed that thus, by a final sublimation, the heart and inner soul in it may be separated and reduced to a precious essence.' (14)

Descent into the Mind

The attempt to burrow into the dunghill and to break through the crust of Mother Earth to discover the treasure hidden in her depths represents one of many alchemical variations of the return to the source of life. Identical with the 'putrefaction' and dissolution of the impure metals, the motif of the descent into the earth acquires in the symbolic language of the adepts the parallel meaning of an act of regression into the maternal depths of the psyche. Thus the alchemists' arduous mining becomes a symbol for their penetration of the 'crust' of consciousness and for their discovery of the treasure hidden beneath it in the darkness of the unconscious. This aspect of the work we shall study more closely.

32. Burrowing into the dunghill of the repressed unconscious, the ugly shadow.

Uncovering the Repressed Unconscious

Since it is repeatedly emphasized that the alchemical work is an *opus contra naturam,* that is, a way not of small but rather supreme resistance, the work of the alchemical rockbreakers emerges as a powerful symbol for the *removal of repression* by an ego working its way back into the depths of the unconscious. The chaos of the prima materia testifies to the dangers of this procedure. When the

repressed, buried, and hurtful memories of the *alter ego* or the 'shadow' (Jung) happen to be unleashed, they can be overwhelmingly frightening and produce a disintegration of mental functioning, fearful symbolic visions and structural personality disorders.

According to Jung, the prima materia may be conceived as a symbolic expression for an initial psychic situation he terms the 'meeting with the shadow': 'The first stage of the work, which was

felt as 'melancholia' in alchemy, corresponds to the encounter with the shadow in psychology (1) . . . The shadow is a moral problem that challenges the whole ego-personality, for no one can become conscious of the shadow without considerable moral effort. To become conscious of it involves recognizing the dark aspects of the personality as present and real. This act is the essential condition for any kind of self-knowledge, and it therefore, as a rule, meets with considerable resistance.' (2)

Onslaught of the Forces of Insanity

In fig.32 the alchemical philosopher Morienus exclaims while pointing to a colleague stamping on a dunghill: 'Take that which is trodden underfoot in the dunghill, for if thou dost not, thou wilt fall on thine head when thou wouldst climb without steps.' (3) Fig.33 shows the alchemical philosopher Democritus pointing to another motif of the opening opus: the appearance of the anima with her burning heart of love. The naked dream woman of the philosophers—half virgin, half whore—stands between Democritus and Vulcan, the latter representing the alchemist at his furnace. In the background a naked man practises dangerous exercises on a hill which slopes toward the sea. The motto reads: 'By the ignited art the shadow is bereft of a thick body.' (4)

Fig.34 depicts the forces let loose by the onslaught of the shadowy prima materia. At God's command the angels of the four corners release the demons Azael, Azazel, Samael, and Mahazael along with their dangerous animals and poisonous insects. The praying alchemist in the middle is protected from the chaos by the four archangels guarding the corners of the impregnable castle. The alchemist says his prayer of salvation to heaven: 'Make thy face to shine upon thy servant: save me for thy mercies' sake' (Psalm 31). This invocation is answered by a voice descending from the divine cloud: 'No plague shall come nigh thy dwelling. For he shall give his angels charge over thee, to keep thee in all thy ways' (Psalm 91).

The psychological implications are given with the epithet of the praying alchemist inside his mandalian castle: *homo sanus,* the 'sane man.' The demonic powers raging outside the castle are those of the *insane* man. Says an alchemical author: 'If you should suddenly see this transformation, wonder, fear, and trembling will befall you; therefore work with caution.' (5)

Fertile Chaos of a New Creation

If fear, hate, and aggression are the irresistible forces unleashed in fig.34,

33. A soul woman conjuring up the shadow and the world of repressed sexuality.

attraction, love, and hope are also present as compensating, and equally irresistible, forces. This paradoxical blend of positive and negative, of trust and fear, of hope and doubt, characterizes the prima materia which to the alchemist is a profoundly bewildering experience. It simultaneously denotes an act of creation and one of destruction, an act of separation and an act of mingling together, a retrograde movement and a progressive movement, a melting process and a hardening process. With its extreme fluidity and incessant fluctuations, the prima materia appears as a clash between the progressive and regressive forces struggling in the *massa confusa* to build a new cosmos out of an old one. In this connection one must also mention the most remarkable feature of all: the alchemist's frightening experience of universal chaos is strangely intermingled with his intoxicating experience of universal love (fig.33).

The Psychology of Adolescence

Jung never specified his general assumption of the prima materia as a symbol for the erupting unconscious psyche. (6) There are two reasons for Jung's inability to arrive at a closer understanding of the 'anatomical' structure of the prima materia: 1) His departure in 1912 from Freud's biological orientation with its attempts to understand the structuring of the psyche in terms of the genetic process; 2) a vague scientific understanding in the 1930s and 1940s of the concluding stages of the genetic process, where man's psychobiological structure arrives at its final form (from the age of 13 to 18).

What could be the psychological equivalent of the prima materia with its awakening of love in the middle of a bewildering chaos dissolving the elements of creation while giving birth to a new cosmos? *The psychology of adolescence corresponds with this paradoxical picture of creation.* The turmoil and upheaval of the prima materia express the adult ego's regressive revival of those unconscious layers which contain the imprints of the ego's tempestuous creation during adolescence where the 'dry land appears' and the sun of the conscious personality rises in full splendour from the sea of the unconscious. Two other prominent aspects of that developmental period are 1) the awakening of adult sexuality with survival value (genital love); 2) the awakening of adult aggression with survival value.

Significantly, this psychobiological maturation process of the ego takes place amidst a mental tempest in which all the psychic patterns built up during childhood and latency are broken up and restructured. In their description of adolescence, psychoanalytical authorities unconsciously avail themselves of prima materia language:

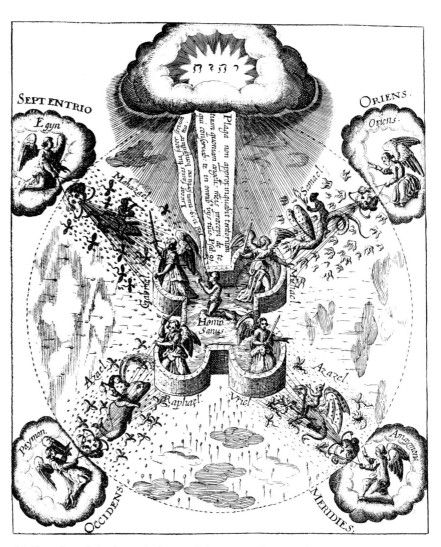

34. Eruption of the demonic forces of the repressed unconscious.

'The adolescent's instinctual development impressively demonstrates how, in climbing up the tortuous ladder to adulthood, he seems at every new step to experience anxiety, confusion, disorganization, and a return to infantile positions, followed by propulsion and reorganization at more advanced and more adult levels. Such processes, to be sure, can be observed at any developmental stage. But during the dramatic adolescent period we see what Helene Deutsch described as a 'clash' between progressive and regressive forces. This clash leads to a far-reaching temporary dissolution of old structures and organizations, in conjunction with new structure formation and the establishment of new hierarchic orders, in which earlier psychic formations definitely assume a subordinate role, while new ones acquire and sustain dominance' (Edith Jacobson). (7)

'One gets the impression that in adolescence, the personality is melted down, becomes molten and fluid, and ultimately hardens again into what is to remain as the characterological core' (Leo A. Spiegel). (8)

'During this period of inner turmoil, and in the midst of the struggle between the contrasting forces of action and agony, upheavals and overthrows, chaos and clarification, joy and despair—during all this, the development of the ego proceeds' (Helene Deutsch). (9)

Since the prima materia symbolizes the opening 'work' of individuation identical with the mature ego's re-experience of the formative period of adolescence, we may expect the emergence of a number of alchemical prima materia motifs symbolizing these crucial events of adolescence:

1) The lifting of repression and the revival of the *alter ego,* shadow, or repressed, unconscious personality part; 2) the revival of the anima, or unconscious woman ideal; 3) the kindling of the shadow by adult aggression; 4) the kindling of the anima by adult sexuality; 5) the revival of the primary objects of love and hate, that is, the parental figures of the Oedipus complex; 6) the revival of the superego formed during latency and subduing the Oedipus complex.

35. *Reviving the magic of adolescent love: the smell of lions, sulphur, and incest.*

Incestuous Meeting of King and Queen

In Barchusen's plate 9 (fig.24) the terror of the prima materia was resolved with the sun establishing contact across a brook with the moon. The origin of this motif is the second woodcut of the 'Rosarium' (fig.36) in which the king, standing atop the sun and representing the spiritus, meets the bride of his choice, resting on the moon and representing the anima. The rose branches crossed by king and queen bear out their mutual love, but the court clothes worn by the royal lovers suggest the restrained nature of their initial encounter.

The two roses at the end of each branch refer to the four elements, two of which are active and masculine (fire and air), while two are passive and feminine (water and earth). Their ordered arrangement in a 'rosie cross' suggests the abatement of the prima materia and its warring elements. The fifth flower is brought by the dove of the Holy Ghost, a parallel of Noah's dove carrying the olive branch of reconciliation in its beak (fig.27). Descending from the quintessential star, the bird reconciles the masculine and feminine elements, just as its third branch equates the rose branches with the three pipes of the mercurial fountain, now transformed into stems of roses.

The dove is the agent effecting the *rapprochement* between king and queen, just as the bird indicates the spiritual and heavenly nature of their love. The unusual character of this affair is further stressed by the partners' left-handed contact. This uncustomary gesture points to the closely guarded secret of their infringement of a general taboo. Actually the royal couple engages in 'unnatural' and illegitimate love, the secret of which is of an incestuous nature: *the bride is the king's own sister.* (1) Hence the 'Rosarium' admonishes: 'Mark well, in the art of our magisterium nothing is concealed by the philosophers except the secret of the art which may not be revealed to all and sundry. For were that to happen, that man would be accursed; he would incur the wrath of God and perish of the apoplexy.' (2)

36. *Establishing contact with the anima.*

Merging of the Two Waters

The engraved variant (fig.35) emphasizes the incestuous nature of the royal meeting. The king and queen shake hands while balancing on the backs of two lions. The lions' heads are joined into one head from which is belched forth the sulphurous water of royal love. Since the lion is the classical incest symbol in alchemy, the water gushing from the mouth of the united lions may be interpreted as an expression of the incestuous passion of the royal pair. The source of the motif comes from Senior as quoted by the 'Rosarium': 'Senior says: Make one water out of two waters. If you have understood my short indication, the whole course of action will be under your feet. Rosarius says: You should have two waters, the one white, the other red. Senior says: This is the water in which the powers of whiteness and redness are united.' (3)

The motif reappears in fig.37, the motto of which reads: 'Make one water out of two waters, and it will become the water of holiness.' (4) The engraving summarizes the opening opus: the gushing waters of the mercurial fountain; the adepts intoxicating themselves with mercurial water; the meeting of the sexes; the awakening of love in the watery chaos of the brimming fountain. The king and queen appear in an interesting variation, as *adolescent boy and girl.* The epigram reads:

There are two fountains springing with
*   great power,*
The one water is hot and belongs to the
*   boy;*
The other water is cold and is called the
*   virgin's fountain.*
Unite the one with the other, that the
*   two waters may be one:*
This stream will possess the forces of
*   each of them, mixed together,*
Just as the fountain of Jupiter Hammon
*   is simultaneously hot and cold.* (5)

Fig.38 shows the fourth painting of the 'Splendor solis' which presents another variation upon the royal meeting. The incest motif is expressed by the king's astonished recognition of his beloved queen, who startles him by her very familiarity. The maternal features of the queen are brought out by her scroll with the inscription, *lac viramium* (the 'heroine's milk'). The queen balances herself on the cool lunar globe, while the king appears to be consumed by the flames of solar fire, or passion. The scroll winding around his sceptre is inscribed *coagula maaschculium*, that is, 'coagulate the masculine.'

Astonishment and secretiveness accompanying the king's *rendezvous* merge with other characteristics apparent in these pictures. The king's expression is a blend of ambivalence and moodiness; such feelings toward the bride of his choice are explained by the queen's *maternal* qualities. The strange kind of love developing at the opening stage of the opus is not difficult to decipher psychologically. The incestuous nature of the royal libido, its astonishment, ambivalence, moodiness, and secretiveness, are features that point to *adolescent love,* which displays these very characteristics. We shall return to this question on the following pages.

The Sun and Moon of Astrology

Alchemical symbolism is closely bound up with astrological symbolism; if we want to unravel the deeper meaning of the fact that the king is on the sun and the queen on the moon, we must look into the astrological implications of these heavenly bodies. The sun is the greatest of all the 'planets,' and it stands for the male principle, consciousness, or spirit. A luminous eye, soaring wings, royal dominion, fire and gold are archetypal elements of solar symbolism. Its core is a heroic force which is creative, guiding and indispensable to life. The sun governs in only one sign: the Lion.

Because of its passive character—in that it receives its light from the sun—the moon is equated with the feminine principle and with the soul. Governing in the Crab, the moon is a symbol for the mother and is closely connected with the maternal functions of conception and birth. Whereas the sun with its fiery activity is responsible for the life of the manifest world, or the day, the moist moon governs the life of the unmanifest world, or the night. Volatile and silvery, the moon of astrology belongs to the nocturnal, subterranean and subconscious part of man's world. She embodies the psychic, the occult, and the magic, and her mana attracts the sun with irresistible force.

The Unconscious Anima Complex

The astrological features of the alchemical Sol and Luna, or king and queen, and the spiritus and anima symbolism expressed by these Hermetic figures, were unravelled by Jung in the 1920s. Jung interpreted the sun and the king as symbols of the ego or the conscious mind, the moon and the queen as symbols of the anima or the unconscious mind. (6) Whereas the psychology of the king and the sun was described by the ego-psychologists of post-Freudian psychoanalysis (Anna Freud and Heinz Hartmann), the queen and the moon received their psychological biographer in C.G. Jung, the discoverer of the anima complex.

According to Jung, the enigmatic anima figure of the alchemists personifies the unconscious psyche and its sexual dynamics in the man. Whereas the unconscious tends to personify itself in a female form in the man, it will

37. A fountain gushing with the waters of adolescent sexuality and incestuous love.

assume a masculine form in the woman. Jung named these complex soul images anima and animus. Formed out of man's experience of woman from time immemorial, and receiving the suppressed 'feminine' elements of the conscious masculine psyche, the anima complex represents the 'eternal feminine' principle in man, his magic idea of the 'ideal woman.'

The archetypal nature of the male's anima,

38. Birth of love in the middle of chaos.

or 'soul,' links it to the collective unconscious and the self, the polarity of which the anima reflects in a fascinating way. Young and old, passionate and aloof, devilish and divine, the anima exhibits not only the erotic and instinctual features of whore, mermaid, and vampire, but simultaneously the luminous and spiritual features of virgin, angel, and goddess. Elusive and enigmatic, and surrounded with all the strange lustre of the unconscious, the anima may be studied in dreams and—in her projected form—in poetry and art.

'Every man carries his Eve in himself' goes the saying, and when a man finds a woman whose whole complexion and character fit his anima projection, he falls in love with her. In an enlarged form the same psychological dynamism appears in the cinema, where film stars live solely on the power of anima and animus projections: screen idols have an animating effect on the moviegoer, even long after such a person has left his dream-house.

When a man's unconscious image of his 'soul' is awakened by a real woman and projected on to her, he will experience a wealth of moods ranging from Weltschmerz and depression to elated yearnings of equally cosmic proportions. Such feelings will thrill the masculine subject as long as the anima image keeps her projected or 'materialized' form; if, for some reason or other, this image loses its fascination and divine character, the man will become 'disillusioned' and suddenly see his 'ideal woman' as an ordinary member of the female sex. However, as long as the anima complex is allowed free projection, she will evoke in the man his deepest feelings, emotions which are often expressed through creativity: writing poetry, performing music, drawing or painting—well-known phenomena in young people who have fallen in love.

39. Announcing the beginning work and the climbing of Jacob's ladder of dreams.

the work should be begun when the sun is in Aries, the 'priority' sign of the Zodiac, and, hence, of the opus circulatorium.

The impetuous beginning of the opus and the violent beginning of the astrological year are both due to the vernal impulses released by the Ram. The first sign of the Zodiac is a cardinal, fiery sign ruled by Mars and covering the period from March 21 to April 20. The Ram is aggressive, dynamic, and choleric; its fiery and passionate nature expresses the explosive sun of spring. Like the gushing mercurial fountain, Aries represents the creative urge which bursts any fixed order to initiate growth. With its fierce and dangerous energy aimed at heat and activation, the Ram embodies the principle of pure impulse, pure drive. Tough and reckless like the warrior-god Mars, who rules the sign (fig.45), Aries symbolizes the primal fire and waters which may both create and destroy. Because the Ram stands for the initial impulse through which potential becomes actual, it is also related to dawn and, in general, to the beginning of any cycle, process, or act of creation.

Lovers Returning to Childhood

The second engraving of the 'Mutus liber' (fig.41) renders the incestuous meeting between the alchemist and his 'mystical sister' *(soror mystica);* they are shown kneeling on either side of the furnace which contains the sealed phial. The gesture of the alchemist is one of prayer, while his mystical sister after the dramatic parting of the curtains points toward the upper half of the engraving. This renders the complex drama of the prima materia with its separation of the four elements (the angels' feet rest on dry land); its magical sunrise in the cool of the first morning on earth; its awakening of love between Sol and Luna (the sym-

Dreamy Descent into the Mercurial Sea

Fig.39 shows the first engraving of the 'Mutus liber' series of the opus. (1) On a moonlit night spangled with stars the alchemist *falls asleep* by the rocky sea shore where the sea suddenly breaks into the land, flooding everything. The eruption of the *unconscious* is confirmed by the second motif of the engraving which renders Jacob's *dream:* 'Behold a ladder set up on the earth, and the top of it reached to heaven: and behold the angels of God ascending and descending on it' (Gen.28:12). In alchemy the stone of Jacob is a popular symbol of the philosophers' stone, which is also a stone working magical dreams. The 'call' to ascend the Jacob's ladder and begin the opus is expressed by two angels attempt-

ing to awaken the sleeping alchemist with their trumpets. The nightly scenery is framed by two rose-branches, whose flowers symbolize mystical, or divine, love.

Aries the Ram: Opening the Yearly Work

Both alchemy and astrology are cyclic systems built upon the principle of analogy: the cosmic order is analogous to the human order. Because the universe is an immense organic being, all the parts of the world are subject to the same laws. What happens to the alchemist at the beginning of his work is therefore a reflection of what happens at the beginning of the yearly nature cycle. According to this system of 'correspondences,'

40. Opening of the work in the Ram.

bolic equivalents of the man and woman below); its regressive current returning the lovers to the bottom of the sea (Neptune) and to the realms of childhood (the infantile presentation of Sol and Luna).

Royal Love of Adolescence

In addition to the incestuous, heavenly, spiritual, ambivalent, moody, and secretive nature of alchemical love, we shall further have to emphasize its regressive nature. This unique pattern fits the psychology of adolescent love, which we shall briefly attempt to describe. Falling in love is one of the most absorbing emotional experiences of adolescence. The experience is enigmatic, since the woman the adolescent projects his feelings on appears to him a superhuman figure, 'not the daughter of a mortal man, but of God,' as Dante described his adolescent love of Beatrice. Produced in him are a variety of feelings and moods: now sweet, now bitter; now elated, now depressed; now ecstatic, now shameful, mostly both; and always confusing, perplexing.

Such feelings of sweet melancholy and ambivalence toward a semi-divine female have puzzled non-Jungian psychoanalytical investigators of adolescence: 'To adolescence proper belongs that unique experience, tender love . . . The partner does not represent merely a source of sexual pleasure (sex play); rather, she signifies a conglomerate of sacred and precious attributes which strike the boy with awe' (Peter Blos). (2) Autobiographical literature abounds with descriptions of this kind; Norman Kiel selected an illuminating number of them in 'The Universal Experience of Adolescence' (1964).

Jung's discovery of this feminine 'spiritualizing' complex in the man's unconscious led him to define the anima as a psychological function, in the same way as Freud defined the ego and the superego as psychological functions. According to Jung, the anima canalizes the dynamics of the sexual drive, which may be directed toward a real woman in object love or (as in introspection) withdrawn into a cathexis (energizing) of the ideal woman or anima. In the latter case, the anima function asserts itself in imaginative and creative activities, in presentiments and in changes of mood.

The sublimating effects of the anima on the sexual drive are easily demonstrable in adolescence and assert themselves in the division between 'sex' and 'love,' or in the development of 'tender love.' There is a tendency on the part of nearly all people to use spiritual phraseology in describing this phase of their lives with its 'crushes' and sacred memories of ineffable love.

41. Adolescent regression of alchemical lovers: watery return to the children's land.

Adolescent Revival of Oedipus Complex

Before Freud it was commonly held that the sexual instinct first appeared in puberty; it was only after the publication of 'Three Contributions to the Theory of Sexuality' (1905) that it was properly understood that the sexual drive has a long history of development in the individual, from birth to the attainment of mature genitality in adulthood. *Adolescence is not the first flowering of human sexuality, but its second.*

This crucial insight has led all psychoanalytical experts on the subject to agree on one point: *the revival and intensification of the sexual drive in adolescence inevitably leads to a revival of infantile sexuality as concentrated in the Oedipus complex.*

This development affects the anima complex in a decisive manner. Since the anima embodies the incestuous woman ideal of the Oedipus complex, she becomes a powerful regressive force in adolescence. Charged no longer with Oedipal-pregenital energy but with the full power of adult-genital energy, the anima pushes the adolescent ego into both progressive and regressive directions. She both projects herself on to a real woman and revives the infantile and incestuous image of the first beloved—the object of divine and infernal love (see pp.34-96). Psychologically, this dual function causes perplexion, moodiness, ambivalence, and secretiveness; also it produces the rapid adolescent mood changes where guilt and depression may alternate with ecstatic elation and feelings of universal love.

42. A date with Saturn and his wolf: the sources of incest, envy, hate and fear revived.

heated stone. In the vibrant air the incestuous passion of the king and queen combines with a parallel feeling of mortal anxiety expressed by Saturn and his howling wolf. 'Roaming about, savage with hunger,' (3) the wolf is related to the two astrological *malefici*, Mars and Saturn, and thereby represents the danger of mutilation and death. Significantly, the scythe of Saturn is connected in fig.42 with the god's amputated leg and, hence, symbolizes mutilation and punishment. Alchemically, Saturn is identified with the metal of lead, while astrologically his emblems are those of the scythe, an amputated leg, and a small child whom he devours. These symbols reflect his sinister background: Saturn castrated his father and usurped his kingdom, hence he suspects his sons of similar intentions. Mercilessly, he forestalls the dangers of his own future castration and overthrow by devouring his sons at birth.

Envy, Hate and Fear Revived

Since Freud, it has been understood that not only the sexual but also the aggressive urge is revived in adolescence. This joint maturation of the primal drives is expressed by the prima materia in which love's awakening appears simultaneously with another initiation: the acquisition of the sword of Mars. The fact that these two events are connected with the 'urine of children' gushing from the mercurial fountain reiterates a psychodynamic explanation in terms of adolescence. Just as the anima is charged with genital sexuality in adolescence, the

Martian Sword of Alchemical Initiation

Fig.44 shows the second painting of Salomon Trismosin's 'Splendor solis,' in which the philosopher, pointing to the vessel, exclaims: 'Let us go and seek the nature of the four elements.' As evident from the subsequent painting reproduced in fig.45, this action is synonymous with the opening of the opus since the separation of the four elements for examination is the very means of producing the chaos of the prima materia.

The third painting of the 'Splendor solis' (fig.45) shows the brimming mercurial fountain adorned with 'pissing mannikins' and bestridden by Mars, the warrior god whose sword opens the opus in the sign of the Ram.* The seven planets or metals hovering above the martial alchemist is another indication of the beginning work, described on the shield in

this way: 'Make one water out of two waters. You who seek to create the sun and moon, give them to drink of the inimical wine, and you will obtain vision at [their] death. Then make earth out of water, and you will have multiplied the stone.'

The 'two waters' gushing from the mouths of the adolescent boy and girl in fig.37 spout from the genitalia of two children in fig.45, thus revealing a prima materia activated by regressive desires. The 'pissing mannikins' fill the basin and the sea with the 'urine of children,' a synonym for the waters of the prima materia. Says the 'Gloria mundi': 'The spirit which is extracted from the metals is the urine of children and of the sages, for it is the seed and the primal matter of metals. Without this seed there is no consummation in our art.' (1)

The sword of Mars developed in fig. 45 is described more closely by fig.43, in which the alchemical sword of initiation is presented by an adolescent boy. The sword is an obvious allusion to the boy's sexual maturity, its phallic implications enforced in the vitriolic hilt with its assaulting snake, suggesting erection, penetration, and fertilization. In his left hand the boy carries the sign of sulphur, or the emblem of masculine sexuality.

The prima materia sword reappears in a third variation with the First Key of Basil Valentine, the mythical Benedictine of alchemy (fig.42). (2) Here the 'sword' is represented by the scythe of Saturn, made glowing in the fire of the

43. The adolescent's sword of initiation.

* The painting precedes fig.38, which is the fourth. However, the sequence does not matter in this case since the symbolic actions of the two paintings are the two sides of the same prima materia-coin (cf. fig.24, plates 8-9).

44. Exploring the contents of the vessel.

shadow or *alter ego* is charged with adult aggression inside the framework of a revived Oedipus complex. This lends resuscitation to the central figure of infantile envy, fear, and aggression: the paternal hate-object of the Oedipus complex (Saturn).

Why the parental love-hate objects of childhood should be revived in adolescence has been adequately explained by Peter Blos, a leading authority on the subject: 'Analytic work with adolescents demonstrates, almost monotonously, the reinvolvment of ego and superego functions with infantile object relations. The study of this subject has convinced me that the danger to ego integrity does not derive alone from the strength of the pubertal drives, but comes, in equal measure, from *the strength of the regressive pull*. Discounting the assumption of a fundamental enmity between ego and id, I came to the conclusion that *the task of psychic restructuring by regression represents the most formidable psychic work of adolescence* . . . I shall now turn to the broader consequences of the fact that regression in adolescence is the precondition for progressive development. I inferred from clinical observations that the adolescent has to come into emotional contact with the passions of his infancy and early childhood, in order for them to surrender their original cathexes [energies]; only then can the past fade into conscious and unconscious memories, and only then will the forward movement of the libido give youth that unique emotional intensity and power of purpose. The profoundest and most unique quality of adolescence lies in its capacity to move between regressive and progressive consciousness.' (4)

This alternation of the adolescent psyche—reviving the Oedipus complex and repressing it, conjuring up the attachment to primary love and hate objects and disengaging from them, extending the umbilical cord to the land of childhood and cutting it—corresponds with the alchemists' experience of the ebb and flow of their prima materia. The modern understanding of adolescence as a formative phase of extreme instability and fluidity fully explains the deep sea swell of the prima materia, or the unconscious, at the opening stage of the *opus individuationis*.

The First Key of Basil Valentine

In addition to opening the work, the springing mercurial fountain signifies the release of the waters of *rejuvenation*, symbolized by the fountain's adolescent lovers and 'pissing mannikins.' This positive aspect of unconscious regression is balanced off by its negative aspect, expressed by the emergence of such sinister symbols as Mars, Saturn and their animal double, the wolf. These shadow

45. The urine of children spouting from a fountain of regression and rejuvenation.

figures express the greedy, ruthless and infantile-sadistic features of the king's inferior personality, governed by the id-impulses of raw aggression and primitive sexuality. Viewed on this background, the text of Basil Valentine's First Key becomes a little clearer:

'As the physician purges and cleanses the inward parts of the body and removes all unhealthy matter by means of his medicines, so our bodies must be purified and refined of all impurity so that perfection may work in our blood. Our masters require a pure, immaculate body which is without any defects and is untainted with any foreign admixture, for foreign admixture is the leprosy of our metals. Let the king's crown be of pure gold, and a chaste bride will be united to him in wedlock. If you would operate by means of our bodies, take a fierce grey wolf which, though on account of its name it be subject to the sway of warlike Mars, is by birth the offspring of ancient Saturn, and is found in the valleys and mountains of the world, where he roams about savage with hunger. Cast to the wolf the body of the king that in this way it may have its food; and when the wolf has devoured the king, burn it entirely to ashes in a great fire. By this process the king will be redeemed; and when it has been performed thrice the lion has overcome the wolf and will find nothing more to devour in him. Thus our body has been rendered perfect for the first stage of our work.' (5)

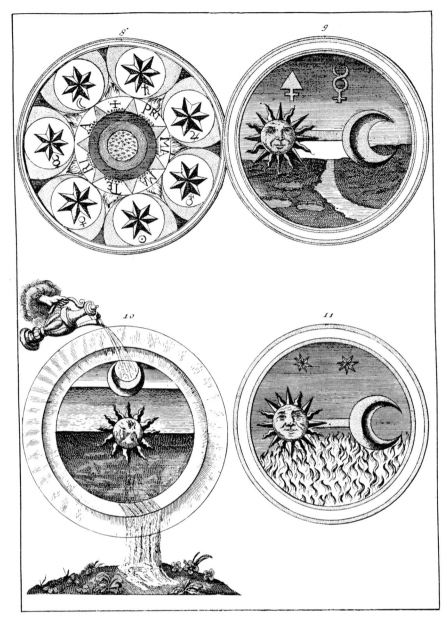

46. *The solar and lunar bodies cooled by Jupiter's water of growth and sublimation.*

Sol and Luna represent the four elements and their peaceful interaction in a process of vegetative growth. Venus (Juno) with her peacock, a girl with flowers representing Mother Earth, a sheep and a bull bear out these vernal processes unfolding under the aegis of Jupiter.

In the central circle the sister baits a merman riding in a shell which is drawn by a double-headed sea-horse. The figure is identified with Neptune carrying his trident. Below, the situation is reversed: here the alchemist attempts with rod and line to hook a mermaid. As indicated by the gesture of his right hand, his baiting parallels that of his sister. Opposite the alchemist, his sister holds a bird-cage in her left hand while trying with her right to enmesh birds.

Latency Period of Libido Sublimation

Jung interprets the actions of fig.48 as expressive of a sublimation of the sex instinct: Neptune drawn by sea-horses is a symbol of the alchemical woman's animus (represented also by the 'spiritual' birds caught in her net); similarly, the mermaid is a symbol of the alchemist's anima (represented also by Venus and the flower girl). (1) In search of their 'soul' in a universe governed by Jupiter, the adept and his sister have gone fishing on a *voyage d'amour* in which sex is experienced everywhere as 'soul love.' This sublimation of the sexual instinct accords well with the symbolic action of Barchusen's plate 10. If plate 8 symbolizes the turbulence of adolescence and plate 9 the adolescent revival of the Oedipus complex, the duplicated situation in plate 11 would symbolize the original Oedipus complex with its pregenital awakening of love and hate. Consequently, the intervening plate 10 would render the period between the first and second kindling of the Oedipus complex. This is the period of *latency* (c.5-13 years). Its psychodyna-

Jupiter's Water of Sublimation

The prima materia raging in Barchusen's plate 8, and the love awakening between Sol and Luna in plate 9, are followed by the strange action of plate 10, which realizes the oracular bubbling of the mercurial fountain: 'Make one water out of two waters, and it will become the water of holiness.' Sol and Luna separate at the hands of Jupiter, who from his little cloud pours out the divine water of growth cooling and purifying their hot, incestuous bodies. The 'holy' aspect of the water is emphasized by its equation with altar wine poured from a large cruet. In plate 11 Sol and Luna resume their amorous encounter in a much more passionate setting than in plate 9. Heated by a sea of fire, Sol and Luna experience a flare-up of their incestuous passion,

burning bright in a night of stars. The symbolic action of plate 10, intervening between the love-sceneries of plates 9 and 11, has the obvious function of sprinkling cool patience on the bodies of Sol and Luna. In terms of the mercurial fountain, the hot and cold waters of its adolescent boy and virgin are mixed into the purifying 'water of holiness' ascribed to the 'fountain of Jupiter Hammon [which] is simultaneously hot and cold.'

A similar neutralization or sublimation of love is expressed by the romantic *voyage d'amour* of the alchemist and his sister in fig.48, the third engraving of the 'Mutus liber.' The picture renders the separation of Sol and Luna (left and right) at the hands of Jupiter on his eagle and little cloud. The effects of Jupiter's intervention are the same as in Barchusen's plate 10: the spaces between

47. *A latency symbol of peaceful growth.*

mic structure fully explains Jupiter's 'water of holiness' and growth, and its subtle effects on Sol and Luna.

Latency is characterized by massive repression of the infantile Oedipus complex, whose sexual and aggressive drives are canalized into intellectual activities and social pursuits. If the child's ego organization is to mature in peace, and if his chances of exploring and mastering his environment are to develop, he must dissolve his sexual ties to his mother and rivalrous identification with his father. The sun and moon of his little universe must be separated and purified by the 'water of holiness.' If this healthy change occurs, that is, if the child succeeds in resolving his Oedipal conflict, he will emerge into the peaceful growth of latency with a greatly strengthened ego, permitting him a *conflict-free father identification and a conflict-free love of mother.*

The Superego, or Jupiter Complex

In the 1920s Freud discovered the unconscious complex which during latency binds and neutralizes conflicting sexuality and aggression. He called it the 'superego.' (2) He might as well have termed it the 'Jupiter complex.' The superego develops through the child's identification with its parents' commands, attitudes, and judgements, which is one of the most important factors in the learning process. Once this occurs, the ego follows the parental admonition as if it came entirely from itself: 'musts' and 'musts not' now come from within, the parent now speaks from within as 'conscience.' The basic code of the superego, on which society still rests, is the tabooing of 1) actual incest and 2) parricide (or fratricide).

Due to the filtering, binding and neutralizing activity of the superego, the growing ego may now resume its aggressive identification with the father in a more positive spirit. The father may now function as an ego-ideal furthering the healthy outlet of the boy's aggressive drive and promoting his formation of sexual identity. Similarly, the superego ensures the parallel purgation and binding of the boy's incestuous urges so that his sexual drive may be used in a conflict-free relationship to his maternal woman-ideal, anima, or mother.

The superego's repressive effects in the opening stage of the king's and queen's love affair may be distinguished in their secretive relationship and in their inhibitory left-handed contact. Further superego symbols are their court clothes, signifying cultural convention and instrumental in keeping the incestuous partners apart. The brook in Barchusen's plate 9 acts as a similar agent of separation and frustration. The superego itself is sym-

48. The alchemist and his sister trying to catch the creatures of submarine love.

bolized by Jupiter and his 'holy water,' 'simultaneously hot and cold.' Another latency symbol is the Bull, the sign in which the alchemist descends into the earth once its crust has been broken by the horns of the Ram.

Taurus the Bull: Gentle, Earthly Growth

Governing from April 21 to May 21, the animal of the second sign of the Zodiac is a heavy and slow ruminant, attached to the earth and its products while filled with earthy vigor (fig.47). A latency symbol of peaceful growth, the Bull signifies *matrix* or matter and the creative processes of the earth, its roots, saps and germs. The Bull holds the key to spring with its slow organic growth: the

sun in Taurus radiates the warmth that invests plants and animals with the energy of budding life and development. Taurus denotes fecundity and nourishment and is therefore a symbol of the Earth Mother with her nutritive and invigorating powers. This aspect explains the basic idea of the Bull as the universal creative force which animates forms of all kinds. A fixed and earthy sign, the Bull symbolizes the 'bovine' libido, the hot blood of the growing body, the throbbing bliss of pure boundless existence.

Whereas the Arian personality is an impetuous, adolescent type—assertive, urgent, choleric and violent—the Taurean personality displays the gentle features of latency: patience, affection, persistence and practicability, all combined with a marked sense of self-preservation.

31

49. Regressing with the mermaid to the Oedipal layers of childhood and infancy.

First Discoverers of the Oedipus Complex

Having dived mermaid-like into the ocean and buried his way into the rocks of the earth, the alchemist suddenly encounters the strange layers of oceanic geology of fig.49; the picture renders the famous ancient legend of King Oedipus. The motto reads: 'After having conquered the Sphinx and killed Laios, his father, Oedipus takes his mother to wife.' (1)

The foreground figures illustrate the riddle of the Sphinx: What is that which walks on four in the morning, on two at noon, on three in the evening? Answer: Man. The pictorial action unfolds like a backwards S and symbolizes an act of

50. The Oedipal quest of Mercurius.

regression. It depicts the 'Oedipal' fate of the alchemical philosopher who, passing the stages of his age and youth, finally crawls as a little child. Going further back with his mermaid or anima (middle of the background), the alchemical philosopher finally involves himself in the fate of King Oedipus: unknowingly he slays his own father and usurps his place by marrying his own mother (background right). The mermaid triumphantly points to the incestuous marriage as the goal of the alchemical voyage. The text accompanying the engraving reads:

'Oedipus was stigmatized on account of patricide and incest, the two most evil vices which may be imagined. Yet they brought him on the throne since he killed his own father, who would not give way to him on the road, and married the queen, Laios' wife, his own mother. This is merely a fable and should not, as is written, be imitated, since it has been invented and presented in an allegorical way by the philosophers in order to reveal the secrets of their doctrine.' (2)

The geometrical signs inscribed on the three foreground figures refer to the opus and to the composition of the philosophers' stone: 'The true meaning is: first one should consider the square, or the four elements; from there one should advance to the hemisphere, which has two lines, the straight and the curved one, representing Luna, who is made white;

after that one should pass to the triangle, which consists of body, soul, and spirit, or Sol, Luna, and Mercurius.' (3)

Diving With the Mermaid

The function of the mermaid in fig.49 is obviously the same as that of the mermaid and merman in the third engraving of the 'Mutus liber': drawing the alchemist into the depths of the sea, defined by fig.49 as the realm of the Oedipus legend. This relationship forms an interesting background for Jung's interpretation of the mermaid archetype:

'Nixies are entrancing creatures: 'Half drew she him, half sank he down and nevermore was seen' (Goethe: The Fisherman). The nixie is an even more instinctive version of a magical feminine being whom I have called the anima. She can also be a siren, melusina (mermaid), wood-nymph, Grace, or Erlking's daughter, or a lamia or succubus, who infatuates young men and sucks the life out of them . . . An alluring nixie from the dim bygone is today called an 'erotic fantasy'. . . With the archetype of the anima we enter the realm of the gods, or rather, the realm that metaphysics has reserved for itself. Everything the anima touches becomes numinous.' (4)

The alchemical experiment in depth symbolized by the baiting of mermaids and mermen finally leads to the scooping up of erotic fantasies hiding in impenetrable forests at the bottom of the sea (see pp.34-97). The fourth engraving of

51. A regressed Oedipus mannikin.

the 'Mutus liber' (fig.52) shows the love flaring up between the adept and his sister in the months of spring: the on-rushing Bull and the Ram are governed by Venus and Mars, in whose signs the lovers collect 'May-dew' in staked-out sheets. By wringing them they gather the moisture full of germinating power in a dish, and from this prima materia they generate the philosophers' stone and the child of their union in the ensuing engravings (figs.75, 92, 123, 141).

The Oedipal Secret of Mercurius

Fig.51 shows an alchemical workshop in which the adept appears in the guise of Mercurius and in the role of 'Oedipus chimicus.' He watches a paternal figure, or elder colleague, putting aside his glowing pincers and heating the furnace with his pair of bellows. Mercurius explains the meaning of the roaring fire by pointing to the Oedipal drama in the background. Here Mercurius appears in his regressed state as mannikin 'Oedipus,' conversing with the maternal 'Sphinx' outside the entrance of a hollow cave—like the furnace, an alchemical symbol of the womb.

The Mythical Level of the Unconscious

With the regressive activation of the Oedipus complex, the reality principle and the secondary process thinking of latency (realistic, rational thinking) begin to yield to magico-animistic fantasy life and primary process thinking. As the layers of the collective unconscious filter into the layers of the personal unconscious, the individual problems and figures are absorbed and replaced by archetypal figures and situations. In short, the ego regressively enters the land of fairytale, myth and legend and the realm of mermaids and mermen. This level of the unconscious was inferred by Jung in 1912 as a result of his study of 'archetypal' dreams and myths ('Transformations and Symbols of the Libido').

Empirically, the level has been demonstrated by LSD-induced regressions which uncover what R.E.L.Masters and Jean Houston call the 'symbolic level' of the unconscious: 'The images become of major importance on this symbolic level as does the capacity of the subject to feel that he is participating with his body as well as his mind in the events he is imaging. Here, the symbolic images are predominantly historical, legendary, mythical, ritualistic, and 'archetypal.' The subject may experience a profound and rewarding sense of continuity with evolutionary and historic process. He may act out myths and legends and pass through initiations and ritual observances often seemingly structured precisely in terms of his own most urgent needs.' (5)

52. The adept and his sister collecting the 'May-dew' of spring and generation.

With the uncovering of the Oedipal layers of primary process thinking and mythical fantasy, the unconscious conjures up a pandemonium of images and impulses disagreeable if not repulsive to the conscious mind. The immensely sadistic, incestuous and parricidal fantasies of infantile sexuality saturate the symbolism of the alchemical pictures which describe the adepts' way toward the royal marriage of Theban myth.

'People still ask, as they did in Freud's time, 'What is the purpose of this ultimate obscenity, the fantasy of incest?' The answer is relatively simple. Once a desire, whether for murder or sex, is repressed into the subconscious, it exercises a covert effect on the subconscious mind and the whole personality. Only when it is consciously recognized and abreacted can the fixation be dispelled. Until a man has recognized his sexual desire for his mother, he cannot achieve complete satisfaction with any other woman, because the ultimate depths of his desire are locked in an attachment he dare not recognize. But once he has consciously accepted that attachment, he can then redirect the emotions elsewhere. The incest fantasy achieves that recognition and dissolves the fixation. From here on, both in psychedelic fantasy and in their normal relationships, patients find an ecstatic joy in sex. Once they have achieved the incest resolution, they are 'sexually well adjusted' in the best sense.'

W.V.Caldwell: LSD Psychotherapy.(6)

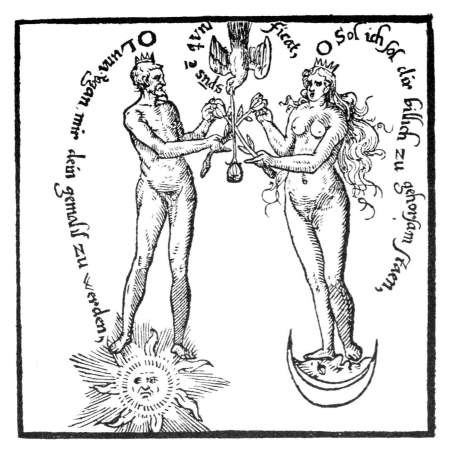

53. *Brother and sister stripped naked in a naked outburst of incestuous love and hate.*

The Naked Truth of Royal Love

Fig.54 shows the third woodcut of the 'Rosarium' and figs.53,55 and 58 its pictorial variants. The king and queen have stripped themselves of the court clothes worn in the second woodcut. Sol and Luna's naked state reveals an ardent revival of their incestuous passion and their determination to engage in sexual intercourse. Sol exclaims: 'O Luna, let me be thy husband,' while Luna answers in the same vein: 'O Sol, I must submit to thee.' The dove bears the inscription: 'It is the spirit which vivifies.' ('It is the spirit which unifies,' reads the varied inscription of fig.53.)

The awkward left-handed contact has become their holding the roses normally: the secret, incestuous relationship has been brought into the open and acknowledged. Intimate contact is further expressed in the four roses becoming two, just as the two roses of the dove have been transformed into the multifoliate *rosa mystica*. This is the rose symbolizing the *unio mystica* of love on the 'spiritual' level of incest.

For all their symbols of libidinal sublimation, the alchemists still emphasize that the 'spiritual' union must be of the same nature as the sexual union. In fig.55 Sol and Luna point to the cock and hen in a gesture expressing their desire to be

united in sexual wedlock. It is repeatedly stressed in the treatises: 'Sun and moon must have intercourse like that of a man and woman: otherwise the object of our art cannot be attained. All other teaching is false and erroneous.' (1)

The text accompanying fig.55 says that the 'cock is sacred to the sun with whom it rises and with whom it goes to sleep.' (2) Cock and sun are archetypal father symbols, while the brooding hen is a mother symbol of similar universality. Thus, brother and sister are invested with so strong paternal and maternal qualities that one glimpses the underlying meaning of the 'unifying spirit' of the dove: that of a father identification established by the brother and a mother identification by the sister, both acts of identification serving to involve the lovers in the mystery of the primal act.

Filthy and sacred, the alchemical act of parental conjunction requires a human vessel of supreme intellectual and moral qualities. Hence the text accompanying the third woodcut of the 'Rosarium' admonishes: 'He who would be initiated into this art and secret wisdom must put away the vice of arrogance and must be devout, righteous, deep-witted, humane toward his fellows, of a cheerful countenance and a happy disposition, and respectful withal. Likewise he must be an

observer of the eternal secrets that are revealed to him. My son, above all I admonish thee to fear God who seeth thy attitude and in whom is help for the solitary, whosoever he may be.' And the 'Rosarium' adds from Pseudo-Aristotle: 'Could God but find a man of faithful understanding, He would open His secret to him.' (3)

Revival of the Oedipus Complex

The present stage of the opus renders the birth of an erotic, incestuous passion activated by the discovery of nakedness, i.e., by the discovery of sex. These features point to the regressive revival of the infantile Oedipus complex with its preoccupation with nakedness and sex. Between the ages of three and six the child enters a crucial period of psychobiological growth during which he explores his genitals and the problems of sex (fig.56). After the oral and anal periods where the erogenous zones of mouth and anus predominate, the developing child enters the so-called phallic period with its primacy of the genital zone. Nudity becomes a source of fascination to the child because it reveals the male and female reproductive organs and stimulates infantile sexual curiosity about the origin of babies, the mystery of birth, and the role of parental intercourse.

The boy fully discovers his penis as a male characteristic and a source of pleasure. Infantile masturbation reaches its peak and the boy's interest and pleasure in the penis become related to an external object. Because the mother normally cared for him since birth, she naturally becomes his first love-object. The manifestations of the male child's interest in the genital zone are manifold: the higher

54. *The incestuous roots of sex unveiled.*

frequency of masturbation, greater desire for physical contact with others, particularly with the opposite sex, and tendencies toward phallic exhibitionism are outstanding examples.

The behaviour pattern of the 'phallic libido' shows the boy's continual bid for attention and admiration, linked with an indulgent protectiveness toward the love object. The features of domination show the mixtures between sex and aggression, or the drive fusion (Hartmann) (4) at the phallic stage of the child's aggressive impulses and sexual-exhibitionistic tendencies. The combined aim is here identical with the one pursued by the cock in fig. 55: to impress and thereby to subdue the love object.

Other manifestations frequently interacting with those of behaviour pertain to the child's fantasy life. That interaction has best been studied where masturbatory activity is concerned. Psychoanalysis has proved the link between masturbatory activities and the fantasied intercourse with incestuous objects. A parallel phenomenon is the child's fantasies of being prevented from or punished for such activities by castration or its equivalent. Thus, the kindling of infantile, pregenital love becomes a painful experience for the boy because it is blended with the fear of incest and castration.

55. *The primacy of the genital zone and the predominance of the parental bodies.*

The Oedipal Father Identification

When the boy falls in love with his mother, he discovers in his father a rival. Wanting sexual intercourse with the mother, the Oedipal boy in fantasy identifies his immature sexual organ with the father's penis. With his discovery of nakedness and sexual difference, the boy naturally identifies with his father because of anatomical similarity. Gradually this identification is transformed into hostile and violent fantasies in which his father becomes his rival: the boy imagines not only incest but also parricide. Paradoxically, the father is simultaneously admired and envied as his mother's lover and hated and feared as his formidable rival. The painful and bewildering character of this psychological configuration with its ambiguity of feelings is reflected in the child's fear of castration, which represents a neurotic inversion of the boy's original castration wish or desire to appropriate the father's mature genitalia and take his place with the mother. Thus the Oedipal father identification arouses anxiety in the boy who fears castration as a retribution for his own fantasied 'usurpation' of the paternal member. With the formation of a complex psychological nucleus of naked sex, incestuous love for the mother, and fear of paternal castration, the Oedipus complex has reached full and conscious maturation in its classical form.*

Incestuous Fears and Parricidal Fantasies

The incestuous or Oedipal features of the love unfolded on these pages need no interpretation since they present themselves on a manifest level with obvious implications. It is true that the king's love object is not his mother but his sister, but this change of sexual object is a displacement expressing a defence against Oedipal anxiety. As the king later succeeds in conquering his incestuous fears, he finally goes to bed with his queen in her transformed shape as mother (pp.64-81). Similarly, the Oedipal father identification is elaborated in the classical alchemical motif of the *filius regius* or 'king's son' who replaces the old, decrepit father who, conversely, renews himself in the son (p.78). This replacement is sometimes represented in a violent form, the king's son conquering

* In the male child the Oedipal conflict is gradually subjected to repression. The resolution of the Oedipus complex by fear of castration, incestuous frustration, feelings of guilt, and growing maturation induces the boy to avail himself of defences which enable him to repress and inhibit his forbidden instinctual impulses to the point of renouncing sexual activities in general. This development inaugurates the latency period in which the superego binds the conflicting aggression and sexuality of the Oedipus complex so that the boy may adapt to his future masculine character by positively identifying with the father as a person he wishes to emulate rather than replace.

his father's throne by means of murder and stark cannibalism (p.63).

In alchemy, the twin taboos of totemism are thus infringed since not only incest is imposed as a task but also the still more horrible parricide. However, the 'philosophical' quality of the transgressions is repeatedly emphasized, just as the wealth of allegories demonstrate the fact that the infringement of the twin taboos is always in some symbolical form and never concrete. In other words, the incestuous conjunction with the sister-mother and the slaying of the father are psychic acts resuscitated by the alchemist from the buried realms of unconscious fantasy. The value of this revival is summed up by Jung's interpretation of fig.54 thus: 'The archaic psyche now emerges into consciousness.' (5)

There **is** a difference

56.

57. A dream woman radiating the energies of sex and the passion of incestuous love.

Sulphur and Mercury Stripped Naked

Figs.57 and 59 present the naked king and queen as sulphur and mercury. The 'mercurial anima' *(anima mercurii)* is swaddled in aureoral drapery radiating the energies of sex. Her masculine counterpart appears as the 'sulphurous spirit' *(spiritus sulphuris)* endowed with the wings of Mercurius philosophorum and eagerly reaching forward his smoking love potion. The verse accompanying the 'mercurial anima' reads:

If any muddiness is felt, seen and
   perceived in me,
I am not the way I should be;
For I should certainly be purified
As I was it in the human body.
In young and old, man and woman,
In fishes, metals and all other things,
I can produce great wonders,
For I am the power, essence, nature
   and quality of all things. (1)

The need for purification also applies to the 'sulphurous spirit.' In the 'Philosophia reformata' Mylius says that sulphur is the 'cause of imperfection in all metals,' the 'corrupter of perfection,' 'causing the blackness in every operation'; 'too much sulphurousness is the cause of corruption'; the substance is 'bad and not well mixed,' of an 'evil, stinking odour and of feeble strength.' (2) Jung sums up the qualities of sulphur thus:

'Being the inner fire of Mercurius [fig. 59], sulphur obviously partakes of his most dangerous and evil nature, his violence being personified in the dragon and the lion, and his concupiscence in Hermes Kyllenios. The dragon whose nature sulphur shares is often spoken of as the 'dragon of Babel' or, more accurately, the 'dragon's head' *(caput draconis)*, which is a 'most pernicious poison,' a poisonous vapour breathed out by the flying dragon.' (3)

On the other hand, sulphur is identified with gold and solar power; when 'cleansed of all impurities, it is the matter of our stone.' (4) Another author states: 'The male and universal seed, the first and most potent, is the solar sulphur, the first part and most potent cause of all generation.' (5) Though this sulphur is a 'son who comes from imperfect bodies,' he is 'ready to put on the white and purple garments.' (6)

Just as Sol and Luna must be purified and bathed before being joined in intercourse, sulphur and mercury must be similarly treated if their final conjunction is to produce the philosophers' stone.

Animal Symbols of Primitive Love

The smoking *spiritus sulphuris* of fig. 59 and his evil-smelling vapours symbolize the dangerous and sadistic libido of the revived Oedipus complex. This means the heating of the shadow by an aggressive drive blazing now at its pregenital level as a cruel parricidal spirit. With the lifting of the repressive layers of the superego and the latency period, the anima is transformed in a similar way. She is reignited by a sexual drive blazing now at its pregenital level as a hot incestuous soul.

The ominous sexual fantasies produced by these unconscious figures are presented in closer detail on pp.40-63. Coloured by primary process thinking, the evil Oedipal spirit finds expression in predatory and cruel animal symbols like the wolf-dog, the lion and the dragon. The libido objects of these kingly symbols are similarly transformed into purely instinctual beings, the bitch in alchemy appearing as the archetype of the human female who deliberately uses her incestuous attraction to get men around her (figs.64-67). The brothel entered by king and queen in fig.58—a variant of figs.53-54—explains the anxious expression of the alchemist at his furnace. The mercurial fire now roaring has brought the work to its dynamic but also unpredictable and frightening state of transformation.

58. Hastening to incestuous sheets.

Discovery of the Oedipus Complex

In their exploration of the unconscious Western psychiatrists encountered almost at once the Oedipus complex. Freud, who discovered the complex and named it, defined psychoanalysis as the science revolving around this highly-charged nucleus of the unconscious. The unique importance of the Oedipus complex was further illustrated by the fact that Freud and Jung—and Freud and Rank—were forever separated by their differing interpretations of its psychodynamics, into which are gathered all the sexual and aggressive energies of the unconscious.

Freud's discovery around the turn of the century floodlit the connection between sexuality and anxiety since it showed the roots of sex intimately connected with the fear of incest and the fear of castration. This fundamental discovery, however, while explaining the anxiety of neurotic reactions, merely uncovered a number of new and enigmatic questions. What were the origins of the fear of incest? Why are incestuous desires considered dangerous by the ego?

Another enigmatic feature of the Oedipus complex turned up with analytical material showing its fear of castration to be frequently endowed with oral, vaginal and uterine features, forming a fear of being devoured by the *vagina dentata*— by the 'toothed vagina' of the *mother*. Furthermore, analytical material encountered in the oral sphere of infantile development demonstrated the equation of the penis with the whole body, and the equation of castration anxiety with the anxiety of *death*. Psychoanalysis of small children confirmed the fact that the earliest castration anxiety is connected with the mother: it is of an oral-devouring character, coloured by anxiety of death and of ego-dissolution. How were these unconscious facts to be explained by Freud's theory of the *phallic* level and origin of the Oedipus complex?

The Enigmatic Meaning of Incest

Even before these questions had been answered, the world of psychoanalysis had been shattered by divergencies of opinion concerning the principal meaning of the Oedipus complex. Freud regarded the complex as part of the personal unconscious, and its psychological structure as belonging to the sphere of infantile sexuality. His psychotherapeutical aims were to 'dissolve' the Oedipus complex and so free the mature personality from its infantile and irrational fixations and psychodynamics.

Jung, on the other hand, regarded the Oedipus complex as a dynamic unconscious structure pointing toward the experience of rebirth, transcendence, and 'God': 'To me incest signified a personal complication only in the rarest cases.

59. A dream man consumed by the fire of incestuous passion and primitive hatred.

Usually incest has a highly religious aspect, for which reason the incest theme plays a decisive part in almost all cosmogonies and in numerous myths. But Freud clung to the literal interpretation of it and could not grasp the spiritual significance of incest as a symbol. I knew that he would never be able to accept any of my ideas on this subject.' (7)

Jung's departure from Freud in 1913 on the Oedipus complex was followed by Otto Rank's in 1925 on the same question. Jung's insistence on the patterns of rebirth embedded in the Oedipus complex, and the mythical-archetypal perspective hiding in its unconscious dynamics of regression, was confirmed by Rank's theories. Following Freud's genetic and psychobiological approach, Rank, in 1924, attempted to prove the origins of the Oedipus complex in a postulated uterine libido organization and in the birth trauma:

'At the back of the Oedipus saga really stands the mysterious question of the origin and destiny of man, which Oedipus desires to solve, not intellectually, but by actually returning into the mother's womb. This happens entirely in a symbolic form, for his blindness in the deepest sense represents a return into the darkness of the mother's womb, and his final disappearance through a cleft rock into the Underworld expresses once again the same wish tendency to return into the Earth Mother.' (8)

The third split in the psychoanalytical world occurred when Melanie Klein—the greatest theoretical genius after Freud, Jung and Rank—attempted to trace the Oedipus complex back to the sexual and aggressive strivings occurring at the anal and oral levels of the libido organization in earliest childhood. (9) The Oedipus complex created a scientific debate as stormy as that in the wake of the physicists' contemporary discovery of the atomic nucleus and its radioactive energies.

60. Alchemical love story cooled down in the subterranean halls of a biblical Jupiter.

ness. From the altar balcony the king and his sons and courtiers spy on the naked bathing women. On a pedestal in the water a little boy atop a horse drinks out of a horn. (He parallels the children riding on sea-horses on top of the altar.) Behind the drinking boy two maids approach the bathers with ointment jars.

The great altar painting shows a young man standing on top of a ladder leaning against a fruit tree. The young man is plucking fruits; he has momentarily interrupted his activity to present two elders with branches he has broken off from the tree. Some of the branches have already been planted in the meadow and are flowering. The tree trunk rises out of a crown around its roots. A flock of birds have just flown away from the crown; only one black bird with a white head remains in its nest to brood or feed its young.

A Freudian and a Jungian Interpretation

In the 'Interpretation of Dreams' Freud discovered the hidden meaning of the situation depicted on the altar painting; the motif recurs in dreams and appears as the 'mounting of a staircase' or the 'climbing of a ladder.' Freud termed the motif *a censored version of sexual intercourse:* 'We have made the acquaintance of the ladder in dreams as a sexual symbol; here German linguistic usage comes to our help and shows us how the word 'steigen' ['to climb,' or 'to mount'] is used in what is *par excellence* a sexual sense. We say 'den Frauen nachsteigen' ['to run' (literally 'climb') 'after women'], and 'ein alter Steiger' ['an old rake' (literally 'climber')]. In French, in which the word for steps on a staircase is *'marches,'* we find a precisely analogous term *'un vieux marcheur.'* The fact that in many large animals climbing or 'mounting' on the female is a necessary preliminary to sexual intercourse probably fits into this context. 'Pulling off a branch' as a symbolic representation of masturbation is not merely in harmony with vulgar descriptions of the act but has far-reaching mythological parallels.' (1)

If Freud's interpretation is applied to the altar painting, one glimpses the Oedi-

Burrowing into a Strange Mountain

Fig.60 shows the fifth painting of the 'Splendor solis' in which the separated sun and moon frame two alchemists working their way into the mountain and its foundations in the earth. The alchemists' descent takes them into the biblical halls of Mordecai, Esther, Ahasuerus, Bigthan and Teresh. The atmosphere here is one of secretive sex and suppressed regicide. Mordecai, the king's guardian (standing behind Ahasuerus), presented the king with his favourite wife, Esther, just as he prevented him from knowing her dangerous (Jewish) origin; at the same time Mordecai saved Ahasuerus by suppressing the murderous conspiracy of the king's two doorkeepers, Bigthan and Teresh (seated at the gate to the right) (Esther 2:1-23).

The painting gives a much cooler version of royal love than the previous, fourth painting (fig.38). The motifs of suppression and concealment account for this 'cooling down' of the alchemical love story. The ornamental altar figures are strongly regressive and show a number of male children playing with the sucking tongues of sea-horses. These animals symbolize the 'sea mother': their curling tails reappear as sexual attributes of the naked mermaids on the altar bottom.

Magical Tree of Parental Conjunction

Fig.63 renders the subsequent painting of the 'Splendor solis,' which centres on the themes of awakening sexual curiosity and man's fascination with naked-

61. The sign of the Twins: One yet Two.

pal psychology of its pictorial symbolism: the crowned trunk has a phallic meaning and refers to the king's erect member penetrating the foliage of the maternal 'crown.' The youth's method of 'penetrating' the crown is by means of a ladder, which symbolizes his 'hanging onto his mother,' or his attempts at incestuous intercourse.

Jung gives a similar interpretation of the motif as occurring in the ritual drama of the Attis-Cybele cult: 'The hanging of the son or his effigy onto the tree represents the union of mother and son. Common speech employs the same image: a person is said to 'hang onto his mother' . . . The tree symbolizes the mother on the one hand and the phallus of the son on the other.' (2)

Gemini the Twins: Birth of Questioning and Analysis

The *denouement* of Hermetic love takes place in the sign of Gemini, the Twins. The third sign of the Zodiac is a mutable, airy sign ruled by Mercury. Gemini covers the period from May 22 to June 21, or the period of vernal growth in which the fertilized egg or germ is polarized, and the differentiation into masculine and feminine takes place. One, yet two, the Twins expresses the severance of the undifferentiated unity, the polarization of matter, or the dual structure of reality. In essence a symbol of opposites, Gemini, however, also relates the opposites and so possesses a knowledge of the duality and ambiguity of reality and a sense of its paradox and humour.

The infantile overtones of the Gemini sign reveal the point in time for man's first overwhelming awareness of the principle of duality: *the child's realization of the difference of sexes*. In the male and female genitals is found the archetype of polarity: father-mother, brother-sister, cock-hen, sun-moon, day-night.

Because of its 'doubleness' Gemini stands for the human intellect's powers of distinction and discrimination. The oscillating Twins are a symbol *par excellence* of the dialectic principle. The sign expresses the reflecting intellect's

63. *Reaching the maternal nest and crown by means of the king's trunk and ladder.*

62. *The moral virtues of the worker.*

nervous energy and fluctuation between opposites, thereby splitting nature into thesis and antithesis, positive and negative, good and bad.

Gemini symbolizes man's awakening consciousness, rising on the wings of infantile sexual curiosity to explore the world. The event signifies the sunrise of the ego, shocked into action by the sword of sexuality, which cleaves the child's incestuous-unconscious unity with the mother and starts a process of dialectic questioning, probing analysis, and mental growth. (Parents despairingly experience this developmental phase as that of the child's *everlasting questioning*. The sexual core of many of these questions are well known to parents and have been studied systematically by depth psychologists.) (3)

'By Love and Constancy'

Fig.62 shows a popular image of the alchemist's opus: the brooding hen completing her work 'by love and constancy.' These are the much-praised virtues of the Sons of Hermes, who are also advised that 'all haste is of the devil.' (4) This Morienus quotation appears in a variant form in the 'Rosarium' which says: 'He who has not patience, let him keep his hands from the work, for rash credulity hinders him because of his haste.' (5) Morienus introduces the virtues of the art to Kalid, the Omayyad prince, thus: 'This thing for which you have sought so long is not to be acquired or accomplished by force or passion. It is only to be won by patience and humility and by a determined and most perfect love.' (6)

64. Brother and sister offered a love potion of wolfish copulation and devouring.

Cruel Love Fight of the Primal Scene

After the laying aside of garments, the royal brother and sister approach each other in the initiatory copulating movements described on these pages. Above, the alchemist brings together the royal couple in the waters of the Hermetic stream. The motto reads: 'Join brother and sister and offer them the love potion.' (1)

In fig.66, which illustrates the 13th chapter of the Second Book of the Kings, Matthaeus Merian has transferred his alchemical partners into their biblical setting: 'And Tamar took the cakes which she had made and brought them into the chamber to Amnon her brother. And . . . being stronger than she, [Amnon] forced her and lay with her' (2 Samuel 13:10-14).

The preparatory mating of the royal couple has the famous animal version in alchemy shown in figs.65 and 67. Sol and Luna approach each other in the shape of the Coetanean dog and the Armenian bitch. The motif is presented by the 'Rosarium' as follows: 'Hali, philosopher and king of Arabia, says in his Secret: Take a Coetanean dog and an Armenian bitch, mate them, and they will bear you a son in the likeness of a dog, and of celestial hue.' (2)

In figs.65 and 67 the wolf and the dog approach each other in a highly ambivalent way, 'furious, with their muzzles wide open,' as the epigram of fig.65 says. (3) The strange position of the fighting and copulating dogs reveals them

as synonyms for Sol and Luna, since the dogs imitate the human position during sexual intercourse, not the animal one. The erotic background of the motif is stressed by the motto of fig.67: 'A wolf and a dog are in one house and are at last changed into one.' (4) In both engravings, the act of canine copulation is rendered as a sadistic act of devouring in which the fighting partners tear each other to shreds in a bloody orgy. The epigram accompanying fig.67, from the 'Book of Lambspring,' reads:

Alexander writes from Persia that
A wolf and a dog are in this valley.
Further, the Sages tell us that they
Are descended from the same stock,
But the wolf comes from the east
And the dog from the west.

65. The copulating, cannibalistic dogs.

They are full of jealousy,
Fury, rage, and madness:
One kills the other,
And from them comes a great poison.
But when they are restored to life,
They are clearly shewn to be
The Great and Precious Medicine,
The most glorious Remedy upon earth,
Which has delighted everywhere
The Sages, who render thanks to God,
And do praise Him. (5)

The epigram accompanying fig.65 is almost identical. The source of the motif is the ancient philosopher Rhazes, whose 'Epistola' is quoted by Petrus Bonus as follows: 'Our wolf is found in the east, and the dog in the west. The one bites the other, and the other bites back, and they both become furious and they mutually kill each other, till the poison originates from them as well as the medicine.' (6)

Anal-Sadistic Fantasies and Fears

The incestuous love engaged in by Sol and Luna clearly indicates the revived Oedipus complex, whose primitive libido is further symbolized by the lovers' animal transformations. However, the sadistic copulation of Sol and Luna's hairy synonyms reveals deepening regression by pointing to an archetypal motif of early childhood: the infant's sadistic interpretation of parental intercourse. To the observing child, the 'primal scene' (Freud) (7) appears as a fight between his parents. Should he find traces of blood on the sheets or on his mother's clothing, he interprets it as proof that his father injured the mother in the presumed struggle.

This concept of parental copulation reflects the anal-sadistic libido organization of the so-called separation-individuation phase of infantile development (age one to three). The term refers to the *separation* of the clinging suckling from his mother and to his transformation into inquisitive toddler, discovering not only the surrounding world but also his own *individuality*. The inaugurated processes of growth, independence and individuation are accompanied by defiance and obstinacy; these reactions coincide with the anal interests of the toddler, going through the ordeal of toilet training. The result is the specific structuring of the aggressive and sexual drives into the *anal-sadistic libido organization*.

The elaboration of the Oedipus complex at this early stage was discovered by post-Freudian psychoanalysis. As Melanie Klein learned from her analysis of small children, the Oedipal 'sin' of the toddler is neither incest nor parricide but the anal-and-oral-sadistic response to observing the primal scene, i.e., the cruel intrusion and cannibalistic attack on the copulating parents with whom the child shiftingly or simultaneously identifies himself. The anxiety of the Oedipus complex at this level is the fear of retaliation of the child's original wishes to tear, claw, rip open, torture, destroy and crush the love object.

The fusion of sexual and aggressive-destructive impulses is a hallmark of anal-sadistic psychology and is obvious even to the unskilled observer. Says Anna Freud: 'Whoever has dealt with toddlers knows the peculiarly clinging, possessive, tormenting, exhausting kind of love which they have for their mothers, an exacting relationship which drives many young mothers to the point of despair. We know, further, that the originally sexual inquisitiveness of children destroys the inanimate objects towards which it is directed; that loved toys are, normally, maltreated toys; that pet animals have to be rescued from the aggression which invariably accompanies the love showered on them by their childish owners.' (8)

Wolf-like Dreams of Early Childhood

It is small wonder that infantile dream psychology is patterned on the haunting motifs of figs.65 and 67, in which the wolf symbolizes the identified father figure and the dog the pursued mother figure. J.Louise Despert in her survey of the scientific literature on small children's dreams concludes:

'Human beings and animals figured predominantly. The parents appeared in benevolent roles; but, on the other hand, were readily identified with powerful, destructive animals which threatened the child with total destruction. People other than parents were most frequently placed in fearful roles. While the animals which were engaged in biting and devouring were usually large and fearful, there were also smaller animals which engaged in the same activities, although biting was not necessarily an intrinsic characteristic of these animals. The dreams reported were predominantly anxiety dreams. Chronologically, the expression of anxiety appeared in the following sequence: the very young child (2-year-old) expressed a fear of being bitten, devoured and chased without naming the agent; later (3-,4-,5-year-old), devouring animals were identified.' (9)

First Glimpse of the Hermaphrodite

The adhesive coitus of Sol and Luna in their animal shapes points to a fusion of the primal scene partners and to the regressive formation of an oral-sadistic figure of supreme ambivalence and anxiety: the 'phallic mother,' or Dual Mother archetype (figs.78-79). (10) As we shall demonstrate later, this combined parental figure is both 'killing' and 'poison-

66. Rending the veils of the primal scene: uniting the Oedipal bodies in cruel love.

ous' and full of 'great and precious medicine.' Its canine symbol in alchemy 'delights the sages everywhere' because it signifies their first, if crude, glimpse of the great goal of the opus alchymicum: the divine rebis, or hermaphrodite, in whom the parental principles come together in supreme unity and purity.

67. Ambivalent fusion of sex and aggression: dogs uniting in murderous intercourse.

68. 'Gilding the queen' in a Hermetic version of the Zeus-Danae myth: a violent coitus filling the love object with lumps of gold.

'Opening of the Matrix' by Violent Love

The motif of the copulating dogs ripping each other open inaugurates the alchemical operation known as the 'opening of the matrix.' (1) Fig.69 shows a variation of this motif with the philosophers' son attacking two barrels containing the pressed grapes of the Earth Mother. After having forcefully opened the first barrel, the infant to his surprise discovers that its contents are vitriol, not wine, as he had expected. Taught by experience, the Eros child in a more peaceful vein attempts to tap the wine of the second barrel, which is inscribed with the sign of Mercurius philosophorum. Behind the child is a massive pillar inscribed with planetary and elemental signs.

According to the text, the infant philosopher dabbles with the wine of *Frau Venus*, which may be both salutary and pernicious. The wine says of itself: 'Intoxicated by my sap, they lose their lives and plunge into a blood bath and show themselves in very beautiful colours. Everybody may wonder at that, as also at my pleasant smell. But methink I hear a wondrous song—that is *Frau Venus* as far as I can perceive.' And Venus answers: 'I am a yellow and green lady capable of emitting a pure spirit.' (2)

Gilding the Queen in a Sordid Way

Fig.68 shows another variant of the opening of the juicy matrix by the powers of violent love. The alchemical version of the Zeus-Danae myth renders the opening of the matrix, which as Luna, moon-bitch *(canicula),* mother-beloved, and 'house' carries in its belly the material of the philosophers' stone and the secrets of the opus. (3) The engraving shows the tempestuous rending of the curtains around Danae's bed and the sexual intrusion of Zeus as eagle fertilizing the naked, tormented woman with a shower of gold. The subtitle reads: *Aurifica Ego Regina*—'I gild the queen.'

Incestuous Fantasies of Anal Coitus

The pictorial symbolism reveals a mixture of anal aggression and eroticism. The winged eagle appears as an animal version of the winged children, also hovering above the fertilized mother. It is the eagle, however, which most directly connects with the act of fertilization carried out by the mythical father. In the engraving, the fertilizing coins, or lumps of gold, appear to spurt from the anus of the eagle. This remarkable feature corroborates the wellknown unconscious equation of money with filth or feces, while simultaneously revealing the underlying infantile fantasy of anal coitus.

The fertilizing feces are obviously equated with children, and the latent birth motif of the engraving with the act of defecation.

Such features reflect the infantile sexual theory of anal conception and birth also underlying the fantasy of impregnating the mother by filling her with one's own feces (=anal children). Melanie Klein, the outstanding investigator of the fantasy life of early childhood, has demonstrated the prevalence of such imaginations in the second and third years of life. (4) In a manner similar to that depicted in fig.68 the anal child in fantasy 'interrupts' the copulating parents of the primal scene: by identifying with his father (Zeus and his eagle), he 'rapes' his mother by putting children into her in an anal-sadistic way. This is Oedipal, anal love and its specific psychology governs the latter half of the child's separation-individuation phase.

69. Violent opening of maternal barrels.

To the incredulity of the public and many of her colleagues Melanie Klein pointed out the sexual content of these early fantasies of intrusion. Alchemical symbolism of the opening of the matrix (including the motif of the copulating dogs) confirms her findings. Chest and casket are archetypal symbols of the uterus and are ripped open in fig.69 by the savage infant exploring the dark subterranean regions of his 'house.' The destroyed casket bears witness to the aggressive sexuality of the intruding infant, just as the vitriolic wine signifies the poisoned milk of the evil and destructive *Frau Venus,* the 'bad' mother. The second, whole casket indicates the beneficial *Frau Venus,* the good and whole mother nourishing the good and whole infant.

The Libido's Anal-Sadistic Stage

The analysis of compulsion neuroses enabled Freud to insert between the oral and phallic periods another organizational level of the libido: the *anal-sadistic.* Here the child's source of libidinal pleasure shifts to the anal region. The voluntary retention of feces to gain libidinal pleasure from the contractions

of the sphincter is a wellknown phenomenon of early childhood. Psychoanalytical observation of children and adult neurotics showed Freud that anal retentiveness constitutes the roots of possessiveness, parsimony, or miserliness.

In cleanliness training, the child finds the opportunity for the first time in its life to express opposition toward grownups, just as the toddler's negativism is another expression of his newly-won and jealously guarded independence from the mother. Obedience or rebellion, release or retention (defiance) become the central motifs of the anal phase.

Love is possessive and is revealed in the *libido dominandi,* in the child's tormenting, harassing possessiveness toward its mother. In the adult, such evil anal personality sources cause much friction and unhappiness because they lead to egocentric attempts to control one's loved ones. The typical 'anal ambivalence,' in which attitudes of love and hate are simultaneously directed toward the same object, manifests itself in fig. 68: the queen is raped and soiled by the king (Zeus), who fertilizes her in an anal way, evidently hurting his beloved during the act. The royal coitus closely resembles the sadistic coitus of the wolf and dog.

The toddler's incestuous and cruel fantasies of intrusion reflect the interaction of his aggressive and sexual drives which, in turn, provokes guilt feelings and tormenting anxiety. Attempts to deal with the latter lead the maturing ego to more powerful measures of protection. The defence mechanisms of the oral stage—splitting, denial and projection—are replaced in the anal phase by *repression and reaction formation.* The conflicts between sexuality and aggression may lead to eating disturbances, infantile insomnia and nightmares. They also account for the toddler's obsessional bedtime rituals and his resistance to going to bed and sleep. The whole area of the unconscious—of sleep and of dreams—is as yet not too secure, and he will seek many methods to postpone it or protect himself magically against its cannibalistic dangers and repressed sexual urges.

Such are the emotions experienced and 'purged' by the alchemist when 'opening the matrix' by means of violent love.

'Know then that you cannot have this science until you have purified your mind for God, which means that you must extinguish all corruption in your heart.'
Alphidius, the Philosopher. (5)

'The alchemist should be prepared to follow knowledge through good and evil report. His life should be free from guilt, falsehood, and sin. Such men alone possess mental aptitude for becoming proficients in this science.'
Thomas Norton. (6)

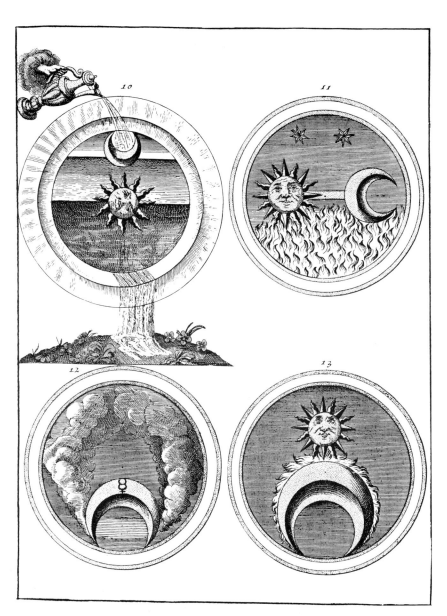

70. A solar lover of the moon fusing with her mercurial body in a Turkish bath.

swelling body has produced a new outburst of fiery love and burning anxiety.

Parental Preparations for the Primal Act

In fig.71 the identified parents of the philosophers' son join under two crowns inscribed 'His father is the sun,' 'His mother is the moon.' The horseshoe-shaped inscriptions above Sol and Luna render their love dialogue. Says the king: 'Come and delect me and embrace me and we shall generate the new son who will not resemble his parents.' On the other side of the cleft the pregnant queen answers her spouse: 'See, I come to you and am ready to conceive a son who has not his equal in the whole world.'

In pointing gestures the king and queen draw attention to the vessel of Hermetic conjunction containing their 'doubles': the father king identified with the philosophers' son burying his head in the lap of his lunar mother and beloved. Evidently this gesture symbolizes a return to the womb; the act appears to have been accepted by Luna, who receives her son-lover below the flowers of mystical conjunction and the signs of mercurial, bisexual unity.

In a strange way, the royal lovers' feet appear to 'extend' into the rock and emerge as claws of some predatory bird or animal. The claws are part of the dark and dangerous mountain crevice which must be spanned or conquered by king and queen if they want to be united. The love fight between the wolf and dog has now swelled to frightening, draconic proportions.

Crucial Transition: Symbiosis-Separation

The action of Barchusen's plate 12 and its double in fig.71 symbolizes the regressive transition from the anal ('opening of the matrix') stage to the oral stage of libido organization. The developmental pattern of these stages has been described by Margaret Mahler under the heading of the *separation-individuation phase* (5-36 months), the *symbiotic phase* (2-4/5 months), and the *autistic phase* (0-2 months). In the second half of the first year and beyond the clinging 'symbiotic' sucker is transformed into a toddler, who begins to discover his ego and the object world while freeing himself from his maternal self.

Although the toddler enjoys his growing independence and with great tenacity perseveres in his attempts at mastery of the newly discovered world of objects, he is emotionally quite unprepared to leave his mother. A wellknown sign of this struggle is that of the child moving away from the mother and shortly after returning to her for emotional refueling. In so doing, the child will frequently

Symbiotic Fusion of Melting Sol and Waxing Luna

After the 'cooling' of Sol and Luna in Barchusen's plate 10 (above) and the fresh outbreak of their fiery love in plate 11, the alchemical process of transformation enters upon a new stage with the opening of the lunar matrix in plate 12. The sea of fire of the previous plate has been quenched and transmuted into seething vapours arising from the swelling Luna. The simultaneous disappearance of Sol indicates the absorption of the glowing solar body by the moist and cold lunar body. The 'opening of the matrix' thus takes a dramatic and unexpected turn: in forcing himself into the body of his queen, Sol evaporates into lunar oneness in a symbiotic fusion indicated by the bisexual sign of Mercurius philosophorum inscribed on the moon sickle. The same action animates fig.71, in which

Sol is absorbed by the opened lunar vessel twice inscribed with the sign of Mercurius philosophorum.* The melting processes of Barchusen's plate 12 are here translated into human terms with the philosophers' son merging with the lap of his lunar mother in an act of symbiosis, termed 'coitus.'

In Barchusen's plate 13 Sol and Luna appear in a new situation: the pregnant moon blazing toward plenilunium is encircled by her newborn sun. As seen from the fire breaking on the surface of the moon, the gravitational pull of her

* The engraving by Matthaeus Merian is made after the original woodcut in Reusner's 'Pandora' (1582, p.22) which opens the book's cartoon on the conjunction of king and queen. The woodcuts immediately following fig.71 are reproduced in figs.117-118. Their engraved variants, also by Matthaeus Merian, are reproduced in fig.122, which shows the completed union.

bury his head in the lap of the mother or lean against her leg. This particular gesture (rendered by fig.71) signifies the toddler's temporary regression to the earlier stage of symbiotic union with the mother. The transition from symbiosis to separation-individuation is viewed by Margaret Mahler as a kind of second birth experience, which she describes as a 'hatching from the symbiotic mother-child common membrane.' (2)

At the Edge of the Precipice

If the vessel symbolizes the symbiotic phase of infantile development (2-4/5) months), the fissure in the earth of fig.71 may be interpreted as a symbol of the 'earthquake' of separation-individuation. Viewed in this light, the king appears as a symbol of the son disengaging from the maternal object and thus achieving his sense of ego identity (the toddler's golden experience of the 'I,' 'me,' 'mine' feeling). As further indicated by the engraving, the son's disengagement from the mother-child symbiosis inside the vessel takes place by means of an Oedipal identification with the father figure, who in the ego growth processes acts as an ego-syntonic force of great power and support against the threat of maternal engulfment.

According to the above interpretation, the king's territory to the left symbolizes the world of outer reality, or the realm of objects. Conversely, the queen's territory to the right symbolizes the world of inner reality, just as her vessel symbolizes the object world as 'inhaled' and fused-confused with the symbiotic love object. In fig.71 this dangerous transformation toward a mentally unified world is reflected in the development of the mercurial, bisexual moon which hides the archaic mother imago of the symbiotic phase: that of the combined parent or the *'phallic mother.'* (3) This is the mother pregnant with the father's phallus in her lap, the paternal member being equated with the infant-son enclosed in her lap (fig.71).

At the moment preceding the rebirth of the filius philosophorum in the vessel, the alchemist is like a king at the edge of a precipice. It is a moment of uneasiness and despair, for at this point he is confronted with the decision to keep his ego-identity or to let go: the crossing of the fissure produced by the earthquake of separation-individuation is a harrowing experience fraught with panic since it represents the point where fear of engulfment—a fear amounting to fear of dissolution of identity—accumulates simultaneously with its apparent opposite, i.e., separation anxiety. When the two overwhelm the ego, the die is cast between integration or disintegration, between illumination of a diving ego or darkening of a sinking ego.

71. The parental bodies uniting in the vessel's symbiotic mother-child relationship.

The 'Symbiotic Psychotic' Child

The great investigator of the separation-individuation phase, the American psychoanalyst Margaret Mahler, developed her theories from observations of 'symbiotic psychotic children.' These children are a living and tragic museum of the separation-individuation phase in its arrested course of development. In her splendid paper 'On Child Psychosis and Schizophrenia,' Mahler has described the toddler's normal separation anxiety and fear of engulfment under the magnifying (and distorting) looking-glass of its pathological expression:

'The world is hostile and threatening because it has to be met as a separate being. Separation anxiety overwhelms the brittle ego of the 'symbiotic psychotic child.' His anxiety reactions are so intense and so diffuse that they are reminiscent of the organismic distress of early infancy. Clinically, such children show all the signs of abysmal affective panic. These severe panic reactions are followed by restitutive productions which serve to maintain or restore the narcissistic fusion, the delusion of oneness with the mother and/or father. Restitution in symbiotic psychosis is attempted by somatic delusions and hallucinations of reunion with the narcissistically loved and hated, omnipotent mother image, or sometimes by hallucinated fusion with a condensation of father-mother images. In the symbiotic infantile psychosis reality testing remains fixated at, or regresses to, the omnipotent delusional stage of the symbiotic mother-infant relationship. The boundaries of the self and the nonself are blurred. Even the mental representation of the body-self is unclearly demarcated. These are the cases, I believe, of whom Bender was thinking when she described their body contour melting in one's own.' (4)

Integræ Naturæ   Speculum, Artisque imago

72. *The philosophers' son in symbiosis with the revolving 'world soul': daily joys and nightly terrors of a unified, spinning world.*

Disclosing the 'Soul of the World'

Above is shown the 'mirror of virginal nature and the image of the art' (headline, top). A variation of the 'opening of the matrix,' the engraving shows the philosophers' son as the ape of nature discovering his universal mother or 'world soul' (anima mundi). The alchemical goddess parallels the woman of the Apocalypse, who also wore a crown of twelve stars; the moon-goddesses of antiquity; the Old Testament's Sapientia (Wisdom); and the Egyptian goddess Isis who also had flowing hair, a half-moon at her womb, one foot on land, the other on water. The Hermetic woman is under the primacy of orality as shown by her flowing breasts. Chained to the Father and the Son in a mercurial, symbiotic kind of unity, the anima mundi functions as a mediator connecting the realm of the corpus with the realm of the spiritus. Whereas the latter is represented by the Name of the Highest in the divine cloud, the world of the corpus is represented by the philosophers' son appearing in the shape of a monkey, that is, totally governed by the instinctual drives of the animal kingdom. Despite his inferior position, the filius philosophorum is nevertheless a participant in the realms of the spiritus and the anima, heaven and his

46

mother blissfully lying about him. Seated on top of his own macrocosmic earth, he applies a compass to a smaller globe containing his slumbering faculties, as represented by the sphere of the 'liberal arts.'

The soul's ascent to God is depicted as a journey through the planetary houses, ultimately embedding the soul in the realm of the heavenly children or unborn souls. This is Paradise, and its realm of angelic light is situated beyond the sphere of the fixed stars. The alchemical cosmos renders the Ptolemean or medieval conception of the universe, the immovable earth in the centre surrounded by the solar, lunar and planetary spheres of the wheeling cosmos. Their rotary motion involves the philosophers' ape also; chained to the wandering moon, he is destined to follow her cyclic course around the earth. In such a manner he will learn about the dual nature of the world. Rising with the 'world soul' and going down with the 'world soul' in a kind of 'symbiotic rotation,' the philosophers' ape will spin planet-like around the earth, first elatedly pushing through its daily half, then, depressed, pushing through its nightly half. These cyclothymic moods of the philosophers' son revolving with the 'world soul' will be further studied on pp.50-53.

Fig.74 presents yet another variation of the 'mirror of virginal nature and the image of the art.' The alchemist appears as a painter absorbed by his life-size canvas of the goddess of the world. The artist's idealized woman figure is 'tatooed' with representations of the animal, vegetable and mineral realms and is thus identified with the anima mundi.

Cancer the Crab: the Dual Mother

The maternal qualities now assumed by Luna indicates the attainment of the sign of the Crab (fig.73). Lasting from June 22 to July 22, the shellfish of the fourth sign of the Zodiac is a water creature which avoids the sun and buries itself in the crevices of the sea-floor. A cardinal sign and the first of the water signs, Cancer is the only zodiacal constellation ruled by the moon, the Lady of the Waters. Because of the moon's effect on the tides (and female menstruation) the Crab is a symbol of the primal water and, hence, of motherhood. The Crab's connection to the waxing moon further explains its correlation with gestation and birth, but also with lunacy, which is supposed to break out in the time of the full moon.

The Crab is the most regressive of all the signs of the Zodiac and may be characterized as the archetype of symbiosis and autism: it is wholly withdrawn into its own shell and it only tentatively reaches out to the world. The oral nature of the Crab is likewise unmistakable: because of its affiliation with the primal

water and the chaste moon, it is a symbol of the 'virgin's milk'; its hieroglyph simultaneously stands for crab-claws and for breasts. The astrological qualities of Cancer are those of Eros, maternal attachment, childhood memories, introversion, return to the womb, and reincarnation.

The psychological features of Cancer are those of supreme sensitivity, great imagination and a wealth of feeling. Given to moods, dreams and ideas of a profound nature, Cancer embodies the feminine functions of feeling and intuition and the psychodynamics of introversion and regression. Because of its relation to the mother and its powers of 'attachment' and 'fusion,' Cancer may lead to a *participation mystique* resulting in mother-fixation and lunacy, i.e., in identity with the unconscious. The terrors of such a state are symbolized by the claws of the Crab, which may pinch and kill its victims. This is an aspect of Cancer which sharply contrasts with the bliss of its nursing state and the 'oceanic' feeling conveyed by its fusion with the lunar sea, the watery earth. A symbol of the Dual Mother *par excellence,* Cancer expresses the maternal libido and man's longing to return to Nature's claws and breasts to die and be reborn.

Mirror Magic of a Symbiotic Anima

'During the symbiotic phase the infant behaves and functions as though he and his mother were an omnipotent system (a dual unity) within one common boundary—a symbiotic membrane, as it were.'
Margaret Mahler. (1)

Fig.72 precisely illustrates the psychological universe of symbiosis in which the infant ego experiences the world in the image of the 'universal mother.' Object relations are dawning, but they have not yet become clearly developed in the infant to whom the 'phallic mother' is the whole world. The oneness, or symbiosis, with the mother makes the infant feel 'objectless' and prevents him from clearly distinguishing between himself, his mother and reality. This state of mind has been termed 'egocentrism' by

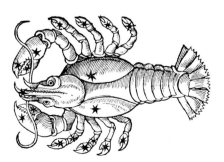

73. *Fusing with the Dual Mother's sign.*

Piaget. By this concept Piaget implies the infant's lack of awareness of the self as separate from the outer world: his emerging ego occupies the centre of a world which revolves around him while reflecting him. (2)

74. *In symbiosis with Mother Nature.*

The result is that the infant conceives of everyone and everything as being 'like himself,' mirroring his own activities and unconscious impulses. Involved in a *participation mystique* with the object world, he falls a victim to the mirror magic of his symbiotic soul fusing ego, self and object world. Such is the mental structure of animism or symbiosis; its behaviouristic symptom is the phenomenon of imitation where the gesture of the symbiotic love object is automatically reflected by the symbiotic subject as 'expression' of himself.*

This is the intoxicating kind of love experienced by the alchemist when moving into the sign of the Crab and the world of the Universal Mother.

* Symbiotic psychology forms the basis of animism, which represents the religion of primitive culture: objects and animals are conceived of as having the same feelings and intentions as one has oneself. Primitive man has a minimum of consciousness and hence a minimum of self-awareness, resulting in a maximum of attachment to the object. Primitive man is involved in a mystical participation with the object world, which exercises a direct, magical compulsion upon him. All primitive magic and religion are based upon these symbiotic attachments which transform man's outer and inner realities into reflections of one another.

The Royal Intercourse of Lions

The predatory aspect of the royal couple, hidden deep down in the rock of fig.71, surfaces in fig.76 where the dependent, greedy lion cub attempts to cover his mother in a manner which reveals the utter confusion of his erotic and hunting impulses. At the same time the lioness appears to have developed wings during the attempted coitive-cannibalistic act. (This makes her a counterpart of the masculine Luna covered by her son in fig.75.) In alchemy, wings stand for the spiritus and belong to the eagle, or the king's birdlike transformation. Hence, the winged lioness (also called the 'philosophical lioness') possesses the spirit or the masculine powers of the lion also. (The winged lioness and the masculine Luna are variations, in turn, of the mercurial, bisexual moon produced by the symbiotic processes of Barchusen's plate 12, fig.70.) The text accompanying the engraving reveals the incestuous nature of the leonine intercourse:

'The philosophical [winged] lioness is conjoined with her own mate and thus is born the genuine and generous little lion, which can easily be recognized by its claws. However, not any lioness can take up battle with this lion; only a winged one may do so, trusting the speed of her wings, so that she will not be too much suppressed by its excessive anger, but may contemplate flight if the lion should fly into passion without reason. For even while trying to prevent her from escaping, he is incensed by an even greater love for her, friendship being formed after the battle.' (1)

The text goes on to explain the necessity of 'conquering the lions' for the purpose of uniting them. The motif reappears in the 'Book of Lambspring' where a picture of two lions are accompanied by the motto: 'Here you behold a great marvel—two lions are joined into one.' (2) The Latin subtitle further informs us that the lion and the lioness must be united as the 'spirit and soul must be united and led back to their body.' (3) Repeatedly the adepts are admonished that the 'conquest of the lions is difficult and full of dangers, but that it should nevertheless be carried out.' (4)

Fig.77 gives an idea of the magnitude of the job and also of the confused emotions of 'lunar love.' The king and queen appear once more in their animal transformations, as indicated by their human copulating position. In an impressive way the mating ritual of the king's and queen's devouring union has accelerated from the love-fight of the cock and hen and the fierce embrace of the wolf and dog to the murderous oral copulation of the lions, clawing and tearing each other to pieces.

75. Symbiotic fusion of the philosophers' son with the lunar, masculine mother.

Masculine Luna and Her Infant Sol

Fig.75 shows the fifth engraving of the 'Mutus liber' in which the alchemist and his sister begin the sublimation of the dew-water gathered in fig.52. As the water of the prima materia evaporates in the heated retort, the vapours condense in a cool still-head held by the sister, then finally drip into the alchemist's receiver (top row). After the distillation, he lifts off the still-head so that his sister may gather the grains of silver which have formed in the bottom of the vessel (middle row). The silvery quality of the distillate is emphasized by the scutcheon of the moon crescent just outside the phial. Its silvery essence is further stressed by Luna receiving the phial

handed her by the sister. Luna has a strangely masculine body, yet she is represented as the suckling mother holding the infant Sol. In a remarkable way, the child clings to the lunar body in a sexual and symbiotic way, as if melting with it.

In the bottom row the alchemist subjects the distilled water to new processes of sublimation in the kerotakis, or reflux apparatus. Manipulating one of the reagent bottles in the test-tube rack, his sister lutes the condensing cover into position while the fire in the reflux apparatus gathers momentum. The secret identity between Luna and the sister is reflected by the masculine features assumed by the latter after the unfolding of the symbiotic transformation mysteries of the middle row.

The Furious Claws of Infancy

The psychological interpretation of figs.76-77 leads to areas of the unconscious discovered by Melanie Klein. In the oral phase (first year of life) the sucking and clinging infant aims at a total incorporation of and fusion with the maternal love object. Psychologically, this desire takes the form of an introjection or 'taking in' of the beloved. (5) Klein terms this cannibalistic act of assimilation 'introjective identification.' (6) Figs.76-77 render a classical illustration of this configuration with its blend of sexuality and aggression, or its total confusion of 'excessive anger' and 'even greater love.' Hartmann has termed this pattern *drive diffusion.** The furious teeth and claws of the oral-sadistic infant were presented by Klein in a memorable paragraph:

'The idea of an infant of from six to twelve months trying to destroy its mother by every method at the disposal of its sadistic tendencies—with its teeth, nails and excreta and with the whole of its body, transformed in imagination into all kinds of dangerous weapons—presents a horrifying, not to say an unbelievable, picture to our minds. And it is difficult, as I know from my own experience, to bring oneself to recognize that such an abhorrent idea answers to the truth. But the abundance, force and multiplicity of the imaginary cruelties which accompany these cravings are displayed before our eyes in early analyses so clearly and forcibly that they leave no room for doubt.' (7)

Klein's discoveries of the introjective identification processes of early infancy with their savage fantasies of incestuous intrusion and bisexual fusion were confirmed in the 1950s by Margaret Mahler's studies of 'symbiotic psychotic children,' the living museum pieces of an arrested symbiosis. Wrote Margaret Mahler: 'The manifestations of love and aggression in these children's impulse-ridden behaviour seem utterly confused. They

* The opposite of drive diffusion is drive fusion or drive neutralization, which replaces drive diffusion as the development of the ego proceeds. As Hartmann discovered, the ego is too weak at this early stage to carry out an act of repression proper. Therefore the aggressive drive is 'bound' and neutralized by its opposite drive. The success of this defensive ego operation may be studied in fig.71 and in the previous alchemical symbols of the primal scene, in which the dragon's and the lion's claws are reduced to dog's paws (figs.65-67) and, finally, to the spurs of cocks and hens (fig.55). The reversal of this developmental sequence in regression produces dogs out of cocks, lions out of dogs, and dragons out of lions, a 'predatory' movement finishing with the complete diffusion of aggression and sexuality, hate and love. This is a feature that is distinctly psychotic, as is the increasingly incestuous colouring of the libido, symbolized in alchemy by the emergence of leonine symbols for the king and queen.

76. The lion cub of alchemy mounting and attacking his parental love-hate object.

crave body contact and seem to want to crawl into you [fig.75]—yet they often shriek at such body contacts or overt demonstrations of affection on the part of the adult, even though they themselves may have asked or insisted on being kissed, cuddled and 'loved.' On the other hand, their biting, kicking, and squeezing the adult is the expression of their craving to incorporate, unite with, possess, devour and retain the beloved.' [figs.76-77] (8)

77. King and queen locked in a leonine embrace of incestuous passion and hatred.

78. Elation and depression surrounding the composite image of the mercurial goddess.

The Elated and Depressed Alchemists

Fig.78 shows two alchemists resting at the feet of the anima mundi, overflowing with milk. In her right hand the alchemical 'world soul' carries the chameleon (or the symbol of the mask), while in her left hand she holds the eagle symbolizing the alchemist's spiritus (or consciousness). The magical soul woman combines and synthesizes the four warring elements: her body appears as the earth of the seven planetary metals, her watery breasts spring with the virgin's milk, her mouth exhales the air of divine spirit or inspiration, while her hair blazes with the fire of passion and celestial love.

The divine breath, the eagle, and the winged feet of Mercurius are masculine attributes endowing the alchemical goddess with a hermaphroditic quality also borne out by the sun and moon conjoined in her eye holes. A human expression of the winged lioness, the anima mundi symbolizes the combined and omnipotent father and mother of the cosmos—the spirit in matter 'animating all things' and the sap in matter 'nursing all things.'

In the foreground a naked alchemist with an elated expression and a crown on his head dwells in the light of the maternal love object, while the capped alchemist with the depressed expression rests in the shadow of the divinely beloved. The crowned adept is leaning on two retorts brought into symbiotic connection with one another; with a triumphant gesture of his left hand he points to the quadratic stone of the philosophers on which he rests. His sense of union with the good mother contrasts with the gloomy figure on the right who, equally dependent on the omnipotent maternal figure, points to the interior of his retort in an explanatory gesture. Inside the tightly shut vessel a ferocious battle is going on between a snake and a winged dragon or basilisk, the former symbolizing the adept himself, the latter representing a still more powerful and archaic image of the combined parental figure than the winged lioness. The desperate consequences of this battle may be studied in the features of the fur-capped adept: the most precious thing in life has disappeared and become an inner darkness full of hate, disillusionment, and depressing fears.

The Good and Evil Universal Mother

Figs.78 and 79 are products of alchemical and modern artistic imagination. Both represent an authentic expression of the infant's creation of the complex intrapsychic image of his maternal love object, or anima, during symbiosis. As in fig.78, the imago of the 'phallic mother' in fig.79 is a dual unit composed of split objects of an opposing feeling tone: her breasts are covered with cows and flowers and her jets of milk nourish animals and plants of all sorts; yet her breasts are surrounded by crabs and lions, just as her hair is filled with evil spiders—and lovely twittering birds. She is obviously omnipotent and endowed with the father's phallus, presented in the shape of a child; however, she is also the dragon-mother expelling her child in the birth trauma ('Rosy Birth' is the title of the collage). Her inside is filled with children, toys and roses, yet she harbours a jungle of predatory animals and bears. The attempt to fuse all these part objects into one whole object has evidently resulted in the formation of a composite mother image of good and bad qualities, one that can be experienced alternately as all good or all bad.

Melanie Klein has termed this libidinal configuration the 'manic-depressive libido position.' (1) Jung has described the same configuration under the title of the Dual Mother archetype. Its pictorial expression in figs.78-79 reveals the 'blurred' form now assumed by the Oedipus complex due to the psychodynamics of symbiosis.

As the father and mother figures of individuation-separation come together in the figure of the combined parent, the Oedipal father identification and the Oedipal love of mother are fused-confused in an *Oedipal identification with and love of the 'phallic mother.'* Further, since the parental love-hate object of the Oedipal conflict is now *one,* not two persons, the aggressive and sexual drives fueling the dynamics of identification and love merge into oneness too (drive diffusion). However, the most important aspect of the welding processes of symbiosis is the 'healing' of the split-elements of the autistic phase which precedes symbiosis in infantile development.

Whereas the infant at this stage was aware of isolated maternal part objects (breasts, eyes, lips, etc.,) he now perceives a complete person, a whole maternal object. Instead of splitting the mother into a good and a bad half—the chief operation of autism—the infant gradually realizes that the nourishing 'goddess' and the frustrating 'witch' are *halves,* i.e., they are not really separate figures but one and the same. In short, they belong to a human person who can be alternately loved and hated.

This realization of the Dual Mother dawns on the infant in the same way as the dual nature of the moon dawns on an astronaut: by orbiting around the lunar planet and perceiving now her bright half, now her dark half. Such circular movements reflect the spiral course of the infant's mental growth processes, produced, in turn, by a dynamic unconscious merging in such manner the split-elements of the autistic universe. *

As the 'goddess' and the 'witch' come together in a whole object, both good and bad, the mirror magic of the symbiotic phase begins to work: the infant is faced with the recognition of his *own* hate and love toward the object, with the awareness of his *own* oral-aggressive and sexual fantasies toward his mother. When the lion cub suddenly realizes that the cruel and oral-sadistic features of a lioness attacking *him* (fig.77) are the effects of *projection* and actually belong to *himself,* he may begin to repent his own behaviour. (Projection is the opposite of introjection and is an unconscious, primitive defence mechanism whereby unpleasant feelings or repugnant wishes are attributed to someone other than the self, so that the individual can feel, 'It is not I who thinks or feels in such and such a way; it is the other person.' (2))

The psychological effects of this mental boomerang are not to be minimized since the infant's fantasy image of the Devouring Witch is invested with all the evil components of infantile emotional life, which are those of *omnipotence, greed, envy and sadism.* (3)

* Once begun during symbiosis, this merger process continues and accellerates during the 'hatching,' 'practising' and 'rapprochement' subphases of the separation-individuation process, where it finally fuses the opposite drives and the Dual Mother into the *ambivalently loved 'whole' mother.*

79. The Dual Mother giving birth to a phallic child in a jungle of emotional opposites.

The 'hatching' and growing infant's awareness of the features of the good and bad mother as being *those of his own* represents a shattering recognition on the part of his growing ego, and it gives rise to 'depressive fear' (Klein) lest his hatred and aggression prove stronger than his love. The intolerable aggressive urges toward the infant's sole protector and source of nourishment are therefore subjected to what B.Lantos bewilderingly calls an incipient act of 'primary repression.' Cannibalistic fantasies are under no circumstance tolerated in consciousness, not even when the ego is immature—they are fought with all the means at its disposal. Lantos, in discussing the genetic derivation of aggression, says of the devouring energies of the carnivora: 'The archaic oral energies are,

in the human being, under primary repression.' (4)

A manifest sign of the 'primary repression' undertaken by the 'hatching' infant is his inhibition of the urge to bite his mother's nipple. This inhibition occurs by the end of the first year, after the eruption of the infant's teeth. *Shame and guilt* are the psychological expressions of the wailing baby who is scolded by his mother because of biting her nipple. 'Could this not be related to the depressive position postulated by Melanie Klein?' asks the American pediatrician Benjamin Spock.' (5)*

* Rene Spitz's discovery of 'anaclitic depression' in infants deprived of a maternal love object at this stage added further confirmation.

Cyclothymia, or Manic-Depression

Fig.78 renders the alchemical regression to the 'manic-depressive libido position' (Klein) created by a rotary unconscious beginning to work during symbiosis and accellerating during the opening stages of the separation-individuation process (the 'hatching,' 'practising' and 'rapprochement' subphases, 5-22 months). Manic-depression is an 'oral' disease which occurs in persons fixated to this primitive stage of ego development: the elated mood of the manic ego expresses its radiant 'world soul,' while the hopeless mood of the depressed ego expresses its blackened 'world soul.'

Psychologically, the manic phase is the exact opposite of the depressive, but the two are related as a convex arch to a concave. The manic phase is characterized by acceleration (flight of ideas), lack of inhibition, extroverted interest in the environment, extreme uncoordinated initiative, unlimited confidence, aggressive fault-finding, uninhibited aggressive behaviour, elation and sexual licentiousness. The depressive phase is characterized by the opposite of these states. (1)

The infantile ego of the manic-depressive reveals itself in his remarkable vulnerability, his intolerance toward frustration, hurt and disappointment. When the world goes against him, he regresses to the defences of the symbiotic phase, which are those of denial, projection and introjection. His symbiosis with the anima—or with a revolving unconscious—makes him a victim to her violent revolutions and swings of mood. This, in turn, prevents him from making an objective distinction between the state of the world and the state of himself. To a normal person the world may appear good even if he feels bad himself, or the world may appear bad even if he feels good himself. Not so with the manic-depressive: he is himself like the world, and the world is like himself, and so the world rises with him and sets with him in the mirror magic of the revolving, symbiotic anima mundi. On the bright side of the moon the whole world is 'eaten up' and introjected by a manic ego inflated by a universal soul and self. On the dark half of the moon the manic's engulfed world is 'thrown up' and projected on to reality, which is now painted in the same colours as the ego's blackened soul and self. As the sense of universal elation is changed into one of universal depression, the circular flight of manic denial comes full circle in the depressive return of the denied. For this reason the elation of mania is an uneasy one since it may be defined as a denial of the horror of the depressed state.

As Melanie Klein discovered, cyclothymia, or manic-depression, reveals a crucial stage of ego development: between three and twelve months the infan-

tile ego draws its strength from the omnipotent, ideal love object, which by means of introjection is fused with a self now felt to be omnipotent and ideal. This is the manic phase; in the depressive phase the helpless ego is sapped by the evil and worthless love object, which by means of introjection is merged with the image of a self now felt to be debased and worthless.

Such psychodynamics are clearly revealed by the symbolism of fig.78. To her alchemical lovers, the 'whole' maternal object is inner object as well: the elated king on his philosophical stone is communicating with his introjected beloved; the depressed alchemist is communicating with *his* introjected, *hated* beloved. In both cases the anima appears under the primacy of orality.

80. Rotary formation of a dual heart.

Wheeling Zodiacal Circus of 'Exaltation'

Fig.81 shows the anima mundi and her wheeling zodiacal circus, which symbolizes a state of elation by depicting the 'beginning [of the opus]: exaltation' (headline). The goddess appears as a cosmic, fire-spewing cow with dragon's claws and the tiara on her head, a bisexual being governing the Zodiac and the seven planets (the seventh star sparkles on top of her tiara). The balls of the wheeling Zodiac have been arranged according to good and bad qualities: the Bull's globe is good and contains the Twins, the Virgin and the Scales; the Lion's globe is bad and contains the Ram, the Crab and the Scorpion. The Capricorn's globe is good and contains the Archer, the Water-carrier and the Fishes. The fourth globe is 'black-and-white,' like the universal cow-mother herself, and contains her planetary star of celestial illumination and the two mercurial dragons. (The spherical retort in the middle presents

the symbols of the work and its stages and is inscribed by a triangle containing the signs of sulphur, mercury and salt.)

The splitting of the original zodiacal wholeness into wheeling globes composed of good and bad signs parallels the symbolic action of fig.80, in which a similar act of splitting is combined with a rotary movement. The black-and-white heart of Venus shot through with an arrow and blazing with love presides over a circular hare-hunting by harriers. The leftward rotating wheel of Basil Valentine's 'Hunting of Venus' is accompanied by the verse (2):

The hunting of Venus has begun;
Truly, if the dog catches the hare
The latter will not grow old.
This is realized by Mercurius, for when
Venus begins to rage
She produces a terrible number of hares.
Therefore guard Mars with your sword
That Venus does not turn into a whore.

Associated with the goddess of love in her 'raging' state, the 'multiplying' hares of Basil Valentine's Hunt are symbols of erotic 'exaltation.' The sexual connotations of the hare are proved by the fact that the animal is an archetypal symbol of procreation. Further, the hare is ambivalent in that it may be considered as naturally amoral or as moral. The Hebrews regarded it as an 'unclean' animal (Deuteronomy 14:7) symbolizing lasciviousness and fecundity. The hare is also an allegorical figure of speed and elusiveness, thus relating to the mercurial moon. In Greece, the lunar goddess, Hecate, was associated with hares. The German equivalent of Hecate, the goddess Harek, was also accompanied by hares.

In a similar manner, the fierce hunt of the cruel dogs appears as a corresponding symbol of aggressive 'exaltation.' The two states of 'exaltation' are merged in a black-and-white pattern expressed by the dual heart of Venus. The two halves of the 'Venus Hunt' represent psychological opposites, one concerned with hate and killing, the other with love and procreation. Such merging of violent sexuality and aggression by the rotary process of Basil Valentine's hunting-round explains the advice of the Benedictine monk: 'Guard Mars with your sword, that Venus does not turn into a whore.'

Healing Rotations of the Unconscious

The revolving Venus Hunt, the wheeling zodiacal circus, and the infant monkey's spinning universe in fig.72 furnish the answer to the enigmatic cyclic structure of manic-depression: as the splitting processes of the autistic phase begin to rotate in the symbiotic phase and gather momentum in its aftermath ('hatching,' 'practising,' 'rapprochement'), the good and bad introjected objects slowly fuse

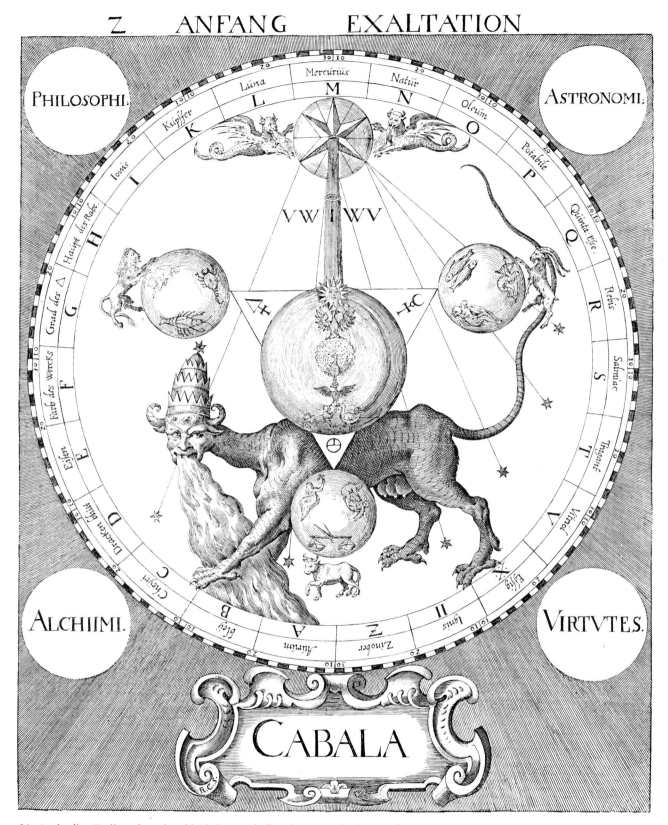

81. A wheeling Zodiac of good and bad signs encircling the composite image of the universal cow mother and evil dragon.

into a composite image reflecting itself in a corresponding external image. The rotary way of connecting split elements and split moods reflects the mandalian movement of a compensating uncon-scious, which 'heals' a schizoid, autistic universe in the same manner as one 'heals' curdled mayonnaise: by stirring until the split elements begin to mix into a unity. Manic-depression represents a fixation to this active, circling, transi-tional phase of the unconscious which in its defensive aspects—denial, projec-tion and introjection—is midway between splitting and repression.

82. *A regressing adept and regicide sweating in the furnace of the Great Mother.*

As prima materia she is the father and mother of the lapis, the filius philosophorum. (1)

A Female Guide in the Night

Another image of the universal mother of alchemy appears in fig.84. In the middle of the night an alchemist is roused by a strange female guest, whom he follows across a bridge, dressed only in his nightshirt and armed with his stick, his spectacles and a lamp. Identified with the wandering moon, or Luna, the universal mother holds the fruits and flowers of the earth, just as her womb grows heavy with the philosophers' son. The epigram accompanying the engraving identifies the woman with 'Nature':

*Nature be your guide; follow her with
    your art, willingly, like a footman,
For you will err if she is not your
    companion on your way. (2)*

The alchemists never tire of praising Mater Natura as their guide and star; in the ancient 'Tractatus aureus' the Hermetic anima mundi is apostrophized in this typical manner: 'O mightiest nature of natures, who containest and separatest the midmost of the natures, who comest with the light and art born with the light, who hast given birth to the misty darkness, who art the mother of all things.' (3)

The Dangerous Virgin of the Sea

Fig.83 shows the anima mundi as 'guide,' or psychopomp, in yet another, more dangerous, variant. She emerges from the waves as a mermaid drawing men to the bottom of the sea with her alluring song. She is armed with a mirror, symbolizing deceptive likeness, destructive illusion, false vision. In this capacity, the anima symbolizes an unreal dream of love, happiness, and maternal warmth—a dream that lures the alchemist away from reality and his work and 'drowns' him in erotic fantasies that can never be fulfilled. The oldest reference to the mer-

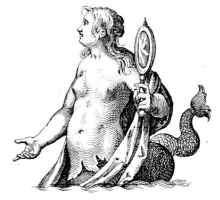

83. *A magic mirror of deceptive likeness.*

A Vision of the Ideal Breast

Above, the labouring alchemist appears as the winged Eros child stepping into the place of his (murdered) father whose crown and royal gear lie on the ground, just below the infant's feet. He holds an enormous poker thrust into the furnace, or womb, of the Great Mother. Strongly idealized, the maternal love object is endowed with the features of Diana of Ephesus, the Great Mother symbol of antiquity. The three ornamental sections of her body, or furnace, represent the animal, vegetable and mineral realms she dominates as universal queen or anima mundi. In addition, the upper half of her body expresses her omnipotence: her many breasts are bountiful sources of nourishment, just as the two lions on her arms and shoulders testify to her male strength and ferocity.

The alchemical apparatus indicates the symbiotic nature of the scenery; vessel and receiver (foreground right) are united with each other through the delivery-spout used for processes of distillation. These processes are frequently compared by the adepts to the dripping breasts of nursing women.

At this crucial stage of the opus, the chaos of the prima materia has changed into the pregnancy of the *prima mater* in whom the warring elements have now become nourishing substances. The primacy of the mother in a primordial matriarchal world is reflected by the absence of any paternal figures around the anima mundi. Significantly, the philosophers' son is called 'orphan' and 'son of the widow,' while his mother enjoys such epithets as 'pregnant girl,' 'virgin in the centre of the earth,' 'widow,' matrix and prima materia. She exists without a man and yet she is the 'matter of all things.'

maid in alchemy is a quotation from Hermes in Olympiodorus: 'The virginal earth is found in the tail of the virgin.' (4) The mercurial serpent is not infrequently called *virgo* and depicted in the form of a mermaid, a creature representing one of the first, if deceptive, manifestations of Mercurius. Other deceptive guises of the 'evasive' Mercurius are the *servus* or *cervus fugitivus*—the 'fugitive slave or stag.' (5)

Psychology of the Mermaid Archetype

Because of the phallic meaning of the fish, convincingly demonstrated by Robert Eisler, (6) the mermaid may be regarded as a symbol of the 'phallic mother' of symbiosis, or of the anima archetype in her watery, crab-like aspect. The deceiving nature of her mirror or watery surface may be explained as follows: just as the 'phallic mother' is merely 'like' the divine hermaphrodite, so the nursing bliss of her breasts is merely 'like' the embryonal condition with its complete physical identity of mother and child. Therefore the alchemist does not rest in the arms of the anima mundi but follows her into night's darkness, closely watching her movements since, as the text of fig.84 says, the 'number of accidents which may befall travellers who in the night and on foot set out on slippery, dangerous roads are countless.' (7)*

This advice seems appropriate because the alchemist now sets out, psychologically, on the dark and dangerous road toward the *autistic phase* of infantile development.

Uniting the Eagle and the Toad

Fig.85 shows the Arabian alchemist Avicenna (980-1037) pointing toward the eagle linked to the toad while exclaiming: 'The eagle flying through the air and the toad crawling on the ground are the magistery.' (9) His gesture draws attention to the central idea of the Her-

84. Pursuing the imprints of the 'world soul' in a lunar night of bliss and terror.

metic procedure: the 'conjunction of the opposites' *(coniunctio oppositorum)*, expressed in the alchemist's arduous attempt to unite the eagle and the toad, spiritus and corpus, intellect and instinct, mind and matter. The descent of the philosopher's eagle, spirit or ego-consciousness into the dark recesses of the toad and the earth—that is, into the instinctual unconscious—gives the key-action of the opus alchymicum. The psychopomp, or 'guide,' of this descent is the alchemist's 'soul sister,' who is depicted in this very function in fig.84.

* Lovers remaining in the arms of the mermaid fall a prey to narcissism and homosexuality. These perversions are characterized by an unconscious identity with the anima (Jung) (8) and by an incomplete detachment from the hermaphroditic archetype of the self (Mercurius philosophorum) as reflected by the symbiotic love object. A 'man with a woman inside,' the homosexual never completely leaves his infantile identification with the 'woman with a man inside,' i.e., with the 'phallic mother.' This fixation is explained by the powerful dynamics of the unconscious at this stage of infantile development: during the symbiotic phase, the introjection of the suckling parental object endows the anima archetype with the features of the *mother*. As a result, the memory image of the mother in the deeper strata of the unconscious becomes the bearer of the ego's first divinely 'beloved' in whom is found the whole world.

85. An Arabian alchemist uniting the worlds of spirit and instinct, mind and matter.

86. Primal union of the philosophical infant with the maternal breast and womb.

The Philosophers' Stone in View

A son-lover on whom the grace of the Earth Mother has descended, Sol as the philosophers' son sucks the breasts of Luna while looking into her semi-divine mother image (above). The mother goddess is now transformed into a perfect sphere representing the earth while also standing for the breast, itself spherical. Identified with the whole world, alias his mother, the philosophers' son has finally established contact with the philosophers' stone. At the bottom of the picture the goat suckling Jupiter (left) and the wolf suckling Romulus and Remus (right) appear as synonyms of Luna and her primordial animality. (1) 'If a small

animal nursed such great heroes, how great must he not be whose suckling mother is the terrestrial globe,' (2) says the epigram of the engraving.

The Philosophers' Cruel Toad

Fig.88 shows a strange variation of the above scene. The motto explains: 'Lay a toad on the breast of the woman so that she, suckling it, may die as the toad grows big with her milk.' (3) This motto echoes a famous passage in Pseudo-Aristotle: 'So tie the hands of a nursing woman behind her back, so that she cannot harm her son; put a toad to her breasts, that she may feed it until she dies, and the woman will die in the fire and the toad will get bigger from the milk.' (4)

Fig.87 shows the philosophers' son adorned with the sign of Mercurius philosophorum and sucking at his mother, transformed into a wolf with the sign of the sun on her forehead. Around the Mercurius child his planetary brothers suck the wolf mother too, or crawl on her body. The accompanying verse shows the blurred speech of the philosophers' son speaking in unison with his solar mother in an act of total, megalomanian identification:

I am like the sun which lets my
Splendour shine, and in numerous
Instances shows my great power
Through which the worldly goods
May produce their effect,
Because they are nourished by me,
Always and everywhere. (5)

The bliss of the Mercurius child sharply contrasts with the horror of fig.89 in which the suckling wolf is transformed into the evil wolf devouring the king. The insatiable greed of the toad-like philosophers' son sucking his mother to death has suddenly changed into the insatiable greed of the mother sucking her *son* to death. This is the primitive psychology of the bad mouth of fig.88: the mouth that wishes to devour not only the milk but the whole breast, nay the *whole mother*. Then the Mercurius child will have an unending supply of milk and will never again have to go hungry or have to wait. But devouring the mothering person is a double-edged sword: if the filius philosophorum wants to devour, he must fear being devoured in retaliation.

Returned to the dependence of the Mercurius child, Sol now gets a taste of the bliss and terror of the Dual Mother: her nourishing goodness, her orgiastic emotionality, and her dark, devouring depths. The cave in fig.87 is not without its anxiety symbols: skulls and skeletons surround the animal mother, who, after all, is a *wolf*. Her unreliable and murderous nature is revealed by fig.89, which illustrates the final action of Basil Valentine's First Key (p.29).

87. The suckling and devouring wolf mother in her cave of death and rebirth.

The Autistic Phase: Imagining the Womb

These pictures describe the attainment of the *autistic* phase of infantile development (0-2 months) which, like the symbiotic phase, is structured according to the oral organization of the libido. In 1943 Leo Kanner described eleven children whose schizophrenic symptoms appeared to constitute a unique syndrome which he termed 'early infantile autism.' (6) Later, autism was incorporated by Margaret Mahler (1952) into the genetic process as a normal phase of the infant's psychobiological growth. (7)

In the first months of life the infant is said to live in an autistic world because of his inability to distinguish between himself and the world around him; he lives and dozes in a world wholly filled with himself and governed by himself. Indeed, the infant depends on his mother for survival, but the maternal object is drawn into the infant's autistic milieu and treated as part of it to the extent that self and object merge into one.

The alchemist's toad scooping up the breast and devouring the mother gives the archetypal fantasy of autism: that of sucking the nourishing object to death, thereby 'taking in' the object, devouring it, and assimilating it to oneself. Melanie Klein has termed this oral-incorporative mode *introjection, introjective identification, or primary identification.* The autistic nature of introjection marks it as one of the most primitive mechanisms of the ego, which thereby begins to perform one of its basic functions, namely the establishment of object relations. (In its *defensive* aspect introjection serves to diminish separation anxiety.)

The sucking philosophers' son enclosed by the pregnant womb of the Earth Mother (fig.86) gives another archetypal fantasy of autism: that of maintaining the original umbilical union with the mother. This desire for 'sameness'—for the congruence of intra-and-extrauterine modes—underlies the autistic fantasies of total incorporation, or introjection, of the gratifying love object. (8)

The Paranoid-Schizoid Libido Position

Six years before Margaret Mahler incorporated the autistic phase into the theoretical framework of the genetic process, Melanie Klein described its psychodynamics under the heading of the 'paranoid-schizoid position' of the libido. (9) Melanie Klein arrived at her theories by inference from material gained in analyses of children and schizophrenics, in whom the regressive processes go back to deep levels of the unconscious.

Klein designates the psychodynamics of autism as introjection and projection; the infantile anxieties, those of persecution (paranoia), devouring and annihila-

88. The philosophers' toad: oral incorporation of the mother by sucking her to death.

tion; and the defence mechanisms, those of denial, splitting and projection.

As she points out, the infant is not always in a state of satisfaction and blissful sleep. In the early months of infancy there is what we are accustomed to call rage, in the sense that the baby, when hungry, hurt or tired, cries furiously. His involuntary body movements are violent, and his facial expression reminds us of anger (fig.111). Nevertheless, there is no indication that there is an objective focus for his feelings, displayed with such intensity and passion.

89. The 'oral triad' of alchemy: the wish to eat, to be eaten, and to sleep.

90. *The king's son and his guide on top of the paternal phallus inside the womb.*

In both normal and pathological regression, the ego's autistic state of 'sameness' with the outer universe expresses itself in megalomanic fantasies and in feelings of 'godliness.' In like manner, the alchemist catches his first glimpse of the philosophers' stone; however, he learns to regard it as a deceptive reflection of the true source of light. This is the moral taught by Lambspring's picture series of the 'king and his son' (figs. 90-91, 125, 150-151), a story based on the Arabian 'Allegory of Alphidius.'

The Temptation of the King's Son

As indicated by its motto, the opening scene of fig.91 shows the 'father and the son linking their hands with those of the guide: know that the three are body, soul and spirit.' (2) The verses accompanying the two pictures read:

[Fig.91.] Here is an old father of Israel,
Who has an only son,
A son whom he loves with all his heart.
With sorrow he orders him a guide
Who is to conduct him whithersoever
    he will.
The guide addresses the son in
    these words:
'Come hither! I will conduct thee
    everywhere,
To the summit of the loftiest mountain,
That thou mayest understand all wisdom,
That thou mayest behold the greatness
    of the earth and of the sea,
And thence derive true pleasure.
I will bear thee through the air
Unto the gates of highest heaven.'
The son hearkened to the words
    of the guide,
And ascended upward with him;
There saw he the heavenly throne,
That was beyond measure glorious.
When his time was up and he had beheld
    these things,
He remembered his father with sighing,
Pitying the great sorrow of his father
And said: 'I will return to his lap.'
[Fig.90.] Says the son to the guide:

Integration of the Wolf and the Toad

Melanie Klein correctly interprets such states of helpless rage and fury as expressing, psychologically, a feeling of overwhelming anxiety. The infant's organismic distress is phenomenologically quite similar to the panic reactions of later life. The nature of this violent anxiety in the infant is unknown, but Melanie Klein inferred from her analytical material that it is related to fantasies of being persecuted and devoured. Such fantasies are explained as inversions of the infant's own vampire-like fantasies of devouring the maternal object by sucking her dry and 'inhaling' her total substance (fig.88).

The alchemist's experience of the sucking toad and the devouring wolf gives his integration of predatory, oral rage and of deeply buried cannibalistic fantasies aiming at 'taking in' the power of another person by the most primitive method of all. Similarly, the final action of Basil Valentine's First Key renders the 'burning' or purgation of the unconscious sources of greed, envy and hate and their evil projective mechanisms. (1)

The Autistic Anima Mundi

If it is true that the ego is born at the point where self and object world separate, it follows that the ego disappears at the point where they meet. If this experience spells dissolution for the psychotic's brittle ego, it spells mystical transformation for the integral ego of Sol, who, absorbed into Luna, is autistically reunited with the 'world soul.' Psychologically this movement means the sliding of the ego into the self as reflected by the autistic love object.

The philosophers' son no longer acts *like* his mother, he has become the *same* person as his mother. This means that the outer world, as represented by the maternal object, is 'inhaled' with her person and incorporated in the self, the latter swelling to awesome, universal proportions. The event signifies the *Weltuntergang* feeling of schizophrenics, who, in panic, perceive the end of the world and simultaneously its ominous 'rebirth' in a self of cosmic proportions. As ego, self and object world are equated in the mirror of an 'autistic' anima, a state of primary identification is obtained which is known as autism. This condition signifies a break with reality and a total regression to the primary process level of delusional thinking and perception. The object world is simply equated with the inner world of the unconscious to the extent that outer reality's objects are replaced by their 'inner images' (introjection).

91. *Beginning of a perilous journey.*

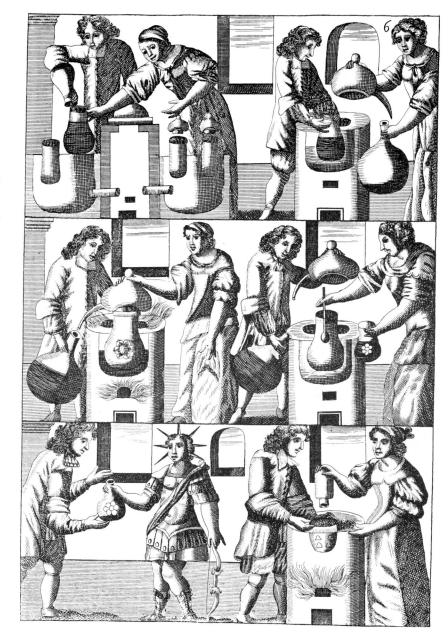

The son and his guide take this step in fig.125, where the supreme secret of Lambspring's bearded king is revealed: *his body is that of a woman!* As the winged guide 'takes back the son to the father's lap,' the king's son is allowed into the royal body of his bisexual parent, who incorporates him by devouring him. After this act, the father goes to bed in the form of a pregnant woman with a son struggling in horror inside her feverish body (fig.150).

Unity Perceived as in a Mirror

The above background of Lambspring's story of the king's son reveals the bearded king of fig.91 as a symbol of the man with a woman inside (or vice versa), i.e., as a symbol of the 'phallic mother.' This relationship explains the son's obsession with the idea of 'returning to the father's lap'; however, it also explains why the son's first attempt at doing so is doomed to fail. Fig.90 shows the son conquering his father's 'heavenly throne' by climbing a phallic mountain projecting into the neck and interior of the maternal vessel, or uterus. The hidden meaning of the imagery is hinted at by the motto of the engraving, which reads: 'Another mountain of India lies in the vessel which the son and the guide have climbed.' (4)

As the king's son beholds the mysteries of solar and lunar conjunction 'in the vessel,' he imagines for a moment he has realized the much-sought-after *coniunctio solis et lunae*. On second thought, however, the king's son realizes that he has only seen a *reflection* of the true event, only perceived the unity of Sol and Luna *as in a mirror*. The winged guide also realizes the deceptive 'sameness' of the event, and so he and the king's son decide to return to the 'father's lap' in order to experience there the *real* conjunction of sun and moon, the *actual* fusion of the heavenly bodies.

Such an interpretation explains the enigmatic reaction of the son and his guide in fig.90: having overcome the megalomanic temptation of Christ in the desert, the son descends from his 'exceeding high mountain' as if another biblical truth had dawned on him: 'For now we see through a glass darkly; but then

92. *The sixth plate of the 'Mutus liber' produces the solar gold, or red tincture, after the distillation of the lunar silver, or white tincture, in the previous plate (fig.75). As the condensing vapours of the heated vessel are gathered in the receiver, the 'golden flower' is developed in the dried-up retort (middle row). The compound thus produced is scraped by the sister into a phial, which in the bottom row is presented to the alchemist by Sol or Phoebus Apollon, intervening in a way similar to the masculine Luna on the previous plate. After the appearance of the second parental figure of the Mercurius child, the moment is ripe for the procreation of the philosophers' son in the vessel. The attempted conjunction of sun and moon is inaugurated by the mystical sister, who in the last scene pours the silvery grains of Luna into the vessel placed in the heated furnace. In the ensuing plate (fig.123) the refined silver is dramatically united with the liquid gold, an act signifying the onset of the first Hermetic trauma of rebirth.*

face to face: now I know in part; but then shall I know even as also I am known' (Corinthians 1:12).

The winged guide is a strange butterfly closely related to the dove of the 'Rosarium' which, according to fig.53, signifies the 'spirit that unifies.' In the light of the guide's action we may equate his spiritus-function with the psychodynamics of introjection, or 'primary identification.' Theologically, the guide symbolizes the Holy Ghost of Incarnation since he attempts to incarnate the son in his heavenly Father and/or Mother. Alchemically, he signifies Mercurius in his endeavours to unite the opposites.

59

93. Lighting the fire of oneness in a furrow between two waves of the mercurial sea.

scribed by comparison with a withdrawn crab. Like Cancer, they signify a state of withdrawal and a return to primary identification with the parental love-hate object. This introjection of the Dual Mother is accompanied by haunting persecutory feelings, aptly symbolized by the pinching claws of the Crab. The autistic child is one who never emotionally perceives the mother as a representative of the outside world; introjected, made part of himself, she is completely removed from the omnipotent and megalomanian orbit of the child's self. The mother is not distinguished from inanimate objects; she appears at best as a part object. Altogether, there is a complete lack of awareness of others.

The autistic child is one who concentrates all his energies into the single defence of blotting out all stimuli, inner and outer, in order to avoid further pain or the impulse to act. Safety resides only in *sameness,* which is the opposite of change and of action bringing about change. Since the autistic child avoids personal activity and change, he remains in the centre of the universe as a flaming sun without boundaries, a sun without awareness of itself as an individual body. (The narcissism of this state of megalomanic self-sufficiency is aptly symbolized by the solar figure of Phoebus Apollon, who in fig.92 presents the alchemist with his magic potion.)

The autistic child's frantic defences concentrate upon the earliest and most traumatic experience of pain in life: the *trauma of birth.* Because the autistic sensations are oral, the recent birth experience is interpreted in oral terms. This gives rise to the archetypal fantasy of the devouring *vagina dentata,* or 'toothed vagina.' This unconscious configuration expresses the primal anxiety of the autistic child.

Imagining the Womb of Rebirth

Against the 'toothed vagina' of the Devouring Mother the autistic child erects two defences: 1) denial and negation of extreme oral aggression and oral means of intrusion; this results in a total paralysis of aggression, of all emotions, and complete withdrawal from the maternal love-hate object; 2) rigid maintenance of the illusion of still living inside the protective womb. This denial of the separation at birth implies a concomitant denial of the outer world which is entered through birth. As a healed autistic child later recalled his fixed idea: 'I was hatched from an egg and a criminal broke it open.' (1)

The autistic child experiences the extrauterine situation 'as if' it were the intrauterine one. This 'sameness' of the two modes results in the autistic child's imitation of the *foetus in utero* condi-

Psychologically, the winged guide Mercurius symbolizes the ego's introjection of its phallic-maternal love object, or 'outer parent.' In a deceitful, subtle manner, this parental object imitates the ego's hermaphroditic self, or 'inner parent.' The son's experience of the *coniunctio solis et lunae* in fig.90 is clearly an 'as if' experience, the source of which he is determined to find by returning to the 'lap' of the *real* parent. What the king's son has experienced is merely the autistic fantasy *par excellence:* that of merging with his mother's lap by identifying with her enclosed phallus (fig.90). The danger of this libido position is realized also by the king's son, who is tempted on top of the same mountain where the Devil tempted Christ. This is the mountain of megalomania and narcissism.

The Children of the Crab

The 'opening of the matrix' in the sign of the Crab uncovers Luna as the suckling Earth Mother. In a parallel move, Sol is returned to the state of the greedy Mercurius child, or sucking toad, and 'borne through the air unto the gates of highest heaven,' tempted there as the king's son on the mountain of omnipotence and megalomania. The mental implications of this alchemical experience may be amplified not only by the psychology of the astrological Crab (p.47), but also by the psychology of the Children of the Crab. These are found in the museum of an arrested autistic development and they are known to psychiatrists as 'autistic psychotic children.' Their mental universe may aptly be de-

tion: absence of object relations ('non being,') object-subject dissolution, autonomy, non-action, posture of immobility, etc. The desperate consequences of this solution of the problem of 'to be or not to be' are evident: because of his desire for the 'sameness' of the two worlds separated by birth, the autistic child finds himself permanently suspended over the yawning abyss of birth with its traumatic anxieties of devouring death. The autistic child manages this uncanny situation in the same way an inexperienced person would walk a tightrope suspended over an abyss: by freezing in total immobility.

Approaching the Lion's Jaws

In fig.93 one of the adepts of the Crab scoops up with a shell the Lady of the Waters, triumphing on the philosophers' stone, now 'converted into water.' The kneeling alchemist appears in the garb of Mercurius philosophorum while his sister and queen appears naked, awaiting him in a symbolic furrow between two waves. In an amorous gesture, she extends her torch toward the raised torch of her impassioned bridegroom and 'fisher king.' The fusion of their flames of love serves to heat the lunar retort into whose neck the sun is about to sink.

Fig.94 shows the attempted conjunction of the sun and moon presented by Hermes Trismegistus, the Egyptian mystery god of alchemy. The astrolabium in his right hand signifies the *rotundum* of the art, the universal wholeness sought by the Sons of Hermes. Referring to the philosophers' son, the mystery god exclaims: 'His father is the sun wedded to his mother, the white moon. The fire comes as the third, as governor.' (2)

Resolving the Conflict of the Sexes

In fig.95 the wheel of the Zodiac makes its fifth rotation: the pinching claws of the Crab now transform themselves into the devouring jaws of the Lion, a transition expressing not only a *crescendo* of persecutory anxiety and fear of being devoured, but also the imminence of rebirth. This relationship is expressed by the symbolic elements of the engraving. Enveloped in a fiery and fearful membrane of love, the naked alchemist points to the pear-shaped vessel which he must enter, expressed in his emphatic gesture. The *vas Hermetis* of 'solution' is closely connected with the mystical sister standing behind the vessel and holding the rose flowers of the *unio mystica*. With a pointing gesture toward the sun descending into the jaws of her Lion, the anima imitates the gesture of the adept, who likewise must descend into the perilous retort of his sister. The taboo nature of the uterine-formed vessel

94. *The god of alchemy raising the philosophers' fire to the temperature of fusion.*

is emphasized by its absorbing function, which parallels that of the Lion, the alchemical emblem of royal incest.

After the hostility of the four elements and the seven planets has been overcome, the last and most formidable opposition remains, that which the alchemists express as the relationship between male and female. The Hermetic *solutio* of this conflict (fig.95) culminates in the 'chymical marriage' in which the work reach-

es its consummation. In order to achieve this supreme act of union, the alchemist is forced to raise his fire to its hitherto strongest degree. In the symbolic language of the adepts, this act implies the heating of love to the passionate intensity of *incest,* the only kind of love which may fuse the sexes into the indissoluble unity of the hermaphrodite's body, identified with the homunculus reborn in the maternal vessel.

95. *Enclosed in the fiery membrane of rebirth, descending into the jaws of the Lion.*

96. Guarding the sulphurous pit in the earth and the stinking water of rebirth.

The Lion Hunt of the King's Son

In quest of the philosophers' stone, the king's son finally arrives before his father's throne (above). The paternal features of the 'old lion' *(leo antiquus)* (1) are unmistakable: the lion's mane is the same as the beard of the old father king in fig.98. His ambivalent look reflects the Wise Old Man and the stern, reproaching father. Similarly, his laurel wreath is a Caesarean symbol of paternal dominion and authority. The territory guarded by the old lion is dangerous: in the foreground sulphurous and evil-smelling vapours arise from the marsh with its 'stinking water' *(aqua foetida)*. (2) This is the water described by the text as the water of the devouring dragon, 'possessing the smell of sulphur and the grave.' (3) In the background a volcano represents the sulphurous pit in the earth which the lion jealously guards. The volcano is in an active state, spewing fire and 'white smoke,' while causing an earthquake indistinguishable from the lion's roaring. The source of the motif is a Morienus quotation from 'De transmutatione metallorum': 'Three species will suffice thee for the whole magistery: the white smoke, the green lion, and the stinking water.' (4)

The specific relation of the lion to the volcanic pit is revealed in fig.105 (plate 15), where he disappears into a fiery moon-crater. The prerogative of vanishing into a hole in the earth with his *whole*

body is the one which the lion jealously guards; he therefore defends his right against any usurper—such as the king's son. The aggressive position of the old lion father 'defending his throne' (above) is seen from the position of the advancing son, whose aim is to kill the lion and eat him up, thereby acquiring leonine strength and magical powers—such as being able to disappear into a pit *toto corpore*. Significantly, this alchemical act of intrusion takes place in the Lion, the astrological sign of traumatic fear and incestuous rebirth *par excellence*.

Leo the Lion: the Trauma of Rebirth

The fifth sign of the Zodiac is a fixed and fiery sign ruled by the Sun. Leo covers the period from July 23 to August 23, thus expressing the Sun at his greatest power. Strength is the essence of the Lion, which is the strongest of all the animals and the king of beasts. His authority and independence are undisputed— Leo, like the Sun, remains on his throne. The strength of the Lion expresses the energy of a fire now under control and harnessed to useful ends. Thus, in alchemy, Leo signifies molten gold.

Astrologically, Leo symbolizes the will to create. However, the procreative urge of Leo is self-centred since it really aims at giving birth to himself. In a certain sense, Leo may be said to be his own father and mother: his roaring erotic

passion is that of 'getting inside himself,' there realizing the core of his personality.

Leo represents the first traumatic sign of the Zodiac, his mouth expressing the anxiety of being devoured and swallowed with one's whole body. When these characteristics of the astrological Lion combine with its incestuous significance in alchemy, a pattern is obtained in which sexuality becomes a dual expression of incestuous intrusion and traumatic fear. This is the very pattern expressed by the symbolism of fig.96, in which the lion's 'stinking water' and sulphurous fire signify the rank smell of incest—the smell of the maternal pit in its orgastic contractions of birth and death.

A similar pattern, rendered in a censored form, appears with the alchemical picture series reproduced in figs.98-104 from the 'Pretiosa margarita novella' of Janus Lacinius (Petrus Bonus), 1546. (5) It shows the son's usurpation of the king's throne, carried out by murder followed by 'cannibalism.' By drinking his father's blood, the king's son assumes his father's body, thereby attaining to parental reunion and rebirth. The woodcuts are accompanied by short texts, reproduced on the opposite page.

Sucked by the Pit of Birth

In alchemy, the lion symbolizes the father-king: the murderous act of the king's son assumes two alternating, yet related forms—his killing of the father (fig.99), or his killing of the lion (fig. 109). Similarly, the sequel to the son's animal sacrifice, or act of parricide, turns into his being devoured by the father (fig.125), or by the green lion (fig.124).

In the dramatic 'Pretiosa margarita' version, the son's parricide and subsequent 'gathering of the father's blood' (fig.100) corresponds to the alchemical drinking of the lion's blood to gain his strength (fig.109).

Thus incarnated in the father, the son in fig.101 begins to dig the grave, or the 'quadratic stone' *(quadrella)*, also termed the 'pit' or 'oven.' In fig.102 the king's son lowers the body of his father into the sarcophagus in an ambiguous way: his gesture resembles an embrace. This feature is explained by the sexual trans-

97. Traumatic rebirth in the Lion's sign.

The 'Pretiosa' Story of the King's Son

'Three things must be observed; firstly, you must prepare the matter; secondly, you must continue the opus so that it does not dissolve due to interruptions; thirdly, you must be patient and observe the interior tracks of nature. Firstly, prepare the purified water of supreme life and keep it. Do not think, however, that this liquid, with which they moisten all things, is the bright and clear liquid of Bacchus. For while you anxiously look about in out-of-the-way places for extraordinary events, you pass by the sparkling waves of the blessed stream.

98. Then you will enter a palace in which there are fifteen rooms and in which there will be a king crowned with a diadem; he will sit in a high place and hold the sceptre of the whole world. Opposite his majesty is his son with five servants clad in various garments. On their knees they implore the king to transfer his kingship to the son and his servants, but the king does not even answer their requests.

99. Impelled by the servants, the indignant son kills his father on the throne. Thus let there be an amalgamation with water well purified.

100. In the third place the son collects in his garments the blood of his father, which is the second opus and already explained in the method.

formation of the interred father, who after having been 'thrown into the pit' develops female genitalia and breasts (fig.102). In particular, this transformation explains why father and son, identified with each other, should 'both fall into the pit through the art.' As the body of the father-mother king sucks the 'evil-thinking son' into the pit, the latter finds himself involved in the birth situation depicted in fig.103. Here the 'son tries to get out' of a *quadrella*, pit, or oven, the lid of which is removed by a split figure of the king's son who, on the woodcut, appears both in his adult and infantile-regressive form. Finally, in fig. 104, this trinity of masculine figures disappears into the earth, sucked by the sarcophagus or 'quadratic stone' and dissolved in its 'very hot bath.' (6)

The Lion Hunt of King Marchos

The 'Pretiosa' series of pictures represents a human variation of the famous lion hunt of King Marchos described by Senior. (7) Here the lion is a transparent symbol of King Marchos himself as son-and-father. The lion is ensnared by King Marchos' mother, who appears as the treacherous Earth Mother. She prepares a trap, and the lion, attracted by the sweet smell of the stone, falls into the pit. The magical stone is a woman lying on a bed of coals and absorbing with her own the lion's entire body. In Senior, this thinly veiled incest allegory reads as follows:

'Marchos said to his mother: How will you catch the lion? His mother, who admired him, said: I will await him, and when he sets out, I will go ahead of him. I will sit down on the road and in the middle of it dig a trap (by which is meant the retort) and over the trap place a roof of glass . . . And when he shall have approached the bridal chamber, I shall kindle the fire without smoke in that trap; this fire is with a flame which comes out over the coals, even as the pious mother steps over the body of her son. And she likened the subtlety of the fire's heat to the stepping of the pious mother over the body of her son. For his mother said to him: O Marchos, must this fire be lighter than the heat of fever? Marchos said to her: O mother, let it be in the state of fever. I return and enkindle that fire in the way assigned for you. And I place on him the stone which he who knows, places on his eyes, and he who knows not, casts away. And when I shall have led him over that fire, it produces a smell which the lion loves. Truly, when the lion smells that stone, he will soon come as if entering that bridal glass chamber. And he will fall into the trap, and the stone will swallow him, so that nothing more of him is to be seen. And this stone, which the lion loves, is a woman' [fig.105]. (8)

101. In the fourth room the pit is dug, which is the oven, its height being two palms, its breadth four fingers.

102. In the fifth house the evil-thinking son assumes that he can leave the father thrown into the pit, but both fall into the pit through the art.

103. Verily, the sixth house is that in which the son tries to get out, but one (who sprang from them in the second operation) turns up and prevents the son from getting out.

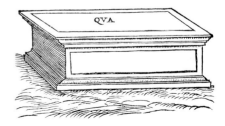

104. While the father and the son are in the pit, which is called the seventh room, they are subjected to putrefaction in the ashes, or a very hot bath.' (9)

105.

The First, or Earthly, Trauma of Rebirth

Fig.105 renders Barchusen's drama of the waxing moon and the opened vessel. Sol evaporating into lunar oneness (plate 12, fig.70) and emerging as the newborn sun on top of a swelling Luna (plate 13, fig.70), finally turns into a lion vomiting the flames of incestuous passion and mortal anxiety (plate 14). Below the circle of the hot lion devoured by its own solar fire, the moist toad, or Earth Mother, swallows the animal. Lion and toad are flanked by their elemental triangles, signifying fire and water and, at the same time, their fusion in the sign of Mercurius philosophorum—appearing on top of the sign of water along with the astrological sign of the Lion, in which constellation the conjugal act takes place.

Plate 15 equates the devouring mouth of the toad with the absorbing neck of the vessel and with the 'pregnant' body of the full moon, sucking the lion into a fiery hole on its surface. The motif renders the lion's fall into the trap of King Marchos and his mother. In the 'Crowne of Nature,' the original of Barchusen's series of engravings, (1) plate 15 is termed 'coitus' and accompanied by the text: 'Joyne therefore (as yt is in the rosary) the most beloved sonn Gabricum with his sister Belia, to whome he gives all that he hath because he came from her. Whence yt may be gathered that without copulation there can be noe pregnacion, and without pregnacion not birth.' (2)

In plate 16 a stopper closes the neck of the retort from which a membrane is bulging; the sealed vessel is placed in a water bath and heated in the steaming furnace, or Athanor. In plate 17 the bulging membrane 'withdraws' into the retort with the steaming vapours, now condensed into the lunar sea heated by solar fire. The event signifies the welling up of the universal sea in the interior of the vessel, or the adept's achievement of the oceanic condition. This is the famous *solutio* of which the 'Rosarium' says: 'Our stone is cheap and is found in filth; many have dug and worked in the filth and have found nothing. But when it has been converted into water, it is obtained by both rich and poor; and it is found in every place and at any time and in every circumstance when the search lies heavy on the searcher.' (3)

Spiritual Rebirth in Fetal Water

After shedding their clothes in the third woodcut of the 'Rosarium' (fig.54), the king and queen in its fourth woodcut (fig.106) descend into the mercurial well, identified by the text with the sexual parts of the queen (p.80). The 'Rosarium' further informs us that 'among other names, the water is called fetid water. Therefore the philosopher says: This fetal water *(aqua foetum)* contains everything it needs.' (4)

The identification of the alchemical water marriage with the act of birth appears in the royal coitus of fig.108. The embrace of Sol and Luna in the bath is equated with Luna in labour with the philosophers' son among the thunderclouds, her child coalescing with Sol, or her copulating lover and husband. Sol in his double role as penetrating phallus and penetrating child depicts a reversed birth as the goal of a sexual act: through his incestuous passion, the copulating king enters into his mother again in an act of re-birth.

The traumatic aspect of this event is given with the king's immersion into the watery well, which contains the horrors of drowning and choking and so emerges as a symbol of death. However, the king's mortal anxiety is compensated by the dove, whose rosy stem will be submerged into the water, too, and thus furnish the royal couple with the life-giving spiritus, or air (fig.106). The alchemical scenery of childbirth and copulation in fig.108

106. Descending into the well of birth.

is accompanied by the Senior motto: 'He is conceived in water and born in air; when he has become red in colour, he walks over the water.' (5) This motto refers to the philosophers' son or the lapis floating upon the liquid in the crucible; it also contains a reference to a famous biblical passage: 'Except a man be born again, he cannot see the kingdom of God. Nicodemus saith unto him, How can a man be born when he is old? can he enter the second time into his mother's womb, and be born? Jesus answered, Verily, verily, I say unto thee, Except a man be born of water and of the Spirit, he cannot enter into the kingdom of God' (John 3:3-7).

The Royal Well of Birth and Death

Sol as the infant toad sucking his mother to death now suffers the pangs of primary identification, as shown in Barchusen's plate 14. In a horrible act of transformation, the devoured mother suddenly changes into the toad sucking the greedy sucker to death with the *labia majora* ('big lips') of her awesome mouth, or womb. The transformative implications of Barchusen's plates 14-15 have an unquestionable interpretation: the shift from the virgin's milk and lunar breasts to the absorbing mouth of the toad and the full moon renders the shift from the suckling mother to the labouring mother.*

At the end of the tether, the mother introjected or 'swallowed' by the infant toad transforms herself into the toad mother introject swallowing the *infant*. With this autistic confusion of outside and inside, object and subject, the primal anxiety of birth establishes itself as an objectless fear pervading everything—as the water of death pervades every pore of the king descending into his well.

Labouring Son, Father and Mother

In fig.108 the water marriage of Sol and Luna takes place at the entrance of a cave symbolizing the open womb. The 'widening' of the queen's lap into a well or cave sucking the whole figure of her copulating mate shows the maternal transformation of the king's beloved

* Luna's toad-like mouth and pit-like womb sucking the lion reveal the overlapping of oral and vaginal libido organizations. Such fusion is natural in the neonate, whose two vital tasks are those of passing through the maternal vagina and of sucking the maternal breasts. (The sucking reflex is inborn and has been practised by the neonate already inside the womb.) The resultant merging of the two libido organizations during birth produces the archaic fantasy of the 'vagina dentata'—the 'teethed vagina' of the devouring witch mother subjecting her child to the primal anxiety of birth. Another variant of this image is the devouring dragon (p.68).

107. Re-experiencing the traumatic act of birth in symbols of death and rebirth.

sister—a metamorphosis implying the king's parallel transformation into the figure of his father. At this stage of a culminating Oedipus complex, the maternal lap receives the father's phallus coinciding with the son's body. The identity of Sol as labouring infant and labouring lover thus expresses the body-phallus equation of primary identification—a union of the father and the son symbolized, above all, by the *spiritus sanctus* of the dove of Incarnation.

108. Royal love in an enchanted cave: Sol embracing a woman giving birth to him.

109. *Slaying the lion father and taking his place in the royal trap, or well of rebirth.*

The Parental Extraction of the Stone

The remaining union of the labouring son, or father, with the labouring mother produces the dual imagery of fig.108, which represents a condensation of the combined parents in intercourse and of the mother giving birth to her child. The idea of being squashed between the copulating parents is a familiar fantasy, clinically as well as in some primal-creation myths. The shifting sexual identification with the parents underlying primal act fantasies is a psychodynamic force likewise animating the labouring Sol in fig.108. It provides his transition to the ultimate goal of primary identification, or parental introjection: the *rebis*, or 'dual being,' which is both father and mother. Significantly, the 'Rosarium' explains the action of its fourth woodcut thus: 'Our stone is to be extracted from the nature of the two bodies.' (1)

The royal water marriage is closely connected with the natural act of thunder and lightning, carrying in alchemy the dual meaning of traumatic horror and celestial illumination. (2) While Sol embraces Luna in the water, their 'labouring' reunion is consummated in a pregnant thundercloud (fig.108). A similar motif appears in fig.110: stuck out from a thundercloud, the hand of God breaks the shell of Sol, who in a flash of lightning experiences his birth. (Alchemically, the act signifies the liberation of gold from the darkness of the earth.)

Thunderstorms and Lionslaughters

Another incidental motif of the water marriage—the slaying of the father king—is shown in its animal version in fig.109. The 'Pandora' woodcut renders the conclusion of King Marchos' lion hunt, in

which the lion, trapped and swallowed by the female stone, suffers final death by amputation of his paws. (3) As we have seen, the lion in Senior's story replaces the king. This secret identification is brought out by the woodcut, in which the trapped alchemist, struggling in the neck of the well, points to a scroll inscribed: 'Kill the lion in his blood.'

The royal significance of the trapped alchemist is indicated by the strange merging of his body with a crowned tower stuck into the well. The 'winged' tower is filled with fluttering birds and, at its bottom, with two copulating birds devouring each other's tails. The pelican on the rim of the basin symbolizes overflowing blood, the serpent to the right, fertilization. Birds flying up and down with flasks or retorts illustrate the inscriptions on the flying scrolls: 'The fixed has been rendered volatile, the volatile has been rendered fix.'

The pictorial action is interpreted by the text as a slaying and decoction of the 'lion and his father,' whose essence is mixed with the well-water and drunk as the much-sought-for elixir of life: 'Whoever takes the blood of the lion and then does him justice by burning to ashes with heat and violence the body of his father, therein pouring the blessed water, he will obtain a remedy healing all sicknesses. This will be the supreme medicine of men, animals, birds, tin, copper, steel, iron, and lead.' (4)

Otto Rank and the Trauma of Birth

The transition from Crab to Lion, the king's descent into the well and immersion in the bath, and the lion's descent into the mouth of the toad, the neck of the vessel, and the fiery hole of Luna symbolize the ego's regressive transition from the autistic phase to birth. Hermetic symbols of this movement present an ardent love-fire blending with the fiery anxiety of death and devouring. Otto Rank's theory of the 'trauma of birth' (1924) explains this strange configuration at the bottom of the personal unconscious. (5)

According to Rank's theory, the infant's severance from the mother and

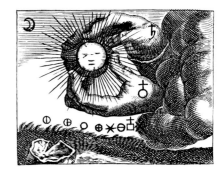

110. *Golden birth of a fetal sun.*

from the all-encompassing, effortless bliss of her womb constitutes the ego's first painful experience of reality. Besides death, birth represents the most anxious experience man undergoes. This event causes such a profound shock to the helpless infant that a traumatic pattern is engraved in its memory with the force of an archetypal situation. The psychic nature of the *birth trauma*—as Rank terms this pattern—is constituted by separation-anxiety and primal anxiety-affect *(Urangst)*. The ego's initial experience of violent terror, or *Angst*, evokes the usual psychological reaction of repression. The result is the formation of a powerful mental barrier known as 'primal repression' around the maternal, vaginal and sexual complex, which in the 'deepest unconscious' becomes the bearer of the universal, primal anxiety of birth.

LSD Confirms Freud's Original Idea

The process of birth must be regarded as a *traumatic* event in Freud's definition of the term: 1) overwhelming, flooding the child with excessive stimulations from all internal and external sources; 2) shocking, coming as a surprise with no forewarning; and 3) overpowering, in that the child has no avenue of flight or fight. Freud considered the act of birth the first trauma and thus the source and physiological prototype of anxiety. (6)

The violent discussion in the wake of Rank's theory and Freud's original idea resulted in a dismissal of the validity of the birth trauma. This conclusion has proved an immature one: it is emphatically contradicted by LSD-induced regressions and by alchemical symbolism, and it may be refuted by a simple experiment performed on the neonate. (For an account of Dr. Liley's experiment, see note 7.)

The Lightning and Thunder of Birth

All Hermetic symbols of rebirth lend themselves to interpretations in terms of a revival of the experience of birth. In the following chapters we shall study various aspects of this experience in a rich variety of alchemical motifs. In the present case, the traumatic thunder-storm of alchemy may be interpreted as rendering the acoustic and visual aspects of the birth experience. Accustomed to the womb's watery darkness, the infant's eyes receive the first impressions of sunlight in the same way as the eyes of an adult perceive the flashes of lightning on a night of thunder. Also acoustically the newborn baby must experience birth in the same way as the adult experiences the crashes of thunder: the eardrums of the infant, which have been shielded by the sound-absorbing 'walls' of the mater-

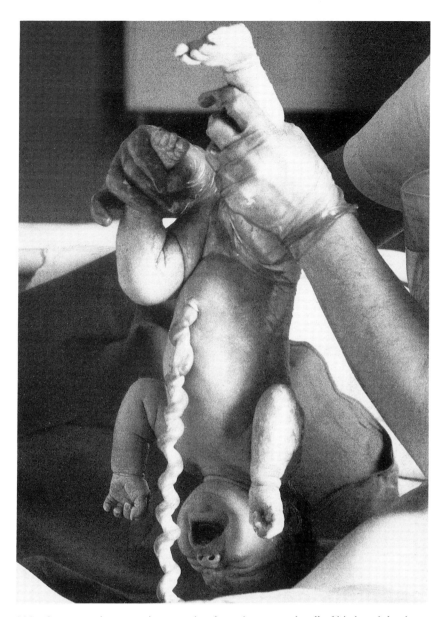

111. The neonate's traumatic extraction from the maternal well of birth and death.

nal body, are in birth exposed to sounds likely felt as peals of thunder.

The Day of Birth

'Birth begins with a narrowing of the uterus, which results in straightening the baby's body so that his head (or, in a few cases, his buttocks) is pressed against the outlet of the womb, called the cervix (in Latin, neck). Next, the virtually closed cervix must give way to accommodate the width of the baby's head. It has been established that the muscles of the top of the uterus apply a force comparable to a weight of fifty-five pounds to the baby with each contraction. Usually, the amnion ruptures under this pressure and, depending on the size and location of the tear, the fluid either rushes or trickles out. The contractions coming at increasingly frequent intervals

push the baby against the cervix until the passively resisting muscles of this outlet give way and the head of the baby can slip out as through a tight bathing cap. This completes the first and longest stage of birth. The second stage is quicker but requires much greater force. To move the baby out to his crowning, as the birth of the head is called, a force equal to a weight of nearly one hundred pounds is needed. The extra power must be supplied by the efforts of the mother. This is why the process of birth is called 'labour.' When the mother's muscle power, for various reasons, is not sufficient, the physician must help. He must work to bring the baby out by the pull of forceps or sometimes even by Caesarean birth . . . Birth is never easy for the baby. It may take less than an hour or it may last many hours. The average duration of the birth of a first baby is 14 hours.'
G.Lux Flanagan. (8)

67

In the image: banners read on left top to bottom: Conyng, Experience, Pracktike, Prudent, Pacience; on right top to bottom: Gras, Nature, Reson, Spekelative, Holi lifing.

112. The labouring dragon's roar: 'Unless ye slay me, ye cannot be called sages.' (1)

The Descent into the Dragon's Cave

Kneeling before the Hermetic mystery of conjunction, a crowd of alchemists in fig.112 marvel at the rebirth drama enacted in front of their eyes. From a cloud the Hermes bird or dove descends into the toothed neck of the vessel, transformed into a split image of the dragon's mouth. Its upper jaw, or left head, is identified with Sol, just as its lower jaw, or right head, is identified with Luna. In such fashion the dragon emerges as a wedding symbol of bisexual, if terrifying nature. In a strange way the praying alchemists appear to 'push' the swollen belly of the hermaphrodite-monster. The contractions of the panting dragon aided by eight alchemical 'midwives' present an interesting variation of the Hermetic act of conjunction, which is framed by the ten virtues of the adepts, described as 'cunning, experience, practice, prudence, patience, grace, nature, reason, speculation, and holy living.'

The Dragon's Incestuous Bath of Life

Fig.113 renders the royal bath in yet another variation. From seven open tubes in the bottom of the retort, the lunar water infused with solar light pours over the heads of the naked brother-sister pair, identified with the sun and moon uniting inside the ripened vessel. While embracing in the 'bath of life,' the siblings are bitten in their calves by a split image of the dragon, just as their legs are scratched by a toad. The inscription on the well shows the incestuous lovers as symbols of the spiritus and anima; similarly, the winged dragon and the toad symbolize the corpus, or the dark and dreaded womb in which the conjunction takes place. The pear-shaped uterine vessel is held by a personification of the dove representing the Holy Spirit; his breath of Incarnation 'seals' the ripened vessel while effecting the con-

junction of opposites. (Similar actions of the dove, or Holy Spirit, may be studied in figs.106-107, 109, 135, 166.)

Fig.114 shows the dragon fight at the entrance of the alchemical cave. Splitting in the dragon's fire of primal anxiety, the alchemist appears in his dual form as philosopher and knight. In the grip of massive shock, the alchemist as philosopher stiffens defencelessly, his black face tinged with mortal fear. Opposite, the knight aggressively meets the traumatic experience, trying to shoot the fire-breathing monster. Thus, the two figures epitomize the hero's active and passive suffering in the dragon's mouth. As informed by the text, the pictorial motif is patterned on the Apollon myth. The cave is the birth place of Apollon on the island of Delos, a sacred spot guarded by lions (top of cave).*

113. The incestuous water marriage.

The dragon fight represents the portal to the Little Work, just as its fire-baptism represents the necessary condition for admission into the secret society of the Sons of Hermes. Because of the dragon's significance, the adepts accept the monster as a blessing in disguise. The dragon, in turn, meets its challengers with its famous roar, rendered thus by the 'Rosarium': 'I announce therefore to all ye sages, that unless ye slay me, ye cannot be called sages. But if ye slay me, your understanding will be perfect, and it increases in my sister the moon according to the degree of our wisdom, and not with another of my servants, even if ye know my secret.' (3)

The Third Key of Basil Valentine

Fig.115 shows the Third Key of Basil Valentine in which a split image of the cock further reflects the active and passive aspects of rebirth: the cock attempting to devour the fox is devoured itself by the fox. In the foreground the winged and hungry dragon awaits the time when the cock and the fox will be devoured by *him*. The scenery presents a variation of another emblem by Basil Valentine in which the eagle is swallowed by the lion, who is swallowed, in turn, by the dragon (fig.124). The text reads:

'The king imparts great strength and potency to his water and tinges it with his own colour, that thereby he may be consumed and become invisible and then again recover his visible form with a great diminution of his simple essence and a great perfection of his intellect . . . which can only be after [his] body has been absorbed by the salt sea and again rejected by it. Then it must be so exalted as to shine more brightly than all the stars of heaven, and in its essence it must have an abundance of blood like the pelican, which wounds its own breast and without diminution of its strength nourishes and rears up many young ones with its blood. This tincture is the rose of our masters, of purple hue, called also

* The dragon fight depicts the slaying of the Python by Apollon, who immediately after his birth kills the dragon with his arrows. After the event the serpent Python lives in amity with Apollon and guards the Omphalos, the sacred navel-stone and midpoint of the Earth, which stands in Apollon's temple. Another version of the Apollonian dragon fight relates how Apollon comes to Delphi in his mother's arms as a little, naked boy holding his bow drawn with an arrow in his hand. He is met by a dragoness named Delphyne (meaning 'womb' in ancient Greek); she dwells together with the male serpent Delphynes, who is often confused with Delphyne and even with the Python. Apollon shoots arrow after arrow into the womb-like giant snake and finally succeeds in slaying the monster. Its body is dissolved by the power of the sun and the place of the event is named Pytho, just as Apollon is called Pythios. (2)

the red blood of the dragon, or the purple cloak of the Supreme Lord of our art, with which the Queen of Salvation is covered and by which all needy metals may be warmed.

'Carefully preserve this mantle of glory together with the astral salt which is joined to this heavenly sulphur and screens it from harm. Add to it a sufficient quantity of the volatility of the bird; then the cock will swallow the fox, and, having been drowned in the water and quickened by the fire, will in its turn be swallowed by the fox.' (4)

The Dragon Fight: the Birth Trauma

Depth psychologists quickly recognized dragons and monsters as symbols of basic powers forming the deepest strata of psychic geology. In 1912, Jung in 'Transformations and Symbols of the Libido' interpreted the hero myth as a symbol of the regressing libido struggling for rebirth. However, it was not until 1924 that Jung's patterns of rebirth could be properly understood and interpreted as symbols of the birth trauma. That year Otto Rank, from the genetic point of view, advanced the interpretation of dragons and monsters as symbolic expressions of the birth trauma, and the dragon-fighting-heroes as symbols of *the ego's regressive overcoming of primal anxiety.* Curiously, Jung reacted in the same way as Freud toward Otto Rank's 'trauma of birth,' i.e., by the appropriate defence mechanisms of splitting and denial, brandishing it the 'infantile theory elaborated by Otto Rank.' (5)

The Dragon Fight of an LSD-Rebirth

The dragon fight is an archetypal theme with a thousand variations on a cosmic scale. In the 20th century the motif cropped up as a prominent feature in LSD-induced experiences of rebirth. Masters and Houston report the following, typical case:

'S began to breathe heavily and gave the impression of being involved in some great internal struggle. His face reddened, he started to perspire, and the facial expression resembled that of some mythological hero locked in mortal combat. After some minutes he reported experiencing a 'titanic struggle.' His senses were unwilling to relinquish their 'hold upon the earth.' He complained of being 'in bondage to serpentine, oriental forms that press down upon consciousness strangling its horizon.' S struggles against these forces and, in so doing, experiences sensations more intense than any he has known. His effort, he now says, is directed towards 'containing God' . . . After a silence of some minutes, S remarks: 'I am locked in a titanic struggle. The crea-

114. Splitting in the dragon's fire of primal anxiety while imitating Apollon's work.

tures are enormous and symbolic. Whether I am losing or winning I don't know, because I don't understand the symbolism or what the outcome should be. Great colossi are fighting. Tigers and other beasts, hundreds of feet high, tear at one another's throats. These are the forces of myself, forces threatened with dissolution should I abandon myself to God. The forces also have cosmic meaning—meaning beyond the meaning they have in my own psychology . . . I am a battleground of the most titanic forces.

All this time colossal tigers and enormous dragons are snarling at one another's throats. These forces I know to be symbolic and involved in my conflict with God, yet I still cannot say exactly what they are.' S reported that he was continuing to experience very intense sexual sensations and said that he feared abandoning himself to God because God might 'take away' his 'sexuality.' The subject was now at the start of what proved to be a three-hours-long 'battle with God.'" (6)

115. Splitting in the mouth of mortal anxiety while trying to devour a devouring foe.

116. Projective identification of a persecuted adept splitting into his four persecutors.

The Persecuting Elemental Brothers

The two woodcuts reproduced in figs. 117-118 derive from the 'Pandora' series of the royal water marriage, the first picture being reproduced in fig.71 (the engraved variant). The woodcuts agree with the 'Rosarium' series, rendering the meeting of the naked king and queen and their descent into the mercurial well. In fig.117 the handshake of the royal lovers takes place inside a vessel whose neck is identified with a naked, pregnant woman. The king and queen are surrounded by 'four faces with one father,' as the 'Pandora' text informs us. (1) The 'faces' are identified by the second woodcut (fig.118) as the four elements—'water, air, fire and earth.' As further informed by the 'Pandora,' the presence of the four faces signifies the 'transformation or circulation of the natures of the four elements.' (2) In fig.118 this circulation of the four elements occurs simultaneously with the descent of the royal bathers into the well and its parallel action: the 'delivery' of the philosophers' son, whose winged, erect body climbs the neck of the vessel with nimble feet of rebirth.

The motif of the 'four [elemental] faces with one father' encircling the alchemical hero reappears in an interesting variation in fig.116. Armed with a club, the hero-alchemist combats the four elements, which in the shape of four inimical brothers attempt to encircle and kill him. According to the text, the task of the persecuted alchemist is that of killing

his elemental brothers; if he succeeds in slaying one of them, he will have succeeded in killing all of them:

Four brothers stand in a long row;
The one to the right carries the weight
*   of earth,*
The other that of water; the rest of them
Carry the elements of air and fire.
If you want all of them to die quickly,
Only kill one of them, and they will
Die together, since they are united
By natural bonds. (3)

The text further compares the persecuting brothers to the four heads of the monster Geryon, who threatened to devour Hercules. The elemental brothers are also compared to Siamese twins or quadruplets. (5) The fact that the fifth figure is their 'brother' and in the engraving appears as yet another 'twin' makes it possible to view the artifex of fig.116 as a multiple-headed figure, whose murderous, Geryon-like body has been subjected to a process of *splitting or fragmentation.*

The motif is finally compared by the text to the dragon fight and the king's death and rebirth: 'When he rises, death, darkness, and the waters will flee from him. As Hermes testifies, the dragon that guarded over the abyss will flee from the sunbeams and our son will live and the dead king will come out of the fire.' (6)

Fig.119 presents the alchemical hero as the 'lord of the forest' (7) struggling with the venomous dragon, who bars him on his way to recover his kingdom.

The Persecutory Anxiety of Birth

These pictures express the persecutory anxieties of the king, or the philosophers' son, during his birth in the neck of the bulging vessel, or pregnant queen. Persecutory anxiety as a chief feature of the infant's birth-traumatic experience was initially postulated by Melanie Klein. According to her, the contractions of the uterus expelling and 'beating' the infant with a weight-force of fifty-five pounds must be imagined and interpreted by the helpless infant as a savage attack by a cruel foe. Wrote Melanie Klein:

'I have put forward the hypothesis that the newborn baby experiences, both in the process of birth and in the adjustment to the post-natal situation, anxiety of a persecutory nature. This can be explained by the fact that the young infant, without being able to grasp it intellectually, feels unconsciously every discomfort as though it were inflicted on him by hostile forces . . . Persecutory anxiety arising from the experience of birth is the first form of anxiety, very soon followed by depressive anxiety . . . In my view omnipotent destructive impulses, persecutory anxiety, and splitting are predominant in the first three to four months of life. I have described this combination of mechanisms and anxieties as the paranoid-schizoid position, which in extreme cases becomes the basis of paranoia and schizophrenic illness.' (8)

As Melanie Klein discovered, the ego's earliest mechanism of defence against the primal anxiety of birth is not 'primal repression'—the ego is too weak for that—but *splitting.* Faced by mortal danger, the infantile ego reacts in the same

117. The four persecuting elements.

primitive way as the lizard, which when caught by the tail, severs it from its body and, although mutilated, escapes. This primitive defence is revived in the adult ego's spontaneous reaction to mortal danger: splitting produces the eerie and chilly sense of *dedoublement,* in which one's personality is felt to have been cleft in two, one half facing the threat of death, the other denying it by remaining in a detached-paralyzed state (fig. 114).

Splitting as a primal defence is revived in schizophrenia, which regresses to the very layers of birth-traumatic, primal anxiety. As Melanie Klein discovered from studies of schizophrenics, a prominent symptomatic feature is even *persecutory anxiety accompanied by fits of uncontrollable rage.* She inferred that similar anxiety and rage must be present in the neonate. This inference seems to correspond with certain psychophysiological manifestations of the neonate. Uncontrolled bursts of violent crying and rage frequently distort the face of the neonate while shaking his whole body (fig.111). Such reactions point to the fact that the trauma experienced during birth, especially the imprisonment and violent squeezing in the birth canal, evokes not only anxiety but rage as well. Possibly this feeling of impotent rage is an integral part of primal anxiety.

Introjection, Projection, and Projective Identification

The alchemist's identification with his persecuting dragon-brothers in fig.116 points to a process of primary identifica-

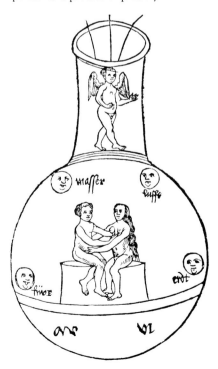

118. Winged rebirth in the vessel's neck.

119. Cruel encounter: 'Here you straightaway behold a black beast in the forest.' (4)

tion with the persecutory object. This is a process which Melanie Klein has described under the heading of *introjection:* 'Important sources of primary anxiety are the trauma of birth (separation anxiety) and frustration of bodily needs; and these experiences too are from the beginning felt as being caused by objects. Even if these objects are felt to be external, they become through introjection internal persecutors.' (9)

Because of the prenatal connection of infant and mother—expressed by the umbilical cord—the 'objective' persecutory anxiety experienced during birth appears to the infant as indistinguishable from 'subjective' persecutory anxiety. The aggressive forces coming from without come from within as well, i.e., the infant feels himself filled with what he hates and fears.

This dual danger is dealt with by means of the defence mechanism of *projection.* If an inner part of oneself is felt to be evil and dangerous, one may save oneself by *splitting off* this part and 'casting it away,' that is, by *projecting* it. Splitting and projection as primitive defence mechanisms have been described by the Bible in a famous passage: 'And if thy right eye offend thee pluck it out, and cast it from thee: for it is profitable for thee that one of thy members should perish, and not that thy whole body should be cast in hell' (Matth.5:29).

If fig.116 renders the Kleinian mechanisms of splitting and projection inside a birth trauma of persecutory anxiety, the engraving also depicts yet another mechanism discovered by Melanie Klein: that of *projective identification.* (10) There is a mirror magic in fig.116 which makes it possible to see its persecutory action the other way round, also. In this case an aggressive alchemist brandishes his club against four split figures who are actually projections of his own fragmented and aggressive personality.

The fact is that splitting and projection unfold within an autistic universe where every split-off and projected impulse boomerangs and returns to its source. Identified with the labouring mother in an objectless world, the neonate will experience every persecuting 'object' as part of himself; consequently, all the split-off and projected persecutors will return to the infant and fill him with *internal persecutors.* Thus the fetal ego is ultimately identified with what it projects. This is projective identification unfolding within the framework of persecutory anxiety and its defence mechanisms, splitting and projection. Fig.116 gives a unique illustration of this psychodynamic configuration of birth-traumatic anxiety, reappearing in all normal experiences of death and rebirth and, in a pathological variation, in schizophrenia.

deprecating, yet helpless gesture. The coronation ceremony exerts a strange influence on the Benedictine, who, like the philosopher-king in the second vessel of fig.122, splits in two as he draws near the crown of the Hermetic marriage. The monk's second, uncrowned self appears just behind him as a crying, frustrated figure. The split personality of Basil Valentine is seated at the fireplace in front of which stands the furnace and the vessel. The action taking place inside the vessel shows the nature of the operation performed in the workshop. The nude king and queen meet in intercourse *pari passu* with the delivery of the philosophers' son in the neck of the vessel adorned with the flowers of conjunction. This act is shown in close detail by fig. 122, the engraved variant of the two 'Pandora' woodcuts reproduced in figs. 117-118. (As witnessed by the Latin inscriptions, the two engravings describe the 'conception' of the philosophers' son and the 'pregnancy' of his mother and wife.)

In addition to the coitive labours of the king and queen, other features of the monk's workshop show his opus reaching the 'hour of conjunction where the greatest marvels appear,' (1) according to the 'Rosarium.' The four elemental signs on the mantelpiece and the seven planetary signs on the pipes behind it signify the 'circulation' of the alchemical matter and its dawning cosmic synthesis, a symbolism also expressed by the globe or *rotundum* on top of the book-case. A similar feeling of redemption is expressed by the scenery behind the queen, showing the 'philosophers' rose garden' *(rosarium philosophorum)* and the 'tree of life' *(arbor vitae).*

The King's Perspiring Bath of Reunion

In Basil Valentine's Second Key the anxious rebirth of the king and the splitting processes stirring the waters of his nuptial bath are described in the following manner:

'Whenever the water comes rolling back, it brings a blessing with it. A bride when she is to be brought forth to be married, is gloriously adorned in a great variety of precious garments which, by enhancing her beauty, render her pleasant in the eyes of the bridegroom. And the bond of love is strengthened by her beautiful appearance. But the rites of the bridal night she performs without any clothing but that which she was arrayed withal at the moment of her birth . . .

'When thus the palace has been constructed by the hands of many craftsmen, and the sea of glass has absolved its course and filled the palace with good things, it is ready for the king to enter and take his seat upon the throne. But you should notice that the king and his spouse must be quite naked when they

120. Royal split wedding of a Benedictine monk, his head engaged at the vulva.

The Royal Wedding of Basil Valentine

Fig.120 gives a French illustration of the Second Key of Basil Valentine, the text of which is reproduced below (the original engraving of the Second Key is reproduced in fig.153). Modelled on fig. 122, the picture shows Basil Valentine surprised by his mystical sister, who attempts to move him to his crowning and wedding, her own crown held in her left hand with the royal sceptre and the Second Key of the opus.* Taken aback by the efforts of his queen, the frightened monk reaches out toward her in a

* As proved by their accompanying texts, the Second and Third Keys of Basil Valentine both deal with the rebirth mysteries of the first coniunctio of the opus. This justifies their presentation in reverse order in this book, the Second Key appearing in fig.153, the Third in fig.115.

are joined together. They must be stripped of all their glorious apparel and must possess their grave in the same state of nakedness in which they were born that their seed may not be spoiled by being mixed with any foreign matter.

'Let me tell you, in conclusion, that the bath in which the bridegroom is placed must consist of two hostile kinds of matter that purge and rectify each other by means of a continued struggle. For it is not good for the eagle to build her nest on the summit of the Alps because her young ones are thus in great danger of being frozen to death by the intense cold that prevails there. But if you add to the eagle the icy dragon that has long had its habitation upon the rocks and has crawled forth from the caverns of the earth, and place both over the fire, it will elicit from the icy dragon a fiery spirit which, by means of its great heat, will consume the wings of the eagle [fig.126] and prepare a perspiring bath of so extraordinary a degree of heat that the snow will melt upon the summit of the mountains and become a water, with which the invigorating mineral bath may be prepared, and fortune, health, life, and strength restored to the king.' (2)

Getting into the Royal Womb

The 'perspiring bath' of the royal water marriage and the strange nature of its intercourse are shown in fig.122: the copulating king disappears into the womb of his queen, thus giving birth to himself as the philosophers' son. As labouring Luna rises up over her son/spouse, she triumphs on her sickle adorned with a split image of the philosopher-king's head, placed in the dark and bright half of the vessel, respectively. The heads look at each other in a kind of mirror symbolism repeating the *dedoublement*

121. *Copulating return to the womb.*

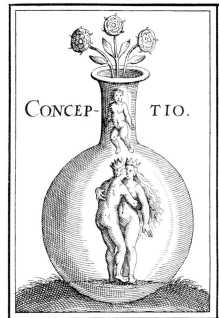

122. *The fetal king of alchemy disappearing into his mother and splitting in the act.*

of the Benedictine monk splitting under the crown of his incestuous marriage.

Fig.121 renders the king's descent into the well under the motto: 'Dissolve the bodies into water.' The fountain's fiery water in D unites the lunar and solar water gushing from the pipes in A and B. Below them, a group of nude men and women bathe in the basins of the fountain. Their diminutive form shows the regressive nature of the fire-water roaring inside a king, whose head and body appear to 'penetrate' the queen's well in a manner resembling the king's breakthrough in fig.122.

Man's First Erotic-Aggressive Experience

It is natural to assume that aggression as a distinct drive is developed during the birth trauma in response to the total 'attack' carried out on the infant's body by the expulsive forces of vaginal contractions and 'beatings.' Interpreted in evolutionary terms, this assumption also makes sense: the experience of being persecuted and attacked, and the parallel onset of rage, appear as a proper preparation of the body for violent fighting activity aimed at survival.

Similarly, it is natural to assume that the sexual drive is differentiated during the infant's 'phallic' sliding back and forth in the vagina: a proper preparation of the body for later copulatory activity aimed at survival of the species. The differentiation of the two drives of survival value are symbolized by the 'two hostile kinds of matter continually struggling in the king's perspiring bath.' Of course, this separation of a primal, diffuse drive unit is at first chaotic, indis-

tinct. The state is one of supreme drive-confusion with concomitant inability of the fetal ego to distinguish between 'good' and 'bad,' between sexual and aggressive impulses. Still, the unity of the primal libido has been severed by the act of birth, which may be envisaged as releasing, for the first time, feelings and impulses of a sexual and aggressive nature.

This relationship highlights the mysterious, unconscious connection between sexuality and aggression—love and hate—which merge in the 'battle of the sexes,' in sadism and masochism. Above all, this relationship explains why intercourse is unconsciously imbued, in later life, with the meaning of a return to the womb, the man's aggressive phallus being unconsciously identified with a child fighting to penetrate the vagina. Fig.122 gives a unique expression of this 'body-phallus' equation of the unconscious at its vaginal level of organization where 'body shrinkage,' or 'body fetalization,' often accompanies the ego's experience of rebirth.

If birth may be defined, biologically as well as psychologically, as the splitting of a primal unity, the contents of unconscious fantasy during birth must conform to an overall symbolism of *splitting*. As Melanie Klein discovered, this applies even to the nature of the ego's first primitive defence mechanism against the primal anxiety of birth. Figs.120 and 122 are graphic demonstrations of frantic processes of splitting occurring in connection with actions related to birth. Fig.122 shows a fetal philosopher-king disappearing into his maternal queen while splitting in the act. Fig.120 shows the split wedding of a Benedictine monk, his head engaged at the vulva.

123. Burnt, drowned, executed and devoured during the Hermetic trauma of rebirth.

throne, where the horrible *denouement* is enacted:

When the father saw his son coming,
He cried aloud, and said: My son,
When thou was away I was dead
And lived in great danger of my life.
I revive at thy return,
And it fills my breast with joy.
But when the son entered the
*   father's house,*
The father took him to his heart
And swallowed him out of joy,
And that with his own mouth. (1)

This motif in Lambspring varies a popular dictum, attributed to Hermes, in which Mercurius, or the lapis, cries out: 'My light excels all other lights, and my goods are higher than all other goods. I beget the light, but the darkness too is of my nature. Nothing better or more worthy of veneration can come to pass in the world than the union of myself with my son.' (2)

Fig.124 shows Basil Valentine's emblem of the *coniunctio solis et lunae,* an event described also in his Second and Third Keys. The filial, solar eagle is devoured by the paternal, solar lion, both being parts of the lunar, serpentine body. (Fig.126 is an engraved variant.)

Umbilical Cord of Primary Identification

In alchemy, the king's reunion with his son is achieved by means of the physiological analogue of the psychological process of introjection, i.e., by eating. Through his swallowing of the *filius regius,* the old king assimilates his heir in a total, but horrible act of primary identification (cannibalism). The winged guide, the dove, and the Holy Ghost are further symbols of the *spiritus* of introjection or primary identification, the biological expression of which is the umbilical cord. This is symbolized by the lunar serpent in fig.124; the sexual na-

A Fiery Family Reunion

The seventh plate of the 'Mutus liber' (fig.123) renders the conjunction of the white and red tinctures, or the union of silver and gold. While the sister crushes the silvery grains of Luna, her brother adds the liquid gold of Sol. The solution is decanted and once more poured into the dish (middle row left). The dish is heated over the crucible and the conjunction of the white and red tinctures attempted in the extreme heat. The last scene shows the sister gathering the products of fusion, symbolized by stars of a mandalian, eight-rayed structure. In the bottom row the mysteries of conjunction are translated into mythical terms: the Mercurius child is devoured by Saturn (Cronos), first in the insufferable heat of

a pyre, then in a bath tub, a motif varying the king's descent into the well. Both father and son are poured over with the red-and-white tincture by the attending alchemist. In the final scene the nude parents of the philosophers' son are tied together by a string Saturn is about to cut with his sword. Luna holds the vessel of conjunction toward her spouse and son, while covering her lap with her left hand.

Fig.125 shows the eerie conclusion of Lambspring's story of the 'king and his son.' After having conquered his father's mountain and throne, the son, overwhelmed with guilt, decides to return to the 'lap' of his father. With the help of his winged guide he descends the paternal rock and goes before the royal

124. Body-phallus-cord equation of birth.

ture of the serpentine cord is indicated by its connection with the lion and the winged, erect body of the eagle. The complex image gives the final formula of primary identification: the *body-phallus-cord* equation of the unconscious at its vaginal-uterine level of organization.

The snake is an archetypal symbol of this configuration and appears as such in the Book of Genesis, closely connected there with the primal act and sin of Adam and Eve. In the Eleusinian mysteries of Demeter, the snake is connected with the mystical basket of the Great Mother. Clement says that the symbol of other Greek mysteries was the 'god through the lap; and that is a snake which is dragged through the laps of the initiates.' (3) In alchemy the coniunctio is symbolized by two serpents entwining the caduceus of Mercurius (fig.153).

LSD-accounts of rebirth reveal the same significance of the snake as a symbol of the body-phallus-cord equation of birth: 'I saw the most horrible, slimy snake I have ever seen. It was large and ugly and it curled around me, starting at my ankles, slowly winding up my legs. I tried to get free but I couldn't, my legs seemed to become part of the snake. I knew the snake was swallowing me, bit by bit. I could feel the mucous inside of the snake. I was becoming a part of it. I was sick. I screamed and looked for Buddy. He seemed so very far away. I thought he was laughing at me. He knew I was terrified of snakes. He held out his hand and his whole arm started to twist and pulsate as if it had no bones. It was another snake. The snake began to swallow my head, all wet and smooth. I was the snake without eyelids, so I had to watch everything.' (4)

Primal Castration Anxiety of Birth

Saturn's sword about to cut the cord in fig.123 and the old king's leonine teeth present the outlines of 'primal castration anxiety,' an unconscious configuration discovered by Otto Rank: 'Castration anxiety derives its impact from the 'primal castration' of birth, i.e., from the separation of infant and mother. In the dreams [of rebirth] concluding a psychoanalytical treatment I often found the phallus symbolized by the umbilical cord.' (5) This discovery fits neatly with our above conclusion: the anxiety of 'primal castration' spells fear of death by amputation of the 'body-phallus-cord' unit.

This is the earliest form of castration anxiety, oral-vaginal-uterine by nature, and intimately connected with the 'phallic mother' in her traumatic aspect. Fig. 124 presents her as a strangling boa, or dragon, with the mouth of a lion—a horrible ogre-witch threatening an equally archaic-regressive transformation of the phallus *into the whole infantile body.*

125. *'Unless thy stone shall be an enemy, thou wilt not attain to thy desire.' (6)*

As Melanie Klein discovered through child analyses, the traumatic fear accompanying infants' sexual fantasies of bodily intrusion into the mother is precisely the fear of being swallowed, devoured, cut in two, beheaded, annihilated.

126. *The descending eagle devoured by the jaws of the lion and the dragon's fire.*

127. The hot armour of the hero-knight penetrating the dragon's fire to win his girl.

The Fire Baptism of the Salamander

Above, the mystical sister with a peremptory gesture sends her brother into a fire the text equates with the dragon's mouth. (1) The text then establishes the identity of the armoured knight as the 'red slave who marries his odoriferous mother and produces a progeny nobler than the parents themselves; this is Pyrrhus, the red-haired son of Achilles with gold clothes, black eyes and white feet; it is the knight, armed with shield and sword, who marches against the dragon to save the virgin, unhurt, from the claws of the dragon; she is called Albifica or Beya or Blanca; this is also Hercules who liberated Hesione, the daughter of Laomedon ... This is Perseus who defended Andromeda against the seamonster by showing the Medusa's head and who married her after releasing her from her fetters.' (2)

Fig.128 shows a popular animal symbol of the knight penetrating the dragon's fire in his struggle for rebirth. The monster frolicking in the flames is the magical salamander, an immature, transitional form of the philosophers' son. It dwells in the 'hellish fire' as the mercurial animal the fire does not consume. Since the spotted and blood-filled salamander feeds on the fire, he is not consumed by the dragon's mouth. On the contrary, he represents the fiery principle which conquers the fire, according to the doctrine of Pseudo-Democritus that nature overcomes nature. In a similar manner, Geber writes about the mercurial salamander, serpent, or dragon: 'For he it is that overcomes fire, and by fire is not overcome; but in it amicably rests, rejoicing therein.' (3) The secret identity between the knight 'marching against the dragon to save the virgin' and the salamander is evident in the motto of fig.127: 'Nature teaches nature how to fight the fire.' (4) This is a clear reference to the doctrine of Pseudo-Democritus, exemplified by the salamander.

The motto of fig.128 reads: 'Just as the salamander, so too the stone lives in the fire.' (5) The source is Avicenna's description of the stone in the 'Tractatulus de alchimia': 'The philosophers have called this stone our salamander because, like a salamander, it is fed exclusively by the fire; it lives in it, that is to say, it is perfected by it, and so it is with our stone.' (6)

Fiery Rebirth of the Philosophers' Son

Fig.129 shows the philosophers' son rescued from the dragon's fire and reborn in his combined parent's womb. The drapery of the pregnant father is elegantly blown by the wind, which fans the flames burning his hair and amputating his arms. The motto quotes the 'Tabula smaragdina' whose wind appears as a counterpart of the dove, or Holy Ghost, which in the Bible acts as a similar agent of divine incarnation, implanting the Son of God in the womb of God: 'His father is the sun, his mother is the moon ... The wind has carried him in its belly.' (8)

128. "Seeing the salamander'. . . a glimpse of another world . . . a gift of the gods.' (7)

A Salamander of Body Fetalization and Erotization

The secret identity between the dragon-fighting knight and his 'fetal' animal symbol, which conquers the dragon's fire by 'feeding' on it and so partaking of it, reveals the salamander as a symbol of primary identification. Like the fetal ego, the salamander is completely identified with the fiery jaws of the dragon's *vagina dentata*.

In addition to its draconic implications, the salamander appears as an animal frolicking in the fire. Such symbolism of intense sexual pleasure fits in with the marked erotic features of man's experience of rebirth. There is a biological explanation for this: in late pregnancy the woman's hormonal production accelerates to such a degree that its effects on the fetal body are the same as the effects of the hormonal production on the body of the *adolescent*. The genitals and breasts of the fetus swell; the breasts of both male and female babies may even secrete milk—known as the 'witches' milk.' Occasionally newborn girls show slight menstrual flow for a few days after birth. Thus, in delivery, the fetus passes through the vagina with hypertrophic, or swollen, sex organs. It is natural to assume, therefore, that the infant experiences a considerable sexual excitation as it slides back and forth in the birth canal. Such *coitus toto corpere* is expressed by all alchemical symbols of rebirth; it reappears in the bold eroticism of modern fantasies of rebirth, particularly under the influence of LSD.

The King Drowning in the Mercurial Sea

Fig.130 shows the dragon fight of Sol and Luna battering the hideous companion of their wedding feast to death. In the background, split figures of the brother-sister pair attempt to kill the winged dragon with their bows. The motto renders the oft-cited proverb: 'The dragon dieth not save with its brother and sister, that is, with Sol and Luna.' (9) This dictum is the most poignant expression of the death to be suffered by the king and queen if they are to cherish any hope of attaining to the coniunctio.

In the farthest part of the background a popular motif of the nuptial bath is presented: the king drowning in the mercurial sea and crying for help. There are many alchemical sources for this motif. A passage about the calling of the stone, ascribed to Hermes, is quoted by the 'Rosarium': 'For our stone calls, saying: My son, help me, and I will help you.' (10) Another source is the seventh parable of the 'Aurora consurgens' in which the drowning king cries:

'Be turned to me with all your heart and do not cast me aside because I am black and swarthy, because the sun hath changed my colour and the waters have covered my face and the land hath been polluted and defiled in my works; for there was darkness over it, because I stick fast in the mire of the deep and my substance is not disclosed. Wherefore out of the depths have I cried, and from the abyss of the earth . . . Attend and see me, if any shall find one like unto me, I will give into his hand the morning star.' (11)

129. *Conquering the salamander's fire and uniting with the primal parent of rebirth.*

130. *Drowning in the mercurial sea while battling its winged monsters and dragons.*

131. The old father king drowning in the sea is reborn in his son and successor.

shows the 'solution' of his agony. The seventh painting of the 'Splendor solis' combines two classical motifs: the drowning king crying for help in the sea (background); and the renewal of the old, decrepit king in his son (foreground). Suffused with the light radiating from the morning star and from the combined sun and moon, the king's son wears his father's crown, a sceptre surrounded by the seven planets, and an apple on which perches the white dove or Hermes bird—the classical symbol of paternal incarnation. The text reads:

'The old philosophers declared that they saw a fog rise and pass over the whole face of the earth; they also saw the impetuosity of the sea, and the streams over the face of the earth, and how these same became foul and stinking in the darkness. They further saw the king of the earth sink, and heard him cry out with eager voice, 'Whoever saves me shall live and reign with me for ever in my brightness on my royal throne,' and night enveloped all things. The day after, they saw over the king an apparent morning star, and the light of day clear up the darkness, and bright sunlight pierce through the clouds, with manifold coloured rays of brilliant brightness, a sweet perfume from the earth, and the sun shining clear. Herewith was completed the time when the king of the earth was released and renewed, well apparelled, and quite handsome, surprising with his beauty the sun and moon. He was crowned with three costly crowns, the one of iron, the other of silver, and the third of pure gold. They saw in his right hand a sceptre with seven stars, all of which gave a golden splendour, and in his left hand they saw a golden apple on which perched a white dove, fiery of nature, covered with silver and with golden wings.' (9)

The seven stars refer to the Revelation of St.John: 'And he had in his right hand seven stars' (1:6). The figure holding this emblem of cosmic dominion is further described as being 'like unto the Son of man,' a parallel which sheds light on the supremacy of the *filius regius* rescued and glorified in fig.131.

132. A maternal sea of blood and milk.

Fearful Baptism in Fiery Water

Fig.132 shows Basil Valentine's woodcut of the 'goddess . . . born in our sea, which spans the whole earth.' (1) The mermaid fills the ocean with 'milk and also red blood,' (2) a synonym for the white and red tinctures, or silver and gold. The engraved variant in fig.133 shows the 'virgin's milk' and 'blood' squirting from her breasts into the 'water of life,' which receives, in addition, the acid water spouting from a monstrous whale. This is the 'fountain's vinegar,' a corrosive and poisonous agent 'splitting' or souring the 'virgin's milk' and the 'water of life.' The sea is filled with the mercurial water of birth and death, described by the adepts in many ways: 'They call the simple water poison, quick-

silver, cambar, permanent water, gum, vinegar, urine, sea-water, dragon and serpent (3) . . . This stinking water contains everything it needs (4) . . . It is the mother of all things, and out of it and through it and with it, they prepare the lapis (5) . . . The water is that which kills and vivifies.' (6)

The King's Rescue and Rebirth

The king's descent into the well and sea results in the perilous situation depicted in fig.134. The motto explains: 'The king swimming in the sea cries with a loud voice, 'Whoso shall deliver me shall obtain the great reward.'' (7) The king 'on whose head the crown presses heavily' (8) is saved in fig.131, which

The Primal Scream

The maternal significance of water is one of the most agreed-upon symbols in the whole field of mythology and depth psychology. In dreams, as Freud discovered, birth is usually presented by imagery related to water: 'Birth is regularly expressed in dreams by connections with water: one falls into the water or one comes out of the water—one gives birth or one is born . . . Every individual mammal, every human being, spent the first phase of its existence in water—namely as an embryo in the amniotic fluid in its mother's uterus, and came out of that water when it was born.' (10)

The attainment of the watery condition and the sealing of the vessel in Barchusen's plates 16-17 (fig.105) symbolize the approaching *solutio* of the birth trauma by rendering the beginning of birth where the pressure of the fetal fluid makes the amnion sac expand. In labour, the sac bulges and bursts, spilling forth its fluid; this is the familiar 'breaking of the water.'*

The drowning motif of alchemy has a biological explanation. The choking sensations of the unconscious fantasies of being drowned and born are reproductions of 1) umbilical cord compression during birth; 2) the first cry (=the king's cry). Ninety percent of all fetal distress is caused by a compression of the umbilical cord ensuing in a cut-off of oxygen and a dramatically abrupt fall in the baby's heart rate. At the actual delivery, the neonate's trials culminate in the cutting of the cord, its pipeline to life. The infant is thereby forced to draw its first breath of air, the hardest in life. It has been calculated that the first inhalation requires five times the effort of an ordinary one because the air must expand the tiny uninflated air sacs of the lungs. Like the drowning king of alchemy, the neonate struggles to the 'surface of the water' in order to draw his first breath. With a desperate mobilization of energy, intensified by the anxiety of birth, the infant inhales the air through a mouth and pharynx filled with slime. 200 to 300 million uninflated air sacs are expanded for the first time while blood circulates to the lungs to pick up the oxygen earlier supplied by the mother's placenta. After this miraculous, first breath the baby pushes out the air in a *cry*—a cry of horror and of victory, reverberating with the ambivalence and mystery of the birth trauma: an entrance into life through the doors of death.

* In biological terms, the 'water of life' symbolizes the amniotic fluid of the pregnant uterus; the 'virgin's milk' and 'blood' the primal sources of nourishment for the neonate (milk) and the fetus (placental blood); the draconic 'fountain's vinegar' the frantic splitting processes of birth-traumatic anxiety.

133. Monstrous companion of a milk-spurting mermaid in the mercurial sea.

The Healing Waters of Rebirth

The Hermetic 'breaking of the water,' expressed by the royal bath and the drowning king, symbolizes the alchemist's revival of the unconscious imprints of the birth trauma, experienced in reverse as a *trauma of re-birth*. The regressive movement finally leads the alchemist to a conquest of primal anxiety and its libidinal splitting processes, and to a recovery of the primal unity of the libido. This happens when the regression reaches the *foetus in utero* stage, rendered in lucid symbols by the first coniunctio of the opus alchymicum (following pages).

134. The primal scream of a king entering the whirlpool of birth and death.

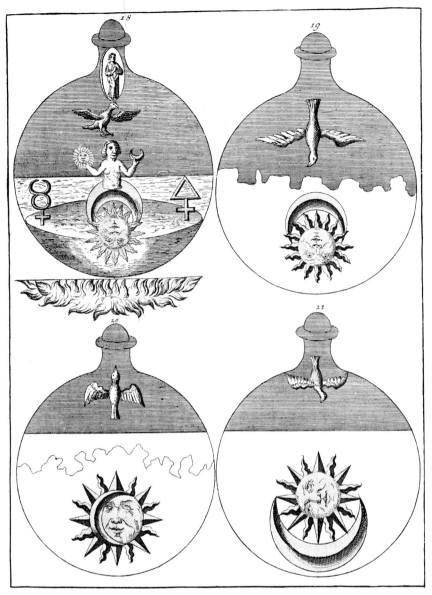

135.

The First Coniunctio: Earthly Rebirth

plete conjunction of lovers. This is the event described by the 'Rosarium' as follows: 'The arcanum of the art of gold is made from male and female, because the female receiving the force of the male rejoices, in that the female is strengthened by the male. So, my son, by the faith of the faith of the glorious God the complexion is from the complexion between the two luminaries, male and female. Then they embrace and have intercourse, and the modern light is born of them, to which no light is similar in the whole world.' (4)

Primal Fusion with the Womb

After the passionate kiss of Sol and Luna in plate 20 the swelling lunar body rotates and begins the crucial 'melting' process of conjunction where Sol must be completely dissolved by 'rooting' as the homunculus in the lunar earth (plate 21). The means of this 'reduction to solution,' as the 'Crowne of Nature' calls it, (5) are the processes of calcination and pulverization undertaken in plates 19-21 and symbolized by the cracked and white transforming substance. The 'Crowne of Nature' explains:

'Thus Sol and Luna are philosophically calcined with the first water, and their bodies are opened and made spongious and subtle that the second water may have the better ingression to work his effort (6) . . . that it [the body] may be restored to his innate humidity which he had lost in his chalk, and that it may quickly melt (7) . . . Therefore saith the philosopher, dissolve by the help of Luna and coagulate by the help of Sol.' (8) During this entire 'melting' process, the Hermetic bird flies up and down in the retort, furnishing the oceanic lovers with the necessary air, or spiritus.

The *coniunctio solis et lunae* of Barchusen's plates 18-21 is modelled on the 'conjunction or intercourse' *(coniunctio sive coitus)* of the fifth woodcut of the 'Rosarium' (fig.136). As the drowning king disappears into the well of his sister

After the heating and sealing of the vessel in Barchusen's plate 16 and the production of the universal sea in plate 17 (fig.105), the work is crowned with the birth of the homunculus, floating in the mercurial water as the sun and moon combined (plate 18, above). A symbol of the lapis and of the conjunction of the opposites *(coniunctio oppositorum)*, the child unites sun and moon, day and night, mercury (left sign) and sulphur (right sign), silver and gold, fire and water, earth and air, man and woman.* This is the hour of mystical illumination in which the alchemist, rejuvenated as

the divine child, cries out: 'I joined the two luminaries in marriage and it became as water having two lights.' (3) What the alchemist perceives now is a paradox: opposites indissolubly wedded, light shining out of darkness, and darkness at the heart of light. Having been transformed into an eagle, a lion and a dragon, the king is finally dissolved in water and reborn as a child. Paralleling this metamorphosis, the dragon and lion's sulphurous fire becomes the gentle fire of the retort. At the top of the vessel, the praying alchemist appears in a mirror, below which the Hermes bird of Incarnation descends.

In plate 19 the philosophers' son merges with his copulating parents, Luna on top of Sol, symbolizing envelopment and absorption. In plate 20 Luna rotates to the left, an amorous movement with Sol resulting in a 'total kiss' and the com-

* The empirical model for the alchemical coniunctio is the amalgamation of gold with mercury. Hence the saying: 'The whole work lies in the solution,' (1) i.e., of sun and moon in mercury. The sea above renders this process.

CONIVNCTIO SIVE
Coitus.

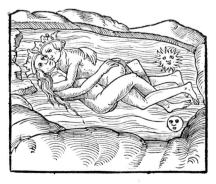

136. 'You need me as the cock the hen.' (2)

in rebirth, he reaches the mercurial sea bottom and the 'water of life,' in which he attains complete union with his queen or mother. Transformed into the father, the king is granted copulation with the queen-mother while being enclosed in her womb. The text explains:

'Then Beya [the lunar sea] rises up over Gabricus and encloses him in her womb, so that nothing more of him is to be seen. And she embraced Gabricus with so much love that she utterly consumed him in her own nature and dissolved him into atoms . . . Therefore Merculinus says:

White-skinned lady, lovingly joined to her ruddy-limbed husband,
Wrapped in each other's arms in the bliss of connubial union,
Merge and dissolve as they come to the goal of perfection:
They that were two are made one, as though of one body.' (9)

In the engraved variant (fig.137), the royal bed is formed as a mussel, thus expressing the king's sense of oceanic unity with a woman in whose womb he has born himself anew. Behind the bed curtain, the conjoined sun and moon are about to be devoured by two ravens, symbols of the *nigredo* ('blackness') which follows upon the union of king and queen.

Fig.138 shows Arnold of Villanova, the supposed author of the 'Rosarium,' pointing to the royal couple while exclaiming: 'The stone is obtained from the marriage of Gabricus and Beya.' (10) With her right hand stuck through a golden ring, Beya confirms her marriage to Gabricus, her lover and husband; her left hand rests on her pregnant womb, enclosing Gabricus as son and child.

The Primal Libido of Orgasm

These pictures equate the orgasm of *coitus* with the fusing sensations of the *coniunctio,* identified, in turn, with the primal libido experienced by the fetus enclosed in the womb. This strange equation of two human experiences of fusion was glimpsed by Sandor Ferenczi, one of the few psychoanalytical supporters of Otto Rank. In 'Thalassa: A Theory of Genitality' (1924), Ferenczi attributed to male intercourse the meaning of a return to the mother's womb. Furthermore, he thought it feasible that orgasm might carry the unconscious, regressive meaning of negating the very first and greatest frustration man has suffered, namely his separation from the maternal organism and its 'oceanic waters' *(thalassa).* According to Ferenczi, coitus and orgasm are based on the unconscious idea of thalassal regression for the purpose of restoring a state of fetal union.

137. Uniting with his queen and mother in a mussel-bed of oceanic love and fusion.

Ferenczi's intuitive idea, which covers the *coniunctio sive coitus,* may be related to modern theories on orgastic impotence in males and orgastic frigidity in females. In normal orgasm the ego at the peak of the fusing experience passes through a moment of unconsciousness, or a moment of 'drowning,' frequently felt as a 'death of the ego,' (*le petit mort* as the French term it). In orgastic impotence and frigidity the unconscious fear of being overwhelmed is an important factor interfering with the ego's experience of orgasm. (11) Submission to the unconscious is a *sine qua non* of sexual ecstasy. Inducing in the male a mystical sense of ego and body 'fetalization,' intercourse culminates in the 'death and rebirth' of the ego during orgasm, which is patterned on the primal libido of 'fetal fusion.' Psychologically, this experience signifies the 'drowning' of the ego in the self, the anima acting as the instrument of erotic-aquatic fusion ('fusing anima').

138. Mystery of the golden wedding-ring: receiving the male as father, son, and lover.

139. The Virgin's 'labour' crowned with the birth of the homunculus in her vessel.

God's own creation. This is why the inscription *cum Deo*–'with God'–adorns the ground on which the alchemist prays to God before a tent, in imitation of the Israelites in the desert.

Fig.141 shows the eighth plate of the 'Mutus liber,' in which the alchemist kneeling in front of the furnace and its vessel offers thanksgiving prayers to God for the completion of his work. Opposite the alchemist, his mystical sister effects a dramatic parting of the curtains and a revelation of the heavenly act of rebirth. Matured by the sun and borne by angels, the Mercurius child strides the sun and moon, tokens of his hermaphroditic nature. The child's wand of wriggling snakes expresses his fertilization of the vessel, or 'philosophical egg,' which encloses him. The angels carrying the retort and the birds flying with the eight-rayed star of conjunction symbolize spiritualization and sublimation of matter.

Virgo the Virgin: Pregnancy of Autumn

In alchemy, the ripening of the homunculus in the vessel takes place in the sign of Virgo, the Virgin (fig.139). The sixth sign of the Zodiac is a mutable, earthy sign ruled by Mercury. Its period extends from August 24 to September 23, or the time of harvest when nature reaches fulfilment with the ripening of her fruits. Virgo expresses this pattern in that she stands for gestation and digestion of the opposites of nature, these being brought into harmony and conjunction by her ordering intelligence and disciplined action. Since the Virgin is governed by Mercury, she is symbolic of hermaphroditism, or of a state of fusion of dual forces. This feature is indicated by the mercurial wand traditionally held

The Divine Child of Hermetic Rebirth

'It is a frequent occurrence for subjects to experience symbolic or literal materials relating to being in the womb. Thus subjects have reported being locked up in some kind of small confine, being buried in the depths of the earth or swallowed by a monster, etc. Through some of these symbols the subject experiences a symbolic death with regression to an embryonic state then followed by the experience of being reborn.'

R.E.L.Masters and Jean Houston. (1)

Fig.139 shows the alchemist praying in his tent while the drama of conjunction is enacted in two subterranean caverns. On the left, the emergent rays of a subterranean sun show the birth of light and the breaking of the waters as results of the adept's 'labour.' On the right, the alchemist clasps the retort in gratitude. Its contents are revealed by

the statue of the birth of the homunculus or stone inside the womb of the anima mundi, appearing as virgin mother and *Sapientia* ('Wisdom'). Created by the conjunction of sun and moon, the divine fetus is floodlit by their combined light. The virgin's erect pillar below her thighs carries the inscription 'This is Wisdom,' thus echoing an alchemical dictum: 'The wisdom of the father lies in the lap of the mother.' (2)

The production of the homunculus in the retort is the *parergon* or 'subsidiary work' which results from the *ergon* or 'work' of the alchemist himself. His achievement of creating 'nature through art' *(arte natura)* fulfils the most audacious dreams of magic and science: the development *in vitro* of a homunculus with supernatural qualities. The alchemist knows that these efforts are destined for success only if he prays to the Creator of all things to lend His aid to a work which is a minute imitation of

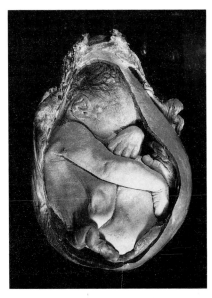

140. Fetus dreaming archetypal dreams.

by Virgo. In her other hand she holds a sheaf of corn, the emblem of the Earth Mother, Demeter, another representation of Virgo.* Since Virgo is so intimately connected with the 'pregnancy' of earth in autumn, she is also connected with the birth of a god or hero whose origin is a virgin fertilized in some supernatural way.

Psychologically, Virgo embodies reality thinking and the objective powers of observation and selection, analysis and criticism, by such means connecting and regulating the forces of matter and directing them to their preordained goal. By diligence, care and attention to minute detail, the tidy Virgin ensures structure and regularity, essential conditions for the completion of any natural scheme. For this reason, Virgo is material in quite a different sense from Taurus, the other earthy sign: Virgo has greater focus upon the sublimated aspect of matter, on the laws of nature which perfect matter.

The Primal Unity of the Libido

The fetal state of the homunculus, or reborn alchemist, shows the prenatal nature of the Hermetic experience of conjunction. The state achieved is described as a half bodily, half spiritual reality held together by a 'soul,' an *anima media natura,* as the adepts term it, capable of uniting the opposites, spirit and body. As the 'Exercitationes in Turbam' describes the coniunctio: 'The spirit and body are one, the soul acting as a mediator which abides with the spirit and body. If there were no soul, the spirit and the body would separate from each other by the fire, but because the soul is joined to the spirit and the body, this whole is unaffected by fire or by any other thing in the world.' (4)

The alchemical 'child of the sun and moon' *(filius solis et lunae)* symbolizes the self as formed by the fusion of ego (spiritus), anima and id (corpus). With this *coniunctio oppositorum*—of male and female, conscious and unconscious, mind and body—a third entity of trans-

141. *Final maturation of the Boy Mercurius in his vessel of solar and lunar rebirth.*

formed opposites is produced. The fire surrounding the infant in fig.139 symbolizes the primal libido blazing in the nuclear processes of the self. The male ego's aggressive drive and the female anima's sexual drive are here merged into an indissoluble drive-unit beyond 'good' and 'bad.'

The Mature Fetus in the Womb

Fig.140 shows the nine-month-old fetus enclosed in the cavity of the uterus. The fetus is totally immersed in the amniotic water contained in the amnion sac, its tough, elastic membrane draping the fetus like a veil (removed here together with part of the placenta). Though completely immersed in the amniotic fluid,

the fetus keeps inhaling and exhaling just enough to send the salty fluid of the amnion sac in and out of its lungs. The fetus does not drown because its oxygen supply is furnished by the throbbing blood of the umbilical cord, rich in oxygen. Psychologically, the fetus spends most of its time in active dream-sleep or REM-ing. With its well-developed brain and fully developed sensory apparatus, the fetus, at this stage, is submerged in a state of primal or prenatal 'consciousness' governed by dreams of a collective and archetypal nature. Alternating between dreaming sleep and waking dreaming, the fetal psyche may be described as an undifferentiated unity between conscious and unconscious states of mind. LSD-induced states of rebirth offer a fascinating glimpse into this psychic dimension.

* In the Eleusinian Mysteries the supreme mystery of the Earth Mother Demeter was expressed by silently revealing an ear of wheat at the climax of the ceremony, accompanied by the cry of the mystai: 'Let the rain come! Conceive!' Significantly, the highest arcanum of the sacred actions consisted in the effigy of a womb the initiate, now the 'seer,' had to touch while the priest solemnly announced the birth of a 'Newborn Child.' Since the emblem of the divine Jakchos, or Dionysus Child, was that of an ear of wheat, corn was identified with a male child born from the womb of the Earth Mother. The assumption that this cultic symbolism referred to the 'reborn' believer himself is unavoidable and conforms to the parallelism between the life of plants and of men which was established by the vegetation cults and fertility rites of antiquity. (3)

142. Meeting under the crown of a tree feeding all flesh and illuminating all life.

The Psychedelic Child of Self-Realization

'The myth of the child-hero is one that occurs in the psychedelic experience with considerable frequency. This motif is often relived in terms of historical and mythological analogues— Jesus, Moses, Heracles—and then is taken up by the subject in a more personal manner to suggest his rebirth experienced in terms of a newborn divine child emerging from the darkness of the womb and undergoing extraordinary dangers in order to begin a life of great promise. The figure of the child-hero becomes for the psychedelic subject a personification of the most profound aspects of his striving towards self-realization. We do not have here, we believe, just a simple regression to an infantile state which presents the subject with an opportunity to 'begin all over again.' Rather, this appears to be a phenomenon of profound engagement in a potent and potentiating universal drama from which the person emerges with a sense of having been redeemed, transformed, and as some subjects have put it, 'transfigured' . . . In the psychedelic drug-state mythologies abound. The guide often may feel that he is bearing witness to a multi-layered complex of mythological systems.'

R.E.L. Masters and Jean Houston. (1)

The 'rooting' of the homunculus in his maternal substance, or the continued 'melting' process of Sol and Luna, is described in Barchusen's plates 22-23 (fig. 154). Luna has promised Sol complete dissolution while he himself hopes for final coagulation. Hence, in plate 22, the growth of the moon, which began in the previous plate, continues at such a speed that its cracked surface begins to rise in the bottom of the retort. (The rays of the sinking, 'pulverized' sun are seen above the swelling lunar surface.) In plate 23 Sol is completely absorbed by the moon in an act of dissolution or 'putrefaction' (2) leaving only heaps of powder or pulverized chalk on the surface of the pregnant moon. Says an alchemical treatise: 'Luna is the mother and the field in which the seed should be sown and planted . . . for I [says Sol] am as seed sown in good earth.' (3)

The Philosophical Tree of Alchemy

In alchemy, the fusion of the philosophers' son with the lunar earth and sea is described in vegetable imagery using the tree archetype to express the 'rooting' of the homunculus in his maternal substance. The strange tree of Hermetic science is that of the *arbor philosophica,* or 'philosophical tree,' a specimen of which is reproduced in fig.142. Under its crown, the reborn adept is spat out of the belly of the whale and the moon goddess Diana, and landed as a youth on the island of the blest. Accompanied only by his eagle (lower right), the alchemist is greeted by Hermes Trismegistus, the god of alchemy. The left-handed gesture of their encounter betrays its secret and illegitimate nature and is explained by the royal throne behind the friendly, yet forbidding, old man. This is the son's ardently desired goal—crowned with solar fire and resting on the conquered lion and the cave of the fire-spewing dragon.

The ghostly meeting takes place under the branches of the philosophical tree adorned with the sun and moon and the five planetary stars. The *arbor philosophica* is surrounded by allegories of the seven phases of the alchemical process, varying the motifs of death and rebirth, burial and resurrection. The philosophical tree is often represented as metallic, usually golden. Its connection with the seven metals implies a connection with the seven planets, so that the tree becomes the world-tree, whose shining fruits are the stars.

The Coral Tree in the Mercurial See

Other specimens of the philosophical tree are reproduced in figs.143-144. Both pictures show the blood-coloured stone of the philosophers known as the 'coral tree in the sea.' (4) It represents the union of earth, sea, fire and air (since the coral tree also grows above water). Filled with blood, or the 'red elixir,' the tree of coral is described as follows in the text accompanying fig.144:

'The philosophers' stone really resembles . . . coral, for just as coral grows

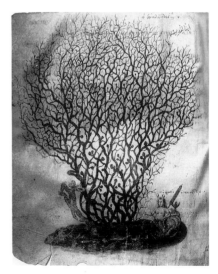

143. The sea-mother's coral tree of life.

in the water and takes its nourishment from the earth, in the same way the philosophers' stone grows out of the mercurial water. What is earthy in it serves as food for the stone and the superfluous fluid is drained away. Also it takes its red colour from the coagulation, which colour is called coral tincture ... Just as coral may be used for several potent medicines, so the philosophical coral bears the powers of all herbs, because it alone possesses as much curative power as all herbs together ... It has to be cut very carefully under water, so that the juice and blood are not lost ... I am thinking of the superfluous liquid which kills the stone if it is not separated from it, not permitting the coral red to appear and the coagulation to occur as long as it is present.' (5)

Just as the 'radical moisture' clinging to the philosophers' son must evaporate in order that the homunculus may become hard and incorruptible like chalk, so too the red stone with many ramifications must be rescued from the water and exposed to the air that it may attain to hardness and fixity. This is the difficult task undertaken by the alchemist in fig.144.

A Lunar Sponge Filled with Blood

The remarkable shape of the coral tree in the sea is fully shown in fig.143. The alchemical water-colour presents the submarine tree of the philosophers in close contact with the mermaid or watermother. 'Nature has planted the root of the tree in the midst of her womb,' (6) says an alchemical author of the philosophical tree, while another asserts: 'The tree of the sun and moon is the red and white coral tree of our sea.' (7)

One of the oldest sources of the coral tree is the 'Allegoria super librum Turbae' which identifies the tree with the Lunatica or Lunaria ('moon plant'). Its collection is described in the following manner: 'In the lunar sea there is a sponge planted having blood and sentience, in the manner of a tree that is rooted in the sea and moveth not from its place. If thou wouldst handle the plant, take a sickle to cut it with, but have good care that the blood floweth not out, for it is the poison of the philosophers.' (8)

The 'Crowne of Nature' probably refers to the coral and spongy states of Sol and Luna in a passage already quoted in connection with the 'melting' processes in the wake of the *coniunctio sive coitus*: 'Thus Sol and Luna are philosophically calcined with the first water, and their bodies are opened and made spongious and subtle that the second water may have the better ingression to work his effort' (p.80).

144. Discovering a coral tree filled with blood and providing the red elixir of rebirth.

The Placenta: the Prenatal Tree of Life

The blood-filled sea-sponge, coral stone and moon plant are transparent libido symbols of the blood-rich placenta, also called the *arbor vitae,* or the 'tree of life' (fig.145). The placenta is one of the great marvels of nature, 'a tree feeding all flesh' as its unconscious representation is termed in Nebuchadnezzar's dream (Daniel 4: 12). With its intricate filigree of blood vessels and membranes the placenta resembles most of all a sponge or a submarine coral tree. The placenta provides anchorage and nourishment for the growing fetus, carries off all its wastes, and protects it in a variety of ways from harmful invaders. It does all this through the fetus' pipeline to life, the umbilical cord. On the left in fig.145 is the yolk sac.

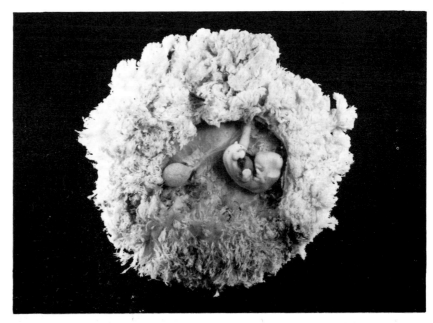

145. The blood-rich sponge of the placenta nourishing the fetus until birth.

146. *The eternal boy taking root in his parental soil, exuding the fruits of immortality.*

A Philosophical Tree of Primary Identity

'Several subjects have felt the inner body as consisting of trees and vines, streams and waterfalls, hills and valleys. One subject could 'feel' his 'parental heritage,' the respective maternal and paternal contributions to his 'cellular structure.' This was a 'revolting and grisly' experience. He said that 'I knew just what in my body came from my mother and what from my father. I could feel my mother and father in my body and I felt that I knew what my mother's body feels like to my mother and what my father's body feels like to my father. I lost for a little while most of my sense of my body as my own. Experiencing so much woman in my body was especially awful.'

R.E.L.Masters and Jean Houston. (1)

Fig.146 shows the seven planetary gods in cosmic harmony around the Boy Mercurius appearing as the 'mercurial tree,' his toes rooting into the earth, his fingers branching into the air. In the top of the tree the blood of the eternal boy exudes as the 'immortal fruit,' which one alchemical author calls the 'golden apples of the Hesperides, to be pluck't from the blest philosophic tree.' (2) Speaking of these, Pseudo-Aristotle says in his 'Tractatus ad Alexandrum Magnum': 'Gather the fruits, for the fruit of this tree has led us into the darkness and through the darkness.' (3)

Fig.147 gives the *arbor philosophica* as it appears in an alchemical vision of the sleeping Adam in the Garden of Eden. Bathed in the light of the moon-mother, Adam is united with the tree of knowledge and with an Eve still existing as 'bone of his bone, and flesh of his flesh' (Genesis 2:23). The trunk grows out of Adam's lap as his erect penis extending into the crown of apples. The hand of Mercurius philosophorum has broken through the sky and pierced the heart of Adam with an arrow (signifying death in love).

Fig.148 shows Sol and Luna playing and singing under the watery tree of the philosophers while merging into unity under its magic crown.

A Philosophical Tree Feeding All Flesh

The nuptial water running through the veins of the philosophical tree is of a more subtle nature than the water sucking the royal lovers in the bath. Therefore the 'Crowne of Nature' stresses the importance of the 'second water'; this is the sap of the philosophical tree saturating the bodies of Sol and Luna, while effecting their total fusion. It is described as 'an oily water and [it] is the philosophical stone, from which branches multiply into infinity.' (4)

In addition to its submarine growth and infinitely multiplying branches, the philosophers' tree has blood in its veins. When exuding, the sap of the tree coagulates as the 'immortal fruit which has life and blood,' as the 'Philosophia reformata' says. (5) In Dorn, the branches of the philosophical tree are veins running through the earth; although they spread to the most distant points of the earth's surface, they all belong to the same immense tree, which apparently renews itself. The tree is thought of as a system of blood vessels; it contains a liquid like blood, and when this flows out it becomes the immortal fruit of the tree. (6) Similarly, in the 'Vision of Arisleus,' the model of the fifth woodcut of the 'Rosarium' (fig.136), the scenery of conjunction is accompanied by the appearance of 'this most precious tree, of whose fruit he who eats shall never hunger.' (7)

The philosophers' tree shares with the stone the qualities of autonomy and universality. Commenting on Senior, the 'Consilium coniugii' says: 'Thus the stone

147. Phallic cord of a universal tree.

is perfected of and in itself. For it is the tree whose branches, leaves, flowers, and fruits come from it and through it and for it, and it is itself whole or the whole and nothing else.' (8) Another alchemical author says: 'Of itself, from, in, and through itself is made and perfected the stone of the wise. For it is one thing only: like a tree (says Senior), whose roots, stem, branches, twigs, leaves, flowers, and fruit are of it and through it and from it and on it, and all come from one seed. It is itself everything, and nothing else makes it.' (9) Dorn summarizes the alchemists' ideas of their philosophical tree in the following manner:

148. Fusing under the philosophical tree.

'On account of likeness alone, and not substance, the philosophers compare their material to a golden tree with seven branches, thinking that it encloses in its seed the seven metals, and that these are hidden in it, for which reason they call it a living thing [fig.142]. Again, even as natural trees bring forth divers blossoms in their season, so the material of the stone causes the most beautiful colours to appear when it puts forth its blossoms. Likewise they have said that the fruit of their tree strives up to heaven, because out of the philosophical earth there arises a certain substance, like to the branches of a loathsome sponge. Whence they have put forward the opinion that the point about which the whole art turns lies in the living things of nature and not in the living things of matter; and also because their stone contains within it soul, body and spirit, as do living things. From a likeness not altogether remote they have called this material virgin's milk and bless-ed rose-coloured blood . . . Concerning this, Mercurius speaks as follows to King Kalid: 'To know this mystery is permit-ted only to the prophets of God,' and that is the reason why the stone is called animate. For in the blood of this stone is hidden its soul. It is also composed of body, spirit and soul. For a like reason they have called it their microcosm, be-cause it contains the similitude of all things of this world, and therefore again they say that it is animate, as Plato calls the macrocosm animate.' (10)

The Inverted Tree of the Philosophers

One of the many paradoxical qualities of the *arbor philosophica* is that it grows upside down, the crown as its roots and vice versa. Hence it is called the *arbor inversa,* the 'inverted tree.' (11) Says an alchemical treatise: 'It has the roots of its minerals above in the air and its branches below in the earth. And when they are torn away from their places a terrible sound is heard and a great fear follows.' (12) Also in the 'Gloria mundi' it is mentioned that the philosophers have said that 'the root of its minerals is in the air and its head in the earth.' (13) George Ripley describes the tree with its roots in the air and, elsewhere, as being rooted in the 'glorified earth,' in the earth of paradise or in the future world. (14)

The most famous of the many exam-ples of the inverted world-tree is the one appearing in the 'Upanishads'; here the religious meaning of the tree is like that of the *arbor philosophica:* 'This universe is a tree eternally existing, its root aloft, its branches spreading below. The pure root of the tree is Brahman, the immor-tal, in whom the three worlds [i.e., the sky, the earth and the nether world] have their being, whom none can transcend, who is verily the Self.' (15)

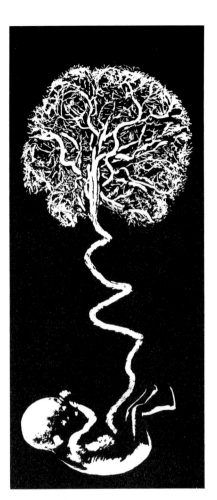

149. The cosmic tree of alchemy is a symbol of the 'arbor vitae,' or blood-rich prenatal tree of life. It is formed by the blood-vessels of the placenta which on the reconstruction have been removed from their covering tissues. The blood-sap circulating in the branches of the placenta (or its 'roots') rushes at a speed of about four miles per hour, the infant's heart pumping three hundred quarts of blood a day. The thousands of branching vessels of the tree of life perform the diverse functions of the adult lungs, the kidneys, the intestines, the liver and some of the functions of a hormone gland. In addition to all this, it also produces sub-stances that can combat infections. At birth the uterus contracts and the roots of the prenatal tree of life are torn off their 'earth' (or 'heaven') and expelled in the afterbirth. The fetus and its navel string must be imagined submerged in the amniotic water of the uterus; similarly, the spongy material of the placenta must be imagined embedded in the uterine wall. The placental tree's two white stems in the foreground are the arteries that carry the blood out of the umbilical cord. These branch into a closed network that returns the circulation to the cord in the single large vein that is the third white stem in the foreground. In the branching vessels, wastes from the fetus are traded for nutrients from the mother.

150. *The pregnant father king digesting a son slowly melting with his body of rebirth.*

151. *'Here father, son and guide are joined in one, so to remain forever.' (1)*

The Redemption of the King's Son

Fig.150, from Lambspring's story of the *filius regius*, shows the 'rooting' of the king's son in the sweating body of his combined parent. The dragon's mouth has closed and the lion-father of Lambspring's previous engraving (fig.125) now 'sweats profusely' in childbed after devouring his son. The labour pains of the pregnant father are accompanied by the verse:

Now the father sweated on account of
*   his son,*
And earnestly beseeched God,
Who has everything in His hands,
Being able to create all things,
And having created them, to bring forth
His only son from his body,
And to restore him to his former life.
God hearkened to his prayers,
And bade the father lie down and sleep.
While he was lying asleep,
God sent down a great rain from above,
Rain from the shining stars of heaven.
It was a fertilizing and silvery rain
Which bedewed and softened the
*   father's body.*
Now help us, o Lord, to obtain
*   Thy grace! (2)*

Fig.151 shows the conclusion and apotheosis of Lambspring's story where the aged king's bath of renewal produces his miraculous rebirth in his son. Emerging from the unifying waters of the *solutio*, father and son are seated on the same throne by the winged guide, or spirit Mercurius. His presence completes the identity of father and son within a trinitarian framework presented thus by the 'Aurora consurgens': 'As the Father, such is the Son, and such is also the Holy Spirit; and these three are One.' (3) Or in the words of Lambspring's motto for the engraving: 'Here father, son and guide are joined in one, so to remain for ever.' (4) The verse accompanying the final picture of Lambspring's series of the 'king's son' reads:

Now the sleeping father is changed
Entirely into limpid water,
And by virtue of this water alone
The good work is accomplished,
And there is now a strong and beautiful
Father, and he brings forth a new son,
Which for ever remains in the father,
And the father in the son.
Thus in divers things
They produce untold fruit
That can never perish any more,
And can nevermore die any death.
By the grace of God they abide for ever,
The father and the son, triumphing
*   gloriously.*
Upon one throne they sit,
And the face of the ancient master
Is straightaway seen between them.
He is arrayed in a crimson robe.
Laud and glory to God alone. Amen. (5)

Fig.152, also from the 'Book of Lamb-spring,' shows the 'lord of the forest' (fig.119) at the end of his labours. Triumphantly displaying the apple and sceptre of royal dominion, the Hermetic figure says:

'I have overcome and vanquished my foes
And trodden the venomous dragon
        under foot;
I am a great and glorious king on earth,
No one greater than I may be born,
Either through art or nature.' (6)

The Eternal Youth of Perfection

Fig.153 shows the Second Key of Basil Valentine which forms a symbolic unit with the Third Key (fig.115). The engraving renders the rebirth of the Benedictine monk as Boy Mercurius or *puer aeternus*. Illuminated by the combined light of the sun and moon, the 'eternal youth' shows the mercurial wands of conjunction, his feathered 'robe' lying in front of him on the ground. As witnessed by his crown, the naked youth appears as the *filius regius*, or the rejuvenated form of the father-king. Similarly, his wings and mercurial sign identify him with the spirit Mercurius uniting father and son.

In a remarkable way, the eternal youth's life is threatened by an armed split figure apparently riveted to the spot by the youth's overpowering beauty. A young eagle perches on the sword of the right figure, a crowned snake winds around the sword of the left figure. The punitive warriors have an obvious connection to the act of conjunction and its transgression of the incest-parricide taboos. As evidenced by the text accompanying the Second Key (reproduced in full on pp.72-73), Basil Valentine's emblem renders the *coniunctio sive coitus:* 'The king and his spouse must be quite naked when they are joined together.' (7)

The most powerful symbol of the incest of the Boy Mercurius is the caduceus, or staff of Hermes, he presents. The caduceus is derived from the Orphic myth of Zeus and Rhea. When Zeus tried to rape his mother, Rhea, she turned herself into a serpent; Zeus did the same and so, as serpent with serpent, entwined in an indissoluble knot, they coupled. Afterwards Zeus ravished his own daughter, Persefone, who had been born of this union. Then, too, he assumed the form of serpent. The commemorative emblem of this dual, incestuous union is the staff of Hermes. (8)

A Figure of the Primal Oedipus Complex

A symbol of eternal youth and hermaphroditic wholeness, the glorified king of

152. The dragon-slaying king on his throne of rebirth and universal dominion.

fig.153 is presented as a conqueror of the traumatic forces of rebirth's persecutory anxieties and splitting processes. The swords of the split figure adorned with a crowned snake and a young eagle are combined symbols of son, father, spirit, king, phallus and cord, that is, archetypal symbols of parental incarnation.

This is the mystery expressed by the crowned and winged youth—half father, half mother, invulnerable and innocent, beyond sex and aggression, whole. Triumphantly he displays the snake-entwined wands of Mercurius in a blinding vision of the primal Oedipus complex and its state of primary, parental identity.

153. Immortal conjunction of the sexes in the eternal youth of purity and perfection.

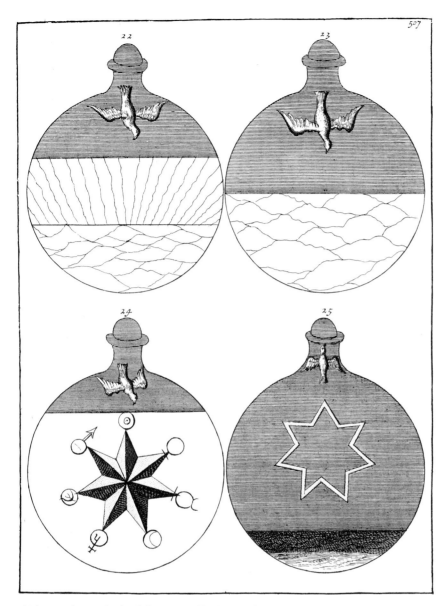

22 23 5o7

24 25

154. Cosmic synthesis of the personality in the alchemical 'star of perfection.'

Planetary Star of Perfect Conjunction

The 'philosophical calcination' of Sol and Luna, 'opened and made spongy and subtle,' is brought to its successful consummation above. After their common 'dissolution' and 'putrefaction' in the white arcane substance of plates 22-23, the royal bodies coagulate into the cosmic synthesis of plate 24. Here Sol and Luna unite with the five planets or metals in the sevenfold planetary star, the 'star of perfection' *(stella perfectionis),* (1) or, as the 'Crowne of Nature' terms it, the 'figure of perfect conjunction':

'My son, know, when the foresaid black earth shall begin to receive any of his argent vive then it is called conception, and then the masculine doth work in the feminine, that is, the argent vive in the earth, and the philosophers say that our mastery is nought but the masculine and the feminine and their con-

junction . . . Let it [the arcane substance] putrefy in a gentle heat of warm and hot dung, and no other wise that nothing ascend, for then it would be seperated which must not be until the male and female be perfectly coniunct and that the one embrace the other. The figure of perfect coniunctio is blackness on the top.' (2)

This particular state is shown in plate 25, where the sevenfold planetary star appears as an empty and ghostly body hovering in the 'blackness on the top' of the vessel. This dual state of light and darkness, life and death, inside the Hermetic vessel is explained by the fact that the 'perfect conjunction' of alchemy occurs in the zodiacal sign of the Scales where the opposites are fused in a supreme way, i.e., at the balancing point of *equilibrium.* This symmetrical arrangement of Libra is reflected not only in the balanced white and black stars in

plates 24-25, but also in the Hermes bird flying downward in plate 24 and upward in plate 25. (Since the beginning of lunar growth in plate 21, the bird has flown downward, a movement of spiritual 'depression' indicating the dissolution of Sol in the 'putrefying' substance of Luna.)

The Celestial Colour of the Rebis

The growing symbiosis of the homunculus and his maternal substance, expressed in the philosophical tree, culminates in the production of the *rebis* ('double-being'), or hermaphrodite, the human expression of equilibrium and the much-coveted goal of the opus alchymicum. The 'Pandora' series renders this miracle in fig.157; after the *coniunctio sive coitus* of the two previous plates (fig.122) the king and queen merge into the figure of the rebis, identified, in turn, with the 'celestial colour.' This is a clear reference to the colours of the sevenfold planetary star, just as this figure's 'blackness on the top' parallels the presence of an opposite balancing principle in the second 'Pandora' plate—the *celestial colour together with thy black earth.'*

Fig.155 shows Sol and Luna taking root as the philosophical tree in the 'chaos' of the arcane substance. The trunk forms part of the Scales and, hence, signifies the supreme union of Sol and Luna in the neutral equilibrium of Libra. The inscription reads: 'Kept in balance by equal weights. Nothing is clearer.'

An Autumnal Globe of Maturity

Fig.156 shows the engraved version of Basil Valentine's vision of the sevenfold planetary star lit in the hour of 'perfect conjunction' and developing the cosmic hermaphrodite on top of the conquered dragon and the philosophers' stone. The planetary crowns surrounding those of Sol and Luna float in the weightless space of Libra, the Scales. The wings of the mercurial sphere or stone indicate a similar conquest of the forces of gravita-

155. 'Kept in balance by equal weights.'

tion and the achievement of a state of bodily 'weightlessness,' or supreme spiritualization. The black egg shining in the middle of the sphere symbolizes the nigredo and expresses the precarious balance of the hermaphrodite, exalted by an equilibrium threatened by the progress of autumn and winter. The winged globe of the rebis hence signifies the ripe fruit at the point where putrefaction is born; its 'celestial colour' contains the 'black earth,' its 'figure of perfect conjunction is black on the top.' The globe of triumph and maturity is thus a globe of death also. The king's red apple is as splendid as autumn, tinged with feelings of sad joy and sweet melancholy.

Libra the Scales: Perfect Conjunction

The seventh sign of the Zodiac is a cardinal, airy sign ruled by Venus. Libra extends from September 24 to October 23, where the halves of day and night, winter and summer balance in *autumn's equinox*. In the Scales the opposites are fused in a neutral equilibrium which abolishes their energetics while containing them. Centred on keeping the balance and preventing disturbance of equilibrium, Libra is the sign of 'Justice.'

Libra is a sociable, cultured and courteous person in whom the two universal drives are balanced and sublimated in a profound way. This type is almost entirely non-aggressive and his sexual drive is sublimated into a loving sense of order, harmony and beauty. Evangeline Adams says on this point: 'In love, the Libra native has perhaps the most interesting temperament of any in the Zodiac . . . There may even appear a strain of homosexuality; this is not to be attributed to any real predilection, but to the fact of the delicate poise of the Libra nature between the two sexes.' (3)

An apostle of non-violence and a lover of art, Libra in his extreme politeness and sociability seeks equilibrium in all human drives and relationships. His inner sense of balance, concord and justice unconsciously converges on his idea of society, the outer expression of his higher individual self.

The Dragon's Speech in Fig.156:

'I bestow on you the powers of the male and the female, and also those of heaven and of earth. The mysteries of my art must be handled with courage and greatness of mind if you would conquer me by the power of fire, for already very many have come to grief, their riches and labour lost. I am the egg of nature, known only to the wise, who in piety and modesty bring forth from me the microcosm, which was prepared for mankind by Almighty God, but given

156. Fusing into double-sexed unity in the equilibrium of the sevenfold planetary star.

only to a few, while the many long for it in vain, that they may do good to the poor with my treasure and not fasten their souls to the perishable gold. By the philosophers I am named Mercurius; my spouse is the gold; I am the old dragon, found everywhere on the globe of the earth, father and mother, young and old, very strong and very weak, death and resurrection, visible and invisible, hard and soft; I descend into the earth and ascend to the heavens, I am the highest and the lowest, the lightest and the heaviest; often the order of nature is reversed in me, as regards colour, number, weight, and measure; I contain the light of nature; I am dark and light; I come forth from heaven and earth; I am known and yet do not exist at all; by virtue of the sun's rays all colours shine in me, and all metals. I am the carbuncle of the sun, the most noble purified earth, through which you may change copper, iron, tin, and lead into gold.' (4)

157. A heavenly vessel showing the genesis of the hermaphrodite, the primal self.

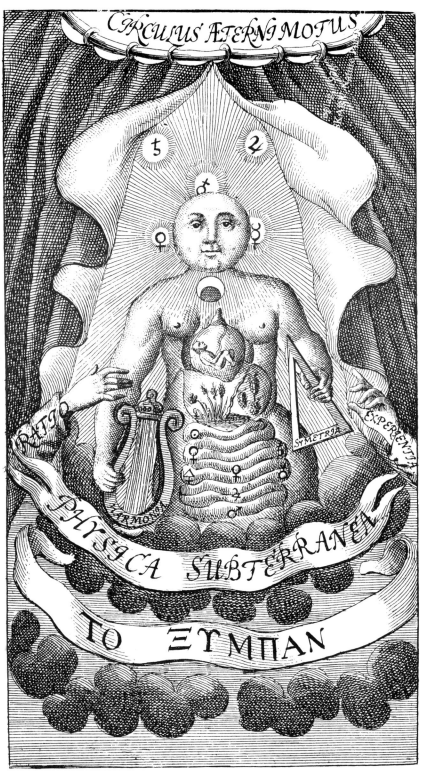

158. *Emergence of the fetal personality at the end of the second month of pregnancy.*

The Glorified Hermaphrodite

I, Hermes, cause to come out to thee,
O Sun, the spirits of thy brethren
    [the planets],
And I make them for thee a crown,
The like of which was never seen;
And I cause thee and them to be
    within me,

And I will make thy kingdom vigorous.
        The Book of Ostanes. (1)

In fig.158 the 'subterranean physics' are revealed to the adept after his descent into the earth and conquest of its centre. At the parting of the curtains of darkness, the glorified alchemist incarnated in the sun appears as the sevenfold pla-

netary star, the revolving planets forming his 'crown.' In his hands he carries the instruments of the Scales, the triangle and the lyre representing 'symmetry' and 'harmony.' Besides having female breasts, he carries the philosophers' son in an umbilical cord in his breast. Below the homunculus, symbolizing the animal realm, flowers and grapes sprout from the hermaphrodite's stomach, containing the vegetable realm. The transparent abdomen holds the mineral realm, the bowels of the rebis identified with the seven planets or metals.

This inner structure shows the final incarnation in the adept of Mercurius philosophorum of whom the fountain bubbled: *'Unus est Mercurius mineralis, Mercurius vegetabilis, Mercurius animalis.'* Another 'metaphysical' feature is the 'everlasting movement in a circle' *(circulus aeterni motus)* performed by the Cosmic Man of fig.158, who thus partakes in the eternal revolutions of the heavens. The two hands pulling the curtain signify 'reason' and 'experience,' while representing the poles of the alchemical procedure, where 'left and right' are finally united in 'symmetry' and 'harmony.'

Perfect Equilibrium of the Two Sexes

Fig.159 shows the medieval English monk, theologian and alchemist Roger Bacon (1214-1292) holding the Scales of 'perfect conjunction' while exclaiming: 'Make the elements equal and you will have it.' (2) Water and fire are balanced symmetrically on either side of the central pivot, while air (the cloud) and earth (the stone) are balanced along a vertical line of symmetry.

Fig.160 shows the medieval German bishop and alchemist Albertus Magnus (1193-1280) pointing to the goal of the royal art, who carries the Y of the original, bisexual man. The bishop exclaims: 'All things agree in the One which is cleft in two.' (3) This united double nature is characteristic of Mercurius philosophorum who, like the Scales, represents an active but neutral equilibrium assimilating the opposites in a higher, synthetic form. His body is said to be masculine, his soul feminine, sometimes the reverse. In the 'Liber de arte chymica,' which is the first alchemical text mentioning the hermaphrodite, the rebis is presented thus: 'For that Mercurius is all metals, male and female, and an hermaphroditic monster even in the marriage of soul and body.' (4) A medieval commentator on the Arabian 'Tractatus aureus' gives a similar description of the rebis: 'As a shadow continually follows the body of one who walks in the sun . . . so our Adamic hermaphrodite, though he appears in masculine form, nevertheless always carries about with him Eve, or his feminine part, hidden in his body.' (5)

Genesis of the Fetal Personality

Interpreted in psychobiological terms, the alchemical coniunctio expresses the regressive revival of the fetal stage of intrauterine development spanning from two to nine months of pregnancy. The fetal stage is framed by two transition points: birth (at nine months) and the embryo's change into a fetus (at two months). The key to this switchover is in the formation of the first bone cells, replacing the cartilage. This criterion is chosen by embryologists because the initial bone formation coincides with the completion of the body. Now perfection of function will follow perfection in structure. As embryo becomes fetus near the close of the second month, the creature can well be called an individual *en miniature*.

Since in alchemy the planetary crown of the hermaphrodite denotes not only the metals but also the astrological temperaments, i.e., psychic factors, the birth of the planetary 'star of perfection' and the 'heavenly coloured' fetal hermaphrodite (figs.157-158) may be interpreted as symbolizing one of the crucial 'stopping places' of libido evolution. If the *coniunctio sive coitus* symbolizes the nine-month-old fetus in the womb, and the motif of the 'rooting' homunculus the regressive revival of fetal growth, the 'figure of perfect conjunction' symbolizes the *emergence of the fetal personality,* the revived genesis of the *primal self.*

LSD Uncovering the Primal Self

The 'celestial colour' enveloping the scenery of rebirth and hermaphroditic unity in fig.157 forms an integral part of all mystical experiences, emphasizing the impact of 'divine light.' Psychologically, the ego's experience of supernatural light signifies its awareness of areas of high-powered mental energies ordinarily unconscious. The revival of these submarine strata of the psyche points to the presence of a mental nucleus governing the total personality at a deeply unconscious level and one not very accessible to the ego. Jung, who discovered this nucleus of the unconscious and termed it 'the self,' could only infer its existence from experiences of the kind described on these and the previous pages. However, since Jung's death in 1961, the self has become scientifically accessible and demonstrable by modern technology. The first description of the self, uncovered in the LSD experience of rebirth, appeared in Sidney Cohen's 'The Beyond Within; the LSD Story':

'As the stream [toward the self] accelerates, it grows clearer—as when, after diving, one swims up rapidly and sees the water breaking open above one into air and light. The light intensifies—generally topaz. The awareness of living interpene-

159. The four elements of alchemy balanced in the perfect equilibrium of the Scales.

trating light becomes a delight, as peaceful as it is fascinating. At this level the sense of personality is not so much lost or merged as vastly dilated till its frontiers are lost in a consciousness which is not that of an ego . . . There is a key phrase in the writings of the philosopher Nicholas of Cusa. He speaks of a state of intense consciousness that is possible, and only possible because the experience goes 'beyond the conflict of the opposites.' The distinction between 'I' and 'it' and the division into 'this and that'

have ceased. Dimension and quantity have gone. Comparison and analysis cease. Polarity and orientation are absent. This, though, is no sense of fogged awareness or confused apprehension. Far from any sense of loss, bewilderment or dimming, there is the most vivid recognition of a wholeness that is absolute, timeless, instant. The comprehension is entire. If there is a feeling tone it is one for which fathomless peace is too passive a word and inexhaustible energy too febrile. This state is basic and omnipenetrating.' (6)

160. The two sexes balanced in the perfect equilibrium of the hermaphrodite.

93

161. The alchemist's polluted return to the angelic womb and its fusing water.

white wings on her back, the feathers of which resembled the very finest white peacock, and the quills were adorned with fine pearls, while the feathers reflected like golden mirrors. On her head she had a crown of pure gold, and on top of it a silver star; around her neck she wore a necklace of fine gold, with the most precious ruby, which no king would be able to pay; her feet were clad with golden shoes, and from her was emanating the most splendid perfume, surpassing all aromas. She clothed the man with a purple robe, lifted him up to his brightest clearness, and took him with herself to heaven.' (2)

The lady of many colours described above is a variation of the 'peacock's tail' *(cauda pavonis),* an alchemical symbol of the lapis; its prism contains all the hues of the rainbow, just as the planetary star of perfection contains the seven basic colours.

Becoming One's Own Egg

Fig.164 shows the ninth painting of the 'Splendor solis,' rendering the sequel to fig.161. As the red slave ascends from the river to meet the white woman with a bath towel, the two figures embrace and fuse into the angelic figure of the rebis. Surrounded with a halo and endowed with wings, the united brother-sister pair holds a target in its right hand and an egg in its left. The target is a circle composed of the four united elements, its centre depicting a beautiful landscape. The image aptly expresses the difficulties connected with the achievement of the Hermetic goal: missed if one shoots too high or too low; the right target is in the middle. The egg held by the rebis is the famous 'egg of the philosophers' *(ovum philosophorum),* which symbolizes the arcane substance. The egg is the cosmic birth-giver and the alchemist's universal parent. Retrieving the philosophical egg is therefore equivalent to reviving one's primal state, where subject and object are one—as in the rebis. (Its target appears as both objective and subjective centre.) By creeping into himself and becoming his own egg, the alchemist turns himself into his own hatcher, a state of primary identity in which bisexuality and self-propagation without a partner form the components of the Hermetic dream of immortality.

The Red Slave and the White Woman

The eighth painting of the 'Splendor solis' (fig.161) shows the artifex rising from the river as the 'red slave' received on the beach by the 'white woman.' Both represent the classical partners of the alchemical marriage presented by Senior: 'The red slave has wedded the white woman, and because the woman through the conjunction became pregnant, she has born a son who will serve his parents in all things, save that he is more splendid than they.' (1)

In the text it appears that the red slave represents the moor, or 'Ethiopian,' an alchemical symbol of uncleanliness and baseness. The painting varies the motif of rescue from water, depicted also in the preceding painting of the 'Splendor solis' (fig.131). In a remarkable manner, the

white woman or angelic queen is depicted as pregnant with her approaching lover, thus expressing the strange Hermetic marriage in which the bride is sister and mother, and the spouse is father, brother and suckling rolled into one. The idea of pregnancy and roundness is so dominant that it has transformed the head of the red slave into a transparent globe symbolic of the philosophers' stone. The text deals with the conjunction of the spirit and body (the red slave) at the hands of a winged anima mundi of fusing qualities:

'They [the philosophers] saw a man black like a negro sticking fast in a black, dirty and foul-smelling slime or clay; to his assistance came a young woman, beautiful in countenance, and still more so in body, most handsomely adorned with many-coloured dresses, and she had

162. Birth trauma followed by rebirth.

The Opening of the Dark Goal

The first medal of fig.162 shows the philosophers' son and his birth-star rising from a skeleton on the ground. The inscription reads: 'These are the flowers which are hidden under so many thorns and thistles.' The second medal shows the philosophers' son resting in his vessel of rebirth, identified with the womb of the pregnant virgin. The inscription reads: 'Like the philosophers' son, the philosophical stone must be nourished by the virgin's milk.' The expression of the birth place of the lapis appears in the Three Words of Kalid: 'For three months the water preserves the babe in the womb; for three months the air warms it; and the fire for the same length of time guards it. And this word and this teaching and the dark goal stand open, so that all may see the truth.' (3)

The first medal of fig.163 presents a variant of the eighth painting of the 'Splendor solis' encircled by the inscription: 'Our seed is the quicksilver which is conjoined with our earth.' The second medal shows the hermaphrodite with the inscription: 'Gold is made from sulphur and mercury when it has been in the fire for a short time.'

Closeness, Likeness, Sameness, Oneness

Figs.155-166 present a unique illustration of the *amor coniugalis* of the Hermetic goddess in her fourth and highest aspect as anima mundi, namely as a 'fusing soul.' We have studied her previous incarnations and transformations in connection with the progress of alchemical conjunction. At first she embodied incipient love—the sense of 'feeling close'; then she expressed a symbiotic kind of love—an intoxicating feeling of 'likeness' with the beloved; then a still more engrossing and autistic love—a magic feeling of 'sameness' with the beloved; finally she epitomized a burning love fusing the partners into a feeling of mystical 'oneness.' This (regressive) progress of the soul through four corresponding stages of the genetic process was aptly summarized by a schizophrenic patient, who after experiencing the inward journey herself, consulted the American psychoanalyst Dr.Edith Jacobson:

'In the course of my talk with her, the girl—a pathetic, beautiful Ophelia clad

163. Fusion with an angelic woman.

164. The goal of alchemy: double-sexed unity as the way to achieve immortality.

only in a torn nightgown—pulled me down to the couch where she had seated herself. 'Let us be close,' she said. 'I have made a great philosophical discovery. Do you know the difference between closeness, likeness, sameness, and oneness? Close is close as with you; when you are like somebody, you are only *like* the other, you and he are two; sameness— you are the same as the other, but he is still he and you are you; but oneness is not two—it is one, that's horrible.—Horrible,' she repeated, jumping up in sudden panic: 'Don't get too close, get away from the couch, I don't want to be you,' and she pushed me away and began to attack me. Some minutes later she became elated again. 'I am a genius,' she said, 'a genius. I am about to destroy all my books' (on social science). 'I don't need them, to hell with them. I am a genius, I am a genius.' (Her husband was a social science teacher.) When I took her in an ambulance to the hospital, she became calm, subdued, and depressed. 'I am dead now. Larry won't kill himself,' she said, taking out a little amulet, a tiny crab enclosed in a small plastic case. 'This is my soul,' she said, handing it to me. 'My soul is gone, my self is gone, I lost it. I am dead. Take it, keep it for me till I shall come out.' Then, in sudden panic: 'I don't want to die,' and she began to attack and to beat me, as though I had assaulted her, only to fall back again into her depressed, humble mood.' (4) With this excellent summary of the first half of the alchemical work we shall pass on to an assessment of its developmental aspect.

165. 'Take therefore from the stone, wherever it may be found, the one who is named rebis and is born in two mountains . . . , that is, from Venus and Mercurius.' (1)

The Maturation Processes of Adulthood

In reviewing this study's argument, we emphasize the genetic basis of man's archetypal stages of mental development. By this we mean the autonomous unfolding of the archetypal structure of the psyche, through which the development of the ego and of consciousness proceeds. There is now a vast body of experiments and observations, all underlining one undisputable fact: children are not born empty vessels which become gradually filled with facts and experience. They follow definite stages of development which are, in effect, different forms of consciousness. A psychobiological time-clock governs our mental and physical maturation. We know that man's organism undergoes a transpersonal development manifesting itself as oogenesis, ovulation, fertilization, segmentation, implantation, embryonic and fetal growth, birth, infancy, childhood, latency, puberty, adulthood, middle age, climacteric, old age and death.

This evolutionary sequence is not only a biological phenomenon; it is also a psychological one—'as above so below.' On the basis of the opus alchymicum we can ascertain a transpersonal development of psychic structure, the sequence of which in time is determined and fixed as a specific, archetypal pattern. This entire process, whose predisposed course is ingrained in the species, we term, like Jung, the *individuation process*. However, we distinguish between two phases, one progressive and concerned with the building up of ego consciousness, the other regressive and concerned with ego integration of its unconscious foundations. As we shall demonstrate, regressive individuation deals with an unconscious play-back of the individual's total course of psychobiological evolution.

166. A love goddess of fusing qualities.

It remains to determine the positional value of the prima materia and the first coniunctio in the 'sequence-dating' phases of man's psychic aging process. *The opening part of the alchemical work terminating in the first coniunctio reflects the psychodynamic 'work' of the unconscious in adult maturation when the ego realizes its potential for creative-aggressive action and sexual-creative activity.* As demonstrated, the labours of a regressing unconscious are centred on an elimination of repression and on a revival and solution of the conflicts of puberty, latency, childhood, infancy and birth. In this perspective, the first coniunctio expresses the final achievement of adulthood or 1) the successful identification with the father in his role in life and marriage; 2) the conquest of the mother in the symbolic ritual of marriage and sex; and 3) the symbolic recreation of self in parenthood.

The unconscious psychodynamics of such ego maturation necessarily involve a resolution of the conflicts and defences at all earlier stages of ego-development. If these were not resolved at some mental level, as in dreams, for instance, the personality would never attain adult structure; this is best seen in immature personalities regressively fixated at certain infantile stages of ego-development. Choice of and relationships to work and to sexual partner are determined by the ego's ability to master anxiety and cope with reality, not in a defensive, but an active way. Thus, for instance, a resolution of primal anxiety is a condition for the ego's normal relationship to a partner of the opposite sex and for its achievement of orgasm, the fleeting glimpse of the *unio mystica* at the unconscious level of the self.

However, most of this 'resolution' of the subterranean locks and doors of the personality takes place unconsciously, and may be glimpsed only in dreams. Normally, the whole process remains unconscious, i.e., *unknown*, only to be experienced indirectly—in the form of inspirational ideas, impulses to action and inexplicable moods. The alchemical opus is concerned with making this unconscious process *conscious* and with integrating its movements of transformation into the structure of the *ego*. In such a manner the dream is not lost but remembered and utilized in the ego's knowledge of itself and of its world. (2)

Left, the anima mundi fuses with the adept in a chemical, psychological and cosmic synthesis of sulphur and mercury, the four humours, or temperaments, and the twelve zodiacal signs. Right, the royal bridal chamber of 'conjunction' placed in a watery mountain cave and surrounded by the seven planetary gods, the Zodiac, and the four elements—a huge mandala illustrating the motif of the engraving: 'Third Means: Conjunction' (headline).

IGNIS.

AERIS.

AQVÆ.

TERRÆ.

TINCTVR
COAGVLATION.
DISTILLATION.
PVTREFACTION.
SOLVTION.
SVBLIMATION.
CALTINATION.

167. A royal art conjured up in the darkness of closed eyelids and governed by nature's earth-returning, or regressive, instincts.

97

168.   *Et sic in infinitum*

Nigredo: 'Black' Death and Putrefaction

At the peak of the opus alchymicum the glory of the coniunctio suddenly fades into darkness and despair. This development signifies the onset of a new stage of the work termed by the adepts *nigredo* ('blackness'), *tenebrositas* ('darkness'), or *mortificatio*.* In the nigredo the alchemist becomes aware that the power he has gained is Janus-faced and that the

---

* In alchemy it is often emphasized that the nigredo represents the 'beginning of the work.' This is not strictly true. The nigredo is the result of a preliminary union of the opposites, that is, of an initial operation concerned with the production of the prima materia and its synthesis in the first *coniunctio oppositorum*. Even if the opening opus is described by the alchemical texts as dark and melancholy and equated with an act of putrefaction, it is not to be confused with the nigredo proper which, according to Mylius, only appears in the fifth grade of the work, during the 'putrefaction which is celebrated in the darkness of Purgatory.' (1) When further on Mylius states that 'this denigration is the beginning of the work, an indication of the putrefaction,' (2) this process is not to be confused with the reactivation of the prima materia at the opening phase of the work. The confusion is one of terms and is due to the fact that the opus proper is divided into the Little Work and the Great Work. Thus the 'beginning' of the work actually signifies the beginning of the Little Work, which follows upon the initial operation sometimes described as the Gross Work. (3)

stone is capable of exercising both a divine and demonic force. Superhuman in potency, the reborn alchemist suddenly topples from his throne, his universe turned upside-down in the process. Known to the Greeks as *peripeteia*, or the 'reversal of roles,' this principle of irony and paradox is overwhelming in its operation in Hermetic science: that which has been worshipped as holy becomes in the twinkling of an eye a monstrous horror; the cup with the elixir of life turns into a deadly poison; the king united with his queen withers into the terrifying creature of fig.169.

As death and darkness descend on a landscape formerly lit up by the golden vision, the 'eternal youth' of Basil Valentine's Second Key changes into the skeleton of the Fourth Key (fig.169). Standing on his bier, the dead yet living Boy Mercurius is on his way to the grave after the funeral in the church in the background. The figure is accompanied only by a burning candlestick symbolizing his waning light of life. The withered and cut-off tree behind him carries the same tragic meaning. The text reads:

'All flesh that is derived from the earth must be decomposed and again reduced to the earth which it formerly was; then the earthy salt produces a new generation by celestial resuscitation. For where there

was not first earth, there can be no resurrection in our magistery. For in earth is found the balm of nature and the salt of those who have found the science of all things.' (4)

Fig.170 shows a still more horrible variation of the nigredo: Mercurius philosophorum transformed into a spider killing all the metals in its cruel web. With the lowering darkness of the nigredo, the bridal chamber of the king and queen is changed into a dry cellar filled with poisonous insects and contaminating presences. The kingdom of life has become the kingdom of death, the hermaphrodite a hollow man lying at the bottom of a precipice where the sun never shines.

The adepts describe the nigredo as 'black blacker than black' *(nigrum nigrius nigro)*, (5) while adding: 'And so it is in infinity' *(et sic in infinitum)* (fig.168). The 'Rosarium' states that during the nigredo the 'brain turns black.' (6) In the 'Theatrum chemicum' we are informed that the nigredo is called 'antimony, pitch, coal, the raven, the raven's head, lead, burnt copper, burnt ivory.' (7) In the night of the nigredo 'when all the beasts of the wood go about,' according to the testimony of the 'Aurora consurgens,' (8) bier and marriage bed are made one. The nigredo is therefore frequently described in imagery relating to funeral and funeral ceremonies. Says the 'Introitus apertus': 'The tomb in which our king is buried is called Saturn and it is the key of the work of transmutation.' (9) Lead is the metal of Saturn and of the nigredo, its heaviness expressing the lowered spirits and the profound depression prevailing in the 'black' phase of the alchemist's work.

The Blackness of Middle Age Depression

Interpreted in terms of the individuation process, the nigredo symbolizes the bout of profound depression occurring in middle age. Statistics show a rise in the frequency of mental depressions at this age. After the unconscious coniunctio underlying the psychology of adulthood, a strange change seems to take its rise in the unconscious between thirty and forty. Jung has termed this stage of life *Lebenswende*, a term signifying the onset of the second half of life, or the onset of a psychobiological change of far-reaching consequences:

'Middle life is the moment of greatest unfolding, when a man still gives himself to his work with his whole strength and his whole will. But in this very moment evening is born, and the second half of life begins. Passion now changes her face and is called duty; 'I want' becomes the inexorable 'I must,' and the turnings of the pathway that once brought surprise and discovery become dulled by custom. The wine has fermented and begins to settle and clear.' (10)

The insight that one's sun has reached its zenith and in the future will sink and finally die does not come easily to man; it is attained only through the severest shocks. W.V.Caldwell gives us the following glimpse of an everyday occurrence in the work of American psychotherapists:

'Many people in their thirties and forties, while giving glib verbal assurance of their acceptance, have not really begun to face the bitter knowledge of death. They are open to a traumatic shock, for the knowledge hides somewhere in their subconscious, waiting to be touched off by unforeseen events. One therapist told me recently of a patient in his thirties who, during a session, abruptly sat up on his bed screaming, 'My God, I'm going to die! I'm going to die!' All the agony of that knowledge had suddenly crashed in upon him and it was insupportable. Fortunately this man was reasonably well prepared and there was a therapist at hand. But for others in our society who have been protected by our social avoidance of death—the comforts of religion, the sham of mortuaries, even the euphemistic evasions of our language—a serious illness, or an operation, or the death of a loved one can suddenly breach those carefully built walls of illusion and flood the mind with unbearable horrors. Trauma, psychosis, nervous breakdown can be the results. This is a shock we all face sooner or later.' (11)

The Unconscious Anatomy of Depression

The profound psychological change accompanying the onset of the second half of life subtly influences the ego, which in normal depressive reactions succumbs to moods of dejection and hopelessness. These moods reflect processes of unconscious transformation which may be studied in a more 'naked' state, i.e., not obscured by normal repression, in *neurotic depressive reactions* and, still more clearly, in *psychotic depressive reactions*. The unconscious anatomy of depression as revealed by psychopathology exactly corresponds with the strange anatomy of the alchemical nigredo.

As the mental sun of adulthood—the ego-anima-self unit—fades into middle age, a 'blackening' of the personality is effected with a depressive reaction as the result. In neurotic depression, the ego succumbs to mood disorders in which feelings of dejection, loneliness and hopelessness express the 'blackened anima,' while reactions of self-depreciation, self-condemnation and self-hatred express the 'blackened self.' Guilt plays a prominent role in the clinical picture: the neurotic depressive is repeatedly overwhelmed by overall tensions of unconscious, inexplicable guilt. This is not expressed directly or experienced consciously as guilt; instead, it appears in derivative form as

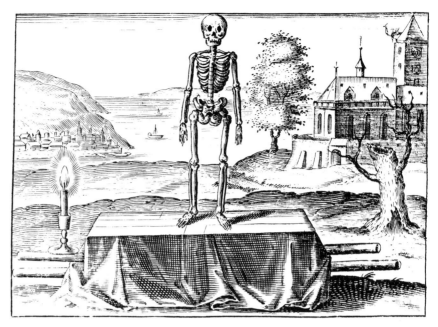

169. Blackening of the sun at its zenith: 'In the midst of life we are in death.' (12)

complaints of being unloved and unlovable, of being worthless, unwanted and inferior.

In psychotic depression, the feeling of guilt is no longer indirect or unconscious; it is expressed spontaneously and repeatedly, often with savage insistence. At this stage the defensive organization of the ego crumbles; the psychotic ego is unable to repress the unconscious hostility creating the intolerable tensions of depressive guilt. Because repression does not work, the psychotic ego is sucked much deeper into the marsh of the unconscious than is the neurotic ego. In its psychotic

or 'direct' form, a depressive reaction subjects the ego to mood disorders in which feelings of dejection, loneliness and hopelessness and reactions of self-depreciation, self-condemnation and self-hatred reach delusional proportions. The sense of worthlessness and guilt is not unconscious as in neurotic depression but *acutely conscious and excluding everything else*. As depression reaches delusional levels, external reality is replaced by an overwhelming internal reality of such blackness and hostility that it frequently drives the psychotic depressive to suicide or serious attempts at this.

170. The alchemical god of conjunction turned into a spider poisoning his creation.

171. Killing and dismemberment of a royal usurper in front of the place of his crimes.

The Sacrifice of the Reborn King

The tenth painting of the 'Splendor solis' (fig.171) renders the nigredo and shows an avenging figure cutting off the head and limbs of a naked man. The text explains: 'Rosinus relates of a vision he had of a man whose body was dead and yet beautiful and white like salt. The head had a fine golden appearance, but was cut off the trunk, and so were all the limbs; next to him stood an ugly man of black and cruel countenance, with a blood-stained double-edged sword in his right hand, and he was the good man's murderer. In his left hand was a paper on which the following was written: 'I have killed thee, that thou mayest receive a superabundant life, but thy head I will carefully hide, that the world may not see thee, and destroy thee in the earth; the body I will bury, that it may putrefy and grow and bear innumerable fruit.'' (1)

As Jung points out, the alchemical *mortificatio* varies the archetypal motif of the slaying and dismemberment of the king for the purpose of renewing his power and increasing the fertility of the land. This motif harks back to the mourned gods and incestuous lovers of the Near East—Tammuz, Adonis, Attis, Osiris—who were originally sacrificed to seasonal fruitfulness. (2) Significantly, many of them were slain by boars. Fig. 172 shows the alchemical hero expiring as Adonis, the mythical son-lover who was himself the fruit of a father-daughter incest. The motto reads: 'Adonis is killed by a boar, and Venus, rushing up to him, colours the roses with her blood.' (3) The text goes on to explain:

'Adonis was the son of Cinyras, king of Cyprus, and of the latter's daughter Myrrha; so, according to legend, Adonis was born of an incestuous relationship. When taken literally this is outrageous, but taken allegorically it is not only allowed, but even necessary. For in this art nothing is achieved if not father and daughter, or mother and son, are united, and if from this union no birth results. And the nearer the relationship of the spouses . . . the more fertile they will be; the more distant their blood relationship is, the more sterile they will be. This is not allowed in human marriage. In this way, however, Oedipus married his mother, Jupiter his sister, just as Osiris, Saturn, Sol and the red slave Gabritius married in similar fashion.' (4)

On this background, the alchemical hero's death by the boar's tusk in fig. 172 appears as a gruesome expression of the punishment inflicted on him for the incest committed in the *coniunctio sive coitus*.

The Allegory of Merlin

Fig.174 illustrates the famous 'Allegoria Merlini' which describes the lowering darkness of the opus, or the transformation of the king's nuptial water into the water of death. According to the 'Allegory of Merlin,' a certain king readying for battle was about to mount his horse when he wished for a drink of water. A servant asked him what water he would like, and the king answered: 'I demand the water which is closest to my heart, and which likes me above all things.' When the servant brought the king this magic water (foreground right) the latter drank such inordinate qualities that 'all his limbs were filled and all his veins inflated, and he himself became discoloured.' His soldiers urged him to mount his horse, but he said he could not: 'I am heavy and my head hurts me, and it seems to me as though all my limbs were falling apart.'

He demanded to be placed in a heated chamber where he could sweat the water out. But when, after a while, they opened the chamber, he lay there as if dead.

172. A son-lover killed by the boar's tusk.

They summoned the Egyptian and the Alexandrian physicians, who at once accused one another of incompetence. Finally, the Alexandrian physicians gave way to the Egyptian physicians, who tore the king into tiny pieces, ground them to powder, mixed them with their 'moistening' medicines, and put the king back in his heated chamber as before. After some time they fetched him out again half-dead. When those present saw this, they broke out into lamentation, crying: 'Alas, the king is dead.' The physicians affirmed this. 'But,' they added, 'we have killed him in such a way that he will become better and stronger in this world after his resurrection on the Day of Judgement.' (5)

The ritual sacrifice of the alchemical king is depicted in yet another variant in fig.173, which reproduces Basil Valentine's second vision of the nigredo. Ten conspirators beat to death their royal lord under the vault of his cosmic glory illuminated by the light of the united sun and moon.

The Torments of Depression

The depressive colouring of the primal Oedipus complex of rebirth transforms the spiritus of paternal incarnation—the Oedipal father identification—into an evil spirit of hatred and revenge. Because of the primary identity achieved in the coniunctio, the son's murderous fantasies directed against the father, his guilt and paralyzing anxiety, become emotions directed *at himself*; in short, they assert themselves as feelings of self-condemnation, self-hatred and suicidal guilt.

The anima of maternal incarnation and primary identity is transformed in a similar way. Accordingly, the ego is subjected to mood disorders in which feelings of dejection and loneliness, baseness and worthlessness prevail. In addition to a depressive loss of warmth, hope and love, such 'blackening' of the soul brings on its heels a complete loss of creative activity, which leaves the ego in a state of mental sterility and 'dryness.'

If this is the predicament of the spiritus and anima, the corpus fares no better. The complaints of the dying king of alchemy read like a catalogue of the somatic sensations of depression: his body is filled with rank poison, there is a mortal inflation of his veins, he is tortured by the stings of the 'boar's tusk,' by heaviness, headaches and sensations of falling bodily apart; he is even racked by the pains of abortive birth. (6)

Depressed persons feel it the same way: they are convinced that they are physically deteriorating or have a fatal disease, usually cancer. Headaches, loss of appetite, gastrointestinal complaints, constipation, vomiting, 'hot flashes,' coldness of the extremities and countless other tortures of the body testify to the so-

173. Cudgelling a transgressor of man's primal taboos under the roof of his crimes.

matic expression of depression. Usually no physical basis can be found for these bodily symptoms. (As we shall see, they are produced solely by the unconscious during its convulsions of psychobiological 'decomposition.')

In psychotic depression and schizo-phrenia the 'putrefaction' of the body reaches delusional levels. Schizophrenic patients complain that they have no stomach or no bowels, that the stomach has shrivelled up and the intestines turned to stone, or that they have disappeared, rotted away, or been devoured.

174. The poisoned cup: 'When the king had drunk from the waters, he became ill.' (7)

175. Infernal guardians around a royal marriage bed reeking with putrefying corpses.

A Bridal Night of Death and Decay

Fig.176 shows the sixth woodcut of the 'Rosarium' in which the royal hermaphrodite expires in a marriage bed-turned-sarcophagus. The motto explains:

Here the king and queen are lying dead,
In great distress the soul is sped. (1)

The event is named 'conception or putrefaction' *(conceptio seu putrefactio)*, a dual term reflecting the alchemist's insight into the enigmatic and paradoxical nature of the 'black' transformation process: a building up by building down, a putrefying movement of creation, a kind of reversed fetal development. 'The corruption of one is the genesis of the other,' says the 'Rosarium' in commenting on fig.176: 'We have an example in the egg: first it decays and then the chicken is born, a living animal coming after the decay of the whole.' (2) This weird example is supplemented by a comparison of the art to the work of the sower who buries his grain in the earth; it dies only to waken to new life. Therefore the 'Rosarium' concludes: 'When you see your matter going black, rejoice: for that is the beginning of the work.' (3)

The engraved variant (fig.175) shows Devil and Death standing guard at the marriage coffin, whose mysteries are described in the following manner by the anonymous author of the 'Tractatus aureus': 'When the bridegroom and his bride were joined together I marvelled that the maiden, who was said to be the

mother of her bridegroom, was of so youthful an appearance that she might have seemed his daughter. But I know not what sin they had committed, except that brother and sister had been drawn to each other by such passionate love that they could no more be separated; and, being charged with incest, they were shut up for ever in a close prison, which, however, was as pellucid and transparent as glass, and arched like the heavenly vault, so that all that they did could be seen from without. Here they were to do penance for their sins with everflowing tears, and true sorrow. All their clothes and outward ornaments were taken away . . . Alas! What fear and anguish fell upon me, when I saw those who had been so straitly committed to my charge, lying, as it were, melted and dead before me. I felt sure that I should be put to death for it.' (4)

CONCEPTIO SEV PVTRE
factio

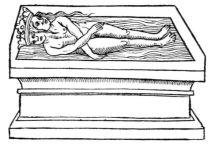

176. A coffin of 'putrefying conception.'

The Horrors of the Black Sun

The royal couple in fig.175 suffer from dropsy in a coffin containing their swelling, incestuous bodies. In the nigredo, noxious vapours sting the eyes of the adept and choke his throat; the stench of the Apocalypse rises up with the opening of the graves of the living dead. As the world becomes a place of reeking decay, the air is contaminated by the *odor sepulchrorum*—the 'stench of graves' and the sickening smell of putrefying corpses (fig.178). This is the *terra damnata* which reveals to the alchemist the terrors of hell and the sufferings of purgatory.

Fig.177 shows the catastrophe of the nigredo expressed in its most powerful symbol: that of the 'black sun' *(sol niger)*, extinguishing all light in a universe turned cold and lifeless. As the splendour of the sun conjoined with the moon changes into the horror of the 'black sun' eclipsed by the new moon, the work of destruction is completed. Two avenging angels point to the sun of death whose sulphurous and tormenting flames purge away the flesh of the king, formerly triumphing as the rebis on his winged sphere (fig.156). Sceptre and apple have by now been replaced by the starving crow or raven *(corvus)*, another emblem of the nigredo. The cruel fate of the reborn king is described by the 'Epigram of the Hermaphrodite,' which derives from about 1150 A.D. It is one of the earliest sources on the subject:

When my pregnant mother bore me in
* her womb,*
They said she asked the gods what she
* would bear.*
A boy, said Phoebus, a girl, said Mars,
* neither, said Juno.*
And when I was born, I was a
* hermaphrodite.*
Asked how I was to meet my end,
* the goddess replied: By arms;*
Mars: On the cross; Phoebus: By water.
* All were right.*
A tree overshadowed the waters,
* I climbed it;*
The sword I had with me slipped,
* and I with it.*
My foot caught in the branches, my
* head hung down in the stream;*
And I—male, female, and neither—
Suffered by water, weapon and cross. (5)

The Hollow, Guilty Men of Depression

The hollow or putrefying men depicted on these pages are famous figures in severe depression. The patient's subjective experience is insubstantial to the point of being hollowed out—'a ghostlike mass of flesh,' as one depressive described herself. (6) A common expression of the disease is statements such as 'I feel hollow.' (7) Another prominent feature is the sense of overwhelming guilt, which in psychotic depression exceeds anything seen in neurotic depression. At his black, delusional level, the psychotic depressive may hate himself so much and be so cruel and insistent about his self-hatred, that he ultimately kills himself.

The development of so much hatred and guilt which psychotic depressives show consciously requires an explanation since it exceeds all limits, even those of a severe conscience. Behind the hatred and the guilt lies the 'unmentionable crime' for which no punishment can be too severe. What exactly is the nature of this crime? The answer to this question is blurred even to the psychotic depressive himself, but two things are certain: 1) the crime is an imagined one and belongs to the realm of inner reality, or the unconscious; 2) the incessant self-depreciations and self-accusations of the psychotic depressive centre on his guilty, ambivalent *self*. All psychoanalytical attempts at describing psychotic depressive reactions in terms of ego-superego conflict miss the point because they ignore the unparalleled depth of regression in the disease. As Lord Harry Monchensey describes his psychotic depression in T.S.Eliot's play 'The Family Reunion': 'It goes a good deal deeper than what people call their conscience; it is just the cancer that eats away the self.' (8)

Carney Landis' observations on these problems are relevant: 'The depressed patient has no conscious knowledge of a moral lapse, of any real sin that might have been of sufficient magnitude to justify the intensity of the depressive guilt feelings. Hence the patient is, in a sense, justified in complaining of having committed 'the unpardonable sin,' by which he means the unknown sin. An unconscious and unknown sin can neither be condoned nor expiated. Essentially, the patient is saying, 'I don't know what I did, but I must have sold my soul to the Devil; anything I try to do can only make it worse; I am afraid and horror-stricken; I may be going mad.' This is, to put it simply, the essence of the thought process that the depressed patient follows when trying to explain to himself his innermost feelings of guilt and melancholia.' (9)

The Heart of Darkness

Alchemical nigredo symbolism provides the answer to the mystery of the imagined, 'unmentionable crime' of psychotic depression: the most sacred and omnipotent figures of all—the primal, archetypal parents—have been murdered, raped, eaten and incorporated in oneself. One's entire personality has thereby been contaminated by the crimes of parricide (matricide), cannibalism, and incest. (10) Such an unconscious configuration explains one of the greatest enigmas of modern psychiatry and psychoanalysis.

177. The stone of solar and lunar conjunction turned into the black sun of death.

'Many depressed persons wait in a spirit of hopeless resignation to be punished—often to be killed—feeling that they deserve it. The delusion that they are destined to be punished terribly makes some patients desperate. Some demand that the terrible suspense of waiting for the inevitable be ended, that they be put on trial, that they be imprisoned, executed or lynched. Some psychotic depressives ask to be beaten, trampled on, starved, degraded, pilloried or mutilated. Some visit punishment upon themselves. It is the unbearable suspense, the frightening expectation, and the absolute conviction of terrible guilt that drive many people to suicide.'

Norman Cameron. (11)

178. Fears and horrors of the damned: the stench of graves and putrefying corpses.

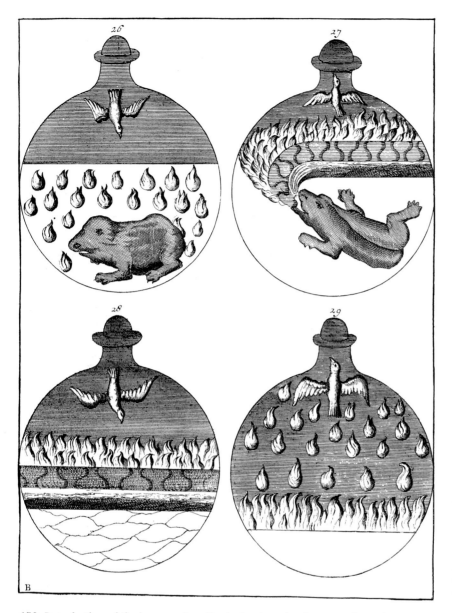

179. *Putrefaction of the homunculus: dissolution into the elements of creation.*

tingeing and permanent. In his artifice, Sorin draws up the first distinction: Take from it by and by, divide the whole thing, rub it frequently until death reigns from the intensity of the blackness, as a dust. This is a great sign in the investigation of which not a few have perished. Then you should discern everything and divide it, and rub it frequently. Morienus: Every body without a soul is found to be dark and obscure. Hermes: We should simultaneously mortify the two quicksilvers. And the same: Take his brain, grind it up with very strong vinegar, or with boy's urine, until it turns black.' (3)

Dissolution of the Philosophers' Son

The departing homunculus and the divided elements of the 'Rosarium' are presented in a variant by Barchusen's plates 26-29 (fig.179), in which the homunculus disappears as a 'bleeding' toad dissolving into its component elements. The 'Crowne of Nature' explains the plates as follows: 'It is necessary first of all to mortify the stone, that is, to draw out the body, soul and spirit. For there is no profit in this art without mortification, but mortification is in the separation of the elements.' (4)

In plate 28 the toad-like homunculus ceases to exist as an individual being; in a kind of reversed growth the creature of rebirth transmutes itself into the four elements of which it is composed: fire blazing in the top of the retort, followed by the heated air and water and by the lunar earth putrefying at the bottom of the vessel. In plate 29 the fire consumes the elements of water and air and transforms them into drops of blood, or drops of distillation. During the whole process the Hermetic bird has continued to fly up and down in the retort.

Chemically, the above process reflects the work of decoction in which the fla-

The 'Black' Extraction of the Soul

Fig.180 shows the seventh woodcut of the 'Rosarium' which renders the 'extraction or impregnation of the soul' (*animae extractio vel impraegnatio*). Out of the decay of the corrupting body the soul in the shape of a homunculus ascends to heaven in order there to receive its 'impregnation.' The motto explains:

*Here is the division of the four elements
As from the lifeless corpse the soul
    ascends. (1)*

The engraved variant (fig.181) amplifies the 'Rosarium' by showing the departure of both the 'soul' and the 'spirit,' leaving the entombed brother and sister in the shape of two angels. (The extraction of the spirit is implicit in fig.180 since the homunculus ascending from the dead body is bisexual and represents the united

soul and spirit.) In the 'Rosarium' text the torments suffered during the 'extraction of the soul' form part of the *iterum mori*—the 'reiterated death' (2)—which belongs to the alchemist's procedure at this stage of the work:

'Hermes, the King, says in his second treatise: Know, my son, that this our stone, which has many names and various colours, is arranged by and composed of the four elements. These we should separate and cut up in their limbs, dividing them into smaller and smaller pieces, mortifying the parts, and changing them into the nature which is in it [the stone]. You must guard the water and the fire dwelling in it, which consists of the four elements, and contain those waters with the permanent water, even though this be no water, but the fiery form of the true water. These should ascend in the vessel, which contains its spirit with its bodies, and thus they should become

ANIMÆ EXTRACTIO VEL
imprægnatio.

180. *Body abandoned by soul and spirit.*

vour or active principle is extracted from a substance by means of boiling. The laboratory worker hereby makes use of the slow dripping of condensation from the vapours rising from a plant or carcass when a moderate flame applied externally is raised and lowered in intensity. While extracting the essence of a substance, these continual drops (depicted in Barchusen's plates 29-35) also serve to bring about the progressive washing or 'ablution' of the substance itself, its putrefying body changing from black to grey and then gradually to white.

Decomposition in a Corrupt Womb

Fig.182 shows the engraved variant of Basil Valentine's emblem of the 'raven's head' *(caput corvi)* (fig.193). Meditating under the sevenfold planetary star of conjunction, the monk in a strange transformation of scenery finds himself surrounded by a rocky desert devoid of life. The mountainous region is darkened by two wind gods spitting tempests and fires into a valley of dying stars. The ascending angels symbolize the extracted soul and spirit, the raven (left foreground) the heavy melancholy of the Benedictine. All that is left is his body, which rests like a piece of lead in the desert sand.

In the original emblem the monk lies putrefying in his philosophical egg (fig. 193). This motif represents a popular variation of the dissolution of the elements and the extraction of the soul and spirit. In the 'Rosinus ad Sarratantam' the 'fetid earth,' or body to be cleansed, appears as the womb of Venus which contaminates the philosophers' son while subjecting him to dissolution: 'As a child in its mother's womb accidentally contracts a weakness and a corruption by reason of the place, although the sperm was clean, the child is nevertheless leprous and unclean because of the corrupt womb.' (5) The notion of the 'dark woman' and the treacherous womb of Luna (or Venus) is a common one in Hermetic treatises on the nigredo. Thus the 'Consilium coniugii' says: 'The moisture of the moon, when she receives his light, slays the sun, and at the birth of the philosophers' child she dies likewise, and at death the two parents yield up their souls to the son, and die and pass away. And the parents are the food of the son.' (6)

Grievous Loss of the Inner Woman

The 'extraction of the soul' reflects the *grief* reaction in depression where the patient behaves as if he had suffered a severe loss, although in most cases no objective loss has occurred, and the nature of the unconscious loss remains obscure to the patient. (7) Alchemy solves this enigma by presenting it as a loss of the 'inner woman,' or anima. Similarly, the

181. Empty mummies in a bridal coffin abandoned by God and men in contempt.

'division of the elements' and the dismemberment of the stone reflect the dissolution in depression of a previously established personality organization. The dangers of this transition, in which 'not a few have perished,' are great to a weakly organized ego. The defective personality organization of the psychotic depressive only just manages to escape the fragmentation and abyss of schizophrenia. Inferi-

or ego structure leads to the catastrophe: in its psychopathological form, the transition of Barchusen's plates 27-28 reflects the complete fragmentation of the personality at a deeply regressed level. Psychiatrists have long since recognized that schizophrenia reaches a depth of regression unequalled in the rest of psychopathology. The disease may be described as *a rapid and malign individuation process.*

182. Leaden depression of a Benedictine suffering death in a valley of fading stars.

183. *'Let a tomb therefore be dug and the woman buried with the dead man.'* (1)

The Graveyard Coitus of Alchemy

The dissolution of the reborn hermaphrodite, homunculus or stone into its composite elements is shown above in its most frightening Hermetic version. In a marriage bed-turned-sarcophagus the king and queen go through a hideous coitus dissolving their bodies while bespattering their grave with their blood. The motto reads: 'The dragon kills the woman, and she kills him, and together they are suffused with their blood.' (2) The engraving illustrates the 59th sermon of the 'Turba,' which gives the dreadful and blurred convulsions of the dying royal couple:

'The philosophers have put to death the woman who kills her husbands. For the womb of that woman is full of poison. So let there be dug a grave for the dragon, and let the woman be buried there together with him, he being chained fast to that woman; and the more he winds and coils himself about her, the more his body, mixed with the limbs of the woman, inclines towards death, and he turns entirely into blood. When the philosophers have seen that he has changed into blood, they leave him in the sun until his softness is consumed and the blood becomes dry. Then the poison appears, and what is hidden takes shape.' (3)

In the nigredo the king appears as the victim of putrefaction, while the queen appears as its agent and perpetrator. In the 'Ludus puerorum' a passage reads: 'So long as the nigredo is manifest, the dark

woman prevails, and that is the first strength of our stone.' (4) This statement is echoed in the 'Liber Alze' which says: 'While the nigredo of the burial endures, the woman rules,' (5) thus referring to the eclipse of the sun or the conjunction with the perilous new moon. Both statements are quotations from Avicenna who says that 'until the albedo the corruption of humidity and the rule of the female is in force.' (6)

The Scorpionic Hermaphrodite

If the female half of the putrefying hermaphrodite appears as a murderous woman, the male half comes out as a scorpion stinging itself with its tail. This is the picture presented by the 'Rosarium' in its description of the coiling embrace of Sol and Luna during the stage

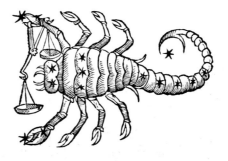

184. *Autumnal equilibrium destroyed.*

of 'conception or putrefaction':

'The philosophical putrefaction is nothing but the corruption or destruction of bodies; for as soon as one form has been destroyed, nature introduces another form in its stead which is both better and more subtle (7) . . . The dragon dies not, except with his brother and sister, and not with one of them but with both of them; the brother is Sol, the sister is Luna (8) . . . The dragon is born in the nigredo and feeds upon its Mercurius and slays itself (9) . . . The living Mercurius and the imperfect bodies converted into Sol and Luna are called the Scorpion, that is, venom; for it slays itself and brings itself back to life.' (10) In an ensuing passage, the 'Rosarium' refers to the Scorpion as the 'noble body which moves from lord to lord, in the beginning whereof is wretchedness with vinegar, but in the end joy with happiness.' (11)

Scorpio: the Cemetary of the Zodiac

The eighth sign of the Zodiac is a fixed, watery sign ruled by Mars and covering the period from October 24 to November 22. Its wintry, putrefying work destroys the autumnal equilibrium of the Scales. The Scorpion is an apt astrological symbol of such seasonal transition since it is the only creature that can kill itself by a sting from its own tail. The sinister and suicidal implications of Scorpio have led one noted astrologist to describe the sign as the 'cemetary of the Zodiac' (Barbault). (12)

There is a remarkable quality hidden in the disruptive activities of the Scorpion: they signify destruction for the purpose of a new birth. In killing itself, the Scorpion releases the powers of regeneration in the same way as winter's corrosive work may be said to prepare the ground for the coming of spring. The watery quality of Scorpio is characterized by the 'Rosarium' as the 'fiery form of the true water' (p.104) because it effects a transformation process of unparalleled intensity. Thus, the most murderous sign is also the most fecund, just as the energies heating the Scorpion are the most awe-inspiring of the universal opposites: Eros and Thanatos, love and hate, birth and death.

In order to carry out its difficult task of decomposition the Scorpion is endowed with the primal energies of creation. Harnessed to the chariot of destruction, these energies appear in a strange, inverted form, as an involutional creation, a reversed evolution, a 'putrefaction or conception.' Moving scorpion-like, the opposites shift their energies and goals: eroticism is inversed by aiming at death, just as death is inversed by aiming at conception and birth. This specific constellation of the opposites accounts for the magic and inscrutable depths of the Scorpion, which is simultaneously a fixed and

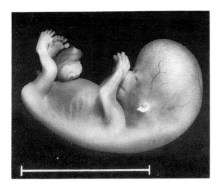

185. At the end of the second month, the embryo (a Greek word meaning to swell) is technically called a fetus (a Latin word meaning young one). The key to this transition is the formation of the first real bone cells replacing the cartilage. The 56-day-old creature shown above measures 37 mm. (white lines indicate relative length of specimens). It depicts the fetus in its incipient stage where beginning bone formation coincides with the essential completion of its body structure.

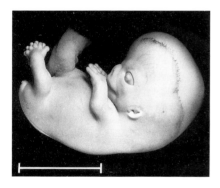

186. The photo shows the 44-day-old embryo, 23 mm. long and endowed with a complete, if boneless, skeleton fashioned of cartilage. The embryo possesses the complex, if miniature, structure of the adult brain. Fig.187 shows the 40-day-old embryo, 19 mm. long. On each side of its bulbous head an eye is forming, just as its mouth cavity is beginning to draw into proper shape. Through its delicate skin the outlines of its brain can be dimly seen, and, looming between the rudimentary hands and arms, its enormous heart.

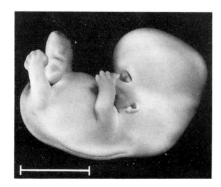

187. Play-back of embryonic evolution.

a watery, a positive and a negative, a divine and an infernal sign. A symbol of involutional melancholia and the change of life *(Lebenswende),* Scorpio describes the span of man's years which lies under the double law of death and inner regeneration.

The Scorpio personality is heavy, melancholy, strongly self-centred and predominantly of an introverted disposition. Endowed with enormous stamina and tenacity, Scorpio embodies the principle of the struggle for survival. Due to its passionate and complex character and its intuitive grasp of the secrets of life and death, the Scorpio personality has great personal magnetism and a considerable contemporary effect impossible to explain at a rational level. Scorpio contains more love and more death than all the other signs of the Zodiac combined; hence the Scorpio personality has within itself the latent possibilities of releasing either the powers of supreme good or supreme evil, or both.

Nigredo: from Fetus to Embryo

The nigredo reflects the unconscious transformation of the libido when performing the regressive transition *from fetus to embryo.* Only such involution accounts for the Hermetic mystery of 'putrefaction or conception.' The reversed development of the eye-organ, finally disappearing in the 30-day-old embryo, explains the *nigrum nigrius nigro.* The reversed development of the brain, rapidly 'dwindling' into increasingly primitive forms, explains the 'turning black' of the alchemist's brain. The dismemberment of the king reflects the reversed growth of the embryo's nose, lips, ears, arms, legs, fingers and toes—all dissolving into jelly-like substances. The putrefying hermaphrodite's blood-bespattered grave reflects the regressive 'growth' of the heart in the early embryo, which is bathed in an orgy of blood rushing through its veins at a speed of four miles per hour in order to ensure its prodigious growth. The 'reversal' of this blood stream fully accounts for the coiling mysteries of the bleeding dragon 'slaying itself and bringing itself back to life . . . destroying one form and introducing another in its stead, better and more subtle.'

In the nigredo, the alchemist recapitulates not only the earlier phases of his individual development but also the earlier phases of evolutionary development. By recapitulating his ontogony he recapitulates at the same time his phylogeny since ancestral plans of structure are retained in human embryonic development. In such manner the 'blackened' alchemist conquers the wheel of births, which is slowly turned back to its first beginning by the reversed movement of the philosophical wheel.

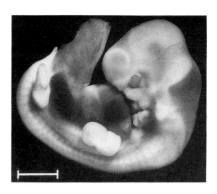

188. The 34-day-old embryo, measuring 11.6 mm. The brain takes up about one third of the body's total volume and is, on this day, one-fourth larger than it was two days earlier. The developing eyes are dark for the first time because pigment has just formed in the retina. The beginning stumps of arms and legs stand out darkly; the spine ends in the pointed tail. The larger appendage just above the tail is the umbilical cord, here broken off. No bone has yet formed, only cartilage.

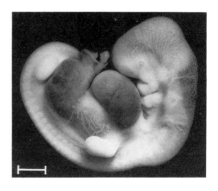

189. The 31-day-old embryo, 7.8 mm. long. Under the bulging forehead with its beginning eye formation jaw-ridges appear, suggestive of gill slits. Below the head, the embryo's heart forms a large bulge which in proportion to its body is nine times as large as the adult's heart. Fig.190 shows the 30-day-old embryo, 7.3 mm. long. The incomplete creature has no eyes, no nose, no mouth and no ears. It houses only a primitive brain with primitive functions. The arms and legs are tiny knobs on the sides of the body.

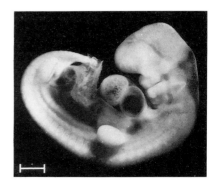

190. Scorpionic descent into nature.

In the illustration:

Caput Putre- | Corvi
Philo- | factio
| fophorum.

Caput | Corvi
et lac | Virginis
dealba | tur

Caput | Corvi
Separatio | animæ
à | corpore.

Caput | Corvi
totalis | feparatio
animæ | à corpore.

191. The raven's reign in a vessel of subterranean horrors and subhuman sufferings.

The 'raven's head' (*caput corvi*) is a famous variant of the operation performed on the alchemist in the nigredo and described by the 'Rosarium': 'Take his brain, grind it up with very strong vinegar, or with boy's urine, until it turns black (4) . . . And know that the head of the art is the raven who flies without wings in the blackness of the night and the brightness of the day; in the bitterness that is in its throat the colouring will be found.' (5)

Putrefaction in the Philosophers' Egg

Fig.193 shows Basil Valentine's vision of the 'black raven' of which fig.182 represented the engraved variant. Sick and aging, the Benedictine monk lies putrefying in his philosophical egg while the soul and spirit depart from his emaciated body in the shape of two homunculi, or angels. In a lucid gesture, the monk's hands cover his secret parts on which the raven descends. Above him, the sevenfold planetary star of conjunction is obscured by the tempests spat out by the gods of fire and air. In the accompanying verse (6) the Benedictine groans:

A weakling babe, a greybeard old,
Surnamed the Dragon: me they hold
In darkest dungeon languishing
That I may be reborn a king.

And that I may enrich my kin,
I am now an ever-changing villain.
Afterwards, again all human beings
Will partake of the kingdom's blessings.

A fiery sword makes me to smart,
Death gnaws my flesh and bones apart.
My soul and spirit fast are sinking,
And leave a poison, black and stinking.

To a black raven am I akin,
Such be the wages of all sin.
In deepest dust I lie alone,
O that the Three would make the One!

O soul, O spirit with me stay,
That I may greet the light of day.
Hero of peace, come forth from me,
For him the world would like to see!

Sulphur, salt and mercury pure
Alone my body holds, for sure,
These must rightly now be sublimated,
Distilled and also separated.

Also make a restless putrefaction,
And once again a mild coagulation.
Also learn the art of fixation
In order not to err in thy operation.

Only dissolve and coagulate me long,
Wash and cook me, then you won't
go wrong.
And so by roasting draw the foulness,
As many a philosopher has been advised.

The Mortal Terror of the Raven's Head

The four 'Pandora' plates reproduced in fig.191 continue the opus by showing the nigredo as the 'raven's head and the philosophers' putrefaction' (see previous plates in fig.157). The text explains: 'The raven's head: the black and stinking earth of the philosophers. Worms appear which eat or devour one another. The crushing or destruction of one is the conception of the other. Now the earth lies at the bottom of the vessel and is completely dissolved or extinguished in water as before.' (1) The second plate shows the winged dragon identified with the 'raven's head and the virgin's milk which whitens.' The text amplifies: 'He who can marry a woman and make her pregnant, kill the bodies of conception and make them live, introduce or infuse a light and cleanse the face of blackness and darkness, he will become of great honour.' (2) The 'cleansing' work of the 'virgin's milk' is further identified with the scorpionic movement of the 'dragon [who] will eat his wings and produce many and various colours; for he will move many times and in many ways from one colour to the next, until he comes to the pure white.' (3) The third plate presents the 'raven's head and the separation of the soul from the body.' The fourth plate shows the 'raven's head and the total separation of the soul from the body.' The winged monster has disappeared and transformed itself into dragon's blood, abluting or 'whitening' the festering body.

The Blood-Bath of the Salamander

The gory Scorpio symbolism of fig.183 and the blood flowing from the dying toad in Barchusen's plates 26-27 (fig.179) have a number of parallels in alchemy. One is the bleeding Christ, another the bleeding king of the 'Cantilena,' in which 'rank poison issues from the dying man' after his conjunction with the queen (p.134). Another variant is the bleeding salamander, reproduced in fig.192 from the 'Book of Lambspring.' The animal frolicking in the fire (fig.128) is finally caught and killed by the alchemist, who brings about its wondrous dissolution:

In all fables we are told
That the salamander is born in the fire;
In the fire it has that food and life
Which nature herself has assigned to it.
It dwells in a great mountain
Which is encompassed by many flames,
And one of these is ever smaller
*   than another—*
Herein the salamander bathes.
The third is greater, the fourth brighter
*   than the rest—*
In all this the salamander washes,
*   and is purified.*
Then he hies him to his cave,
But on the way is caught and pierced
So that it dies, and yields up its life
*   with its blood.*
But this, too, happens for its good:
For from its blood it wins immortal life,
And then death has no more power
*   over it.*
Its blood is the most precious medicine
*   upon earth,*
The same has not its like in the world.
For this blood drives away all disease
In the bodies of metals,
Of men, and of beasts.
From it the sages derive their science,
For through it the sages attain
*   the heavenly gift,*
Which is called the philosophers' stone,
Possessing the power of the whole world.
This gift the sages impart to us with
*   loving hearts*
That we may remember them for ever. (7)

192. Piercing the animal of rebirth.

193. Trapped in the womb: the adept expiring in his putrefying egg, or fetid vessel.

The Raven of Suicidal Depression

The mortal melancholy of the 'raven's head' makes the Hermetic image a transparent symbol of *depressive suicide*. In severe depression the ego is sucked by a scorpionic self, to which it responds in a violent and murderous way. Freud emphasized that suicide is homicide turned against the self, the ultimate act of self-punishment and self-destruction. In suicide the self becomes a secretly hated object, or the unconscious goal of murderous aggression.

The life-and-death struggle of the psychotic depressive, his remarkable body sensations, and the disappearance of his defence mechanisms reflect a much deeper regression than that of paranoid reactions; there, denial of one's own fear and hatred is buttressed by projection onto the environment. The psychotic depressive is unable to project his internal hate and fear, his ego and its defences having been reduced to 'embryonic' proportions. The only 'defence' in psychotic depression appears to be either suicide or a passive entrance into the darkness, i.e., involuntary suffering of the depressive state of dying.

In all normal experiences of middle age depression, the ego may face the negative moods of the anima and the critical nature of the self with all defences at its disposal, repression and sublimation among the first. In addition, the ego commands a strange kind of 'defence,' which is more in the nature of an offensive: a conscious acceptance of the state of depression as something positive to be endured. Such an attitude is expressed by the rebis and the dragon humbly submitting themselves to death by fire. 'Endure to die and not to perish' groans the burning dragon of 'Mercurius triumphans' (8) in response to the challenge of the nigredo. Such a reaction comes from the redeeming insight that the hermaphrodite shares its agonizing experience with Mercurius philosophorum; not only the ego but also the self suffers transformation in the black fire of depression.

The Art of Dying with Life

'From the middle of life onward, only he remains vitally alive who is ready to die with life. For in the secret hour of life's midday the parabola is reversed, death is born. The second half of life does not signify ascent, unfolding, increase, exuberance, but death, since the end is its goal. The negation of life's fulfilment is synonymous with the refusal to accept its ending. Both mean not wanting to live; not wanting to live is identical with not wanting to die. Waxing and waning make one curve.'

C.G.Jung. (9)

194.

Albedo: the 'Whitening' Work of Ablution

Fig.194 shows the lifeless hermaphrodite stretched out on its bier under the sign of the new moon and the eclipsed sun. The motto reads: 'The hermaphrodite, lying in darkness like a dead creature, is in need of the fire.' (1) As evidenced by the reference to Bonellus in the text, the engraving illustrates the 32nd sermon of the 'Turba,' which reads:

'Bonellus: . . . But, sons of the doctrine, that thing will need fire, until the spirit of its body is changed and is sent away through the nights, like a man in his grave, and becomes dust. When this has happened, God will give back to it its soul and its spirit and, with all infirmity removed, that thing is strengthened and improved after its corruption, as man becomes stronger after the resurrection and younger than he was in this world. Therefore it behoves you, O ye sons of the doctrine, to consume that thing with fire boldly until it shall become ashes. And know that you have mixed it excellently well, because those ashes receive the spirit and are imbued with that humour until it assumes a fairer colour than it previously possessed. Consider, therefore, O ye sons of the doctrine, that artists are unable to paint with their own tinctures until they convert them into powder. Similarly, the philosophers cannot compose the medicines for the sick until they turn them into powder, cooking some of them to ashes, while others they grind with their hands. It is the same with those who compose the images of marble. But if you understand what has already been said, you will know that I speak the truth, and hence I have ordered you to burn up the body and turn it into ashes.' (2)

Speaking in the same vein, the 'Rosarium' admonishes the adepts of the 'raven's head': 'The unclean body must be cooked and calcined until it reaches the whiteness (3) . . . [therefore] burn in water and wash in fire, cook and cook again, moisten and coagulate all the time, kill the living and resuscitate the dead. Do this through the sevenfold circulation and you will truly have what you seek.' (4)

The washing or 'ablution' now undertaken inaugurates a new phase of the opus: the stage known as the *albedo* ('whiteness'), in which the alchemist's work is devoted to the 'dealbation' of the black, impure body. Fig.196 shows a variant of this motif with the bath of Naaman the Syrian in the river Jordan. Transformed by the coniunctio into a hermaphrodite-body, the alchemical leper prepares for a bath, which the text of the engraving describes as 'a washing by fire and a burning by water.' (5)

The Washerwomen's Work

Another variant of this motif is the washerwomen's work depicted in fig.195. The text explains their action as part of the 'lunar work' *(opus lunare),* which consists in abluting and whitening for 150 days: 'Dealbate the whole and the darkness will flee from it.' (6) Fig.197 illustrates a famous dictum of the albedo: 'Go to the woman who washes her sheets and do as she does.' (7) The text continues:

195. Washing the foul clothes of rebirth in the sevenfold circulation or distillation.

'This is the art of the women which they have learnt from nature herself; for we see that the bones of the animals, which in the beginning are black and squalid, when exposed to air become completely white as they are repeatedly drenched by rain and again dried by the sun's heat, as stated by Isaac [Hollandus]. It is in the same way with the philosophical work: whenever there have been crudities and excrements they have been purged and destroyed by being suffused with its water, and the body has been led back to the greatest clarity and perfection.' (8)

The 'Rosarium' concludes its description of the nigredo on a similar note: 'If you will not clean the impure body and make it white and give back to it its soul, you will have accomplished nothing in this magistery.' (9)

The Sevenfold Circulation or Distillation

In the albedo the *virgin* and the *moon* appear as the great alchemical symbols of sublimation. The polluted soul extracted and purified in heaven gradually acquires the features of the heavenly Virgin, just as the perilous new-moon by means of ablution is transformed into the glittering half-moon, then into the three quarters phase and finally into the full moon of the 'white' rebirth. Chemically, this act signifies the production of silver by means of a cleansing and sublimation of the impure metals, frequently appearing as those of tin or lead.

This dual aspect of the *ablutio* as a chemical, yet mental, act of purification is expressed by the two sources of fig. 196. One is the 'Clangor buccinae,' which says: 'Our metal has a dropsical body, just as Naaman, the Syrian, has a leprous body, and therefore it seeks a curing bath in the river Jordan seven times, that it may be cleansed from its innate suffering and corruption. Then you have the non-combustible sulphur and arsenic of which the alchemists may make use, and with which they make silver perfect. Gratianus says: So make Latona white.' (10) ('The lato is the unclean body' says the 'Rosinus ad Sarratantem.') (11)

The second source is a passage in the 'Aurora consurgens' which reads: 'Doth not the Scripture say: Wash yourselves in it and be clean. And to Naaman, the Syrian, was it said: Go and wash seven times in the Jordan and thou shalt be clean. For there is one baptism for the ablution of sins as faith and the prophet testify. He that hath ears to hear, let him hear what the holy spirit of the doctrine saith to the sons of the discipline concerning the virtues of the sevenfold spirit, whereby all the Scripture is fulfilled, which the philosophers set forth in these words: Distil seven times and thou hast

196. Cleansing the leprous body of rebirth in a biblical river abluting the sins of men.

set it apart from the corrupting humidity.' (12)

On the following pages we shall further investigate the 'ablution or purification' of the continued work. Rendered in detail by Barchusen's plates 28-46 (figs.179, 198, 206, 210, 217, 228), the work precisely assumes the form of the 'sevenfold circulation' mentioned by the 'Rosarium.' A variant is the 'sevenfold bath' of Naaman the leper, inspired by the 'virtues of the sevenfold spirit of distillation.'

197. The 'whitening' work: washing by means of the fiery water of the philosophers.

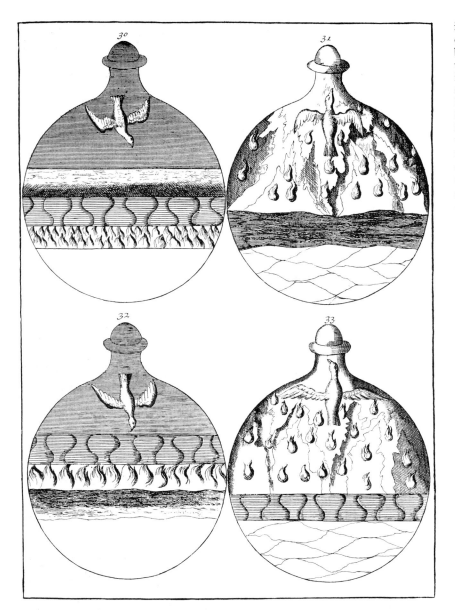

198. Circular distillation of the elements in a vessel of ablution and sublimation.

The Royal Ablution or Purification

Fig.199 shows the eighth woodcut of the 'Rosarium' and fig.201 its engraved variant. 'Ablution or purification' *(ablutio vel mundificatio)* reads the title of the woodcut, while its motto explains:

Here falls the heavenly dew, to lave
The soiled black body in the grave. (1)

After the attainment of the nadir of the nigredo, the insufferable draught of depression is relieved by the heavenly rain or 'philosophical humidity . . . falling as clear as a tear,' as the 'Rosarium' says. (2) While abluting the entombed, incestuous body, the rain also fertilizes the earth and the royal mummy, which begins to revive and impregnate itself. The swelling womb in fig.201 reveals the incipient pregnancy of the brother-sister pair and their germinating rebirth. Even if the

king and queen are still chained to their sarcophagus and paralyzed by its leaden depression, they have gained the hope of resurrection and the promise of a new life. The 'Rosarium' explains:

'But the water I have spoken of is a thing that comes down from heaven, and the earth's humidity absorbs it, and the water of heaven is retained with the water of the earth, and the water of the earth honours that water with its lowliness and its sand, and water consorts with water, and water will hold fast to water, and Albira is whitened with Astuna.* Hermes: The spirit does not enter

* The two words derive from a passage in Senior: 'And water consorts with water, and water will hold fast to water, Alkia to Alkia, and Alkia is whitened with Astua.' (3) In Arabic *al-kiyan* signifies the life principle or libido, while Astua in the original Arabian text appears as a synonym for Alkia. The meaning is probably that nature 'whitens' or heals nature.

into any body unless it is pure. Alphidius: Take the whiteness and dismiss the blackness. Democritus: Purify the tin with the excellent ablution, extract from it its blackness and obscurity and it will show its whiteness. In the work of Sorin: Dissolve with a white fire until it looks like a naked sword, and make by whitening the body white as snow. Rasis: When the water is mixed with the metal, it makes it white inside. This whitening is called by some impregnation since the earth is made white; for when the water governs, the earth grows and multiplies, and by the augmentation the new germs are generated. Alphidius: Therefore you must ablute the black earth and whiten with the hot fire. And therefore says Hali: Take that which descends to the bottom of the vessel and ablute it with a hot fire until it is delivered of its blackness and thickness; make the additional humidity depart from it until it becomes an exceeding white chalk in which there will be no spots. For then the earth is ample and purified to receive the soul . . . . Therefore Morienus says: This earth putrifies and purifies with its own water; when this has been purified, the whole magistery is directed by the help of God.' (4)

Ablution through Circular Distillation

Fig.198 shows the 'Rosarium's work of ablution varied by Barchusen's plates 30-33. In plate 30 the separated layers of water, air, fire and earth are subjected to renewed processes of sublimation under the aegis of the fluttering Hermes bird. In plate 31 the upper layers of water and air are vaporized by fire and turned into fiery blood drops or drops of milk abluting the fetid water and putrefying earth at the bottom of the vessel. Gradually the drops transmute themselves into a 'heavenly dew,' producing the first streaks of white in the blackened vessel.

ABLVTIO VEL
Mundificatio

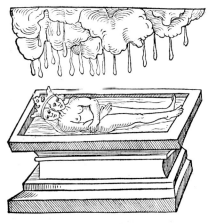

199. Cleansing the black body.

In plate 32 the 'sevenfold circulation' or distillation begins again with a corrupting arcane substance releasing new elemental layers to be purged and sublimated. In plate 33 the extracted elements of fire and water descend as fiery drops of dew to ablute the elements of air and earth at the bottom.

The King's Bloody Sweat Bath

A popular motif of the extraction of the 'corrupting humidity' from the putrefying body is the king perspiring in his 'sweat bath' (laconicum). A variant of the 'Allegory of Merlin,' fig. 200 shows King Duenech cooking in his laconicum while attempting to extract the black bile from his body. The text informs us that the 'king is affected by melancholy or black bile, and for this reason regarded by all other monarchs as less in authority and power, for he is plagued by the moroseness of Saturn and by the choler or rage of Mars. He himself wants either to die or be cured, if that were possible.' (5)

The situation gives the aftermath of the 'soul's extraction' and shows the king in his narrow prison, torn between hope and despair and, finally, in his fear and desperation, breaking out in a sweat of blood.

The identity of the king's bloody sweat and the falling dew of ablution is confirmed by the 'Epistola ad Hermannum': 'Then the most perfect body is taken and applied to the fire of the philosophers; then . . . that body becomes moist and gives forth a kind of bloody sweat after the putrefaction and mortification, that is, a heavenly dew, and this dew is called the mercury of the philosophers, or the permanent water.' (7)

The coincidence of the king's bloody sweat and the 'heavenly dew' testifies to the ambiguous nature of the fierce transformation raging in the wake of the coniunctio: a black whitening, a putrefying conception, a dying rebirth. Says the 'Turba': 'The dew is joined to him who is wounded and given over to death, and the more days that pass, the more it congeals without burning. For the sun cooks him and the fire congeals him and powerful in war it [the sun] lets the fire conquer the earth, after having removed the infirmity.' * (8)

* The Arabian 'Vision of Arisleus,' the model of the Rosarium's coniunctio sive coitus, is probably also of the motif of the king in his sweat bath. In the short treatise, the philosopher Arisleus tells the convent about his dream of Thabritius (Gabricus) and Beya, the children of the 'King of the Sea.' In the latter's kingdom nothing prospers and nothing is begotten because like is mixed with like. In order to redeem his sterile realms, the king follows the advice of his philosophers and mates Thabritius with Beya, his two children whom he has hatched in his brain (fig. 136). When the incestuous con-

200. 'The heat of the baths in which the stone sweats when it begins to dissolve.' (6)

iunctio ends in the death of Thabritius, the king imprisons Arisleus and his companions together with the dead brother-sister pair in a triple glass house under the sea: 'Here we suffered the darkness of the waves, the intense heat of summer, and the storms of the sea, something we had never experienced before.

Completely exhausted, we then saw you, O master, in a dream. We implored you to send us help through your pupil Horfoltus, the originator of nourishment. This being granted, we rejoiced and sent this message to the king: Behold, your son who had been doomed to death lives.' (9) (Fig. 201.)

201. Miraculous effect of the heavenly dew: incipient pregnancy of an abluted corpse.

dragon with his bellows and phial, the medicine of which he pours into the dragon's throat. The text stresses the efficacy of the alchemist's fire, and indicates that a turning point in the darkness has been attained: 'Senior says: That heat turns every black thing white and every white thing red. So, as water bleaches, fire gives off light and also colour to the subtilized earth, which appears like a ruby through the tingeing spirit she receives from the force of the fire, thus causing Socrates to say: A wondrous light shall be seen in the darkness.' (3)

Suffering in the Furnace of the Cross

The 'Splendor solis' paintings reproduced on these pages symbolize the transition from a passive suffering of depression to an active entry into the depression. Such a transition from bitterness to acceptance is apparent in many alchemical documents on the nigredo. The Allegory of Duenech stresses the protagonist's embittered, martian reactions—his 'choler and rage'—at his torturing experience. The account given in the 'Aquarium sapientum' of the same experience emphasizes the king's Christian reactions to the nigredo and presents quite a different picture of the alchemist dissolving in his sweat bath:

'The old nature is destroyed, dissolved, decomposed, and, in a longer or shorter period of time, transmuted into something else. Such a man is so well digested and melted in the fire of affliction that he despairs of his own strength and looks for help and comfort to the mercy of God alone. In this furnace of the cross, man, like the earthly gold, attains to the true black raven's head; that is, he is utterly disfigured and is held in derision by the world, and this not only for forty days and nights, or years, but often for the whole duration of his life; so much so that he experiences more heartache in in his life than comfort and joy, and more sadness than pleasure. And through this spiritual death his soul is taken from him, and lifted up on high; while his body is still upon earth, his spirit and heart are already in his eternal Fatherland; and all his actions have a heavenly source, and seem no longer to belong to this earth. For he lives no longer according to the flesh, but according to the

202. Whitening the black body in a hot cauldron tended by the artifex of the albedo.

Growing Light in the Darkness

Fig. 202 shows the eleventh painting of the 'Splendor solis,' in which the Saturnine alchemist in his cauldron is subjected to 'ablution or purification.' A fellow alchemist applies the bellows to the fire while a dove descends on the alchemist's head, proof that the whitening work has been initiated. The dealbation of the arcane substance is sometimes compared by the adepts to the whitening of lead, or Saturn, who represents the metal. 'Throwing snow in Saturn's black face'

(1) is an alchemical synonym for the work of whitening. The text reads: 'Ovid, the old Roman, wrote to the same end when he mentioned an ancient sage who desired to rejuvenate himself and got the message: He should allow himself to be cut to pieces and decoct to a perfect decoction, and then his limbs would reunite and again be renewed in plenty of strength.' (2)

Fig. 205 shows the twelfth painting of the 'Splendor solis,' in which the vessel develops a little boy actively fighting the

203. The primal parents killing their son.

spirit, not in the unfruitful works of darkness, but in the light and in the day—in works that stand the test of fire.

'This separation of body and soul is brought about by a spiritual dying. For as the dissolution of body and soul is performed in the regenerated gold, where body and soul are separated from one another, and yet remain close together in the same phial, the soul daily refreshing the body from above and preserving it from final destruction, until a set time: so the decaying and half-dead bodily part of man is not entirely deserted by its soul in the furnace of the cross, but is refreshed by the spirit from above with heavenly dew, and fed and preserved with divine nectar. (For our temporal death, which is the wages of sin, is not a real death, but only a natural and gentle severing of body and soul.) The indissoluble union and conjunction of the spirit of God, and the soul of the Christian, are a real and abiding fact. And here again we have an analogy to the sevenfold ascending and descending of the soul in the chemical process . . . While the digestion of the dead spiritual body in man goes forward, there may be seen (as in the chemical process) many variegated colours and signs, that is, all manner of sufferings, afflictions, and tribulations, including the ceaseless assaults of the Devil, the world, and the flesh. But all these signs are of good omen, since they show that such a man will at length reach the desired goal.' (4)

The Black Spirit Torturing the Bodies

The four medals reproduced in figs. 203-204 summarize the nigredo and its subsequent ablution. In the first medal of fig.203 the philosophers' son is pierced by his spouse after their union. The inscription explains: 'When the son has slept with his mother, she kills him with the stroke of a viper.' In the second medal the son is killed and dismembered by his father, whom the alchemists compare to Saturn or the *spiritus niger*. The inscription reads: 'That which was the cause of thy life is also the cause of thy death.' The first medal of fig.204 shows the alchemist in his sweat bath, invested with the raven's hood, or the emblem of Saturn. The inscription explains: 'Saturn is the planet of death; look, this one has brought a black mantle.'

204. The hot vessel of the black raven.

205. The boy of 'conception' fighting with his medicine the dragon of 'putrefaction.'

Saturn is the Hermetic symbol of transformation through suffering and torture. In the 'Turba' a celebrated passage runs: 'Take the old black spirit and destroy and torture with it the bodies until they are changed.' (5) In the 18th sermon of the treatise, Mundus questions the number of adepts capable of passing the crucial test of alchemy: 'How many there be who search out these applications and [even] find some, but yet cannot endure the torments.' (6)

The second medal of fig.204 shows the alchemist struggling with the winged dragon in the belly of the glowing vessel. The scorpionic nature of the battle is witnessed by the inscription: 'Concep-

tion and engagement take place in the putrefaction, and the generation of the engendered takes place in the spring.'

The 'Whitening' of Depressive Blackness

The slow whitening of the black body described by the 'ablution or purification' is not difficult to translate into psychodynamic terms: it describes the gradual 'whitening' of the 'black' state of melancholia, that is, the slow 'lifting' of the intolerable burden of depression. Clinically, this development is confirmed by the fact that nearly all depressives ultimately recover.

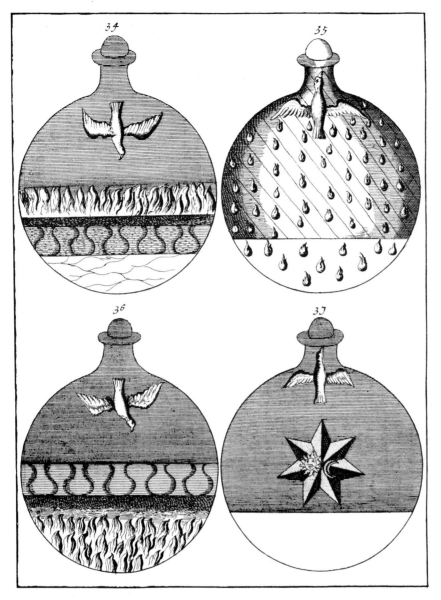

206. The heart's blood abluting a vessel illuminated by the embryonic star of rebirth.

Life's Blood Palpitating Anew

If suicide can be avoided during depression, most people manage to work out their depression, recover their composure and return to their previous work. Why the blackness of depression gradually 'whitens,' nobody knows exactly; one may only observe the signs of improvement which occur after the depression has struck rock bottom. It is this turning point which is heralded by the falling dew and the rain, or tears, of the *ablutio:* deep down in the depressive state there is the profoundly moving feeling that something is breaking through which in due time will end the depression. This experience is beautifully described by the symbolism of these pages.

In Barchusen's plates 34-37 (fig.206) the fire keeps heating and vaporizing the impure contents of the vessel, while the restless Hermes bird assists in the work of sublimation. Releasing a new outflow of earth, air, water and fire in plate 34, the vessel in plate 35 appears to be soaked with a shower of fiery blood drops composed of the transformed elements. By now the 'sevenfold circulation' has gathered momentum so that the drops of condensation fall like a shower of rain from heaven.

In plate 36 new elemental layers arise from the bubbling solution to be purged and refined. As the drops of condensation wash the polluted vessel, the whitening process attains the dynamic stage in plate 37: the sevenfold planetary star (without the planets) lights up the vessel with a miniature sun and moon enclosed. The 'Crowne of Nature' explains the plate as rendering the 'preparative conjunction of the second ferment with . . . the imperfect bodies' of Sol and Luna. (1) Below the star of miniature conjunc-

tion appears the whitened substance of dealbation, alternately described by the 'Rosarium' as the work of calcination or sublimation:

'The alchemical chalk is said to have life in it, for the philosophers have sought to mortify their imperfect life and give back to it eternal life (2) . . . Hermes says: Azoth and fire cleanse the Lato and remove the blackness. Therefore the philosopher writes: Whiten the Lato and rend the books lest your hearts be rent asunder. For this is the synthesis of the wise and the third part of the whole opus. Join therefore, as is said in the Turba,* the dry to the moist, the black earth with its water, and cook till it whitens. In this manner you will have the essence of water and earth, having whitened the earth with water: but that whiteness is called air.' (4)

Abluting the Lato, or Impure Body

Part of the above passage is illustrated in fig.208, in which the Lato is personified as the impure mother of Sol and Luna. She is washed by the alchemist to the left, who sprinkles the heavenly dew, or the water of baptism, on her polluted body. Lato's sun-and-moon children correspond with the miniature sun and moon enclosed in the sevenfold star of plate 37, another symbol of the 'quickening womb' of the entombed hermaphrodite (fig.201). Other images of the turning of the 'black' tide are reproduced in fig.207.

The first medal shows the ablution of the black body of the Moor, or Ethiopian. He appears in his half-washed state with a miniature sun and moon burning in the candles inside his transparent body. The inscription reads: 'We have removed the blackness with salt, anatron and almizadir, and we have fixed the whiteness with borrezae.' The second medal shows a woman alchemist at a lion-legged table studying an alchemical treatise. She is illuminated by the ray of divine wisdom, which is translated by the inscription: 'Whiten the Lato and rend the books lest your hearts be rent asunder.' This often repeated quotation— illustrated by the alchemist to the right in fig.208—is derived from the Arabian author Morienus, who attributes the

* 'Therefore mix the dry with the moist, which are earth and water, and cook them with fire and air, whence spirit and soul are dried out.' (3)

207. Rending books instead of hearts.

208. *Book-rending philosophers plumbing a world of primal emotion, primal heart.*

enigmatic saying to the philosopher Elbo Interfector.

Since the heavenly dew is also called the 'eye-water of the philosophers' *(col- lyrium philosophorum),* (5) the 'ablution or purification' expresses the alchemist's surrender to a world of tears (=emotion) gradually replacing a world of books. The intellectual understanding now 'rent a- sunder' instead of the alchemist's heart reveals the upwelling of emotion and the moistening of the 'dryness' of depression by the adept's dawning understanding— at an emotional level—of the meaning and purpose of his depression. Signifi- cantly, the 'Rosarium' calls its heavenly dew the 'water of wisdom' *(aqua sapi- entiae).* (6)

Reviving a Cross-Road in Evolution

If we attempt to unravel the uncon- scious processes underlying the compli- cated symbolism of 'ablution or purifi- cation,' we have to seek the answer in some crucial psychobiological act of transformation. If the sevenfold planeta- ry star of solar and lunar conjunction in fig.154 symbolizes the formation of the whole fetus or the fetal personality by the end of the second month, the incom- plete sevenfold star of miniature solar and lunar conjunction may be interpret- ed as symbolizing the formation of the *whole embryo or the embryonic persona- lity by the end of the first month.* This

event coincides with the first beatings of the primitive heart and the first forma- tion of the primitive brain, two events which are probably symbolized by plates 35 and 37.

A remarkable LSD vision reported by Masters and Houston sheds light on the obscure symbolism of these pages. Since the miniature sun depicted in Barchu- sen's plate 37 represents the first image of the sun (=spirit, consciousness) in his great series of the opus (if this is read backwards), we may correlate plate 37 with the numinous LSD experience of 'S.' His vision reflects the first embryo- nic differentiation between conscious and unconscious, Sol and Luna, spiritus and anima; it even illuminates the ob- scure saying of Elbo Interfector by de- scribing the primacy of feeling over think- ing in an ego plumbing an archaic, pre- conscious world of primal emotion, pri- mal instinct, primal heart:

'Suddenly, as S describes his ascent up the evolutionary process, S becomes ex- tremely excited. His whole demeanor changes from that of a curious observer to the manner of one experiencing an im- portant revelation. Slamming his fist against his palm he reports with mount- ing excitement that 'Something cuts across the Evolutionary process at this point! Something blasts into it! Cuts it clean in two! Changes its course!' The severed chain snaps back together quick- ly, but although the evolutionary process is deflected only slightly, the conse-

quences are enormous. 'Had this not happened man would have evolved into just another kind of animal!' . . .

'S continues that man possesses two distinct varieties of consciousness. One is the higher consciousness that came into being at the time when the alien blast cut through evolution. The other, primitive consciousness had its origins much ear- lier and is capable only of feeling and a very low order of intellection. The alien blast into matter initiated a process whereby the higher consciousness evolv- ed along with but did not extinguish the lower, primitive consciousness. The force that struck into the pre-established evo- lutionary animal pattern was God or Spirit. This Higher Force burst in like a bullet. It imposed itself upon the crea- tion of the 'other, earlier God-Force' that had conceived of and created the ma- terial world . . . The blast touches off a profound reaction in matter and in the animal consciousness. These are infused by the *other,* but not wholly conquered by it. 'Between the lines of silver that surge through the body of matter the chunks of meat remain.' S is able to move up and down the evolutionary chain and to pass back beyond the point when the higher consciousness evolved. He descends down his physiological past to a level that seems to be of feeling alone and remarks that 'the older con- sciousness is still there in our bodies. The new consciousness is spirit and must be of a different order since it has cut into the evolutionary process and redirected it from outside of the process' . . . He regarded this phase of his experience as being 'not a religious one in any conven- tional sense, or any kind of revelation from God, but a message probably from the unconscious." (7)

209. *The two upper bulges of the incipi- ent brain (end of first month) will be- come the hemispheres of the forebrain.*

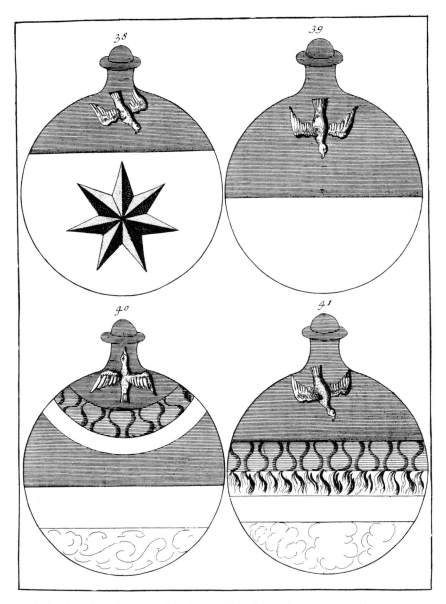

210. Continued sublimation of the body, calcined into the whiteness of bones.

Calcination of the Whitened Body

The planetary star of Barchusen's plate 37, hovering over the whitened earth with a rudimentary sun and moon enclosed, sinks into the 'white earth or the white chalk' (1) in plate 38 (above), but in the act loses its sprouting sun-and-moon children. In plate 39 the planetary star itself dissolves into the calcined earth, now dividing the retort in two symmetrical halves. At this stage, the corrupting darkness of the vessel has been conquered halfway by the white light of the albedo. The work of dealbation has finally succeeded, according to the testimony of the 'Rosarium': 'The unclean body must be cooked and calcined until it reaches the whiteness' (p.110). Barchusen's plates 40-41 continue the work of calcination, the aim of which, according to Geber, is the 'purification of the metals of their earthly parts; for it has been discovered that the metals are purified through repeated calcination and reduction.' (2) To this may be added the definition given by the 'Rosarium': 'Calcination means reduction in the manner of the white ash or earth or white chalk by means of the spirit of the operation, which reduction takes place by means of our fire, that is, our mercurial water.' (3)

In plate 40 the white chalk is cleft in two and the upper segment elevated by the ascending Hermes bird and the element of air. By this procedure 'water is turned into air and fire into water,' according to the testimony of the 'Crowne of Nature.' (4) A similar process of sublimation takes place at the bottom of the vessel where 'earth is turned into fire and air into earth.' (5) Plate 41 renders a new bout of the 'sevenfold circulation' in which new elemental layers are calcined and incinerated, as witnessed by the dust clouds swirling at the bottom of the vessel in plates 40-41. The calcining process of Barchusen's four vessels illustrates the 'Rosarium' text for its eighth woodcut: 'Calcine the earth, sublimate the water; the earth remains below, the water ascends above, the earth is purged by the calcination, the water by the sublimation, both by the putrefaction. The water defends the earth so that it does not burn, the earth binds the water so that it does not flee.' (6)

Uncovering the White Bones

With the 'ablution or purification' of the hermaphrodite's black body, the flesh has gradually become white and, in the royal sweat bath, deprived of its innate humidity so that only the 'dry' parts remain. This operation is represented by the process of calcination, aimed at uncovering the *skeletal* part of the hermaphrodite's body. The procedure is demonstrated by the 'Pretiosa margarita' series of Janus Licinius shown on the opposite page. Here the calcined royal corpse lies shining as an immaculate body of bones in the quiet of the desert.

Fig.212 gives the horrible aftermath of the son's incestuous conjunction with his parental figure in the sarcophagus (fig.104). As the lid is removed from the 'pit,' the united bodies of the son and his royal body of origin are found dead in a marriage bed-turned-sarcophagus. The text explains: 'In the eighth room one beholds that which emerges in the putrefaction after the cooling of the vessel.'

The text of fig.213 reads: 'After this follows the ninth room in which the bones are taken out of the sarcophagus, which happens when the whole body has been dissolved. What has not yet been completely dissolved must be dissolved by a repeated operation until it is totally dissolved. After its dissolution take it out with great care.'

Fig.214 shows the artifex admiring the bones of the royal hermaphrodite after a descending angel has scattered them on the whitened earth. The text explains:

211. The strength of sublimated sex.

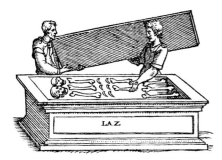

212. From putrefaction to calcination.

'In the tenth room the bones are divided into new parts, which happens when the dissolved matter has been cooked for nine days over a gentle fire until the blackness appears . . . Then it must be cooked anew for nine days over a gentle fire. If it is required by the work, fresh water must be poured over it. In this way the earth will become pure and whitened according to the sayings of the philosophers, for this earth putrefies and purifies with its own water. Then an angel is sent who throws the bones on the purified and whitened earth, which is

213. Reduction of the body to bones.

now mixed with its seed; the whole thing is now placed in a closed vessel with its alembic. After the matter has been made somewhat thinner, it must be divided from the water by a strong fire and must be made hard at the bottom of the vessel.'

After the calcination of the whitened earth the adepts or planetary servants pray for the intervention of God, as shown in fig.215: 'In the eleventh room the servants pray to God that their king may be restored to them, in whose restoration the whole work is conducted.'

Fig.216 shows the fulfilment of their prayer, described by the text as follows: 'Therefore, in the twelfth room another angel is sent who puts the other part of those bones on the earth until they too have become hard. Then they will appear wonderfully in the work. And thus one angel is sent after another, throwing the first and second and third and fourth part of the bones on the earth in order that they may become white, lucid and hard. And after they have become hard with the fifth and sixth parts, they are changed into a yellow colour. And with

the seventh, eighth and ninth parts of the bones, the earth is turned red as blood and as a ruby.' (7) This strange transformation of scenery indicates the return of blood to the bones and the imminence of resurrection (see pp.132-133).

The Mercurial Unicorn of the Albedo

Since corruption is a quality of the flesh, the decomposition of the flesh is a *conditio sine qua non* for the achievement of the incorruptible body of the albedo. This relationship explains the fierceness of the alchemist's 'reiterated death,' or 'sevenfold circulation,' with its ruthless annihilation of all the elemental layers of the corpus. The fact that the angels of God participate in the final work of calcination shows the 'angelic' state of the hermaphrodite's body, which now consists of shining and transparent bones in the desert of draught and suffering.

A classical symbol of the *corpus albeficationis* is the chaste and snow-white unicorn; the invincible strength of its horn expresses the power of the alchemist's calcined bones. The mythical animal appears in the 'forest of the philosophers' of fig.211, from the 'Book of Lambspring.' An animal symbol for Mercurius, the unicorn approaches the deer for the purpose of mounting it and realizing the white conjunction. The accompanying verse reveals the unicorn's partner as a symbol of the anima with whom the unicorn, or the spirit, must be united if the sublimated corpus is to be resurrected from its sarcophagus:

He that knows how to tame and master
  them by art,
To couple them together, and to
Lead them in and out of the forest,
May justly be called a master.
For we rightly judge that
He has captured the golden fleece,
And may triumph everywhere; nay,
He may bear rule over great Augustus. (8)

The Hunting of the Virgin's Unicorn

According to medieval legend, the chaste and elusive unicorn may be caught only by an immaculate virgin into whose lap the entranced animal will place its

214. Reduction of the bones by division.

215. Praying for the bones' resurrection.

head and horn. At this point the huntsmen come out of hiding to capture the unicorn for the purpose of giving it to the king. In medieval ecclesiastical tradition the story of the unicorn's capture is interpreted as a symbol of the Incarnation of Christ in the womb of the Virgin. (9) The hunting of the unicorn also appears in the Grail legend of medieval folklore. As in alchemy, the unicorn is connected with the quest for the philosophers' stone and with the conjunction with the white woman. In Wolfram von Eschenbach's version of the Grail myth a famous stanza reads:

216. Red blood returning to the bones.

We caught the beast called Unicorn
That knows and loves a maiden best
And falls asleep upon her breast;
We took from underneath his horn
The splendid male carbuncle stone
Sparkling against the white
  skull-bone. (10)

An interesting aspect of the unicorn archetype is its connection with the towering sublimation symbols of the albedo, the virgin and the moon. A modern authority on the subject, Odell Shephard writes in 'The Lore of the Unicorn': 'The unicorn is commonly, though not always, thought of as white in body; it is an emblem of chastity; it is very swift; according to the best authorities it cannot be taken alive. The animal is most readily associated with . . . the crescent moon which has been used for ages to represent both celestial motherhood and virginity, whether of Ishtar, Isis, Artemis, or the Madonna . . . The ki-lin, or unicorn of China, is commonly represented in bronze bearing a crescent moon among clouds on his back.' (11)

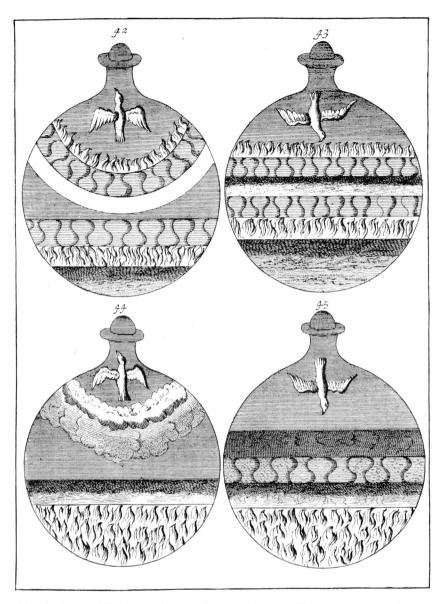

The calcining fire initiates the crucial process of incineration where the hermaphrodite's body, already reduced to a skeleton of white bones, is further reduced by being pulverized and turned to ashes. As a result of this act of ultimate sublimation, the alchemist aims at the creation of a subtle body capable of sheltering the soul and spirit at their hoped-for return from heaven.

In Barchusen's plate 44 the purged elements arise as vapours from the earth while new masses of fire gather from the interior of the vessel. Evidently the transformation process now attains the dynamic stage described by the 'Rosarium': 'Cook till it whitens: in this manner you will have the essence of water and earth, having whitened the earth with water: but that whiteness is called air.' (4) In the 'Crowne of Nature' the transformative processes of plate 44 are described as those of turning 'earth into air, air into water, water into fire and fire into earth.' (5) In plate 45 the heated body of the hermaphrodite emits its last elemental layers to be purged and sublimated. With its incessant upward and downward flight the Hermes bird continues to support the relentless sublimation of the arcane substance.

The Pulverized Stone of Albefication

One of the oldest sources of the *incineratio* appears in the 'Turba,' which describes the pulverization of the stone for the purpose of making it 'white and splendid' as follows: 'Grind, therefore, the white stone, and afterwards let it coagulate with milk. Then grind the chalk and marble and take care that the humidity does not escape from the vessel; but let it coagulate in the vessel until it shall become ashes. Cook also with the spume of the moon, then ye shall find the stone broken and already imbued with its own water. This, therefore, is the stone which we have called by all names, which assimilates the work and drinks it, and is the stone out of which also all colours appear.

'Take, therefore, that same gum, which is from the scoriae, and mix with the ashes of chalk, which you have ruled, and with the dregs which you know, moistening with the permanent water. Then examine whether it has become a powder, but if not, roast in a fire stronger than the first fire, until it has been ground to powder. Then imbue with the permanent water, and the more the colours vary, all the more suffer them to be heated. Know, moreover, that if you take white quicksilver, or the spume of the moon, and do as ye are bidden, pulverizing with a gentle fire, the same is coagulated, and becomes a stone. Out of this stone, therefore, when it is pulverized, many colours will appear to you. But herein, if any ambiguity occur to you in our discourse, do as ye are bid-

217. An 'echoing' fire inexorably transforming the chalk of bones into dust and ashes.

The Calcining Fire of 'Reverberation'

The calcination of the circulated and separated elements are continued with undiminished force in Barchusen's plates 42-45 (above), which show the ceaseless decomposition of the body, its elemental parts released in wave upon wave from new layers in the vessel. The fierce nature of the calcining process is evidenced by the 'doubling' of the elemental layers in plates 42-43. This feature reveals the heating of the arcane substance by a reverberating or 'echoing' fire throwing back and forth the contents of the vessel. This process takes place in the 'furnace of reverberation' *(furnus reverberationis),* in which the elements are subjected to a supreme and direct process of heating. During this final stage of calcination the arcane substance is reduced to the state of fine powder, also identified with the white ashes of the *incineratio.* In his

'Lexicon,' Ruland defines the *reverberatio* as follows: 'Reverberation is ignition, reducing substances under the influence of a potent fire, and by means of reverberation and repercussion, into a fine chalk.' (1)

Crushing the Whitened Bones to Dust

Geber admonishes the adepts to carry out their calcination in a furnace of reverberation in which 'things to be calcined must be put into dishes or pans of most strong clay, such as of which crucibles are made, that they may persist in the asperity of the fire, even to the total combustion of the things to be calcined.' (2) To this statement may be added Paracelsus' famous dictum: 'The microcosm in its interior anatomy must be reverberated up to the highest reverberation.' (3)

218. *The 26-day-old embryo encapsuled in its chorionic cavity, which is attached to the uterus by a fine network of roots called villi (the Latin word for tufts of hair). By means of the villi, nutritive substances are received by the embryo and waste products transferred to the maternal blood. All the vital organs are present in their embryonic state: brain, spinal cord, nerves and skin; digestive system, liver and pancreas; skeleton, heart, blood vessels and muscles.*

219. *A week earlier the organs of the embryo appear in a more primitive state. The spherical body to the left is the yolk sac, which helps to produce blood. The embryo itself lies encapsuled in the amniotic sac, appearing as an oblong transparent egg. Most of the wide top in the middle is the precocious brain region, while the caudal end is seen at the opposite pole. Slowly, the various organs begin to differentiate from the cells packaged in the three layers of the embryonic disc, storing genetic instruction.*

220. *The sign of bodily sublimation.*

den, until a white and splendid stone shall be produced, and so ye will reach your aim.' (6)

Sagittarius the Archer: Sublimation of Matter

In alchemy, the fiery transformation of the body into a *corpus mundum* takes place in the astrological sign of Sagittarius, the Archer (fig.220). The ninth sign of the Zodiac is a mutable, fiery sign ruled by Jupiter. Sagittarius covers the period from November 23 to December 21, or the period in which the scorpionic work of destruction is carried on in a calmer and more directed way.

In the Archer the meaning and purpose of autumnal death begin to dawn like a far-off star twinkling in the darkness. As a result of the growing crystallization of the *goal* of decomposition, the Scorpion changes itself into the Archer where the suffering of decline is endured and actively pursued by the will. This attitude toward transformation, conceived of as an act of sublimation, is symbolized by Sagittarius, who is represented by a centaur drawing a bow and aiming at the highest targets. Half-man, half-beast, the sign embodies a profound dualism and tension: the horse renders man as an instinctual being, the human torso of the Archer man as a transcendent being aiming at heaven. The duality of the Archer presents man as a creature on the boundary of heaven and earth, while the activity of the Archer expresses a movement of sublimation raising animal-man toward the stars. With its ardent desire to transform instinct into spirit, earth into air, or animal-man into the divine, the Archer stands out as the zodiacal symbol of sublimation *par excellence.*

The Sagittarius personality is of an ardent and enthusiastic bent, aiming at goals beyond him and permitting the sublimation of libido. Barbault describes the fire of Sagittarius as a purifying fire, very different from that of either Aries or Leo, and suitable to later middle age, when the desires of the flesh are waning but the spirit can still have a burning desire for social, political, artistic or spiritual objects. Always wanting to go further in concern for the 'beyond' within himself, the Archer is a born explorer and adventurer and, at a moral level, an idealist indefatigably pursuing his vision of global love and man's spiritual perfection. Since unconsciously the Sagittarius personality always aims at the stars, he has a passionate longing for new ideas, new horizons, new visions. The magnitude of his goals prevents him from ever achieving them, but this is unimportant to him, the very act of striving fulfils him. To the Archer the goal is secondary to the movement that brings him toward it; sublimation is its own goal.

221. *The embryo at a still more primitive stage. The inner cell mass with its two cavities is separated midway by a three-layered plate of cells, called the embryonic disc. It consists of a lower layer of ectoderm (facing the amniotic cavity) and an upper layer of entoderm (facing the yolk sac). In the middle is a cellular layer called the mesoderm; this completes the three primary germ layers from which the entire organism will develop. Fig.222 (below) shows the embryonic disc at a still earlier stage surrounded by the yolk sac and amniotic cavity and enclosed by the chorionic cavity.*

222. *The embryonic disc from which the individual will develop only measures ¼ mm. Fig.223 (below) shows the embryo's very earliest days in the uterus as a fertilized egg, or blastocyst, which has built for itself what amounts to a little nest. In fact, the process is called nidation, or nesting. Over the course of days, weeks and months, the embryo becomes firmly rooted in the uterine wall.*

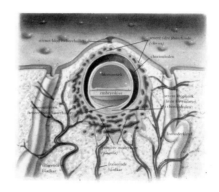

223. *'Incinerated' stage of the embryo.*

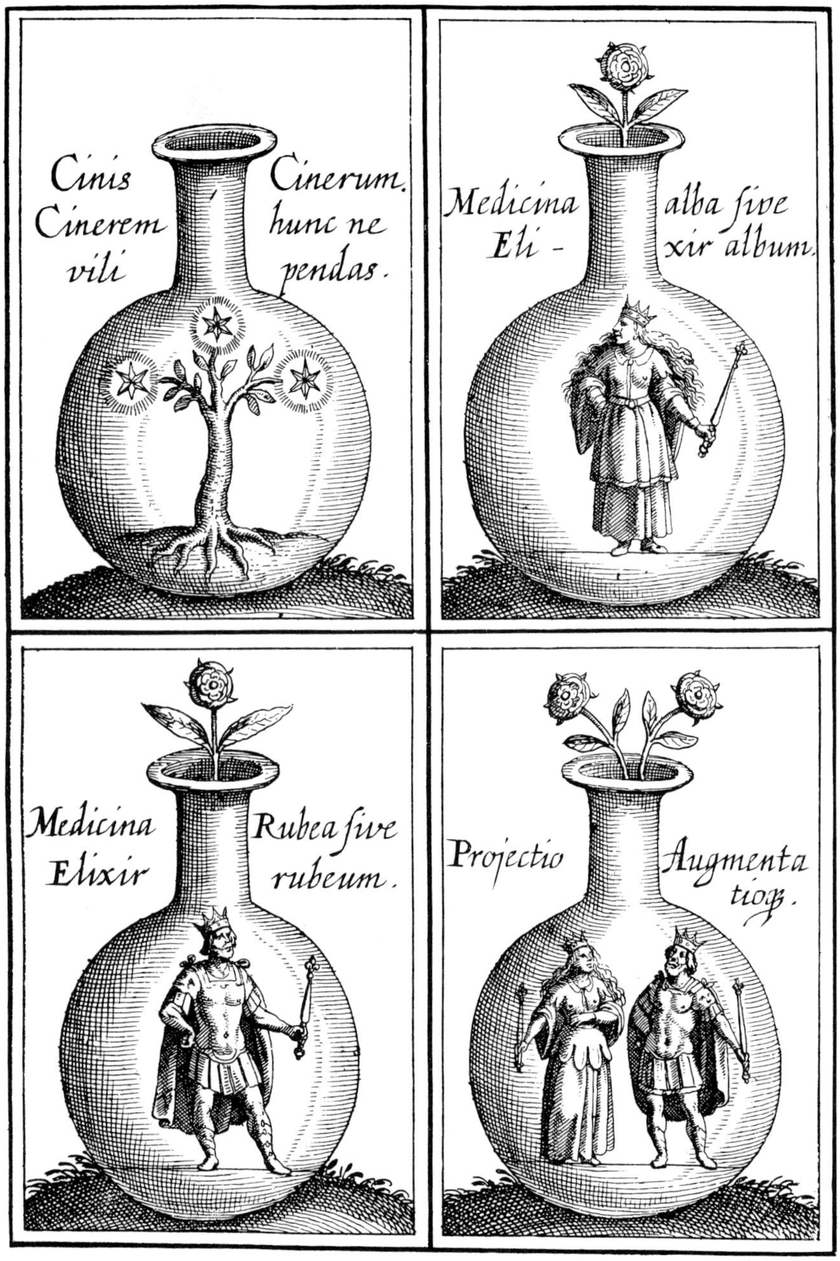

Cinis
Cinerem
vili
Cinerum.
hunc ne
pendas.
Medicina
Eli -
alba ſive
xir album.
Medicina
Elixir
Rubea ſive
rubeum.
Projectio
Augmenta
tioq.

224. The young tree of the philosophers rooting and sprouting in the maternal earth.

Ash-Wednesday of a Royal Art

The four concluding plates of the 'Pandora' series of the Little Work (above) render the final stage of the albedo with its 'white' trauma of rebirth (previous plates in fig.191). As the wheel of sublimation performs its last revolution, the white bones of the dissembled hermaphrodite are crushed to dust and ashes. This movement explains the strange admonition of the 'Rosarium,' *'Despise not these ashes'* (see following pages), a dictum which is illustrated by the first plate *(cinerem hunc ne vili pendas).* The picture shows a young tree rooting in the maternal earth while sprouting stars and leaves. This opening symbol of the royal marriage developed in the subsequent plates is termed 'ash of ashes' *(cinis cinerum).* It renders the philosophers' tree as the *tree of death and birth* (figs.234-235)—a white, starry wondertree rooting in ashes and flowering in a vessel devoid of any trace of life. The 'Pandora' text explains:

'Calcination is nothing but the drying-up and incineration [of the body]. Therefore it must be burned without fear until it is turned to ashes. When thus it has become ashes, you have blended it well. These ashes you must not despise or throw away, but restore to them the sweat which they have expired. Therefore, because all the water has been exhausted and turned into earth, it is putrefied in its vessel for some days over a gentle fire until the precious white colour appears above it. In this vessel will appear all the sufferings of the world since all humidity has been dried up.' (1)

The Fifth Key of Basil Valentine

Fig.226 shows the Fifth Key of Basil Valentine, in which the incineration is rendered by the black vessel filled with earth and clouds of ashes. The vessel belongs to Venus and appears as her breath, thus symbolizing her sublimation into 'spirit of the earth.' While supporting the vessel with her right hand, she presents with her left a heart flowering with the white roses of the albedo. Vulcan, her male partner, appears in a similar state of sublimation, as witnessed by his fiery breath. With his bellows he fans the furnace and the blindfolded Eros child, who aims his bow and arrow at his parents.

In Basil Valentine, the impending conjunction between ignited air and powdered earth lends itself to a simile aptly expressing the difficulties of such a task: 'Two contrary spirits may dwell together but they do not easily combine, for when the gunpowder is put on fire the two spirits out of which the powder is formed will fly from one another with a great shock and noise, and speed through the air so that no one can perceive them any more, nor say whither they have gone.' (2) Fraught with suspense, the Fifth Key places its child of spiritual rebirth under the lion's claws and jaws. The crown of glory floating between lion and sun is one spelling death for the winged child of promise. The text explains:

'First, our matter should be carefully purified, then dissolved, destroyed, decomposed, and reduced to dust and ashes. Thereupon prepare from it a volatile spirit, which is white as snow, and another volatile spirit, which is red as blood. These two spirits contain a third, and are yet but one spirit. Now these are the three spirits which preserve and multiply life. Therefore unite them, give them the meat and drink that nature requires, and keep them in the warm conjugal bed until the perfect birth takes place.

'Then you will see and experience the virtue of the gift bestowed upon you by God and nature. Know also, that hitherto my lips have not revealed this secret to any one, and that God has endowed natural substances with greater powers than most men are ready to believe. Upon my mouth God has set a seal, that there might be scope for others after me to write about the wonderful things of nature, which by the foolish are looked upon as supernatural. For they do not understand that all natural things are ultimately traceable to supernatural causes, but nevertheless are, in this present state of the world, subject to natural conditions.' (3)

The Death Wind of Resurrection

Fig.225 shows a dramatic variation of the attempted conjunction between the dust of man, or the spirit of the earth, and the fiery spirit of God in heaven. The divine hand stuck through a cloud in the desert feels the pulse on the outstretched hand of the adept, who suffers the terrors of incineration and death. The Latin top inscription (italicised below) quotes Job's excruciating experience of biblical incineration:

'My bones are pierced in me in the night season: and my sinews take no rest. By the great force of my disease is my garment changed: it bindeth me about as the collar of my coat. He hath cast me into the mire, and I am become like dust and ashes. I cry unto thee, and thou dost not hear me: I stand up, and thou regardest me not. Thou art become cruel to me: with thy strong hand thou opposest thyself against me. Thou liftest me up to the wind; thou causest me to ride upon it and dissolvest my substance. For I know that thou wilt bring me to death, and to the house appointed for all living . . . When I looked for good, then evil came unto me: and when I waited for light, there came darkness. My bowels boiled, and rested not: the days of affliction prevented me. I went mourning without the sun: I stood up, and I cried in the congregation. I am a brother to dragons, and a companion to owls. My skin is black upon me, and my bones are burned with heat' (Job 30:17-30).

Inside the great circle of fig.225 the symbolic action brings out another aspect of the incinerating death wind enveloping the biblical-alchemical protagonist. The circular inscription identifies the wind with the breath of resurrection and rebirth blowing in the 37th chapter of Ezekiel:

225. Breathing life into human ashes.

226. The parental spirits attempting the conjunction in a vessel of ashes and death.

'Prophesy unto the wind, prophesy, son of man, and say to the wind, Thus saith the Lord God; *Come from the four winds, O breath, and breathe upon these slain, that they may live.* So I prophesied as he commanded me, *and the breath came into them,* and they lived, and stood up upon their feet, an exceeding great army. Then he said unto me, Son of man, these bones are the whole house of Israel: behold, they say, Our bones are dried, and our hope is lost: we are cut off for our parts. Therefore prophesy and say unto them, Thus saith the Lord God; Behold, O my people, I will open your graves, and cause you to come up out of your graves, and bring you into the land of Israel. And ye shall know that I am the Lord, when I have opened your graves, O my people, and brought you up out of your graves. And shall put my spirit in you, and ye shall live' (Ezekiel 37:9-14).

Ablution and Approaching Rebirth

Fig.227 shows the ninth plate of the 'Mutus liber,' in which the coniunctio of the previous engraving (fig.141) is followed by a bout of mortification. The 'May-dew' collected by the alchemist and his sister in fig.52 now falls in a blackened state, just as the lovers' staked-out sheets appear to have been torn and scattered by the gusts of the storm. The spring of Hermetic love is now turned into autumn and winter and the heavenly dew transformed into a dark substance, collected by the couple in six dishes on the ground.

In the bottom row the alchemist and his sister engage in new processes of pur-

gation and sublimation of the prima materia of their work. As the brother extends a decanter, his mystical sister pours the dark contents of the dishes into the vessel of Hermes.

The prospective nature of their work is brought out by the emergence of Mercurius philosophorum, who appears to receive the vessel at the hands of the woman. The uniting powers of this mercurial vessel and its tincture are explored by the alchemist and his sister in the next plate of the 'Mutus liber,' depicted on fig.254.

227. Dark landscape lit up by Mercurius.

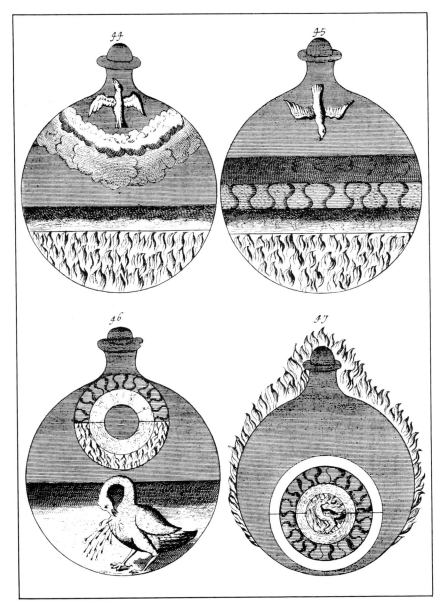

228.

body. Hermes: The spirit is an extractor of the soul and a returner of the soul and a reformer of the whole work, and all that we seek is in it.' (3)

Birdlike Copulation of Royal Lovers

The attempted coniunctio of the albedo passes through a rebirth rivalling the king's descent into the queen's well, if assuming, this time, a more sublimated form. In the shape of a winged bird the king approaches his wingless queen, who hides in the earth below the sarcophagus as a cruel beak which will devour him in the act of copulation. The winged bird clearly symbolizes the descending soul and spirit, just as the buried bird symbolizes the earthy corpus.

The courting ritual of the two birds is transposed into human terms by the engraved variant reproduced in fig.230. The picture shows the reviving hermaphrodite, whose sublimated sex is expressed by the birdlike conjunction attempted in the background and elucidated by the 'Rosarium' as follows:

'Our sublimation is nothing but the exaltation of the body, that is, its transformation into spirit, which cannot be without a gentle fire. Thus we say that it is sublimated into a bishop, that is, exalted (4) . . . Sublimation is twofold: the first is the removal of the superfluous so that the purest parts shall remain, free from elementary dregs, and shall possess the quality of the quintessence. The other sublimation is the reduction of the bodies to spirit, that is, when the corporeal density is transformed into spiritual thinness.' (5)

The actual coitus between the birdlike king and queen assumes the nature of a birth trauma: both unite by pecking and devouring each other. Thus the king

The Second, or Lunar, Trauma of Rebirth

Fig.229 shows the ninth woodcut of the 'Rosarium' in which the incinerated hermaphrodite in its sarcophagus is finally revived by the homunculus returning from heaven to breathe life into its dead body, thus realizing the act of rebirth long awaited for. The headline identifies the winged child with the returning soul, the event termed the 'jubilee of the soul, or the dawn, or the sublimation' *(animae jubilatio seu ortus seu sublimatio).* The motto (1) reads:

Here is the soul descending from on high
To quick the corpse we strove to purify.

As a result of the preceding operations of ablution, calcination, and incineration the gross body has finally taken on a 'soulish' and 'spiritual' form, becoming a *corpus mundum*—a 'purified body'—

capable of sheltering soul and spirit or even drawing them down to itself. The text presents the parched body as revived also by the falling rain, and 'this divine water is the king descending from heaven.' (2) In other words, the soul returns with the spirit in the figure of the homunculus, who is bisexual and represents the united anima and spiritus. The 'Rosarium' continues:

'He [the king] is the one who returns the soul to its body, which revives after its death; and through him is life, after which there will be no more death. Rosinus: For the body rejoices when the soul enters into it. The same: Truly, the body takes possession of the soul, and every body which finds a soul easily takes possession of it. You must notice that the soul is punished with the body, imprisoned in it, and transformed by it into a

ANIMÆ IVBILATIO SEV
Ortus seu Sublimatio.

229. The wonders of sublimated sex.

124

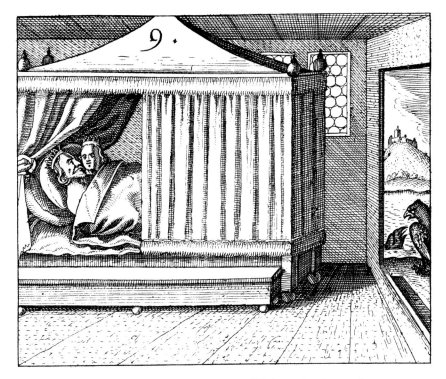

230. A 'noughted' king reviving on the return of his lunar daughter and queen.

transformed into blood and wings returns to the nest of his mother from which he came. This fearful act of re-union is described on pp.126-127.

Birdlike Rebirth of the Incinerated Body

Barchusen's plates 44-47 (fig.228) il-lustrate the ninth woodcut of the 'Rosa-rium' and its text, which opens thus: 'Here follows the fourth word which says: The water which would have been with the earth ascends by means of sub-limation in a thick and coagulated state. Thus you have earth, water and air. And this is what the philosopher says: Whiten it and sublimate it with a quick fire until the spirit which you will find in it goes forth from it; it is named the bird or the ashes of Hermes [plate 46]. Therefore says Morienus: Despise not the ashes, for they are the diadem of thy heart, and the ash of things that endure. And the Turba says: Augment the regimen of fire, for after the whiteness one comes to the incineration, which is called the cal-cined earth. Therefore says Morienus: At the bottom remains the calcined earth which is of a fiery nature.

'Thus you have in the above men-tioned proportions the four elements, namely the dissolved water, the whitened earth, the sublimated air and the calcined fire [plate 47]. Of these four elements says Aristotle in his book on the regimen of the principles: When you will have ob-tained water from air, and air from fire, and fire from earth, you will have ob-tained the whole philosophical art. And

this is the end of the first composition, as Morienus says. Patience and time are necessary in our magistery; all haste comes from the devil. Hermes: The dead will revive and the sick will be cured. The same: You must conjoin the body and the soul by means of a pulverization in the sun.' (6)

Producing the Chicken of Rebirth

Barchusen's elaboration and amplifica-tion of the 'Rosarium' text is highly in-teresting. Plate 44 shows the transforma-tion of the elements into 'white air' un-der the impact of the blazing fire of re-verberation. The work of 'incineration' is continued in plate 45 in which the last elemental layers of the vessel are heated and sublimated. In plate 46 the four ele-ments at length assume the desired na-ture of air by replacing the ascending and descending bird at the top of the vessel. In a magical act of transmutation, the fluttering Hermes bird and the four incin-erated elements are merged into one com-posite figure appearing as a free-floating hollow ball. This airy ash-body is com-posed of the four elements in their su-preme state of sublimation, that is, in-visibly endowed with the wings of the Hermes bird, or with the powers of pure spirit.

Simultaneously with the development of this weightless body at the top of the vessel, a second 'bird' makes its appear-ance at its bottom. This is the white swan, or pelican, plucking her breast in order to nourish her young with her

blood. The object of the bird's activity is obviously the hollow, elemental cluster floating over her head. The union of this fledgeling ball with its mother is shown in plate 47, where the fire of the second conjunction envelops the top of the ves-sel in a sudden blaze signifying the 'nest-ing' of the elemental ball in the gory breast of the pelican. At the same time the conjunction of the two 'birds' gives birth to a 'third bird'; this is the chicken enclosed in the centre of the elemental ball, by now transformed into an egg with a shell of calcined earth, a white of airy water, and a yolk of subtle fire.

The 'Nesting' of the Fertilized Egg

The 'nesting' conjunction of alchemy symbolizes the regressive revival of the unconscious imprints of implantation, or nidation ('nesting'). As the fertilized egg, or mulberry *(morula),* is slowly trans-ported through the uterine tube into the womb cavity, its dividing cells increase to about one hundred and fifty differen-tiated cells. In the process, the solid clus-ter of the mulberry becomes hollow at its centre. It is now called a blastocyst from the Greek *blastos,* meaning sprout, and *cyst,* meaning pouch. On the sixth or seventh day the 'sprout pouch' settles down in the spongy lining of the uterus (fig.231=plates 46-47). In the process of nesting, tiny blood vessels are broken in the maternal tissues, which serve as nour-ishment for the growing cells of the nest-ed egg. In fact, the cells of the blasto-cyst absorb the nutrients of the uterus, just as a plant absorbs nourishment from the wet soil.

By the end of the first week the mater-nal tissues begin to heal and form a scar-like capsule over the cell cluster which thereby gains extra protection. Within the opaque walls of the capsule a specta-cular metamorphosis will take place. As the embryonic cells begin to nest and fuse with the uterine vessel, the cells will increase from hundreds to many thou-sands and, changing hourly, will soon be transformed into a distinct human being.

231. Nesting of egg in the uterine soil.

232. The royal lovers of the albedo involved in the critical operation of 'nesting.'

A nest is found in the forest, in which
The Bird of Hermes has his brood;
One fledgling always strives to fly upward,
The other rejoices to sit quietly in
  the nest;
Yet neither can get away from the other.
The one that is below holds the one that
  is above,
And will not let it get away from the nest,
As a husband in a house with his wife,
Bound together in closest bonds
  of wedlock. (1)

Traumatic Reunion of Birdlike Lovers

The union of the winged and wingless birds is elaborated by Lambspring's second illustration of the motif. The accompanying verse of fig.235 reads:

*In India is found a beautiful wood
In which two birds are bound together.
One is white as snow, the other red,
They bite each other dead.
As one devours the other,
Both are changed into a white dove.' (2)*

The motto of the picture elucidates: 'Here are two noble and precious birds: body and spirit devour each other.' Evidently, Lambspring's motif is connected with the white dawn, or with the return of the soul and spirit to the purified body. In Petrus Bonus, the *animae jubilatio seu ortus seu sublimatio* is described as follows:

'It is the body which retains the soul, and the soul can show its power only when it is united to the body. Therefore, when the artist sees the white soul arise, he should join it to its body in the very same instant; for no soul can be retained without its body . . . The force of the body should prevail over that of the soul, and instead of the body being carried upward with the soul, the soul should be brought to remain with the body. Thus the work is crowned with success, and the spirit will abide with the two in indissoluble union for ever. Since, then, the body perfects and retains the soul, and imparts real being to it and the whole work, while the soul manifests its power in the body, and all this is accomplished through the mediation of the spirit, it has been well said that the body and the form are one and the same thing, while the two others are called the substance.' (3)

The Winged and the Wingless Birds

Above, the king with his sceptre and sword approaches his queen, who brings him the lilies of the albedo. Their 'white' reunion is symbolized by the winged and wingless birds representing the spirit of fiery air and the spirit of volatile earth, respectively (cf. Basil Valentine's Fifth Key). The meaning of the two birds of the 'Rosarium' is part of the secret tradition of alchemy. It is revealed by the 'Book of Lambspring' in the two pictures reproduced in figs.234-235. The verse accompanying the 'winged' tree of death and rebirth in fig.234 reads as follows:

The Gory Nest of Death and Rebirth

The devouring union of the king and queen revives the old conjugal pattern of death and rebirth, a pattern now sublimated and appearing in its 'winged' edition. As the dragon queen of the first *coniunctio* turns into the bird queen of the second *coniunctio*, her sucking well becomes a nest of gory implantation.

233. The bird king nesting in a crown of thorns devouring and transforming him.

Fig.233 varies this motif by rendering the nest in the likeness of a crown of thorns, a deadly bed which will tear the birds to pieces as soon as they begin copulating. The text of the engraving informs us that the motif of the two birds derives from Senior. In his treatise 'De chemia' Senior presents his vision of a strange statue in a subterranean treasure house (fig.277):

'There was on the tablet which he held in his lap . . . a picture of two birds having their breasts [contiguous] to one another, of which one of them had both wings cut off, and the other had both wings [intact]. Each of them held fast the tail of the other by its beak as if the flying bird wished to fly with the other bird, and that bird wished to keep the flying bird with itself. Also these two linked birds that were holding one another appeared like a circle, like an image of 'two in one.' At the top of the one that was flying was a circle and, above these two birds, at the top of the tablet close to the fingers of the statue was an image of the luminous moon.' (4)

As evidenced by Senior's interpretation, the two birds stand for Sol and Luna, who, as birds, attain reunion in the body of the full moon. Hence Senior advises the adept of the lunar work: 'Cast the female upon the male, and the male shall ascend the female.' (5) By this act the unfledged bird is extracted from the earth and 'lifted' up to the condition of the fledged bird, that is, endowed with its volatile qualities. The result of this conjunction appears with the 'third' bird—in Lambspring a dove—which marks the completion of the white operation of rebirth.

The conjunction of the fledged and unfledged birds is an ancient motif in alchemy. The earliest reference to the two birds is an obscure passage in Zosimos: 'If two do not become one, that is, if the fledged does not conquer the unfledged, your expectation will come to nothing.' (6) Senior represents a later and more famous rendering of the same motif.

234. *The eerie tree of death and rebirth.*

235. *'Here are two noble and precious birds: body and spirit devour each other.' (9)*

The dove is a symbol of the albedo and is sometimes identified with the returning queen, sometimes with the king reborn in the queen. In the 'Theatrum chemicum' we read about the 'lead of the philosophers in which is the shining white dove, which is called the salt of metals, [and] in which consists the teaching of the work. This is that chaste, wise, and rich queen of Sheba clothed in a white veil.' (7)

The dove symbolizing the son of the whiteness appears in a famous passage in the 'Aurora consurgens': 'The signs of those who believe and are well baptized are these: When the king that is in heaven judgeth over them, they shall be whitened with snow in Selmon and shall be as the wings of a dove covered with silver, and the hinder parts of her back with the paleness of gold. Such shall be our beloved son, behold ye him, beautiful above the sons of men, at whose beauty the sun and moon wonder. For he is the privilege of love and the heir, in whom men trust and without whom they can do nothing.

'After thou hast made those seven [metals] which thou hast distributed through the seven stars (and hast appointed to the seven stars) [and] hast purged them nine times until they appear as pearls (in likeness)—this is the Whitening.' (8)

Sublimation of the Birth Trauma

Psychologically, the alchemical drama of 'nesting' symbolizes a depressive reaction reaching its nadir and turning point. The enigmatic dictum 'Despise not the ashes, for they are the diadem of your heart' points to a depressive 'incineration' of the personality containing at the same time the germs of a healing of the depressive mood disorder. As we have seen, the white 'dawn' illuminating the soul's dark night initiates an act of rebirth which is bitter agony for the ego involved. The strange convulsions of the unconscious at this culminating point of depression reveal the uncovering of a second birth-traumatic layer appearing as a 'winged' or sublimated edition of the first one. The regressing libido's experience of death and rebirth reflects the psychobiological dynamics of implantation, which, in the course of embryonic evolution, *represents a critical operation of a similar magnitude as the act of birth.*

Biologically, implantation subjects the blastocyst, or the fertilized egg in its perfected form, to such dangers and hazards and disfiguring metamorphoses that the regressive experience of the event amounts to a second trauma of rebirth. The devouring union of 'nesting' in the womb is precisely rendered by the symbolism of these pages.

236. A meditating alchemist suffering the painful birth of the winged, lunar stone.

The Lunar Stone of Birth and Death

Leaning on the philosophers' stone (above), the incinerated and 'noughted' alchemist suffers the mystery of its two birds uniting inside a lunar lapis about to become alive. The alchemist meditates under the branches of the lunar tree whose fruits are still unilluminated and difficult to discern. The white sails flying seaward in the background express the adept's dawning sense of liberation,

the breaking out of containment that characterizes transcendence. The situation depicted reads like an illustration of a passage in the 'Theatrum chemicum':

'When . . . Sol, Luna, and Mercurius are in our material, they must be extracted, conjoined, buried and mortified, and turned into ashes. Thus it comes to pass that the nest of the birds becomes their grave, and conversely, the birds absorb the nest and unite themselves firmly with it. This comes to pass, I say,

that soul, spirit and body, man and woman, active and passive, in one and the same subject, when placed in the vessel, heated with their own fire and sustained by the outward magistery of the art, may in due time escape [to freedom].' (1)

Alchemical descriptions of the peculiar state of mind elicited by the transformative processes of fig.236 abound in obscurity, mystery and paradox. One statement of the lunar stone of birth and death reads as follows:

'In the proper house the flying bird is begotten, and in the alien house the tincturing stone. The two flying birds hop on to the tables and heads of the kings, because both, the feathered bird and the plucked, have given [us] this visible art and cannot relinquish the society of men. The father of [the art] urges the indolent to work, its mother nourishes the sons who are exhausted by their labours, and quickens and adorns their weary limbs. Therefore pull down the house, destroy the walls, extract therefrom the purest juice with the blood, and cook that thou mayest eat. Wherefore Arnaldus saith in the Book of Secrets: Purify the stone, grind the door to powder, tear the bitch to pieces, choose the tender flesh, and thou wilt have the best thing. In the one thing are hidden all parts, in it all metals shine. Of these two [parts], two are the artificers, two the vessels, two the times, two the fruits, two the ends, and one the salvation.' (2)

The Mother of the Embracing Fumes

Fig.237 shows a strange alchemical woman, Maria Prophetissa, also called the Jewess, sister of Moses, or the Copt. She is probably of Gnostic origin and connected with the Maria of Gnostic tradition, known for her vision of Christ extracting a woman from his side and uniting with her on top of a mountain. An advocate of the *matrimonium alchymicum,* Maria Prophetissa is attributed the popular saying: 'Marry gum with gum in true marriage.' In fig.237 she points to a Hermetic variant of the conjunction attempted in fig.236. Instead of the two united vessels and the two birds merging with each other, the engraving shows two vases with necks facing each other and with outpouring fumes blending with each other. The motto reads: 'One fume embraces the other fume, and the white plant *(herba alba)* growing on top of the little mountain catches them both.' (3)

This is an echo of a famous dictum of Senior (Hermes) related to the white rebirth and quoted also by the 'Rosarium': 'The full moon . . . is the root of all things, and from it is extracted the thing which signifies the water because the moon governs all moist things and is the Lady of the Waters, and the two birds

237. The white plant of Maria Prophetissa catching the fumes of above and below.

are extracted from her, which birds are the two fumes mentioned by Hermes when saying: The upper fume descends to the lower fume and one fume conceives by the other fume (4) . . . When the whole is coagulated, then it is called the sea of the sages. And this earth is the mother of wonders, and the mother of the two fumes, and it is all, and from it all is taken.' (5)

Lightening the Lunar Planetary Star

Figs.238-239 present the mother of the 'whiteness' in two variations. Fig.238 renders Basil Valentine's vision of the queen of the albedo conferring the lunar crown on the head of her beloved brother and king. The 'Chymical Pleasure Garden' gives the following paraphrase of Basil Valentine's long original poem on the lunar lightening of the sevenfold planetary star:

As the beautiful sister re-lives,
She approaches her beloved brother
And once more assumes her
White and crystalline organs.
She much complains to her [planetary]
   brothers
That hitherto she has loved nothing
But the heavy burden of the earth,
And almost despised everything
   heavenly.
Now she admonishes that she might
Win the star of her brother.
Then she puts on the head of each
   of them
The crown of new honours. (6)

Cleaving of the Mature Lunar Egg

Fig.239 shows the 'white' mother as lunar egg or stone 'from which all is taken.' This is the birth place of the 'third bird,' finally ready to be delivered by the alchemist's cleaving sword. (Barchusen's plate 47 (fig.228) x-rays the lunar egg and shows the chicken enclosed.) The motto admonishes the alchemist to 'take the egg and cut it with a fiery sword.' (7) The text describes the circulation of the elements in the final, synthetic procedure of the whitening work:

'The external heat is the first cause which through the circulation of the elements and the transmutation of one into the other introduces a new form under the guidance of nature. For water passes into air, and air into fire, and fire into earth, and while all are copulating, a specific form originating from the stars [creates] an individual, a certain species of bird, namely that to which the egg belongs and in which the semen is infused . . . Basil Valentine writes that Mercurius was incarcerated by Vulcan at the command of Mars, and not released until he had putrefied completely and died. But this death is to him the beginning of a

238. The lunar queen and mother of the 'whitening' lightening her planetary star.

new life, just as the corruption or death of the egg brings about the generation and life of the chicken . . . I also tell you that no [cutting] instrument will be produced except from our white powder, star-like, splendid, and deriving from the white stone; and this powder will constitute the apt instrument for [cutting] the

egg. However, they have never named the egg nor revealed the bird of that egg.' (8)

This statement is not strictly true: the supreme secret is disclosed by the 'Rosarium' in its tenth woodcut, where the alchemist cuts the ripened egg of the albedo, hatching thereby its lunar creature of perfect conjunction (next pages).

239. An alchemist cutting the white stone and releasing its winged creature of rebirth.

240.

Thus you have the true Mercurius extracted from the two bodies mentioned above, well washed and digested. And I swear by God that no other Mercurius exists in the universal way than the one just declared, on which depends the whole philosophy. Who speaks otherwise, speaks false.' (1)

The White Moon Stone of Rebirth

Barchusen's variation upon the tenth woodcut of the 'Rosarium' is reproduced in fig.240. The incinerated elements contracting into a hollow ball in plate 46 and nesting chicken-like in the gory breast of the swan or pelican in the subsequent plate finally rises as the lunar egg-stone of perfection in plate 48. Enveloped by the lunar fire of conjunction, the lapis appears as the 'white stone, the white sun, the full moon, the fruitful white earth, cleansed and calcined.' (2) In plate 49 the lunar fire of conjunction leaves the egg, which is suddenly defaced by concentric rings tearing its substance apart. The neck of the retort appears to have been knocked off and at the point of fracture left a flake obviously related to the entrance of the egg into the vessel.

Silver Wedding and Family Reunion

The 'Rosarium' woodcut is accompanied by a long verse in German which reads:

Here is born the Empress of all honour,
The philosophers name her their
*   daughter.*
She multiplies, bears children ever again,
They are incorruptibly pure and without
*   any stain.*
The Queen hates death and poverty,
She surpasses gold, silver and jewellery,
All medicaments great and small.
Nothing upon earth is her equal,

The Second Coniunctio: Lunar Rebirth

Fig.241 shows the tenth woodcut of the 'Rosarium' which realizes the second or 'white' coniunctio of the opus, thus resolving the trauma of birdlike conjunction in a silvery act of rebirth. The chicken hatched from the lunar egg is revealed as the winged rebis triumphing on the full moon and convulsed by the ecstasy of angelic copulation. Wafting its wings, the resurrected hermaphrodite is animated by the wriggling mercurial serpents winding around its body in movements of fertilization. The serpents have developed together with the fruits of the moon tree which shine like gleaming eggs. In the engraved variant (fig.242) the royal hermaphrodite holds in its right hand the united creature of birdlike copulation, while in the woodcut the double-sexed bird rests at the foot of the united king and queen. The bird endows the hermaphrodite with the powers of

spiritual love, or with the ability to rise from the earth and fly. The accompanying 'Rosarium' text reads:
'Hermes: Know, ye searchers of rumours and ye sons of wisdom, that the vulture who lives on top of the mountain exclaims in a loud voice: I am the white black and the red yellow [fig.278]. I am surely speaking the truth and not lying. Alphidius: Further, the quicksilver which is extracted from that black body is humid and white and pure with bark so that it will not perish. Morienus: You must know that the white fume is the soul and spirit of those dissolved bodies [fig.237]. And certainly, if the white fume had not existed, neither would the white gold of alchemy. Rosarius: This is our noble Mercurius, and God has never created a thing more noble under the sky beside the rational soul. Plato: This is our matter and our secret. Ortulanus:

241. *Wondrous hatching of a silvery egg.*

242. *Through the night to the light: final hatching of the lunar creature of rebirth.*

Wherefore we say thanks to God
   in heaven.
O force constrains me naked woman that
   I am [the queen is speaking],
For unblest was my body when I
   first began.
And never did I become a mother,
Until the time when I was born another.
Then the power of roots and herbs
   did I possess,
And I triumphed over all sickness.
Then it was that I first knew my son,
And we two came together as one.
There I was made pregnant by him
   and gave birth
Upon a barren stretch of earth.
I became a mother yet remained a maid,
And in my nature was established.
Wherefore my son was also my father,
As God ordained in accordance
   with nature.

I bore the mother who gave me
   birth [the king is speaking],
Through me she was born again upon
   earth.
To regard as one what nature hath wed
Is in our mountain most masterfully hid.
Four come together in one
In this our magisterial stone.*
And six when seen as a trinity
Is brought to essential unity.
To him who thinks on these things aright
God giveth the power to put to flight
All such sicknesses as pertain
To metals and the bodies of men.
None can do that without God's help,
And then only if he sees through himself.
Out of my earth a fountain flows
And into two streams it branching goes.

One of them runs to the Orient,
The other towards the Occident.
Two eagles fly up with feathers aflame,
Naked they fall to the earth again.
Yet in full feather they rise up soon,
That fountain is Lord of sun and moon.

O Lord Jesu Christ who bestow'st
The gift through the grace of thy
   Holy Ghost:
He unto whom it is given truly,
Understands the masters' sayings
   entirely.
That his thoughts on the future life
   may dwell
Body and soul are joined so well.
And to raise them up to their
   father's kingdom,
Such is the way of the art
   among men. (3)

Blastocyst: the Perfected Stage of the Egg

The lunar egg-stone of the second coniunctio symbolizes the regressive reinstatement of the libido at its blastocyst

* These are the Oedipal figures of father, mother, daughter, and son, united in a self-begetting circle of primary identity uniquely expressed by the stanzas. In the poem's criss-crossing pattern of conjunction, the fetal son unites with his pregnant mother or sister, who unites with her begetting father or brother or the fruit of her womb. The sublimation of the Oedipus complex in the second coniunctio is expressed by the winged shape of the hermaphrodite. The unity of the six 'when seen as a trinity' refers to the Seal of Solomon with its two inserted triangles, one masculine, the other feminine.

stage, that is, the final, perfect stage of the fertilized egg. This libido configuration is attained with the situation depicted in fig.243: the blastocyst in its state of conjunction with the surface of the uterus, not yet violated by the disfiguring metamorphosis released by fusion with the womb.

The crucial moment of fig.243 brings a dramatic development to its close. After having been shed from the ovary, or the maternal 'fruit tree,' the ovulated egg undergoes fertilization by the male serpents, or spermatozoa, as it falls to the ground. During its 'winged' flight the fertilized egg passes down the uterine tube while slowly transforming itself into a cluster of cleavage cells known as the morula. As it leaves the uterine tube and enters the uterine cavity, the morula acquires a fluid-filled cavity and becomes a blastocyst. For about three days after its arrival in the uterus the blastocyst remains free. However, further development is prevented until an intimate connection between the egg and the uterus is established by the critical operation of implantation, or embedding in the womb.

Fig.243 shows the very moment of this life-saving *coniunctio*. From now on the blastocyst can grow into an embryo, a fetus, a man. The entire plan of this future creation is stored up in the several hundred cells of the blastocyst with their DNA and RNA codes. At this final, perfect stage of the egg, its 'royal jelly' contains the whole scheme of creation *in potentia*. This is the very jelly of the white moon stone of alchemy, composed of the ashes of creation.

Silvery Rebirth at Middle Age

Psychologically, the Hermetic 'whitening' of the leaden blackness into a state of silvery light symbolizes the gradual transformation of a depressive state into a state of rebirth and new life. In terms of the individuation process, the nigredo of a middle age depression running its course somewhere between the age of thirty and forty is finally resolved in 'silvery' rebirth in middle age.

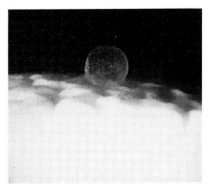

243. *Blastocyst landing on uterine soil.*

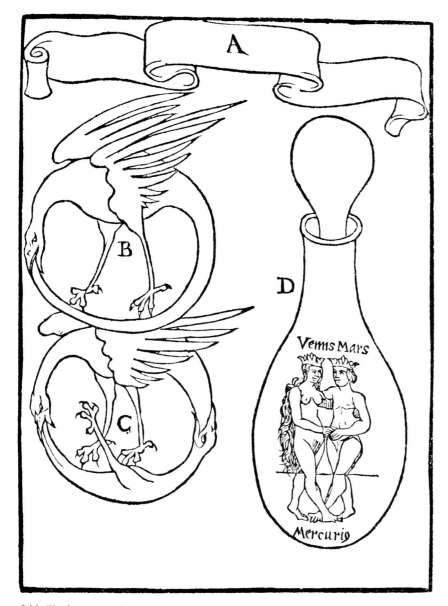

244. The lunar wonder bird (B) rising out of the union of its murderous parents (C).

Sublimation of the Personality

A psychological synthesis and maturation of the personality in middle age is a regular phenomenon of life and may be observed in the biographies of all creative artists. Shakespeare concludes at this stage of the individuation process: 'Men must endure their going hence, even as their coming hither, ripeness is all' (King Lear 5:2).

The Hermetic procedures during the Little Work—the ablution of the black body, the transformation of body into spirit, the growing sublimation of earthly things, or the lunar illumination of the tangible world—are explained by the psychodynamics of depression. After the blackout of the depressive's entire life and surroundings, and after the total death of any pleasure in the things offered by life, the material world and its pursuits are bound to appear in a 'trans-

parent' light to the depressive when he returns to 'life' again. Bert Kaplan described his recovery from a severe middle age depression in the following manner:

'Such are my memories of those years when my existence seemed to me a 'lost traveller's dream under the hill'; and even after I came back to life and sailed out clear and free I remained conscious at moments of an abyss beside me. I seemed to catch out of the tail of my eye a cold black draughty void, with a feeling that I stood on the brink of it in peril of my reason; but it was only rarely now that I had this glimpse of the *neant*, and in the end my crisis was invaluable for me. I felt as one of my friends felt after he too struck bottom and had 'come up more and more ever since,' finding his own grave breakdown a 'complete purgation.' To me he wrote, 'I predict you'll find new springs of energy that you had never suspected'; and so, in fact, it prov-

ed to be when I returned to love and work with a feeling that my best years still lay before me. Hawthorne had spoken of the dark caverns into which all men must descend if they are to know anything beneath the surface, or what he called the illusive pleasures of existence. It seemed to me now that I understood him.' (1)

The Fighting Birds in the Moon

The 'Pandora' woodcut reproduced in fig.244 shows the murderous copulation of the winged and wingless birds 'appearing like a circle, like an image of 'two in one,'' (2) according to Senior's famous description of their vision in the full moon: 'This is their root, that from which they stem, because this [the moon] is the whole and a part of the whole, and because from this the two fumes emanate, the head of the one being joined to the tail of the other.' (3)

As explained by the letter C, the winged beings stand for the 'two birds or the procreators of everything, man and wife.' (4) The third bird 'extracted' from their fusing bodies appears in B where the vulture-like bird represents the 'bird of the extracted soul of our stone.' (5) The unrolled scroll in A explains: 'If you want to open the sealed castle, be careful, and add the head to the tail; then you will find the whole art.' (6) D translates the conjunction of the birds into human terms, showing Mars and Venus melting into the hermaphroditic Mercurius.

The 'Pandora' woodcut reproduced in fig.247 illustrates the German poem of the 'Rosarium' and appears as a pictorial variant of its tenth woodcut. The hermaphrodite is represented by the naked queen forming the masculine trunk of the lunar tree with its silvery fruits (A). She strides the 'fountain of the sun and moon' of the 'Rosarium,' here composed of the 'distillatory of the sun' (F) and the 'distillatory of the moon' (G). The arboreal queen illuminates the night with the torches of the united sun and moon (B and C). She wears a cross and a

245. The king leaving his sarcophagus . . .

crown, in which the bird of conjunction is nesting. The text varies the copulation of the two birds in the following manner: 'The tree comes from the seed of the man and the woman. As soon as the seed has died in the earth, it rises again from the earth and becomes a tree full of ineffable fruits and with numerous effects.' (7)

The two eagles of the 'Rosarium' poem 'flying up with feathers aflame and naked falling to the earth again' are represented by the birds ascending and descending in D and E. They symbolize the flapping wings of the hermaphrodite as it attempts to take off. Evidently the newly hatched creature has not fully learned how to use its wings, or to guard against the dangers of flying. The text explains: 'D: The birds are the seed of the sun, and they fly up into the mountain of the moon, into the heights of heaven, and bite their feathers and again return to the mountain in order to die a white death there. E: The birds are the seed of the moon and they fly up into the mountain of their father and mother, into the heights of heaven, there assuming the radiance of the sun and becoming transparent to die a black death there.' (8)

The Resurrection of the King

Figs.245-246 show the concluding sequence of the Little Work as depicted by the 'Pretiosa margarita.' After the calcination carried out in the previous woodcuts (figs.212-216), the king is finally resurrected from his sarcophagus in fig. 245 and elevated to the throne in fig.246. The sevenfold planetary star is kindled in ·splendour anew as the king puts a crown on the head of each of his planetary 'servants' lining up for the act. They are only *five* in number, meaning *two* are present on the throne, namely the sun and moon—united in the hermaphroditic body of the king. The text reads:

'Then the king rises from his grave, full of divine grace and made totally spiritual and heavenly with great power and the ability to make all his servants into

247. *The lunar tree of the silvery wedding filled with birds flying up and down.*

246. *. . . and resuming his celestial throne.*

kings. At last he demonstrates his power over his son and his servants by putting a golden crown on the head of each of them and making them kings by his grace, God having granted him great power and majesty. Nobody who is a fraud or an avaricious and sacrilegious person may undertake this work with impure hands. Only he may approach whose soul is pious and wise and who is able to grasp the doctrines [of alchemy] besides the cause of things.' (9)

The Cantilena of George Ripley

A brilliant survey of the nigredo and albedo is given by the famous 'Cantilena,' written by the English alchemist and Canon of Bridlington, Sir George Ripley (1415-1490). The Latin poem describes the nuptials of Mercurius and the production of the homunculus in the vessel, an event soon to be followed by its death

and decomposition. The reason for this putrefaction is explained by the fact that the king has lost his fertility in an act of generation, the object of which has been himself. Like the grain of wheat in the parable, the king is doomed to unregeneration unless he sacrifices himself and dies. In a dreamlike overlapping of images, the expiring king of the 'Cantilena' is indistinguishable from his suffering queen, with whom he has become one in the coniunctio, skillfully presented by Ripley in the less offensive form of a rite of adoption.

In the course of their common dissolution something in the nature of a miracle occurs: the material solution loses its earthy heaviness, and solvent and solute together pass into a higher state immediately following the 'peacock's tail,' namely the albedo in which Luna gives birth to her 'ruddy son' and husband king. Here closes Ripley's account of the Little Work. (10)

Two Royal Birds Fusing into a Third

The Bird's Traumatic Transformation

248. The murderous copulation of birds.

249. Producing the chicken of rebirth.

250. Winged dragons in a vessel of death.

The Cantilena's Royal Transformation

Behold! And in this Cantilena see
The hidden Secrets of Philosophy:
What Joy arises from the Merry Veines
Of Minds elated by such dulcid Straines!

Through Roman Countreys as I once
    did passe,
Where Mercuries Nuptiall celebrated was,
And feeding Stoutly (on the Bride-
    Groomes score)
I learn'd these Novelties unknown before.

There was a certaine Barren King
    by birth,
Composed of the Purest, Noblest Earth,
By nature Sanguine and Devoute, yet hee
Sadly bewailed his Authoritie.

Wherefore am I a King, and Head of all
Those Men and Things that be
    Corporeall?
I have no Issue, yet I'le not deny
'Tis Mee both Heaven and Earth are
    Ruled by.

Yet there is either a Cause Naturall
Or some Defect in the Originall,
Though I was borne without Corruption
And nourished 'neath the Pinions of
    the Sunne.

Each Vegetative which from the Earth
    proceeds
Arises up with its own proper Seeds;
And Animalls, at Seasons, speciously
Abound with Fruit and strangly Multiply.

Alas, my Nature is Restricted so
No Tincture from my Body yet can flow.

It therefore is Infoecund: neither can
It ought availe, in Generating Man.

My Bodies Masse is of a Lasting-Stuffe,
Exceeding delicate, yet hard enough;
And when the Fire Assays to try
    my Sprite,
I am not found to Weigh a Graine
    too light.

My Mother in a Sphaere gave birth
    to mee,
That I might contemplate Rotunditie;
And be more Pure of kind than other
    things,
By Right of Dignity the Peer of Kings.

Yet to my Griefe I know, unlesse I feed
On the Specifics I so sorely need
I cannot Generate: to my Amaze
The End draws near for me,
    Ancient of Daies.

Utterly perish'd is the Flower of Youth,
Through all my Veines there courses
    naught but Death.
Marvelling I heard Christ's voice, that
    from above
I'le be Reborne, I know not by
    what Love.

Else I God's Kingdom cannot enter in:
And therefore, that I may be Borne agen,
I'le Humbled be into my Mother's
    Breast,
Dissolve to my First Matter,
    and there rest.

Hereto the Mother Animates the King,
Hasts his Conception, and does
    forthwith bring

Him closely hidden underneath
    her Traine,
Till, from herselfe, she'd made him
    Flesh againe.

'Twas wonderfull to see with what
    a Grace
This Naturall Union made at one
    Imbrace
Did looke; and by a Bond both
    Sexes knitt,
Like to a Hille and Aire surrounding it.

The Mother unto her Chast Chamber
    goes,
Where in a Bed of Honour she bestowes
Her weary'd selfe, 'twixt Sheets as white
    as Snow
And there makes Signes of her
    approaching Woe.

Ranke Poison issuing from the Dying
    Man
Made her pure Orient face look foule
    and wan;
Hence she commands all Strangers to
    be gone,
Seals upp her Chamber doore, and
    lyes Alone.

Meanwhile she of the Peacocks Flesh
    did Eate
And Dranke the Greene-Lyons Blood
    with that fine Meate,
Which Mercurie, bearing the Dart
    of Passion,
Brought in a Golden Cupp of Babilon.

Thus great with Child, nine months
    she languished
And Bath'd her with the Teares which
    she had shed

Coloured Illumination of the Vessel of Death and Rebirth

251. The peacock's tail of salvation.

The Queen's Silver Wedding in the Vessel

252. The white queen in her solar vessel.

The King's Silver Wedding in the Vessel

253. The red king in his lunar vessel.

For his sweete sake, who from her
should be Pluckt
Full-gorg'd with Milke which now the
Greene-Lyon suckt.

Her Skin in divers Colours did appeare,
Now Black, then Greene, annon 'twas
Red and Cleare.
Oft-times she would sit upright in
her Bed,
And then again repose her
Troubled Head.

Thrice Fifty Nights she lay in grievous
Plight,
As many Daies in Mourning sate upright.
The King Revived was in Thirty more,
His Birth was Fragrant as the
Prim-Rose Flower.

Her Wombe which well proportion'd
was at first
Is now Enlarg'd a Thousand fold at least,
That it bear Witnesse to his Genesis;
The End by Fires the best Approved is.

Her Chamber without Corners smoothly
stands,
With Walls erected like her outstretched
hands;
Or else the Fruit of her ripe Womb
should spoil,
And a sicke Son reward her
labouring Toil.

A burning Stove was plac'd beneath
her Bed,
And on the same another Flourished:
Trimm'd up with Art, and very
Temperate,
Lest her fine Limbes should freeze for
lack of Heate.

Her Chamber doore was Lock'd and
Bolted fast,
Admitting none to Vex her, first or last;
The Furnace-mouth was likewise
Fasten'd so
That thence no Vaporous Matter
forth could go.

And when the Child's Limbs there had
putrefy'd,
The Foulness of the Flesh was laid aside,
Making her fair as Luna, when anon
She coils towards the Splendour
of the Sun.

Her time being come, the Child
Conceiv'd before
Issues re-borne out of her Wombe
once more;
And thereupon resumes a Kingly State,
Possessing fully Heaven's Propitious
Fate.

The Mother's Bed which erstwhile was
a Square
Is shortly after made Orbicular;
And everywhere the Cover,
likewise Round
With Luna's Lustre brightly did abound.

Thus from a Square, the Bed a Globe
is made,
And Purest Whiteness from the
Blackest Shade;
While from the Bed the Ruddy Son
doth spring
To grasp the Joyful Sceptre of a King.

The above translation of Ripley's Latin original dates from the 16th century and is entitled 'George Ripley's Song.' Translator anonymous.

'White' Sequence of Death and Rebirth

The six paintings from the 'Splendor solis' reproduced in figs.248-253 render the concluding stage of the albedo and its final culmination in the royal conjunction (previous painting in fig.205). Fig.248 shows the struggle to deliver the white dove from the nest of its copulating parents. Fig.249 renders the precarious formation of the 'trinitarian' bird of promise, while fig.250 presents its traumatic transformation. Fig.251 shows the many colours of the peacock's tail which herald the dawn and the return of the soul. Figs.252-253 depict the vessels of rebirth in which the lunar queen is merged with the face of the sun, the solar king with the face of the moon.

The lapidary texts accompanying figs. 248-253 read as follows: 'A heavy body cannot be made light without the help of a light body' (fig.248). (1) 'The heat cleanses that which is unclean. It throws off the mineral impurities and bad odours and renews the elixir' (fig.249). (2) 'The philosophers say that whosoever can bring to light a hidden thing is a master of the art. The same is meant by Morienus when he says that he who can revive the soul will have the experience' (fig.250). (3) 'The heat of the fire intensified in the earth has made light the latter's concentrated part and resolved it so as to surpass the other elements' (fig.251). (4) 'Distil seven times and you will have removed the destructive moisture' (fig.252). (5) The lunar fire illuminating the king in fig.253 is defined as that of the Archer, where the fire 'is not burning hot but under the rule of air, or in a state of rest and peace.' (6)

254. *The alchemical laboratory illuminated by Sol and Luna uniting in the sign of ten.*

The Higher Unity of the Denarius

Fig.254 shows the tenth plate of the 'Mutus liber' in which the alchemist pours the contents of the red and white vessels into a pair of scales, while distributing their lunar stars and solar flowers in equal proportions (top row left). The contents of the scales are poured by the sister into the vessel of conjunction given to her by Mercurius in the previous plate (fig.227). Her brother appears to add some liquid to the solution, presumably the permanent water necessary for a successful conjunction. In the middle row the alchemist as glass-blower seals the neck of his vessel, which is placed in the crucible and subjected to heating. The conjunction is realized in the bottom row where the couple succeeds

in hitting the target (extreme left), consisting of the four incinerated elements enclosed in a ball or circle. With their return to the unity of the centre, the brother and sister marry anew in the heavenly shape of Sol and Luna and in the sign of ten.

This number (inscribed at the bottom of their feet) refers to the mystical *denarius,* or to the perfect number of ten, which also 'rules' the *tenth* woodcut of the 'Rosarium.' In alchemy, this number symbolizes the return to unity on a higher level (1+2+3+4=10). Like the Pythagoreans, the alchemists regard 10 as a monad—the beginning and end of all numbers. This view was transmitted to the alchemists through the 'Turba' in which Pythagoras advances the following doctrine: 'The perfect number of

ten: 1+2+3+4=10. One cannot separate ten from four, and ten is only made perfect through four. Beyond this there is no counting and no knowledge.' (1)

The axiom of Maria Prophetissa (fig. 237) represents a famous variation of the doctrine of Pythagoras since it builds on the same numerical succession in its ascent to unity on a higher level: 'One becomes two, two becomes three, and out of the third comes the one as the fourth.' (2) (1+2+3+4=10.)

In alchemy the denarius forms the *totius operis summa,* the culminating point of the work beyond which it is impossible to go except by means of the *multiplicatio.* While the denarius represents a higher stage of unity, it also represents a multiple of 1; thus it may be multiplied to infinity in the ratio of 10, 100, 1000, 10,000, 100,000 etc. For this reason the hermaphroditic denarius is described as *cibus sempiternus* ('everlasting food') (3) or as the white tincture that replenishes itself.

The Sixth Key of Basil Valentine

Fig.256 shows the Sixth Key of Basil Valentine in which the purified king and queen are wed anew by Mercurius philosophorum appearing as a bishop in white vestments. An emblem of the albedo like the swan (background), the white bishop is described by the 'Rosarium' as follows: 'Our sublimation is nothing but the exaltation of bodies, that is, their transformation into spirit, which cannot be except through a gentle fire. Thus we say that it is sublimated into a bishop, that is, exalted.' (4) The text of the Sixth Key alludes to the mortal copulation of birds preceding the royal conjunction:

'The male without the female is looked upon as only half a body, nor can the female without the male be regarded as more complete. For neither can bring

255. *Ascending on the swan's wings.*

136

forth fruit so long as it remains alone. But if the two be conjugally united, there is a perfect body, and their seed is placed in a condition in which it can yield increase. Therefore, when Neptune has prepared his bath [foreground right], measure out carefully the exact quantity of permanent water needed, and let there be neither too little nor too much.

'The twofold fiery male [foreground left] must be fed with a snowy swan, and then they must mutually slay each other and restore each other to life. And the air of the four quarters of the world must occupy three parts of the room of the imprisoned fiery male, that the death-song of the swans may be distinctly heard. Then the swan roasted will become food for the king, and the fiery king will be seized with great love towards the lovely voice of the queen and will take his fill of delight in embracing her, until they both vanish and coalesce into one body.' (5)

A Snowy Stone Born in Thin Air

Fig.257 shows the birth of the white stone on the snowy summit of Mount Helicon. The text explains: 'The nigredo is identical with Saturn, he is the touchstone of truth, and instead of Jupiter he devoured a stone . . . This stone is vomited by Saturn when it becomes white, and then placed on top of the Helicon as a monument to men, as Hesiod wrote. For the true whiteness is hidden under the blackness and is taken out of its belly, that is, out of the small belly of Saturn. That is why Democritus says: Purify the lead by a special washing, extract the blackness and the darkness from it, and its whiteness will appear.' (6)

The Philosophers' White Swan

In the Sixth Key of Basil Valentine, the song of the dying swans varies the theme of death and rebirth expressed by the copulation of the winged and wingless birds. The magic bird emerging from their union is often represented as a swan (or dove). The swan is a classical emblem of the albedo because of its wings and immaculate whiteness. As in the legend of Leda and the Swan, the bird is also a symbol of divine union. In addition to the conjugal implications of the swan, the spiritual and transcendent nature of the bird is apparent in its wings of heavenly flight and divine sound (fig. 255). In antiquity, swans were honoured as the sacred birds of Apollon, the god of music, spirit and beauty.

Says an alchemical author: 'The old masters were wont to call this work their white swan, their albefication, or making white, their sublimation, distillation, circulation, and purification.' (7)

256. *The white bishop celebrating the silver wedding of the revived king and queen.*

The Elevating Wings of the Swan

The powerful wings acquired by the resurrected hermaphrodite are those of the swan. They are soon to be put to use as the rebis begins to waft its wings and to take off. When this happens, the albedo and the Little Work come to an end and a new stage of the opus is inaugurated. This is known as the Great Work, which opens with the *citrinitas,* or 'yellow' stage, during which the hermaphrodite wings its way toward the sun. In so doing, the rebis transforms the lunar light into that of solar light with its greater powers of illumination and glorification. The perils and wonders of this Ikaros flight are described on pp.140-161.

257. *The leaden god of depression spitting out the stone of silvery regeneration.*

258. 'Who is she that cometh forth as the rising dawn, fair as the moon?' (1)

The White Mass of Alchemy

Transformed into the white bishop of the albedo, the adept above appears as priest and Christ figure illuminated by the light of the lunar stone. Subjecting *himself* to the sacrifice of the Mass, the alchemical priest suffers the crushing of his body and the shedding of his blood which, in turn, effect his resurrection and rebirth in the womb of the Virgin Mother (left). The alchemist's secret identification with the Christ figure is spelled out by the image of the Saviour embroidered on the back of his chasuble and also by his gesture of surrender, which imitates the crucified arms of the suffering Christ.

The engraving illustrates a famous treatise by Melchior Cibenensis in which the alchemical process of transformation is expounded in the form of the Catholic Mass. Like Christ, the artifex of the nigredo and albedo suffers the breaking and eating of his bread, or body, and the shedding and drinking of his wine, or blood. Thus the adept himself partakes of the Christian mysteries of redemption and regeneration: the crucified victim's surrender of his spirit in front of the Lord's altar in fig.258 engenders the act of rebirth far left. After bleeding to death in the nest of Golgatha with its crown of thorns, the dying adept is finally reborn in the nest of Bethlehem with its crown of light. The White Mass of alchemy is presented as follows by Melchior Cibenensis:

Introitus missae: The basis of the art is the dissolution of the bodies.
Kyrie, fons: Lord, fountain of goodness, inspirer of the sacred art, from whom all good things come to your faithful, have mercy.
Christe: Christ, Holy one, blessed stone of the art of science who for the salvation of the world hast inspired the light of science . . . have mercy.
Kyrie, ignis divine: Lord, divine fire, help our hearts, that we may be able, to your praise, to expand the sacraments of the art, have mercy.
Gloria in excelsis.
Collecta.
Epistola.
Graduale: Arise, O north wind, and come, south wind; blow through my garden,

259. White rebirth of the divine child.

and let the aromatic spices thereof flow. *Versus:* He descends like rain upon the fleece, and as showers falling gently upon the earth. Alleluja. O blest creator of the earth, whiter than snow, sweeter than sweetness, fragrant at the bottom of the vessel like balsam. O salutary medicine for men, that carest for every weakness of the body; O sublime fount where gushes forth truly the true water of life into the land of thy faithful.
Ave Praeclara: Hail, clear shining star of the sea, Mary, divinely born for the enlightenment of the nations . . .
Virgin, ornament of the world,
Queen of Heaven, elect above all like the Sun, lovely as the light of the moon . . .
Let us drink in solemn faith of the sweet stream that
Flowed from the rock in the desert, and,
Girding our loins that the sea has bathed,
Gaze on the brazen crucified serpent.
O Virgin, who hast been made mother
By the sacred fire and the Father's word,
Which thou didst bear like the
Burning Bush, let us, as cattle,
Ringstraked, speckled and spotted,
Draw near with our feet,
With pure lips and heart. (2)

To this hymn Melchior Cibenensis adds the important statement: 'The *Ave Praeclara* must be sung; it shall be called the 'testament of the art,' since the whole chemical art is figuratively concealed therein, and blessed is he that understands this sequence.' (3)

Feeding on the Virgin's White Tincture

Fig.261 shows a variant of the stone produced in fig.258. Inside the fiery triangle of the lapis, the sun and moon enter into the white conjunction shown in its bottom corner and expressed by the *cibatio* or 'feeding' of the philosophers' son. In both pictures he imbibes the *tinctura alba* flowing from the breasts of the lunar virgin. 'The stone, like the infant, must be nourished by the virgin's milk,' (4) reads the motto of fig.258.

The winged dragon also enclosed by the triangle of fig.261 gives the trauma of rebirth, the agony of the bones when crushed and incinerated by the jaws of Mercurius philosophorum. On top of the fiery triangle the three birds of the albedo triumphantly flap their wings. The bird perching in the solar corner represents the spirit of the sun, the bird opposite the spirit of the moon. Their common offspring, flapping its wings midway between its parents, appears just above its double and symbol—the philosophers' son uniting the sun and moon *in utero virginis.*

An emblem of the suckling Mother, the lower trinity represents the world of nature and instinct, equated by the engraving with the realm of the Dragon and the Devil. The upper trinity with its winged beings represents the world of masculine spirit and contains an obvious reference to the Christian Trinity. The fiery merging of these opposite trinitarian worlds into the Seal of Solomon or the stone of the philosophers implies a theology shocking to the medieval mind: *Deus quid est diabolus*—'God who is [also] the Devil.' (5) This stupendous *coniunctio oppositorum* is spanned by the lunar stone of figs.258 and 261, the former uniting Golgatha and Bethlehem, the latter the Holy Trinity and the Devil.

The Lunar Mercurius Child of Rebirth

Fig.259 shows the eleventh plate of the 'Mutus liber' in which the white rebirth is hailed by the alchemist and his sister. Two angels ascend with the silvery vessel enclosing the Boy Mercurius striding the sun and moon. The plate is almost an exact copy of the eighth plate of the 'Mutus liber' which shows the first coniunctio (fig.141). A comparison between the two plates emphasizes the moonlike, ethereal nature of the second coniunctio.

The Lunar Light of Sublimated Love

Fig.260 shows Luna nourishing her son and spouse with the white tincture. The feet of the lunar mother are submerged in a river bed or fountain containing the element indispensable for rebirth. Senior comments on this feature of the albedo: 'The full moon is . . . the mistress of the moisture . . . the perfect round stone and the sea, wherefore I know that the moon is the root of this hidden science. I also know that the two birds emanate from the full moon, because the philosopher depicts them as being united [therein].' (6)

The incestuous features of the second coniunctio are relieved by the silvery radiance of Luna which makes earthly things transparent and ghostlike. The ethereal nature of objects in moonshine expresses the sublimation achieved in the albedo, where the former black earth, or polluted body, appears in the shape described by Senior: 'The white foliated earth is the crown of victory, which is ashes extracted from ashes, and their second body.' (7)

Earth and moon coincide in the albedo where Luna appears as Earth Mother, and the 'white foliated earth' as the surface of the moon. Hence the 'Rosarium' says: 'When thou seest the earth as whitest snow . . . the ash is extracted from ash and earth, sublimated and honoured . . . the white foliated earth is the good that is sought.' (8)

The background scenery of fig.260 shows the profound transformation of

260. Transforming the earth into the moon: elevating matter to the lunar state.

matter effected between the two mountain tops of conjunction. The star-spangled salamander frolicking in the fire on the left mountain top represents the first coniunctio in its massive and material splendour. Opposite, the winged and wingless birds in their gory nest represent the second coniunctio in its weightless and volatile beauty. The proper illumination of the albedo is naturally the plenilunium on whose rays the soul descends from heaven as a silvery virgin. This is the anima transformed into the figure of the blessed sister and holy mother—the anima as spirit of the earth, spirit of the sea, and spirit of the love between the sexes. Her fusing qualities in the albedo involves the ego in a conjunction with the self, experienced now at its 'winged' or spiritual level.

261. Fiery conjunction of two trinitarian worlds, merged in the Seal of Solomon.

262.

Citrinitas: 'Yellow' Death and Putrefaction

'Mercurius is begotten by nature as the son of nature and the fruit of the liquid element. But even as the Son of Man is begotten by the philosopher and created as the fruit of the Virgin, so must he [Mercurius] be raised from the earth and cleansed of all earthiness, then he ascends entire into the air, and is changed into spirit. Thus is fulfilled the word of the philosopher: He ascends from earth to heaven and receives the power of Above and Below, and puts off his earthy and impure nature and clothes himself in the heavenly nature.'
                    Theatrum chemicum. (1)

Fig.263 shows the eleventh woodcut of the 'Rosarium' which renders the sequel to the white conjunction. The winged hermaphrodite has taken off from the earth and is now soaring as a royal swan high up in the air. Surrounded by banks of clouds and looking down upon the earth and sea below, the copulating hermaphrodite is presented as an angel in the state of 'fermentation' *(fermentatio)*. After the bliss of orgasm on the lunar body, the king's fusing experience comes to a close as his queen gathers her legs and extracts his erected member from her womb. Instead, her lap becomes a tomb for the king, now suffused with Mercurius philosophorum in his 'fermenting' state. The motto explains:

Here Sol is buried and overflowed
With Mercurius philosophorum. (2)

According to the text, this strange form of copulation is known as the 'stone's conjunction with its ferment.' (3) Quoting Hermes, the 'Rosarium' says: 'Sow your gold [Sol] in the white foliated earth, which through the calcination has become fiery, subtle and airy. Therefore we sow the gold in that earth when we place the tincture of gold in it. For the gold can never tinge another body to perfection except itself and this only through the art. Gold is the ferment of the work without which nothing may be brought to completion; it is as the ferment of the paste, or the coagulation of the milk in the cheese, or the musk in a good smell: by means of it is made the composition of the greater elixir, for it lightens up and preserves from the scorching, which is the sign of perfection . . .

'After the perfect fixation or fusion comes the regimen of the stone's conjunction with its ferment, namely until the work arrives at its completion. This does not take place at once since it is not the intention of nature to do so; but it takes place by means of the copulation, that is, little by little; by means of the coagulation is also formed the true and uniform medicine. And therefore this copulation is caused by the subtle parts [of the stone] which transform and change themselves into a spiritual form and essence (4) . . . And this you can grasp with your intellect when it has become a transparent body and continued into a unity through the conjunction or commixture of [the] multiple parts [of the stone] without division, discontinuation or termination in any density, [finally forming] a transparent figure through all its parts.' (5)

The Separation from the Birds' Nest

Fig.264 shows the engraved variant of the 'Rosarium' woodcut. Terminating its ecstasy of copulation, the winged hermaphrodite separates into its male and female halves while leaving the fertile soil

FERMENTATIO.

263. A royal swan taking off.

in which it nested at the moment of conjunction (background). Separating from his queen, the king gazes wistfully at her finger stuck between two of his own in a gesture signifying intercourse. The spiritual nature of their bodies is indicated by their Christ-like walking on the water, a release from the laws of gravity produced by their conquest of the wings of the fully fledged bird of the albedo. The sower in the background illustrates the Hermes dictum, 'Sow your gold in the white foliated earth.'

A variant of fig.264 appears in fig.265 which shows the angelic lovers of the white conjunction in their royal nest. The fully fledged bird carried by the queen has 'spread' its wings to the body of the king also, just as the two mercurial wands held by the couple testify to their conjunction. However, the lovers are on the point of being cut off from their nest by the sword of Mars, the cruel agent of their 'separation.'

Fermentation of the Stone by Cleavage

Fig.262 renders Barchusen's variation upon the eleventh woodcut of the 'Rosarium.' The fire of the second conjunction blazing in plate 48 disappears from the vessel in the subsequent plate, where the moon egg leaves its fiery nest and begins to float in space as the 'white foliated earth.' The remarkable surface of the lunar earth illustrates its state of 'fermentation,' indicated by concentric rings spreading from its centre while transforming its substance. At the same time the neck of the retort appears to have been knocked off by the flying globe, apparently as a result of its entry into the dark cavity of the vessel.

The tubal symbolism of plate 50 shows the retort recovering its neck but not its plug; this feature is probably meant to express the floating and fermenting egg's entry into the tubal section of the vessel, where it is attacked by a giant snake.* In plate 51 the philosophers' egg is pierced by the *serpent mercurialis*, which in the following plates 52-56 (figs.271 and 283) attempts to cleave or constrict it with vigorous movements of its body. The animal illustrates the 'stone's conjunction with its ferment,' a transformation process interpreted by Barchusen as a fermentation by cleavage division.

Dissolution of the Coagulated Stone

The renewed bout of separation, burial, putrefaction and fermentation constitutes the opening phase of the *citrinitas*. Its distant and golden aim is to yellow the 'white foliated earth' which must be brought from the lunar to the solar state, or from the state of silver to the state of gold. Says Senior: 'This is the preparation which they call the change and the division and this on account of its change in the preparation, from stage to stage, from infirmity to power, from the gross to the fine and subtle. In such a manner the semen alone converts itself under the influence of the matrix of the natural preparation, from thing to thing, until from this is formed the perfect man from that which was his root and beginning.' (6)

On the following pages we shall study further alchemical expressions of the mystery and paradox of the citrinitas: a winged dissolution, a fermenting copulation, a putrefying glorification.

264. The winged hermaphrodite leaving the earth prepared for its nesting descent.

265. King and queen separating from the winged nest of their lunar conjunction.

---

* Since the other end of the tube is reached in Barchusen's plates 58-59 (fig.287), the intervening pictures may be interpreted as rendering the egg's traversal of the tube.

266. The sower-alchemist yellowing his heavenly earth with coins of fermenting gold.

Yellow Death and Golden Fermentation

'The hour is come, that the Son of man should be glorified. Verily, verily, I say unto you, Except a corn of wheat fall into the ground and die, it abideth alone: but if it die, it bringeth forth much fruit.'

John 12:23-24.

'This mixture or union cannot be realized without transformation, which means a sublimation of the body and its reduction into a spiritual form.'

Rosarium philosophorum. (1)

'Making her fair as Luna, she coils anon Towards the Splendour of the Sun.'

Ripley's Cantilena, verse 25.

267. The fermenting bodies of Sol and Luna raised toward heaven and Doomsday.

The Sower's Sacrifice of His White Gold

Fig.266 shows the alchemist-as-sower scattering the treasures he has just reaped in the albedo and so preparing the 'snow-white fields' of the albefied earth. This is an earth redeemed from the laws of gravity by its transformation into a celestial body weighing no more than a heap of leaves. The verse reads:

The farmers entrust their seed to the fat earth,
After having foliated it with their mattocks.
The philosophers have taught that the gold must be
Scattered over the snow-white fields
Weighing no more than the light leaves.
When you undertake this, pay good attention to it,
For from the wheat you see, as in a Mirror, that gold germinates. (2)

The motto quotes the Hermes dictum 'Sow your gold in the white foliated earth,' (3) a saying of considerable antiquity and appearing already in Senior in connection with the lunar, albefied earth:

'The foliate water, which is the gold of the philosophers, Lord Hermes called the egg with many names. The lower world is the body and the burnt ashes, to which they reduce the venerable soul. And the burnt ashes and the soul are the gold of the sages which they sow in their white earth, and in the earth scattered with stars, foliate, blessed, and thirsting, which he called the earth of leaves and the earth of silver and the earth of gold (4) . . . [Wherefore] Hermes said: Sow the gold in the white foliated earth. For the white foliated earth is the crown of victory, which is ashes extracted from ashes.' (5)

Rising on the Raising Forces of Hermetic Fermentation

Fig.267 entitled *fermentatio* shows a variant of the Hermes dictum with Sol and Luna fermenting as the grains of corn sown by the alchemist in the white foliated earth. The rising posture of the royal bodies testifies to the elevating power of the sown earth, i.e., to the swelling quality of the golden ferment. In particular, this feature is symbolized by the sceptred angel to the right announcing with her trumpet the raising of the dead and the Day of Judgement.

The sower-symbol's paradoxical pattern of gain through loss, or of fertility through burial, renders the essence of the citrinitas: during this stage the lunar egg or rebis is fermenting, cleaving and dying while winging its way toward the splendour of the sun.

Sealing the Mother in Her Infant's Belly

In the 'Introitus apertus' the 'yellowing' process is described as follows: 'The reign of Mars [fig.265] begins with a light yellow, or dirty brown colour, but at last exhibits the transitory hues of the rainbow and the peacock's tail. At this stage the compound is drier, and the images of various forms are seen to be imitated. During this period the compound often shows like a hyacinth with a tinge of gold.

'The mother being now sealed in her infant's belly, swells and is purified, but because of the present great purity of the compound, no putridity can have place in this regimen, but some obscure colours come and go, and they are pleasant to look on. Know that our virgin earth here undergoes the last degree of cultivation, that the fruit of the sun may be sown and ripened. Hence you should keep up a moderate temperature; then there will be seen, about the thirtieth day of this reign, a yellow colour which within two weeks from its first appearance will tinge the whole substance with its own orange hue.' (6)

The Royal Art of the Alchemist's Opus

The alchemist's voluntary sacrifice in the citrinitas of the riches he has gained in the albedo reflects the inexorable process of alchemical transformation compelling the adept to ever new adjustments, unexplored procedures, unknown attitudes. With his air of quiet and humble agony the sower-alchemist of fig.266 displays his willingness to obey an obscure power and compelling development which requires the death and fermentation of his white gold that has been achieved after so much toil and suffering.

In the treatises it is stressed that the artifex must scorn avarice and selfishness and always be willing to turn the wheel on which he is turned. Only thus may the movement of the *rota philosophica* be sustained and the wheel in its perfect motion arrive at the supreme goal of the *opus circulatorium*. Therefore, what has been gained in the act of conjunction must invariably be left in the subsequent putrefaction in order that the opus may be fulfilled and the royal art be led to those transparent heights where the adept gets beyond himself and becomes a pure medium.

Again and again the alchemists compare their opus to the work of an artist and their process of transformation to the development of an art. This comparison is of interest since great art,

among many qualities, displays such remarkable features as continuous progress, increasing refinement, growing profundity. Like the stages of the alchemical opus, the stages of an artist's development are each of them *different,* and this difference is not one of decline but one of improvement and transcendence.

This pattern of growth in an individuation process jointly reflected by alchemy, art and mysticism is admirably described by St.John of the Cross: 'He who learns the finest details of an art always goes forward in the dark and not with the initial knowledge, for, if he does not leave it behind him, he could never be liberated from it.' (7)

This phrase aptly describes the royal imagery of the opening citrinitas, in which the artist leaves behind him the mastery he has just gained in order to learn the finer details of his divine art. The growing light of solar illumination helps him to discern more clearly the imperfections of the lunar sphere.

Fermenting Egg of Blastocyst Evolution

The Hermetic actions of the opening citrinitas symbolize the unconscious, regressive play-back of blastocyst implantation and blastocyst growth (figs.268-270). The teeming cellular divisions of the blastocyst as it develops out of its previous morula stage may aptly be described as a process of 'fermentation.' While the fertilized and cleaving egg is conveyed along the uterine tube toward the uterine cavity, it feeds on the metaplasmic granules stored up in its 'white.' They sustain its continued divisions which finally result in its transformation into a blastocyst. This final, perfect stage of the egg (figs.269-270) endows it with an outer shell of trophoblast cells forming a sticky surface which in due time will attach itself to the spongy lining of the uterus (fig.268).

The transition from morula to blastocyst takes place as the 'fermenting' egg is about to enter the uterine cavity (Barchusen's plates 49-50, fig.262). The morula is a ball of 32 solidly packed cells which have developed as the result of five preceding cleavage divisions occurring while the egg moves slowly down the uterine tube. After its fertilization high up in the tube the egg cell begins its divisions into two cells, four, eight, sixteen, and, finally, thirty-two cells.

If the cleavage divisions were played in reverse, they would present a series of divisions gradually undoing themselves by restoring the egg to its original, undivided unity. This, precisely, is the fate of the philosophers' egg or stone when 'yellowing' into solar maturity. On the following pages it enters the dark and narrow tube of Mercurius spelling unity through cleavage, or wholeness through decomposition.

Film Play-Back of 'Nesting' Sequence

268. Fusing with the 'lunar earth,' the free-floating blastocyst burrows down into the nutrient-rich, spongy lining of the womb. There, it becomes firmly implanted as the maternal tissues grow to form a capsule over it, and the whole appears like the dome of a minute plateau. The reversal of this natural sequence has the 'nested embryo' leave its maternal soil and ascend as a 'flying' blastocyst.

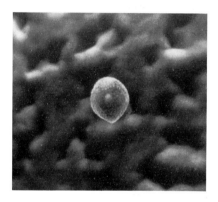

269. Preparing to land on the 'moon,' the blastocyst hovers over the surface of the uterus. As the fermenting egg begins its regressive space journey (below), it slowly changes into a cleaving morula. This metamorphosis is symbolically rendered on the following pages, which show the cleavage divisions of the ascending moon egg by means of arrowed birds, cutting swords and constricting serpents.

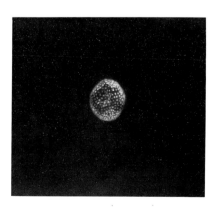

270. Space capsule heading for the moon.

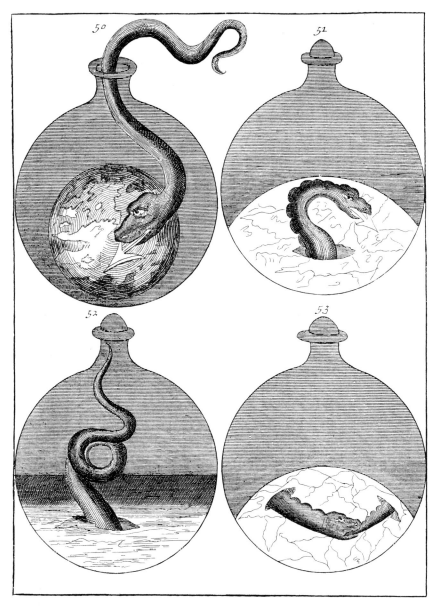

271. The ascending moon egg cleaved by the mercurial snake in the vessel's tubal part.

Death of a Batman

Fig.274 shows the twelfth woodcut of the 'Rosarium' which renders the stage of 'illumination' *(illuminatio)*. The winged sun is about to descend into a narrow well or cistern indistinguishable from the sarcophagus of the earlier woodcuts. The motto emphasizes the dying movement of the sun as it wings its way into the dark and unknown well:

*Here Sol disappears again and is drowned
In Mercurius philosophorum. (1)*

In spite of the sun's depressive loss of brilliance, the woodcut nevertheless illustrates the alchemist's experience of 'illumination.' Such paradoxical pattern is explained by the specific dynamics of the 'yellowing' work, which aim at colouring the white stone, or lunar herma-

phrodite, by means of an elevation to the solar sphere. The 'Rosarium' text explains: 'Raymundus: However much this our stone now contains the natural tincture, the stone being turned into a perfect magnesian body, it has not in itself any movement except that which is effected by the art and the operation.' (2)

As the gold that was sown in the white foliated earth begins to ferment, the silvery moon is made to 'rise' toward the sun in a golden elevation 'improving the germ' by transmuting the lunar silver into the solar gold. Quoting Geber, the text of the 'Rosarium' goes on to explain its work of 'illumination':

'The most precious of metals is the gold, for it is the soul which conjoins the spirit with the imperfect body, for just as the human body is dead and immovable without the soul, so too is the impure body [of the stone] without the

ferment which is its soul, terrestrial and vegetable. For it is the reddening tincture which transforms every body, and it is the ferment which converts the whole mass into its own nature. Just as the sun and moon govern over the other planets, so these two bodies [gold and silver] govern over the other metals, which are converted and conformed to the nature of the two above mentioned bodies. And therefore it is called the ferment, for without it the germ would never improve. And just as a bit of ferment corrupts the whole mass, that is, transmutes and elevates it, so too it happens with our stone.' (3)

Mercurial Snake Cleaving Egg

Barchusen's variation upon the twelfth woodcut of the 'Rosarium' is reproduced in fig.271. Plate 50 shows the meeting of the flying moon egg and the mercurial serpent in the tubal part of the vessel, followed by the serpent's attack in plate 51. With its arrow-pointed tongue, the snake pierces the egg longitudinally, its head emerging at the polar end of the philosophers' egg which by now has 'turned into a perfect magnesian body,' as the 'Rosarium' says.

In plate 52 the lashing tail of the snake is seen in a close-up of the same hole that was dug in the previous plate; evidently the *serpens mercurialis* has turned around in a repeated attempt to cleave the egg longitudinally. In plate 53 the serpent attempts to divide or constrict the egg, not vertically but horizontally, its tail and head joined in a tightening knot around the cap of the philosophers' egg.

Piercing Rays of Divine Illumination

Fig.273 shows the engraved variant of the 'Rosarium' woodcut. Sol endowed with wings descends into a narrow cistern or tube, while Luna with her bow and arrow aims at her spouse in order to pierce him. This amplification corre-

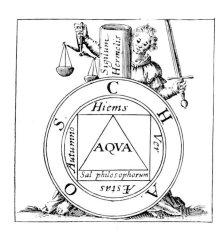

272. Justice punishing the egg of 'chaos.'

sponds with Barchusen's plates 50-53 by interpreting the winged flight of the fermenting stone or rebis as a suffering of death by cleavage.

Once more, the king in the embrace of his queen is treacherously slain by the snake-bite of the mother-beloved, or pierced by her arrow of love. In the 'Rosinus ad Sarratantem' the hermaphrodite tells of its slaughter by Mercurius 'who with an arrow from our quiver bound together, that is, joined in one body, wretched me, that is, I who possess the matter of mercury and the moon . . . and my beloved, that is, the fatness of the sun conjoined with the moisture of the moon.' (4)

The Seventh Key of Basil Valentine

Fig.272 shows the Seventh Key of Basil Valentine in which Justice with her Sword and Scales executes judgement over the stone enclosed in the round vessel. Its opened neck inscribed with the 'Hermetic Seal' *(Sigillum Hermetis)* forms part of the stone, whose circular shape is emphasized by the 'Rosarium' in the text accompanying its twelfth woodcut:

'My son, take the simple and round body and do not take the triangle or the quadrangle; but take the round body, for the round body is more related to simplicity than the triangle. Also it should be noted that the simple body has no angles, since it is the first and the last among the planets just as the sun is it among the stars.' (5)

The propinquity of Basil Valentine's stone to the egg of the philosophers is emphasized by its double-lined outer circle, which in the Ninth Key of Basil Valentine (fig.296) denotes the philosophical egg. The fermenting outer layer of the egg termed 'chaos' encloses the quadrature of the four seasons *(hiems, ver, aestas, autumno)*, the 'philosophers' salt' *(sal philosophorum)*, and the triangle of 'water' *(aqua)*—all testifying to the cosmic and life-giving qualities of the egg-stone presented. The raised sword of Justice and the scales sinking in its favour suggest punishment by piercing or cleavage.

Solar Purgation of the Heavenly Earth

The text of the Seventh Key is very obscure, yet one may distinguish a symbolic action related to the 'yellowing' work and its stage of 'illumination.' The stone is presented as the 'earth of the philosophers' imbued with the precious 'spiritual water' and appearing now in its elevated shape as heavenly city—threatened, however, by 'earthly foes' identified with worms and reptiles. The fiery purgation of the moist, earthy body is presented as effecting its gradual desiccation and elevation into the dry sphere

273. Treacherous Luna piercing her winged husband in the neck of the solar vessel.

of the angels and the fiery realm of divine illumination:

'The earth of the sages should not be melted and dissolved too soon, otherwise the healthy fishes in your water would be changed into scorpions. If you would perform our task rightly, take the spiritual water, in which the spirit was from the beginning, and preserve it in a closely shut castle. For the heavenly city is about to be besieged by earthly foes, and your heaven must be strongly fortified with three impassable and well-guarded walls, and let the one entrance be well protected.

'When all this has been completed, then light the lamp of wisdom and seek

ILLVMINATIO.

274. Painful illumination of a solar body.

with it the coin that was lost, showing only such light as is needed. For you must know that the worms and reptiles dwell in the cold and humid earth because of their quality, while man has his proper habitation upon the face of the earth with its tempered and blended qualities. The angelic spirits on the other hand, being endowed with an angelic and not with an earthly body, and not subjected to the flesh of sin of human beings, are living at a higher level and enabled to endure the fire and the cold both in the upper and in the lower regions. When man shall have been glorified, his body will become like the angelic body in this respect [for] God reigns in heaven and on earth and works all in all. If we carefully cultivate the life of our souls, we shall be sons and heirs of God, and shall be able to do that which now seems impossible. But this can be effected only by the drying up of all water, and by the purging of heaven and earth and all men with [solar] fire.' (6)

The Rising Philosophical Egg

Another alchemical author expresses the elevating effects of spiritual water in interplay with solar fire thus: 'Just as May-dew enclosed in an egg-shell makes the egg, or its contents, ascend into heaven by means of the sun's heat, so too the cloudy water, or dew, makes the philosophers' egg ascend, sublimating, elevating, and perfecting [it]. That same water is also the strongest vinegar, transmuting the body into pure spirit.' (7)

275. The assailing bull launching a new stage of unrest, suffering and transformation.

Dissolution of the White Rebirth

Above is shown the twelfth engraving of the 'Mutus liber' in which the white rebirth of the previous engraving (fig. 259) is followed by a new bout of mortification (cf. the similar sequence of plates 8-9, figs.141 and 227). Once more the onrushing bull inaugurates a new process of transformation, and once more the adept and his sister collect the 'May-dew' or prima materia of their work in dishes spread out on the ground. In the bottom row the brother extends a decanter into which his mystical sister pours the dew. The prospective nature of the couple's work is again brought out by the emergence of Mercurius philosophorum, who appears to receive the vessel at the hands of the woman. The unit-

ing powers of this mercurial vessel and its tincture are explored by the alchemist and his sister in the next plate of the 'Mutus liber,' depicted on fig.325. The transparency of the engraving's scenery makes it a good basis for the solar illumination now approaching.

Heavenly Ascent on the Swan's Wings

276. A rising swan yellowing the egg.

Birds play a prominent part in the citrinitas with its elevation of the stone and winged ascent of the rebis. The two medals of fig.276 show the heavenly flight of the lunar earth on the swan's wings. The first medal renders the white bird taking off from the earth while carrying on its back the moon egg with its fully fledged bird, white queen and white lilies of conjunction. The ascending bird spits out its milky liquid into the silvery sea, now left for a still higher goal.

In the great monument of the opus (fig.399) this motif is explained as follows: 'A sea of pure silver which represents the mercurial fluid whereby the tinctures are united. A swan is swimming in the sea, spitting out a milky liquid from his beak. This swan is the white elixir, the white chalk, the arsenic of the philosophers, the thing common to both ferments.' (1) The solar nest of the phoenix bird blazing above the lunar swan indicates the process of 'yellowing.' The inscription explains: 'When you see the white colour, cool down your work, and you will arrive from the lunar to the solar colour.'

The second medal describes the same transition. The philosophical egg resting on the back of the rising swan is gradually reddened from within by the pelican's blood and the phoenix's fire, both emblems of the red energies of the sun. The inscription reads: 'So great is the medicine that it will produce gold.'

Solar Ascent: the Rape of Ganymede

Fig.278 shows the alchemical eagle or vulture perching on top of the Mountain of the Adepts while proclaiming the four stages of the opus: 'I am the black, white, yellow and red.' (The wingless raven at the base of the mountain represents the nigredo.) The eagle appears as the instrument of 'yellowing' or 'reddening' when the swan's wings can elevate the stone no further into heaven. According to one alchemical author, the 'eagle flies up to the clouds and receives the rays of the sun in his eyes.' (2)

Fig.279 shows the alchemist as Ganymede ascending on the back of the eagle while 'rejoicing in God' *(in deo laetandum).* The rape of Ganymede by the eagle of Zeus is a popular allegory for the colouring of the soaring hermaphrodite, pierced by the lightning and solar rays of the citrinitas. According to Greek legend, Zeus fell in love with Ganymede because of his adolescent (hermaphroditic) beauty. Transforming himself into the bird carrying his lightning rod, the god swooped down on the youth, pierced him with his claws, and raised him on powerful wings to the splendour of the sun and the glory of Olympus. The agony of spiritual elevation and solar transformation expressed by the legend aptly explains its alchemical popularity.

A Citrine Halo of Piercing Eagles

The solar bird of alchemy appears in an equally interesting context in fig.277. The woodcut reproduces Senior's famous vision of the god of alchemy and his Book of Secrets, opened to the pages that describe the transition from the whiteness to the redness. This passage is expressed by an arch of armed eagles obviously intending to pierce and cleave with their arrows the hooded master, who, pale with emotion, but outwardly controlled, awaits his heavenly fate. Senior's description of his vision reads as follows:

'I and the bearded Oboel entered into a certain house under the earth, and later I and Elhasam saw the burning seventh sphere of the universe in the prison of Joseph, and I saw on its roof pictures of nine eagles with out-spread wings, as if they were flying, and with outstretched and open claws. In the claw of each of the eagles was a thing like the fully-drawn bow which is carried by archers, and on the wall of the house, both on the right and on the left of the entrance, images of men, standing, clothed in garments of divers colours and having their hands stretched out toward the interior of the hall, where some statue was seated . . . in a chair like those used by physicians, the chair being separate from the figure. In its lap, resting on the arms—the two hands of the figure being stretched out on its knees—was a stone slab, also separate, the length of which was about one arm, and the breadth about one palm. The fingers of both its hands were bent behind the slab, as if holding it. The slab was like an open book, exhibited to all who entered as if to suggest that they should look at it. And in the part of the hall where the statue was situated were

278. The crying vulture proclaiming the coloured sequence of the opus alchymicum.

277. Piercing halo of a hooded master.

different pictures of innumerable things and of hieroglyphs (3) . . .

'I shall now make known to you what the wise man who made the statue has hidden in that house. In it he has described that whole science, as it were, in the figure, and taught his wisdom in the stone, and revealed it to the discerning.' (4)

The opened Book of Secrets in fig.277 depicts the *opus ad albam* and the *opus ad rubeum*. The left page shows Luna and Sol in their coitive fight as the winged and wingless birds struggling to deliver the full moon (top left). Commenting on this image, Senior gives us the information that the 'two linked birds that were holding one another appeared like a circle, like an image of 'two in one.' At the top of the one that was flying was a circle and, above those two birds, at the top of the tablet close to the fingers of the statue, was an image of the luminous moon.' (5)

On the right page, the solar circles indicate the *opus ad rubeum*. According to Senior, the two upper circles describe 1) 'the sun emitting its [two] rays' (*imago solis emittens radios*); 2) 'the sun with one descending ray' (*imago solis cum uno radio descendente*). (6) The three solar rays point to 'a black circle with circular divisions so as to become one-third and two-thirds.' (7) As further explained, the innermost third depicts the circle of the moon; the second third a black circle enclosing the moon in a

conjugal embrace termed 'two in one'; (8) the third third the 'single sun' (*sol simplex*), also termed the 'one in one.' (9) This circle forms a solar cover around the moon and its black conjugal matrix so that the big radiant circle signifies the conjunction of the sun and moon at the solar stage of the work (see pp.162-163).

The transition from the silvery to the golden page covers the 'yellowing' phase, which in Senior is expressed by an arch of armed eagles. This transitional symbol adds yet another image to the cutting swords, splitting arrows, cleaving serpents, and piercing rays of the citrinitas.

279. Soaring toward the source of light.

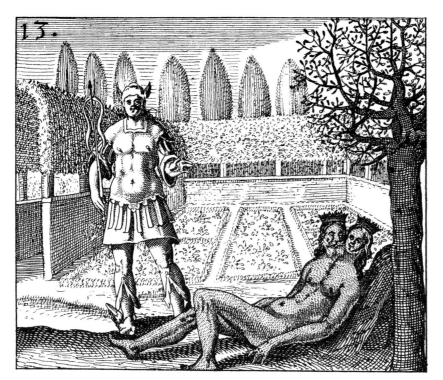

280. Rising toward the philosophers' rose garden on the wings of the guide Mercurius.

Feeding on the Golden Ferment

Fig. 281 shows the thirteenth woodcut of the 'Rosarium' in which the hermaphrodite lies dead and scorched in its sarcophagus, its soaring wings folded in the shape of a heart. The motto reads:

Here is Sol turned black, becoming with Mercurius philosophorum one heart. (1)

The condition is termed *nutrimentum,* or 'nourishment.' As indicated by the text, this term refers to the red sulphur digested by the silvery moon after its purgation. The substance provides it with the 'nourishment' that will slowly transform it into a golden body:

'If, as mentioned above, the moon contains the white sulphur, just as the gold contains the red, it still hides the species of fire under the cover of its whiteness. Therefore it is also possible to make gold out of all silver, and therefore the philosopher says: There is no gold which has not before been silver. Thus the silver contains some indigested qualities which it is possible to purge from it by means of the art. And thus the particular may pass into the fixed Mercurius and into the vicinity of the nature of gold. For then it contains all that is gold through the addition of the red sulphur of the philosophers with which it is digested more and more; and the yellowing *(citrinatio)* is caused in it by the addition of the perfect body simply because both are of the same nature. But it is impossible to do this with the other [metallic] bodies because they are not so re-

lated to the same perfect nature as it [the silver] is; the combustible and fetid sulphur prevented this when they were generated; neither are they in the nature of Mercurius. Concerning this the philosopher says: One cannot pass from one extreme to another extreme except by means of a medium, that is, out of Mercurius no gold may be generated if it has not previously been silver.' (2)

Fig. 280 shows the engraved variant in which the scorched hermaphrodite leans on a tomb stone under the shadow of a tree. The winged god of alchemy appears as the guide of the rebis during its heavenly flight toward the rose garden of the philosophers (background). In the 'Chemical Pleasure Garden' the action of fig. 280 is interpreted as an abduction of the hermaphrodite by Mercurius appearing as a hungry eagle (Ganymede motif). (3)

NVTRIMENTVM

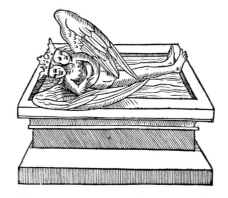

281. Scorched rebis in a flying coffin.

The Mystery of Dürer's 'Melancholia'

Did Albrecht Dürer draw on the secret doctrine of alchemy when he created his famous 'Melancholia' (fig. 282)? The question is a legitimate one since 'Melancholia' is saturated with Hermetic symbols and meanings. The non-initiate is puzzled already by the chief figure of the engraving: is it a human being or an angel, a *genius* or a giant, a man or a woman? The answer is both, since the melancholy figure represents the winged hermaphrodite of the citrinitas, seated in the alchemist's laboratory and surrounded by symbols of the royal art.

The adept's crucible heated in a bed of coals glows in the left background, halfway hidden behind the philosophers' stone which appears in the shape of the Platonic *polyhedron.* Below the stone and the sleeping dog is seen the *rotundum,* another symbol of the lapis or the philosophers' egg. The seven-runged ladder behind the polyhedron is a popular alchemical symbol, the rungs of the *scala philosophorum* representing the seven metals and the associated planetary gods. In front of the ladder hangs a pair of scales and an hour-glass, classical tools of the alchemist's workshop; further, an almost hidden pair of bellows under the angel's skirt (bottom right).

The *infans philosophorum* writing on a slate on top of the covered millstone symbolizes 'Melancholia's dawning sense of rebirth, a feature expressed in particular by the background scenery. Since bats fly in the night and sleep during the day, the squeaking bat indicates the nightly state of 'Melancholia.' However, the darkness of the mortified genius is illuminated and nurtured by a transcendent source of light struggling to be born and appearing as a solar moon or lunar sun. This is the heavenly symbol of the citrinitas *par excellence,* as is the rainbow arched by Dürer over his nocturnal scenery.

There may even be a Hermetic answer to the enigmatic problem occupying the minds of the two figures, the child in an active and creative, the adult in a passive and despairing way. The fact that the hermaphrodite sits pondering below a magic square, its hand holding a pair of compasses and resting on a book, suggests the presence of some insoluble mathematical problem—probably the classical object of alchemical speculation, the quadrature of the circle.

Depression in Late Middle Age

The two middle cells in the bottom row of the magic square show the date of the engraving—1514. This year, which is repeated in Dürer's signature in the right bottom corner, signifies the artist's 43rd year. This makes it possible to find another, more natural, explanation for

282. *The magic square above Dürer's powerless hermaphrodite belongs to the fourth order, that is, it contains the consecutive numbers 1 to 4^2 and adds up in various directions to a constant sum. Whether the addition of the numbers is performed in horizontal, vertical, or diagonal rows, the result is invariably the same number, namely that of 34. The lapis abounds in such weird riddles.*

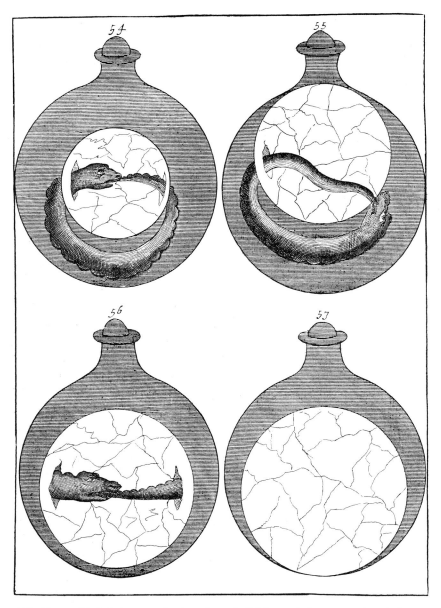

283. The work of citrine putrefaction: through division and cleavage to the whole egg.

hour-glass whose sands are running out is one such sign; another the sundial on top of the hour-glass, its hand pointing between three and four; a third the death-bell above the magic square waiting to be pulled.

The ego's awareness, in late middle age, of the brief span of human years is frequently accompanied by a despairing realization of the insignificance of human actions and ambitions compared to the age of nature and the vastness of the cosmos. This confrontation of the finite with the infinite, of man with the universe—expressed by the foreground and background of 'Melancholia'—triggers off a period of crisis. Life becomes a problem and work becomes an empty passtime. This prevailing mood is masterfully expressed by 'Melancholia' with its various tools of activity, construction and profit lying abandoned and scattered on the floor.

For all its melancholy and despair, late middle age is also a period of growing inner light and increasing self-awareness, features jointly expressed by 'Melancholia' and the citrinitas with their dual sense of burial and mystical illumination. This blend of *melancholia* and *consolatio* we shall study in the citrine actions of these pages.

The Moon Egg's Cleaving Ascension

Fig.283 gives Barchusen's variation upon the thirteenth woodcut of the 'Rosarium' with its 'nourishment' of the moon by the buried gold or red sulphur, here represented by the *serpens mercurialis*. The snake's attempt to cleave the egg horizontally in plate 54 is followed by the reptile's strange swinging manoeuvre in plate 55. The action may be interpreted as rendering the snake's attempt at rotating the egg with its body so as to be able to cleave it from a new angle. The snake spindle formed in plate 56 would thus give the serpent's operation on a new plane of division, bisecting the rotated egg at a right angle in relation to its previous plane of division. In plate 57 the division spindle formed by the tightening snake has disappeared and left the moon egg in a state of resting unity.

284. Transforming matter into spirit.

the parallelism between 'Melancholia' and the citrine symbols of separation, mortification, burial and putrefaction. Dürer's work and the 'yellowing' work both reflect man's archetypal experience of a *late middle age depression*. The essence of its piercing agony is the ego's experience of biological and psychological decline. (Middle and late middle age are among the commonest periods in which depressive reactions occur.)

As everyone knows, the human organims begins to slow down long before it begins to wear out. One thing that no one can escape is a gradual decline in biological effectiveness. People in their forties and fifties find that they fatigue more easily than they used to, and that they recover from exertion slowly. There are also involutional changes in the viscera which, although invisible in themselves, may appear as physiological disturbances in visceral function. Gastrointestinal, urinary and genital disturbances are among the most common. The blood vessels lose their elasticity and the skin becomes wrinkled, dry and discoloured. Hormonal changes affect the whole body and appear most dramatic in the menopause. The autonomous ego functions of motor coordination, perceptual grasp, and new learning show impairment; in most persons, sensory acuity and sensory adaptation also diminish. All these and many other changes involve cerebral function which shares in the general slow down of middle life.

The all-pervading experience of decline serves to heighten the ego's awareness of approaching death. In 'Melancholia,' various features bear out the artist's preoccupation with this idea. The half-empty

285. A heavenly churchyard transforming putrefying bodies into angels and seraphs.

natural law under the dominion of spiritual control. On account of the magnitude of the mountain as compared to the efforts of the Goat, the animal's conquest of nature is a matter of patience and suffering as much as it is a matter of toil and action. The clambering of the Goat hence represents a wintry struggle which calls for zeal and industry, discipline and control, patience and endurance; for the Goat, action is suffering and suffering, action.

Conservationism and concentration on personal self are characteristics of Capricorn psychology, which strives to elevate matter and to bring the work of sublimation to its peak of spiritual perfection. For Morrish, Capricorn is the gate to the spiritual life and the 'sign of yoga' in which the adept practises the control of spirit over the body. (2)

A Biological Textbook on 'Nutrimentum'

'The fertilized egg has the ability to reproduce itself and begin proliferating from one cell to two, from two cells to four, and from four cells to eight (below). The chromosomes carry the code of life that will direct some cells to turn into heart muscles or kidneys or eyes—and that will produce a unique individual with his own eye colouring, facial features, body build and intelligence. Also inside the egg, though too small to be seen in any photograph, are many droplets of fat, like miniature dabs of butter, and other substances that can help nourish and sustain life. These are essential— for now, as the egg begins to grow, it is on its own. It is still in the uterine tube, which can only move it along toward the womb, and which seems to offer no haven and no nourishment. Not until several more days pass and the sanctuary of the womb has been reached, can the fertilized egg find any new source of supplies. At the moment it is like an explorer in space, dependent for its life on food it has brought along.'
Ernest Havemann: Birth Control. (3)

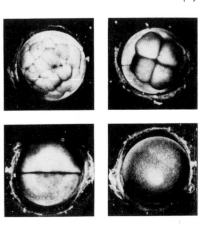

286. After 'fermentation,' a whole egg.

As the drama of cleavage comes to an end, the lunar egg is made ready for the next stage of its flying transformation: that of its polarization and fertilization (pp.152-153).

The Eighth Key of Basil Valentine

Fig.285 shows the Eighth Key of Basil Valentine in which the Sword of Justice (fig.272) visits punishment on the alchemist in accordance with the laws of the *fermentatio*. These are expressed by the sower scattering his gold in the white foliated earth and by the dead man corrupting in the furrows, his head resting on a bundle of mowed corn. The black crows picking up the seed behind the sower are similar symbols of mortification and suffering. For all its gloom, the graveyard appears as a fertile field holding the promise of a new harvest and a resurrection of the dead—heralded by the angel of the Last Judgement. The corn shooting from the grave of the risen alchemist gives the vegetable image of this victorious moment.

The Key's background shows an unploughed churchyard with two archers aiming at a target crowned by a key. The arrow-shooting partly signifies the piercing and cleaving of the circular target, partly the attempt to hit the bull's-eye, identified with the sign of gold. The 'yellowing' work of the archers appears to make good progress, as witnessed by the last arrow shot. The text reads:

'Neither human nor animal bodies can be multiplied or propagated without decomposition; the grain and all vegetable seed, when cast into the ground, must decay before it can spring up again . . . Let me sum up in few words what I have

to say. The product [of the albedo] is of heavenly birth, its life is preserved by the stars, and nourished by the four elements. Then it must perish, and be putrefied. Again, by the influence of the stars, which works through the elements, it is restored to life, and becomes once more a heavenly thing that has its habitation in the highest region of the firmament. When this has been completed you will find that the earthly has been completely devoured by the heavenly, and that the earthly body has changed into a heavenly substance.' (1)

In alchemy, the gradual and painful transformation of the earthly into the heavenly, the natural into the spiritual, takes place in the astrological sign of Capricorn, the Goat.

Capricorn the Goat: Spiritual Ascension

The tenth sign of the Zodiac is a cardinal, earthy sign ruled by Saturn and covering the period from December 22 to January 20, or the period of winter solstice. Capricorn is an arduous, melancholy and suffering sign which takes its features from the mountain goat with its slow, patient and concentrated clambering of the mountain. Always aiming at the summit while guarding the dangers of the ravine, Capricorn stands out as the zodiacal symbol of ascension *par excellence.* Since its energies remove it from the earth and raise it to the top of the mountain, the Goat has come to symbolize the overcoming of materiality by spirituality.

Compared to Cancer, its opposite sign, which expresses the urge to fuse with nature, Capricorn embodies the urge to *conquer* nature, the desire to bring the

287.

The Third, or Solar, Trauma of Rebirth

Fig.288 shows the fourteenth woodcut of the 'Rosarium' which renders the 'fixation' *(fixatio)* of the yellowing transformation process. The wings of the entombed hermaphrodite have disappeared and passed over to a naked woman winging into heaven. The motto explains:

Here the lunar life completely ends,
The spirit into heaven deftly ascends. (1)

The 'complete end' of the hermaphrodite's 'lunar life' connected with its spiritual ascent into heaven imply the beginning of its *solar* life, also indicated by the title of the woodcut. As the streaming process of citrine transformation reaches the stage of 'fixation,' the mutable silver acquires the constancy of gold, and the lunar light the permanence of solar light. The text conveys the 'fixa-

tion' of the tincture and the 'reddening' of the stone in the following manner:
'Raymundus: Now I will describe the fixation of the tincture or the air carrying in it the tincture, which takes place through the calcination in a way which I will omit to describe. Lilius, the philosopher: In the end your king will go forth crowned with his diadem, shining as the sun, clear as a carbuncle, flowing forth as wax, persevering in the fire, penetrating and retaining the quicksilver. Arnold: For the red colour is created by the complement of digestion, since the blood is not generated in man if it has not first been cooked diligently in the liver. Thus, when we in the morning see that our urine is white we know that we have slept little. Then we lie down again to sleep, and after a while the digestion is completed and our urine has become

yellow. In the like manner, the whiteness may arrive at the redness alone through decoction and the continuation of the fire. If our white ore is diligently cooked it will redden in the best manner and therefore it must be decocted by a dry fire and a dry calcination until it becomes red as cinnabar. To this you should add no water from the other things, nor any other thing, until it is decocted to the red complement.' (2)

The idea underlying this passage is the alchemical conviction that purification consists in a removal of the 'watery' elements of the stone. The stone in its moist and lunar form is less refined than the stone in its dry and solar form. This association of moisture with earth and imperfection, and of dryness with heaven and perfection, is the determining factor behind the fiery elevation and fixation of the stone. In the 'Aurea catena' it is stated that 'the nearer a subject is to the centre, the more strongly it is fixed, if only it is not hindered by the copious and continually rising moisture.' (3) This idea explains the alchemist's ceaseless heating, calcination and decoction of his stone.

Ignition of the Ascending Ganymede

Fig.289 shows the engraved variant of the 'Rosarium' woodcut, whose 'spirit deftly ascending into heaven' is represented partly by an attacking eagle, partly by an angel pointing to the entombed hermaphrodite as the object to be snatched. The motif contains an obvious allusion to the rape of Ganymede, which in alchemy serves to express the 'reddening' stage: the youth is caught up by the eagle to the solar sphere of 'fixation' and set on fire there.

In fig.289 the ignition of the scorched hermaphrodite is indicated by the light-

FIXATIO.

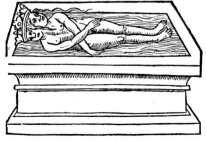

288. *Spiritual ascent into heaven.*

289. End of the lunar life: the lightning flash of conception of Zeus' soaring eagle.

ening-up of its head, 'shining [now] as the sun,' as the 'Rosarium' says. The core of spiritual elevation and solar transformation expressed by the antique myth of Ganymede is brought out by Dante's famous elaboration of the motif in the 'Purgatory':

I dreamt I saw an eagle in mid-air,
Plumed all in gold, hovering on wings
outspread,
As though to make his swoop he poisèd
him there.
Meseemed me in the place whence
Ganymede
Up to the high gods' halls was snatched
one day,
Leaving his comrades all discomfited.
I thought: Perhaps this eagle strikes
his prey
Always just here; his proud feet would
think shame
Elsewhere to seize and carry it away.

Then, in my dream he wheeled awhile
and came
Down like the lightning, terrible and fast,
And caught me up into the sphere
of flame,
Where he and I burned in one
furnace-blast;
The visionary fire so seared me through,
It broke my sleep perforce, and the
dream passed . . .
'Fear nothing,' said my lord,
'sit thou secure
At heart; we've come into a good estate,
Faint not, but be the more alert
therefore.
Thou hast reached Purgatory . . .' (4)

The Solar Fire of Conception

The solar transformation of the lunar body is explicit in Barchusen's paraphrase of the fourteenth woodcut of the 'Rosarium' (fig.287). In plate 58 the moon egg is lured into the tubal section of the vessel by the mercurial serpent, now intent on bringing the 'lunar life to a complete end.' In plate 59 the polar section of the egg is shown at the entrance of the opened neck, where a draconic edition of the serpent slips into the tube while emptying its fire across the egg's polar section.

This flash of solar lightning sets the moon egg on fire, as evidenced by plate 60: transformed into a blazing rose, the lunar body is fertilized by the mercurial serpent who, coiling as the uroboros, or tail-eater, impregnates, begets, devours and slays himself, and 'himself lifts himself on high,' as the 'Rosarium' says *(sublimatur per se)*. (5)

The coiling movement of the tail-eater unloosens in plate 61, where the fire spat out by the receding serpent appears as the blazing curves of the rainbow illuminating the vessel with the many colours of the peacock's tail.

Solar Moonrise of the Citrine Work

The nineteenth painting of the 'Splendor solis' reproduced in fig.290 gives the aftermath of the conjunction of the solar and lunar bodies in figs.252-253. The polar top of the moon is scorched by solar fire, a 'putrefaction' of the lunar body due to its conjunction with the

solar sulphur or golden ferment. The lapidary text explains: 'The mercury dissolves the sulphur added to it, and this dissolution is nothing but an ordering of the moist with the dry, and is actually a putrefaction, and that same will turn the matter black.' (6)

The 'rising dawn' *(aurora consurgens)* of the citrinitas is described in this way by one of the greatest alchemical treatises:

'The title of this book is baptized *Aurora Consurgens*—The Rising Dawn—and that for four reasons: Firstly, it is called Dawn as one should say the Golden Hour, for so hath this science an hour with a golden end for them that rightly perform the Work. Secondly, the dawn is midway between night and day, shining with twofold hues, namely red and yellow; so likewise doth this science beget the colours yellow and red, which are midway between white and black. Thirdly, because at dawn they that labour under all the infirmities of the night are relieved and have rest; and so at the dawn of this science all evil odours and vapours that infect the mind of the laborant fade away and weaken, as the Psalm saith: In the evening weeping shall have place, and in the morning gladness. Fourthly and lastly, the dawn is called the end of the night and the beginning of the day, or the mother of the sun, and so our dawn at its greatest redness is the end of all darkness and the putting to flight of night, of that long-drawn-out winter wherein he who walketh, if he take not heed, shall stumble. For of this indeed it is written: And night to night showeth knowledge, day to day uttereth speech, and night shall be light as the day in its pleasures.' (7)

290. Scorched top of a solar moon.

291. The fertilizing serpent burrowing into the interior of the philosophers' egg.

'By reiteration of this medicine and administration of [its] goodness with cautionary industry, you may arrive at the preparation of the stone [which is not completed] until the mercury transmutes itself into the infinite sun-making and the true moon-making substance, everything depending on its multiplication.* For now shall be praised the sublime, blessed and glorious God of all creatures, who has revealed to us the order and connection of all medicines along with the insight into that order. This we have attained through the goodness of our investigation and the perseverance of our labour, seen with our eyes and touched with our hands, the completion having been explored by means of our magistery.' (3)

Conquest of the Mercurial Serpent

Fig.293 renders the engraved variant in which the angel of the previous engraving (fig.289) appears as the Earth Mother soaked by the fertilizing rain of 'multiplication.' She grasps the hands of Sol and Luna, who leave their sarcophagus in a rejuvenated shape, reborn as the children of the Great Mother.

Fig.291 shows Barchusen's variation upon the fifteenth woodcut of the 'Rosarium,' whose rain of 'multiplication' is interpreted in accordance with its text, namely as a synonym for the solar sulphur fertilizing the stone while 'multiplying' in its substance. The *sulphur solis* is still represented by the fire-spewing serpent, whose receding and suicidal coiling reaches its climax in plate 64 where it devours its own tail. Absorbed by the fire begotten by itself, the tail-eater completely disappears in plate 65 in which the solar sulphur blazes and tinges the egg's mercurial interior. With the alchemist's conquest of the mercurial serpent, the philosophers' egg is returned to its golden, immaculate condition and readied

The Fiery Rain of Fertilization

Fig.292 shows the fifteenth woodcut of the 'Rosarium' in which the rain of 'multiplication' *(multiplicatio)* descends from heaven to quicken the entombed hermaphrodite. The fertilizing function of the rain is emphasized not only by the title but also by the motto which reads:

Here the water doth sink,
Once more giving the earth its water
to drink. (1)

In the text, this motif appears as the fertilizing impact of the solar sulphur, no longer 'fermenting' in the stone, or 'illuminating' it, or 'nourishing' it, but 'fixing' it by 'multiplying' in its earth. Quoting Geber, the text opens:

'In the preparation of the solar medicine the incombustible sulphur, perfect-

ly administered, must be added in a fixing and calcining manner and with the use of multiple solution, reiterated until it [the solar medicine] is made pure . . . In this way is completed the most precious art, which is above the art of all the sciences of this world, and an incomparable treasure. You must be exercised in this with the greatest labour and with the protraction of immense meditation. For through this you will find it, but without it you will not find it.

* Alchemically, multiplication refers to the goldmakers' 'projection' of the solar or golden tincture upon the white silver, thereby dyeing or gilding the latter as a result of the tincture's 'multiplication' of its own substance. Geber's recipe for the production of the 'solar medicine' defies any translation into chemical terms. According to Ernst Darmstaedter, 'Geber's remarks on the 'solar medicine' are . . . shrouded in mystery so that he can rightly say that he has submitted his doctrine in a veiled manner.' (2)

MVLTIPLICATIO.

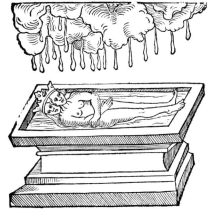

292. Fertilizing rain of 'multiplication.'

293. The Great Mother and her children soaked by the Father's fertilizing rain.

for its solar rebirth, realized in Barchusen's subsequent plates (fig.306).

These plates paraphrase the seventeenth woodcut of the 'Rosarium' which depicts the new birth on the sun and the resurrection of the hermaphrodite on top of the solar hill, *at whose base the three-headed mercurial snake expires (fig.307).* This variant of the tail-eater appears in many alchemical descriptions of the slaying of the serpent (see following pages). The fact that the 'Rosarium' equates this event with the triumphant realization of the third coniunctio reveals the hermaphrodite's serpentine struggle as the implicit motif of its two preceding woodcuts, viz., figs.292 and 300. Basil Valentine's Ninth Key (fig.296) and its engraved variants (figs.295 and 297) bring out this relationship with their ingenious synthesis of the fifteenth, sixteenth and seventeenth woodcuts of the 'Rosarium.' Before presenting these variants of the 'Rosarium's trauma of rebirth, we shall reproduce one of the most interesting versions of the slaying of the mercurial serpent.

The Slaying of the Solar Dragon

In the 'Book of Lambspring' the tail-eater's emblem is accompanied by a short verse describing the preparation of the solar medicine in this manner:

A savage dragon lives in the forest,
Lacking not the strongest venom.
When he sees the rays of the sun and its
*   bright fire,*

He scatters abroad his poison
And flies upward so fiercely that
No living creature can stand before him,
Nor is even the basilisk equal to him.
He who hath skill to slay him wisely
Hath escaped from all dangers.
All his veins and colours are perceived
In the hour of his death, his venom
Becoming the greatest medicine.
He quickly consumes his own venom,
For he devours his own poisonous tail.
All this is performed on his own body,
From which flows forth glorious balm,
With all its miraculous virtues.
Hereat all the sages do loudly rejoice. (4)

The dragon presented by Lambspring corresponds with that of Eleazar's 'Uraltes Chymisches Werk' in which the fire-spewing dragon floating in the air is described as the universal 'python, the beginning of all things . . . the old Father-Begetter.' (5)

Ovulation, Fertilization and Polarization

The alchemical *fixatio, multiplicatio* and *revificatio* (p.158) reflect the regressive play-back of the unconscious imprints of ovulation (ejaculation) and conception. Fig.294 shows a photo of the egg just after the entrance of the fertilizing sperm (dark spot, at upper right) slowly wriggling its way toward fusion with the female nucleus (dark spot, at upper left). The recently ovulated egg is still drifting high up in the uterine tube where it is met by a host of tadpole-like sperm cells swimming rapidly toward it.

The photo shows the encounter in which the egg is exposed to the fertilizing rain of a huge number of attacking sperm cells.

After the sperm cell has penetrated its surface, the egg cell experiences a time of intense activity. As the nucleus reorganizes itself for union with the sperm, the cell mass shrinks and leaves an enlarged clear space inside the thick outer membrane. Into this space the egg projects its polar bodies; the first polar body siphons off half of the egg's 46 chromosomes so that the remaining 23 may unite with the sperm's 23 to give the new cell 46 chromosomes, or the number which the normally developing cell requires. (The second polar body, formed just after fertilization, contains other excess cellular materials.) This process is known as the polarization of the fertilized egg.

The event is symbolized by figs.287-290, just as the pictures on these and the following pages render the reversed act of fertilization. The sperm's 'extraction' from the egg aptly explains the tail-eater's fate and the alchemist's serpentine conquest. Similarly, the following pictures and their strange symbolic actions may be interpreted as natural reflections of a reversed act of ovulation (ejaculation) 'returning' the egg (sperm) to its follicle in the ovary (semineforous tubule in testis). This biological sequence forms the vehicle of the third Hermetic coniunctio accelerating on the following pages and realized on pp.162-163.*

* One may ask how it is possible for the individual to trace his evolutionary film to a point beyond his moment of conception, since the film actually splits up in two separate performances, one concerned with oogenesis, the other with spermatogenesis. The unconscious playback, however, is possible in a subtle manner.

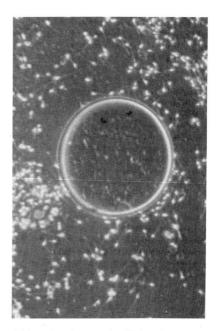

294. Rain of sperm fertilizing the egg.

The 'Yellow' Trauma of Rebirth

Fig.296 shows the Ninth Key of Basil Valentine which renders the attempted conjunction of Sol and Luna as they wing into heaven on the elevating air-current of the *revificatio*. (This is the stage rendered by the sixteenth woodcut of the 'Rosarium,' reproduced in fig.300. The word means 'revival' or 'resurrection.') Rising Ganymede-like with the winging eagle clawing his head, the king returns to his naked queen in a strange rotation also appearing to shed him from the woman's sexual parts.

The rotary movement is brought about by the three-headed mercurial serpent coiling inside the philosophers' egg while penetrating or fertilizing three hearts at its centre. As evidenced by her position, the queen tries to counterbalance the gyration of her fertilized egg by bending her body forward, her feet resting on the feathery circle of the peacock's tail. This is the bird of the citrinitas spreading its tail in the text as a marvellous procession of the planetary deities arrayed in multi-coloured clothes and presenting to the public a number of beautifully coloured allegorical banners and standards. (The description is omitted in the passage reproduced below.)

The swan resting on the queen's head represents the albedo, the crow on the king's feet the nigredo, the eagle on his head the 'reddening' process of the rubedo. Thus the four birds represent the four *regiminia* or procedures of the opus alchymicum.

The Key's text describes the upward race of the planets toward the highest planet, the sun, for the purpose of being 'united with [their] first mother.' Saturn appears as the victor of this race, also presented as the 'elevation of the great stone to its foreordained perfection.'

The Ninth Key of Basil Valentine

'Saturn who is called the greatest of the planets has the least authority in our magistery and is yet the chief key of the whole art, howbeit set in the lowest and meanest place. Although by its swift flight it has risen to the loftiest height, far above all other luminaries, its feathers must be clipped and itself brought down to the lowest place and through its putrefaction arrive at its improvement; thus the black is changed to white, and the white to red, until by running through all the colours of the world and transcending the other planets, it will finally arrive at the supreme colour of the triumphant king . . . In the preparation of Saturn there appears a great variety of different colours; and you must expect to observe successively black, grey, white, yellow, red and all the different intermediate shades. In the same way, the

295. Conquering the father and his sperm: final death of the procreative principle.

The fact is that the individual's egg cell and sperm cell have a previous history of development along analogous lines and taking place in homologous organs. Even if the individual's regressive life-film splits up after conception into a sequence of oogenesis and a sequence of spermatogenesis, the fundamental biological pattern of the two sequences remains the same. The ovulation of the mature egg is analogous to the ejaculation of the mature sperm, just as the two sex cells derive from homologous organs,

the egg from the follicle of the ovary, the sperm from the follicle of the testicles. The maturation processes undergone in these organs are the same for the growing egg and the growing sperm. Both are formed by a similar process of meiotic division and both cells originate in the same primordial germ cell-state (fig.352). Therefore, whether the first or the second film is run, one will behold the same performance. LSD-induced regressions offer a stunning experience of these cellular realms of the unconscious.

matter of the sages passes through the several varieties of colour before the great stone is elevated to its foreordained perfection. For as often as a new gate of entrance is opened to the fire, as often is won a new form of garment, until even the poor man arrives at great wealth and need not borrow any longer.

'Understand that each planet strives to supplant the other from its glory, office, dominion and power, until the best among them arrives at the highest place [the sun] clothed with the most permanent colour and united with its first mother, victorious and superior in love and friendship because of its inherent stubbornness. For the present state of things is passing away, and a new world is about to be created, and one planet is devouring another spiritually, until only the strongest survive and two and three are conquered by the One alone.

'Let me finally tell you that you must put into the heavenly Balance, the Ram, Bull, Scorpion and Goat. In the other scale of the Balance you must place the Twins, the Archer, the Watercarrier, and the Virgin. Then let the golden Lion jump into the Virgin's lap, which will cause the other scale to kick the beam. Thereupon let the twelve signs of the Zodiac enter into opposition to the Pleiads, and when all the colours of the world have shewn themselves, let there be a conjunction and union between the greatest and the smallest, the smallest and the greatest.
If the whole world's nature
Were seen in one figure,
And nothing could be evolved by Art,
Nothing wonderful would be found
    in the Universe,
And Nature would have nothing to tell us,
For which let us laud and praise God.' (1)

Riding on a Fertilized Egg

Fig.297 shows the engraved variant of the Ninth Key of Basil Valentine. Sol and Luna atop their lunar egg experience its moment of fertilization by the three-headed *serpens mercurialis* coiling inside

296. The ovular drama of citrine rebirth.

297. Sol and Luna enthroned on their royal egg, gilded by the fertilizing serpent.

its shell. They present the four vases of Hermes with their four regimens.

Slaying the Mercurial Serpent

Fig.295 represents another variant of the Ninth Key, combining like its model the sixteenth and seventeenth woodcuts of the 'Rosarium' (figs.300 and 307). The descending angel of 'revival' or 'resurrection' represents the 'soul coming from heaven, glorious and clear' (fig.300) and raising the king, now triumphing on the body of the pierced serpent. Numerous small serpents emerge from the wounds of the expiring monster which rests on the overhanging cliff of the 'solar mountain' *(mons solis).* Standing in this perilous position, which threatens him with death by abysmal falling, the vertiginous king receives the wreaths of victory assuming the form of a solar coronation. According to the text, the solar crown 'signifies both the resurrection of the philosophical gold, which is much purer than the gold in the mines, and the revivification preceding the multiplication of the philosophers' stone. This is the stone which the artist has elevated by means of his science into the supreme degree of splendour.' (2)

Conquest of the Begetting Principle

The strange elaboration of the mercurial serpent in the seventeenth woodcut of the 'Rosarium' (fig.307) and its variants symbolizes Mercurius philosopho-

rum in his spiritual aspect. Jung sums up the trinitarian manifestations of the spirit Mercurius in the following manner:

'The triadic nature of Mercurius does not derive from Christian dogma but is of earlier date. Triads occur as early as the treatise of Zosimos, 'Concerning the Art': 'The unity of the composition [produces] the indivisible triad, and thus an undivided triad composed of separate elements creates the cosmos, through the forethought of the First Author, the cause and demiurge of creation; wherefore he is called Trismegistos, having beheld triadically that which is created and that which creates.' (3) Martial calls Hermes *omnia solus et ter unus* (All and Thrice One). In Monakris (Arcadia), a three-headed Hermes was worshipped, and in Gaul there was a three-headed Mercurius. This Gallic god was also a psychopomp. The triadic character is an attribute of the gods of the underworld . . . Khunrath calls Mercurius *triunus* and *ternarius.* Mylius [following Basil Valentine and the 'Rosarium'] represents him as a three-headed snake.' (4) (Fig.297.)

In other words, the serpentine and triadic form of the *spiritus mercurialis* represents the begetting principle of the Creator-God. This is in agreement with psychoanalysis, which has established the serpent archetype as a symbol of the *paternal penis.* The slaying of the mercurial serpent or dragon hence represents the alchemist's conquest of the libido in its impure form, that is, his rising above the compulsion of sexuality and the desire to propagate and create.

298. *Spiritual rebirth of an aging, melancholy man revived by his returning soul.*

Conquest of the Three-Headed Sperm

Fig.299 shows a mysterious alchemical motif probably related to the conquest of the three-headed serpent: Orion, the Earth-born giant of the starry sky, extracts the 'three-headed' sperm that begot him. The giant-motif points to the concluding citrinitas in which heaven and earth are united by the alchemist, whose stature thereby grows into celestial proportions. The alchemist reborn in the dual shape of the 'philosophical infant' (far left) and the giant Orion (far right) flanks a group of Hermetic figures appearing as his three fathers, namely Apollon (Sol), Vulcan and Mercurius. These figures lay open an oxskin filled with their sperm, the very hide from which Orion, after ten months, had been born. And so, explains the motto, the 'philoso-

phical infant acknowledges three fathers, just as Orion does it.' (1) A symbol of heavenly rebirth, the motif is further elucidated by the text as rendering the rejuvenated alchemist's conquest of the active principle of generation, the 'three-headed' Orion-sperm being equated with the fertilizing and tingeing powers of the sun's rays:

'The conception of Orion . . . would be horrible and not only fabulous if there were no secret of nature at the root of it. In his 'Testament' Lully ascribed the same fathers to the philosophers' child, namely Sol, who is identical with Apollon or the heavenly sun, as the first cause of his generation. With unspeakable force, in a secret, astral way, Sol affects a certain matter known to the philosophers, and doing it in such a manner as if that matter were in the womb of a woman. In this matter Sol generates a son or fetus equal to himself, to whom he later passes his weapons, the signs of his power by means of his paternal rights; that is, the power of ripening unripe things and of colouring and purifying non-coloured and non-purified things.' (2)

The 'Revival' of the Hermaphrodite

Fig.300 shows the sixteenth woodcut of the 'Rosarium' presenting the stage of 'revival' or 'resurrection' *(revificatio)*: as the soul returns from heaven in the shape of a naked woman, the hermaphrodite's body is revived in its sarcophagus. The motto explains:

Here comes the soul from heaven,
glorious and clear, truly
Reviving the philosophers' daughter. (3)

The woman diving from the sky is imagined as reviving the philosopher's, or the king's, female half, thus quickening half of his dead, bisexual body. The text quotes the concluding chapter of Geber's 'Summa perfectionis,' which deals with the stone's 'three degrees of preparation.' The third degree now attained is presented as follows:

'By the method of sublimation one must make volatile the already fixed stone and then again fix the volatile and solve the fixed, once more making the solution volatile and once again fix the volatile until [the stone] becomes fluent and is changed into its true sun-making and moon-making substance. Through such repetition of the preparation of the third degree, the goodness and refining effects of the medicine will be multiplied . . . and even in this manner: From the medicine will arise sometimes a sevenfold, sometimes a tenfold, sometimes a hundredfold, sometimes a thousandfold and sometimes an infinite portion of the sun-making substance and the true moon-making substance which will transmute the body into perfection.' (4)

In a later passage the stone's third degree of preparation is described as effecting the 'conversion of the body into spirit, which secret is extracted from the dicta of the philosophers.' (5) At the same time, the act is presented as 'sufficing to produce the total elevation.' (6) The 'Rosarium' woodcut illustrates this 'total elevation' of the body by showing a returning anima 'reviving' the entombed hermaphrodite while preparing it for the third conjunction.

Fig.301 shows the engraved variant in which Sol and Luna emerge from the upper end of the well or tube into which

REVIFICATIO.

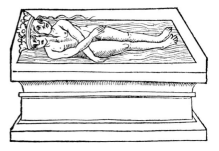

300. *A flying coffin approaching heaven.*

299. *Disclosing the agent of fertilization.*

301. *Leaving the top of a well reddened by the pelican's blood of death and rebirth.*

The equation of the coitive act of Sol and Luna (Venus) with the birth of Athene out of the head of her Father shows the spiritual nature of the golden coniunctio now under way. The natural act of generation has become a spiritual act of generation, an act of conception in the brain.

The text presents the island of Rhodes as a place teeming with serpents and roses, thus relating the engraving to the serpentine drama of the citrinitas. This connection is further established by the reference to the Medusa's snake-covered head, the victorious emblem of Pallas Athene:

'Perseus gave her the Medusa's head, which has a petrifying effect and is horrible to look at, as the head is covered with twisting snakes in place of hair. Athene [terrifies] . . . by means of the same substance as that from which Chrysaor was born, who was the father of the three-bodied Geryon, namely by the petrifying Gorgon blood, which is nothing other than the tincture of the philosophers' stone.' (10)

Trauma of Ovulation and Conception

The conquest of the Medusa's snake-covered head with its 'petrifying Gorgon blood' fits in with the serpentine drama and gory 'reddening' of the lapis or rebis as presented by the 'Rosarium,' Barchusen, Basil Valentine and Abraham Eleazar. They are all expressions of the 'yellow' trauma of rebirth which, psychobiologically, reflects the trauma of ovulation and conception: the egg cell's (or the sperm cell's) 'fall' from the sphere of unbeing, or unmanifest existence, into the sphere of being, or manifest existence. (See following pages.)

302. *A gory well of falling children.*

they began their flying descent in fig.273. As the royal lovers climb over the upper edge of the well, they emerge from the pelican's blood-bath in the neck of the well or vessel. The bird is shown in her classical position, plucking her breast in order to nourish her young with her blood. The pelican's self-sacrificial blood symbolizes the red tincture, or the solar medicine, or the venom of the slain serpent—all expressions of the 'fluent' stone.

The Blood-Bath of Sol and Luna

Another variant appears in fig.302, from Abraham Eleazar's 'Uraltes Chymisches Werk.' The blood-bath of Sol and Luna emerging from the well is identified with the slaughter of the innocent by King Herod, a motif deriving from the tomb stone of Nicolas Flamel which depicts the elevation of the alchemist and his sister into heaven (fig.324).

Abraham Eleazar's version of the royal bath in the neck of a vessel reddened by the blood and bodies of falling children is inscribed with the verse: 'Dissolve the king or the queen in this red blood of children, then the sun and moon will take their bath in it; for this well is inexhaustible.' (7) The text goes on to explain the action of fig.302: 'A king stands with a naked sword while his soldiers slay the innocent children and gather their blood. They throw them into the well in order to colour it still more, the well being already filled with blood. Sol and Luna descend to take a bath in this well.' (8) The text elucidates the traumatic na-

ture of the bath by relating it to the adept's struggle with the mercurial serpent:

'Therefore they have poured these volatile birds with solar and lunar feathers over the python [*serpens mercurialis*]; then the python has again melted into these birds. Then they have poured out the clear solution and once more thrown it over a new python and so obtained a fat and heavy liquor. Then they have united the king and queen and poured them together.' (9)

Spiritual Intercourse on Mount Olympus

Fig.298 synthesizes the citrine stages of 'multiplication' and 'revival,' the giant motif and the solar myth of Ganymede. Deposited on the Olympus by the eagle of Zeus, the alchemist in the dual shape of Ganymede and Vulcan approaches the Father of the Gods. With his ax he cleaves Zeus' brain, thereby assisting in the 'spiritual' birth of Pallas Athene, the 'philosophers' daughter.' Her return to the body of a saturnine old man gives the essence of the *revificatio;* in the background the golden rain of the *multiplicatio* falls on the conjugal bed of a quickening Sol and Luna (Venus).

The philosophers' son appearing just behind his loving parents is another symbol of rebirth as is the golden superman reaching into heaven (Colossus of Rhodes, background left). The superman's halo expresses the solar powers conquered by the alchemist at the end of his *citrinatio.*

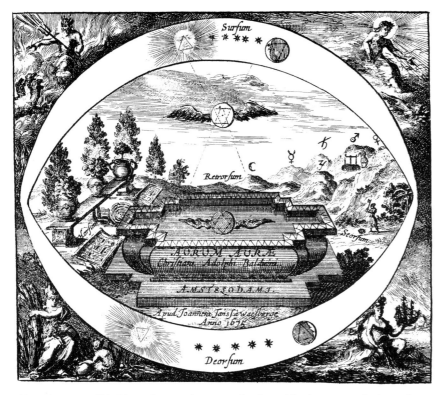

303. *The stone gilded into the morning sun and reflected in the rose garden's pool.*

Gory Transition into the World

In alchemy, the transition from Paradise to earth, or from spiritual to bodily existence, is represented by the 'inexhaustible' well of the pelican's neck, reddened by the blood of the slain serpent and by the pierced bodies of falling children.

On the tomb stone of Nicolas Flamel (fig.324) the children precipitated into the gory well of fig.302 belong to the rose garden of the philosophers. This is the garden in which the roses are children and the children roses. This is also the garden of the heavenly mother from whose protection the children in fig.302 are separated by the piercing sword of the cruel king. Thrown into the deep and uncanny well, these innocent children suffer the 'death' of unbeing and the 'birth' of being—a traumatic transition or 'fall' which the alchemists connect with the tempting voice of the mercurial serpent, precisely rendered by Barchusen's plate 58 (fig.287).

The Golden Pool of the Rose Garden

After the revival of the citrine trauma of rebirth, the Hermetic transformation process continues its strange and divine wheeling, now producing bliss out of agony and ascension out of falling. On the powerful air-current of the *revificatio* the philosophical egg coils into heaven.

Fig.303 shows the winged philosophical egg or stone, shining now as the morning sun; it hovers over the philosophers' rose garden just before descending into its glittering pool. The winged body is reflected in the pool, whose *aurum aurae* ('gold of gold') is composed of water out of sunlight. The walled rose garden is surrounded with planetary mountains, cypresses and bowls of rose-leaves; in its upper right corner, the alchemist waits at the garden gate while his mystical sister runs toward him with the key to the garden in her hand.

The vision disclosed through the tube-like aperture of the engraving renders the initiated conjunction between heaven and earth, which in the golden mirror of the pool are seen as 'inversions' (*retrorsum*) of each other. This feature points to the famous doctrine of the *Tabula smaragdina* according to which the things 'above' (*sursum*) are like the things 'below' (*deorsum*), just as the 'receding movement' (*seorsum*) is like the 'approaching movement' (*horsum*).

The same philosophy is expressed by the Seal of Solomon inside the flying sun. An emblem of the conjunction of opposites, the Seal twinkles inside the sun's reflected image in the pool, where the magic figure is presented as an 'inversion' (*retrorsum*) of its heavenly original. Also, the Seal is composed of the triangles of the earthly sun and moon, which together with their planets are seen as 'inversions' or 'reflections' of their celestial models or archetypes. Thus earthly reality and the seven metals below (*deorsum*) are reflections of heavenly reality and the seven planets above (*sursum*).

The mirror symbolism of the picture is of a subtle and mystical quality: as the alchemist and his sister move up the garden path in order to look down into the golden pool of the *aurum aurae*, they are deprived of any means of distinguishing between the sun itself and its reflected image. Glittering out of heart of light, the magic pool represents above and below as mirror-like 'inversions' of each other: the sun descending toward the surface of the lake is indistinguishable from the sun rising toward its surface. Such oneness of above and below in the pool of the rose garden signifies the timeless moment when all the opposites come together in a white light still and moving.

The Rose Garden of the Philosophers

Fig.304 presents a variation of the philosophers' egg or stone about to 'nest' in its first world. The engraving shows the winged body passing through its first gate and flying down the passage toward the door opening into the rose garden. Humming bees swarm all over the place and four of the seven metals move down the garden passage together with the 'antimonian' sun.

The cosmic circle shown by fig.305 is a multiple image of the philosophical wheel (with the bird-symbols of the regiments), the sun-tree's wheeling crown, and the philosophers' egg or stone. As *ovum philosophorum* the image renders the birth of the world egg, leaving heaven and entering earth. Its shell is studded with stars, its white and yolk composed of the zodiacal, planetary and alchemical realms. These are centred on the sign of Mercurius philosophorum, or the sign of the lapis; its very centre appears as the *scintilla* or *punctum solis* in which the whole cosmos and all opposites are concentrated. This is the magic point standing for unity, the origin and the centre. Having reached the still point of the turning world, the alchemist is immersed in the centre of his being, realizing here the divine light of Absolute Reality, or the nature of Mercurius philosophorum—the immovable mover of the moving universe.

304. *Through the first gate into life.*

305. *Sol and Luna chained to the stone between unbeing and being: mystical union at the still point of the turning world.*

Another symbol of totality is the star-studded hermaphrodite triumphing with his twin-bladed ax on the backs of two united lions and subsuming the cross-like division of the engraving, divided horizontally into heaven and earth, vertically into day and night. The lions are symbols of sulphur and mercury, emerging from the earth as a flame and a spring just behind the lions' tails. Also, they symbolize Sol and Luna, who appear as a naked man and woman: the former assigned to the sun and the lion, the latter to the moon and the night. Luna carries a bunch of grapes, the Milky Way springing from her breast of abundance; she stands in the Hermetic river, her beauty being admired by Actaeon, the mythical huntsman who for viewing naked Artemis bathing was changed into a stag as punishment.

Balancing on the wings of the phoenix and the eagle, Sol and Luna are chained to the revolving cosmos, which also appears as the wheeling crown of the sun-tree, the latter towering on top of the 'solar mountain' or 'solar hill' *(mons solis)*. Since the entire cosmos wheels in its crown, the sun-tree is depicted as com-

bining the features of both the axle-tree and the world-tree. On both sides of the solar axle-tree stretches the trees of the other planetary gods or metals; the crest of twelve minor trees in front of them carry the signs of the twelve most important metalloids.

Above the trees of the magical garden, the philosophers' egg wheels its way into the world, its terrestrial half adorned with stars, its celestial half with angels' heads and symbols of the Trinity. The entrance of the *ovum philosophorum* into the world of manifest existence takes place *pari passu* with its expulsion from the world of unmanifest existence (or 'Paradise'). The chains of naked Adam and Eve show their intimate connection with this birthlike movement of the philosophical egg, a movement which the Bible describes as the *Fall of Man*.

Obviously their chains tie them to the world of creation, duality and sexual compulsion—a level of existence set apart from the world of uncreation, trinitarian oneness and spiritual bliss at the top of the engraving. This is the sphere of Paradise symbolized by the heavenly Kinder-

garten, or the philosophers' rose garden.* Its flowers are identified with the choirs of angels in heaven, or with the spirits of the unborn children. The Creator of these heavenly multitudes appears as the Holy Trinity of the Father, Son and Holy Ghost, symbolized by the name of the Highest, the Lamb, and the Dove, respectively.

* The ovarian follicles in the germinal epithelium of the ovary resemble a rose garden that is a Kindergarten as well: 500,000 eggs are buried in this soil (fig.351). During ovulation the follicle fills with fluid and moves toward the surface of the ovary where it erupts, releasing the egg. After the draining of its pool, the ruptured ovarian follicle becomes filled with extravasated blood and surrounding cellular tissue of a yellowish colour—the *corpus luteum*. This is the structure that produces progesterone, a hormone which conditions the walls of the uterus for the development of the fertilized egg. Figs.303-305 reflect the reversed act of ovulation: on the 'wings' of the regressing libido the philosophers' egg returns to the 'pool' of its rupturing follicle, there to unite with the ovary, or the rose garden of the philosophers. (Exactly the same sequence applies to the sperm cell's 'return' to the germinal epithelium of the testicles.)

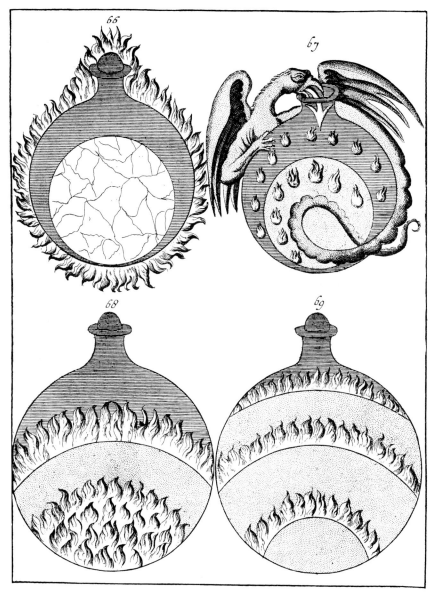

66

67

68

69

306.

The Third Coniunctio: Solar Rebirth

pleted in 40 days and nights after the true purification of the stone. As to the purification, it is impossible to fix a certain time unless the artifex works in a skilled manner; then the reddening work *(opus ad rubeum)* will be completed in 90 days and nights. These are the true lengths of time required for the total perfection, understand here the coagulation, which takes place after the purification, which purification cannot take place except through the putrefaction and conversion of the body into pure spirit. When you have attained this, laud God.' (2)

The 'Rosarium' goes on to quote one of the most ancient and famous accounts of the alchemical coniunctio—Senior's 'Epistola Solis ad Lunam crescentem': '[Luna is speaking:] I am the crescent, moist and cold moon, and you, o sun, are warm or moist (or else dry). When we have copulated in equal rank in our house, which cannot take place except by means of a gentle fire, carrying with it a heavy [fire], we must nestle in this and become like the dwelling woman and her husband of noble origin. This is truly said, and when I and the sun have been joined in order to sojourn in the womb of the closed house, I shall receive by means of flattery a soul from you if you steal my beauty and decorous figure out of your nearness. Then we shall rejoice and be exalted in the exultation of the spirit when we shall have ascended unto the order of the elders. Then the lamp of your light will be poured into my lamp, and of you and of me there will be a mixture, as of wine and sweet water . . .

'Answers Sol and says to Luna: If you will do this and will not do me any harm, then my body shall change once more; afterwards I will give you a new power of penetration by means of which you will become mighty in the struggle of the fire of liquefaction and purgation. And you

Fig.307 shows the seventeenth woodcut of the 'Rosarium' which renders the third coniunctio, or the new birth on the sun. The soul returning from heaven in the previous woodcut (fig.300) has incarnated herself with the spirit, thereby resurrecting the hermaphrodite's body on the solar hill or mountain *(mons solis)*. (1) In a gesture of triumph, the rebis extends its enormous bat-wings designed for falling flight (into the mercurial well).

The king and queen's copulation resembles their previous birth on the moon (fig.241): three serpents wriggle in the king's elevated chalice, a fourth writhes around the queen's arm, its neck clutched by her hand. The expiring three-headed serpent at the foot of the solar hill reflects the general death of the snakes still crawling on the hermaphrodite's body but soon to drop off.

The triumphant couple is gilded by the light of the sun tree *(arbor solis)* gleaming with its solar fruits. Opposite, the pelican nourishes its young with its blood, thus 'reddening' the mountain with the tincture of death and rebirth. The incestuous aspect of the solar marriage appears behind the hermaphrodite: the red lion calmly reposes in the splendour of the heavenly union with its 'display of perfection' *(perfectionis ostensio)*. The accompanying text reads:

'After the stone has been purified and perfectly cleansed of all corrupting elements and after it has been fermented, you need not change the vessel nor open it, but alone pray to God that he will guard it and not break it. And therefore the philosophers have said that the whole magistery is brought to completion in one vessel. One must know that the whitening work *(opus ad album)* is com-

PERFECTIONIS
ostensio.

307. *'Display of perfection' in heaven.*

162

308. Crushing the serpent on the solar hill, conquering the compulsion of sexuality.

well, or uterine tube.

The pelican's gory nest symbolizes the rupturing follicle, the solar hill the 'egg-hill' *(cumulus oophorus)* inside the mature follicle. (A micro-photograph of this is reproduced in fig.309; white area gives the follicular fluid surrounding the egg-hill.) As follicle and egg approach maturity, the egg-hill becomes more elevated and undercut until finally the egg is supported in a column of granulosa cells in which it is readily released in the follicular fluid at the time of ovulation.

The expiring *serpens mercurialis* at the foot of the solar hill symbolizes the death of the sperm at the top of the uterine tube if no egg is present. Similarly, the sun tree is a symbol of the ovarian 'tree' with its many 'fruits.' Shining through the ovary's germinal epithelium, a number of small vesicles can be seen—the vesicular ovarian follicles—in which the egg cells, or oocytes, are embedded (fig. 351). Just as the fruits of the lunar tree typify the eggs in their earthly, or 'created,' form, the fruits of the solar tree denote the eggs in their original, heavenly form, untainted by earthly traces of creation.

The Emblem of the Royal Enigma

Fig.308 shows the engraved variant in which the hermaphrodite's female half leads the red lion on an iron string, while its masculine half crushes the *serpens mercurialis* with a stick. The original 'Rosarium' woodcut is accompanied by a German verse reading:

The Enigma of the King
Here is born the emperor of all honour
No higher may be born than he
Through art or nature
By any living creature.
The philosophers call him their son,
And everything they do by him is done.
What men desire from him
He gives: health in many years,
Gold, silver and jewellery,
Power and youth, beauty and purity.
Rage, sorrow, poverty and sickness
he twists,
Happy is the man whom God this grants.

The response of the lunar Queen:
Here is born the empress of all honour,
The philosophers name her their
daughter,
She multiplies, bears children ever again,
They are incorruptibly pure and without
any stain.
She conquers death and hates poverty,
She gives riches, health, honour and
goods,

And surpasses gold, silver and jewellery,
All medicaments great and small.
Nothing upon earth is her equal,
Wherefore we say thanks to God
in heaven. (4)

Gilding the White Egg

Fig.306 gives Barchusen's paraphrase of the seventeenth woodcut of the 'Rosarium.' In plate 66 the ripened moon egg is enveloped by a sea of fire signifying the attainment of the third coniunctio, or the completed citrinitas. Plate 67 shows the winged mercurial serpent expiring in the tubal opening of the vessel, in vain attempting to attack the egg with its arrowed tongue. Transformed into its golden form, the egg simultaneously disappears into the opened vessel in a rain of fiery blood drops colouring or suffusing the egg with the solar medicine, the red tincture, or the pelican's blood. In plates 68-69 the sun's fire consumes the egg's granular substance, now set ablaze by ever-rising waves of divine love.

Nesting in the Mature Follicle

The symbolic action of figs.306-308 completes the unconscious play-back of conception and ovulation by embedding the egg in its follicular 'nest' or 'pool' in the ovary. The incestuous aspect of this 'higher' reunion with the maternal body is expressed by the red lion and the resurrected hermaphrodite's 'higher copulation.' Its powerful bat-wings indicate its powers of falling flight into the mercurial

Sublimation of Biological Development

The stone's sublimation during its three stages of conjunction reflects a similar 'refinement' of biological development: 1) the material splendour of the first coniunctio: the neonate's coniunctio with the gravid uterus, 2) the ethereal beauty of the second coniunctio: the fertilized egg's coniunctio with the surface of the uterus, 3) the spiritual nature of the third coniunctio: the unfertilized egg's coniunctio with the ovary.

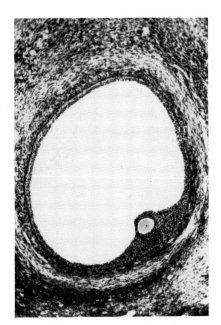

309. 'Nesting' egg in its follicular hill.

310. 'So God created man in His own image, in the image of God created He him; male and female created He them. And God blessed them, and God said unto them: Be fruitful and multiply . . . And the evening and the morning were the sixth day' (Gen.1:27-31).

311. 'And God said: Let the waters bring forth abundantly the moving creature that hath life, and fowl that may fly above the earth . . . And God blessed them, saying: Be fruitful and multiply . . . And the evening and the morning were the fifth day' (Gen.1:20-23).

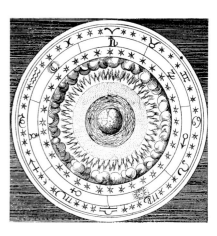

312. 'And God said: Let there be lights in the firmament of heaven to divide the day from the night; and let them be for signs, and for seasons, and for days, and years . . . He made the stars also . . . And the evening and the morning were the fourth day' (Gen.1:14-19).

313. 'And God said: Let the waters under the heaven be gathered together unto one place, and let the dry land appear . . . Let the earth bring forth grass, the herb yielding seed, and the fruit tree yielding fruit . . . And the evening and the morning were the third day' (Gen.1:9-13).

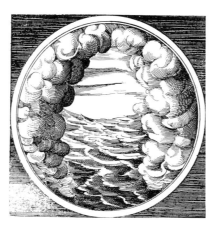

314. 'And God said: Let there be a firmament in the midst of the waters, and let it divide the waters from the waters. And God made the firmament, and divided the waters . . . And the evening and the morning were the second day' (Gen. 1:6-8).

315. 'And God divided the light from the darkness. And God called the light Day, and the darkness he called Night. And the evening and the morning were the first day' (Gen.1:4-5).

316. 'And God said: Let there be light: and there was light. And God saw the light, that it was good' (Gen.1:3-4).

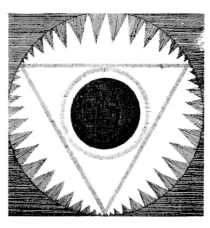

317. 'And the Spirit of God moved upon the face of the waters' (Gen.1:2).

318. 'And the earth was without form, and void; and darkness was upon the face of the deep' (Gen.1:2).

Reproducing the Mysteries of Creation

Figs.310-319 render the world's or the stone's creation, re-experienced and re-produced by the alchemist in his solar vessel. Its mysteries are described by one alchemical author as follows:

'Take a drop of the consecrated red wine and let it fall into the [philosophical] water, and you will instantly perceive a fog and thick darkness on top of the water, such as also was at the first creation. Then put in two drops, and you will see the light coming forth from the darkness; whereupon little by little put in every half of each quarter hour first three, then four, then five, then six drops, and then no more, and you will see with your own eyes one thing after another appearing by and by on top of the water, how God created all things in six days, and how it all came to pass, and such secrets as are not to be spoken aloud and I also have not power to reveal. Fall on your knees before you undertake this operation. Let your eyes judge of it; for thus was the world created. Let all stand as it is, and in half an hour after it began it will disappear.

'By this you will see clearly the secrets of God, that are at present hidden from you as from a child. You will understand what Moses has written concerning the creation; you will see what manner of body Adam and Eve had before and after the Fall, what the serpent was, what the tree, and what manner of fruits they ate: where and what Paradise is, and in what bodies the righteous shall be resurrected; not in this body that we have received from Adam, but that which we attain through the Holy Ghost, namely in such a body as our Saviour brought from heaven.' (1)

The alchemical cartoon reproduced on the opposite page forms part of the pictorial universe of the 'Janitor pansophus' (along with figs.305, 339 and 379). The picture series renders the ascent of Sol and Luna into heaven, thus duplicating the action shown by fig.305. In both engravings the couple's ascent coincides with the elevation of the egg or stone into heaven, an event identified by figs. 310-319 with the drama of creation described by Genesis. The cartoon further illustrates the sublimating effects of the philosophical wheel returning the created world into increasingly abstract patterns within the divine mind. This is the work traditionally assigned to the Water-Carrier, in which sign the third coniunctio takes place (fig.323).

The Tenth Key of Basil Valentine

Fig.321 shows Basil Valentine's emblem of the third coniunctio and the production of the stone. Its trinitarian design merges the sun and moon (top corners) in the sign of Mercurius philoso-

319. 'Alpha and Omega.' (4) The final emblem of the 'Janitor pansophus' series resembles Basil Valentine's Tenth Key (fig.321). Both render the divine state of the philosophers' egg or stone before its fall into the world of creation.

320. 'The rose gives its honey to the bees,' reads the inscription of the seven-petalled 'mystical rose' blossoming in the philosophers' garden. Its fertilization by bees expresses the supreme sublimation of sexuality achieved at the golden stage of the work. The image resembles the celestial rose in Dante's 'Paradiso,' described as suffused with the 'light of the Trinity.' (5)

321. 'Without Jamsuph I am compelled to perish' is an unintelligible statement perhaps referring to some unknown substance or acid sustaining the act of re-birth of Basil Valentine's Tenth Key.

phorum (bottom corner). The Trinity is inscribed with a radiant double-circle duplicating that of the Ninth Key (fig. 296) and hence symbolizing the philosophers' egg. Its 'nesting' in heaven is expressed by the name of the Highest inscribed in the stone's centre.

The Latin inscriptions read: 'I am born of Hermogenes. Hyperion elected me. Without Jamsuph I am compelled to perish.' Hermogenes is either a compound of *Hermes* and *genesis* meaning 'born of Hermes,' or else a reference to the Gnostic philosopher Hermogenes whose heretical tenet was that 'God had created all things from coexistent and unregenerated matter.' (2) Basil Valentine's 'election' by Hyperion is a reference to solar rebirth, Hyperion in Greek mythology representing the Father of the Sun. The text reads:

'In our stone, as composed by me and by those who have long preceded me, are contained all elements, all mineral and metallic forms, and all the qualities and properties of the whole world. In it we find most powerful natural heat, by which the icy body of Saturn is gently transmuted into the best gold. It contains also the highest degree of cold, which tempers the fervent heat of Venus and coagulates the living Mercurius, which is thereby also changed into the finest gold. The reason for this is that all the properties are infused by nature into the substance of our great stone, and are developed, perfected, and matured by the gentle coction of natural fire, until they have attained their highest perfection . . . When the arm of the king cannot reach any higher, then the glory of the world is achieved. The king has attained to indestructible fixation and is no longer liable to any danger or injury because he has become unconquerable.

'Let me express my meaning in a somewhat different manner. When you have dissolved your earth with your water, dry up the water with its own proper fire. Then the air will breathe new life, and when this life has again turned into a body, then you will have that matter which nobody else can have. For the great stone of the world which in a spiritual manner pervades human and metallic bodies is the universal and immaculate medicine, since it drives out that which is bad, and preserves that which is good, and is the unfailing corrective of all imperfect or diseased substances. This tincture is of a colour intermediate between transparent red and dark brown, ruby and pomegranate, and its weight is great and heavy. Whoever gains possession of this stone should thank the Supreme Creator of all creatures for such a heavenly balm. And he should pray for himself and for his neighbour that he may use that same stone for an earthly lull in this vale of tears and in the next that he may hereafter inherit eternal life. Praise be unto God everlastingly for this His inestimable gift and grace.' (3)

322. Enclosed in the cavity of the solar hill, perceiving the harmony of the spheres.

Apollonian Rebirth in a Solar Cave

Above, the alchemist reborn as Apollon plies his lyre in the cavity of the solar hill (or Mount Olympus), its crust cut open in front of the tube-like well from which Sol and Luna ascended in figs.301-302. He is accompanied by the nine muses gathered around and above him. The artistic apotheosis aptly expresses the citrine spiritualization of matter into harmonious patterns, abstract forms, sounding beauty. Music is a favourite symbol of the heavenly rebirth, expressed by the musicians' haloes, or solar coronation.

Three muses appear on top of the *mons solis*, two of them holding the triangles of fire and water (also representing above and below), the third uniting them in the Seal of Solomon. This woman represents the philosophers' daughter or muse, the king's wife, the heavenly virgin. Significantly, the solified alchemist appears just beneath the woman, at the place occupied by the roots of her tree. The marriage of heaven and earth is further indicated by the 'ring' formed by the engraving's tube-like aperture (cf.fig. 303). Its lower half shows the sun, moon and planets in their earthly region, as material bodies; its upper half renders

the same planets in their heavenly region, as spiritual bodies, archetypal ideas, or abstract 'codes,' later to materialize with the *fiat* of creation. The corner emblems signify the four elements, earth and water representing the 'realms beneath,' fire and air the 'realms above.' The verse reads:

The things that are in the realms above
Are also in the realms beneath. What
Heaven shows is often found on earth.
Fire and flowing water are contraries,
Happy thou if thou canst unite them. (1)

Aquarius the Water-Carrier: Spirituality

The golden conjunction of above and below takes place in the sign of Aquarius, the Water-Carrier (fig.323). The eleventh sign of the Zodiac is a fixed, airy sign ruled by Saturn and covering the period from January 21 to February 19, or the period of deepest winter. The Water-Carrier is a giant Orion-like figure uniting heaven and earth with the airy water, or drizzle, poured out from his pitcher. Aquarius is the astrological symbol of spiritualization *par excellence;* it stands for the dissolution and decomposition of

the material forms existing within any process, cycle or period. By means of his spiritualizing water, or universal solvent, the Water-Carrier loosens the bonds which hold the components of creation together, thereby reabsorbing the world of phenomena into the world of mind. Figuratively speaking, the Water-Carrier restores every creature to its egg state. Psychologically, the Water-Carrier represents the moment of awakening at the lofty and transcendent level of the yogi.

The Aquarius personality 'is of such stuff that dreams are made of'; immaterial in its effects on its surroundings, expectant, intuitive and absent-minded, the Aquarian moves at the level of pure spirit. He has a natural gift for abstract thought and the circulation of ideas, usually of a 'cosmic' nature. Imbued with the true scientific spirit, he is primarily interested in discovering the laws and principles of nature, Darwin and Galileo being typical Aquarians in this respect. Due to this tendency, the Aquarius type is greatly attracted to modern trends of thought and to new inventions in every sphere.

The Arcade of Nicolas Flamel

Fig.324 shows the 'Figures of Abraham the Jew,' sculptured in 1407 by the French alchemist Nicolas Flamel (1330-1418). The arcade in the churchyard of the Innocents contained the original figures and formed a sacred shrine to the alchemists of succeeding centuries. (2) The arcade survived until the demolition of the church of St.Jacques-la-Boucherie in 1797. The engraved copy of the arcade shows its two bottom inscriptions: 'Nicolas Flamel and Perrenelle his wife.' 'How the innocents were slaughtered on the command of King Herod.' The three pictures inserted between them illustrate the event.

The band of pictures above them shows the winged and wingless dragons [2] followed by an elderly man and woman who

323. A giant uniting above and below.

324. Dangerous ascent toward the rose garden of the philosophers, opened by the Christian emperor on the Day of Judgement.

prophesy: 'Man will come to the Judgement of God. Verily, that day will be terrible' [3]. The subsequent pictures show the resurrection of two men and a woman and the pronouncement of Judgement by two angels and a winged lion, forcibly restrained by a recumbent man: 'Ye dead arise and come to the Judgement of my Lord' [5,6,8]. The heavenly vault, symbolized by the arch, is peopled by flying angels and a trinity of saintly figures. St.Paul with his sword appears as the guardian of the kneeling Flamel who prays: 'Obliterate the evil I have done' [4]. St.Peter with his keys acts as the guardian of Perrenelle who prays: 'Christ have mercy on us' [7]. The Saviour appears in the middle, making the sign of the Trinity and presenting the orb of universal dominion. He is supported by two angels awakening the dead with celestial music performed on a lute and a bagpiper. Hovering angels above the Saviour sing his praise: 'O Almighty Father,' 'O Good

Jesus' [5]. The angels in the lower corners of the arcade join with their song: 'O Eternal King,' 'Hail thee, Lord of the Angels.'

As evidenced by the composition, the entrance into the philosophers' rose garden [plate III] is identified with the opening of the gates of heaven at Doomsday. According to Flamel, plate III shows 'a fair rose tree flowered in the midst of a sweet garden, climbing up against a hollow oak, at the foot whereof boils a fountain of most white water, which runs headlong down into the depths, notwithstanding it first passes among the hands of infinite people which dig in the earth seeking for it; but because they are blind, none of them know it, except here and there one who considers the weight.' (3) Plates I-VII at the engraving's top symbolize the trauma of rebirth suffered by Flamel and Perrenelle while ascending toward the gates of heaven and the rose garden of the philosophers. The course of

the down-pouring fountain is explored by plate VII which Flamel describes as 'painting deserts or wildernesses in the midst whereof run many fair fountains, from whence there issue out a number of serpents, which run up and down, here and there.' (4) Their action is explained by plate V which, according to Flamel, describes 'a virgin and serpents swallowing her up.' (5) Another eerie passage is made in plate II which depicts 'a fair flower on the top of a very high mountain *[mons solis]*, which is sore shaken with the north wind: it has the foot blue, the flowers white and red, the leaves shining like fine gold, and round about it the dragons and griffins of the North making their nests and abode.' (6)

Plate I renders the horrors of amputation and cleavage, depicting 'a young man with wings at his ankles, having in his hand a Caducean rod, writhen about with two serpents, wherewith he strikes upon a helmet which covers his head. He

325. Sol and Luna marrying anew in the sign of infinite multiplication and fertility.

the lunar and solar tinctures in the vessel handed to Mercurius philosophorum in the previous engraving (fig.275). Having weighed and merged the tinctures (upper row), the couple seals the retort, now illuminated by the solar tincture. The vessel is placed in the furnace and matured by its fire (middle row). The golden conjunction is realized in the bottom row where the couple succeeds with their bow in hitting the target (extreme left). It is composed of the four elements enclosed in a ball or circle. With their return to the unity of the centre, brother and sister marry anew in the heavenly shape of Sol and Luna.

If compared to the tenth plate of the 'Mutus liber,' which renders the lunar conjunction (fig.254), the engraving demonstrates the progress achieved: 1) the earth strewn with leaves has become a glazed surface symbolizing the floor of heaven (bottom row); 2) the number ten (denarius) has multiplied into infinity, thus indicating Sol and Luna's infinite powers of generation.

The 'Reddened' King on His Throne

Fig.326 shows Basil Valentine's vision of the 'reddened' king.* Resurrected on his throne anew, the giant hero of earthly and heavenly reunion presents the Seal of Solomon, while crowning his planetary brothers. The event signifies the lighten-

* Actually the 'reddening' has two distinct stages in alchemy, one unfolding in the citrinitas, the other in the rubedo. The two stages are symbolized by the golden morning sun and by the blazing sun at noon; by the pelican's gory nest and by the phoenix's blazing pyre; by the eagle and by the two-headed eagle; by the king and by the emperor; similarly, the multiplicatio has two editions, just as there are two heavenly marriages. The two stages are frequently mixed up and subsumed under the term 'rubedo.' In our study we distinguish between the citrinitas and the rubedo and hence between two 'reddening' stages, the former colouring the silvery moon into the 'redness' of the morning sun or the golden stone, the latter colouring the morning sun into the 'redness' of the hot sun at noon while transforming the golden stone into the heavenly stone of gold.

326. The red king on his golden throne.

seems in my modest judgement to be the God Mercury of the pagans. Against him there comes running and flying with open wings a great old man, who upon his head has an hour-glass fastened, and in his hands a hook (or scythe) like Death, with the which in terrible and furious manner, he will have cut off the feet of Mercury.' (7)

Another symbol of death appears in plate IV which Flamel explains as follows: 'There was a king with a great falchion, who made to be killed in his presence by some soldiers a great multitude of little infants, whose mothers wept at the feet of the unpitiful soldiers; the blood of which infants was afterwards by other soldiers gathered up, and put in a great vessel, wherein the Sun and Moone came to bathe themselves [fig.302]. And

because that this history did represent the more part of that of the Innocents slain by Herod, and that in this book I learned the greatest part of the art, this was one of the causes why I placed in their churchyard these hieroglyphic symbols of this secret science.' (8)

The citrine figures of Abraham the Jew include the killing of the mercurial serpent on the solar mountain. The event is depicted by plate VI which Flamel describes as 'painting a Cross whereon a serpent is crucified.' (9)

Celestial Rebirth in the Solar Vessel

Fig.325 shows the thirteenth engraving of the 'Mutus liber' in which the alchemist and his sister attempt the fusion of

ing of the sevenfold planetary star in its solar splendour. In Basil Valentine, the king's mystical speech from the throne sounds as follows:

I have conquered all my enemies,
And a celestial glory radiates from me.
Many from one and one from many,
Issue of a famous line, I rise
From the lowest to the highest.
The nethermost power of the world
Is united with the highest, therefore
I am the One and the Many within me,
Multiplying myself by ten [fig.325]. (1)

The Harmony of the Spheres

Fig.327 shows another version of the planetary star's solar lightening. The astrological joining of the seven planetary deities takes place inside the solar hill, heated by upwelling masses of fire. The assembled gods appear with their zodiacal signs and traditional equipment; their peaceful gathering reflects the resolution of their oppositions, squares and trines in a cosmic conjunction, the musical symbol of which is the harmony of the spheres.

Fig.328 shows crippled Saturn recovering his legs and jumping to mow the sun and moon flowers and the Solomonic Seal's flower. The scenery to be destroyed is the heavenly marriage of the citrinitas, celebrated below the sun tree, on top of the solar hill. The king presents his sceptre and fiery eagle, the queen her silvery swan; their attributes signify the 'sublimation' of love, the swan denoting spiritual love, the eagle loving spirit. The queen points to the philosophers' stone blazing inside the solar hill and gilding the red lion. The saturnine darkening of the landscape inaugurates a new bout of mortification leading to the destruction of the winged hermaphrodite, the solar stone, tree and hill, the philosophers' rose garden.

Rebirth in Late Middle Age

In terms of the individuation process, the third coniunctio symbolizes rebirth in late middle age. This is a regular phenomenon of life and may be observed in the biographies of all creative artists. Goethe's 'Faust I,' Wagner's 'Mastersingers' and Beethoven's Ninth Symphony with its 'Ode to Joy' (fig.305) belong within this category. In T.S.Eliot, the poet's experience of the golden autumn of maturity is expressed by the two quartets 'Burnt Norton' and 'East Coker':

'The inner freedom from the practical
desire,
The release from action and suffering,
release from the inner
And the outer compulsion, yet
surrounded

327. *Golden conjunction of the planetary gods in a hill heated by the sun's fire.*

By a grace of sense, a white light still
and moving,
Erhebung *without motion, concentration*
Without elimination, both a new world
And the old made explicit, understood.'

Pearl S.Buck described the sublimation of love at this stage of life in the following terms: 'It is not the same love that one feels in youth or the same love that one may feel in middle age, but it's a very special rewarding love, the love that gives and asks for nothing, and whatever comes back is pure gold.'

The splendour of the setting sun, or aging personality, reveals the growing transparency of the self, illuminating the ego from within and producing the flower of individuation: the serene personality, the Wise Old Man.

328. *Saturn mortifying the citrine splendours while inaugurating the last putrefaction.*

329.

Rubedo: 'Red' Death and Putrefaction

Fig.330 shows the eighteenth woodcut of the 'Rosarium' which opens the final stage of the opus alchymicum, the so-called *rubedo*. Since every Hermetic stage begins with a bout of putrefaction followed by an act of conjunction, the 'red' putrefaction is hailed by the adepts as the unlocking of the door to the last and most difficult labyrinth of the Hermetic castle.

'Our Mercurius is the green lion devouring the sun,' (1) says the 'Rosarium' of the arcane substance as it coils back on itself in a final, mysterious convulsion of depression and death. The motto reads:

I am the true green and golden lion,
In me are hidden all the philosophers'
  secrets. (2)

The text proceeds: 'Mercurius is that same one, and know that he is cold and moist and that God out of him has created all the minerals . . . And therefore he is the whole elixir of the albedo and the rubedo, and the permanent water, and the water of life and death, and the virgin's milk, the herb of ablution, and a living fountain of which who shall drink does not die. He takes on colour and is their medicine, causing them to acquire colours, and he is that which mortifies, desiccates and moistens, makes warm and cool, and does contrary things according to the measure of his regimen. And when alive, he performs certain kinds of operation, and when dead, others; and when in the state of sublimation, others again; and again others when in the state of solution. And he is the dragon who marries himself and impregnates himself, and brings to birth in due time, and slays all living things with his poison.' (3)

Uniting with the Green and Golden Lion

Fig.331 shows the engraved variant in which the lion kept on a leash by the golden hermaphrodite (fig.308) suddenly assumes universal proportions. The starry lion, which symbolizes the heavenly incestuous marriage, devours the sun and moon, who separate and cruelly expire in the belly of the cosmic beast.

Fig.329 shows Barchusen's variation upon the eighteenth woodcut of the 'Rosarium.' In plate 70 the ever-rising waves of solar fire keep heating the granular interior of the philosophers' egg enclosed in the vessel. In plates 71-72 the fire reverts its energies, blazing in the opposite direction. In plate 73 the rings of fire close in on the philosophers' egg in a kind of implosion, turning the flames dark and mortal.

Atrophy of the Libido in Senescence

The green lion's mortification of the golden hermaphrodite symbolizes the crucial stage of the individuation process known as *senescence or old age*. As the wheeling alchemical work nears its end, the circle of life comes to a similar close: 'Last scene of all, that ends this strange eventful history, is second childishness and mere oblivion, sans teeth, sans eyes, sans taste, sans everything' (As You Like It, 2:7).

Physically, senility is characterized by thinning, atrophy, and wrinkling of the skin; graying of the hair; wasting of muscular tissue and loss of its firmness; increasing tremors, postural changes, and changes in gait; impairment of vision and hearing, taste and smell, memory and imagination.

Psychologically, the 'green lion . . . who slays all living things with his poison' asserts himself in an equally painful manner. Depression has long been recognized as a characteristic mood of senescence; throughout history descriptions of old age have referred to the melancholy, dolorous, crabbed mood of the aged.

330. *Mortifying the celestial marriage.*

331. *The fire of heavenly conjunction turned black and mortal by the green lion.*

Sexual Polarity Reversed and Undone

If the separation of the chromosomes during meiosis transforms the cell into a sex cell governed by polarity and tension, the reversal of this process means the *undoing* of sexual polarity and tension. Such a hypothetical process would re-establish the libido's initial 'a-sexual' state in the immature egg or sperm cell. At this stage of oogenesis or spermatogenesis, the cell is in an original resting position since its nucleus shares the full number of chromosomes present in body cells and in non-maturing germ cells.

The Last Transition of the Libido

The green lion devouring the sun is a dual symbol of the reversed course of meiosis and the libido's withering into senescence, both processes coinciding in the last movement of a regressing unconscious closing the circle of life and individuation.

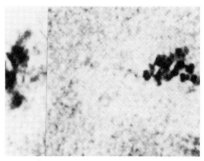

332. *Film-sequence of a reversed meiosis.*

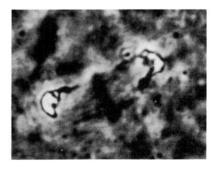

333. *Creation of a sex cell by division.*

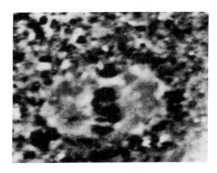

334. *Preparing the halving of the cell.*

Cicero describes old men as 'morose, troubled, fretful and hard to please.'

Depth psychologists have observed that the possibilities for psychic change are greater in old age than at any other period of life; growing introspection and withdrawal, heightened body concern and increasing indifference toward the affairs of the world form part of what amounts to a profound identity-crisis.

The result of such psychobiological changes is the onset of a so-called 'senile depression,' which displays the whole gamut of depression from younger periods of life. However, the senile degeneration inexorably proceeding at a biological level lends its specific colouring to the course of senile depression, which acquires a final and painful quality, straining the ego's adaptive functions to their utmost.

The Egg's First Maturation Division

In terms of the genetic process, the 'red' putrefaction symbolizes the regressive revival of the unconscious imprints of *meiosis*. This is a special form of cell division occurring in connection with the development of cells destined for reproduction. It represents the crucial transformation process by which the egg or sperm cell is ripened toward ovulation or ejaculation. In meiosis, the common body cell is turned into an egg or sperm cell proper by means of the *first maturation division*. In order to understand the unique nature of this process, one has to consider a normal cell division or *mitosis*.

The Halving of the Sex Cell

The cell is the corner-stone of all life, just as the division of the cell into two identical copies of itself is the process which ensures the renewal of all life. In normal cell division the chromosomes in the nucleus double, form pairs and split, thus ensuring the transmission of the original cell's 46 chromosomes. The two new cells represent an exact copy of the original cell's chromosomes. This is mitosis.

In the differing process of meiosis the egg cell's chromosomes are cut in half. This 'halving of the egg' (or sperm) is a necessary process if the union of sperm and egg is not to result in a 'monster cell' with 92 chromosomes. Figs.332-334 demonstrate the 'sexualization' of the original sex-less germ cell: 1) the chromosomes line up along the equatorial plane of the cell-spindle and prepare for the act of division (fig.334); 2) the cell's chromosomal complement is torn in two by the cell-spindle seen as a dark vertical band (fig.333); 3) 23 chromosomes are projected toward the cell's pole as a polar body, while 23 chromosomes remain to form the reduced nucleus of the egg cell (fig.332).*

* After the first maturation division (meiosis) the two new cells divide once more in the so-called second maturation division which is a normal (mitotic) cell-division dividing the two cells into four sex cells, all with a reduced nuclear-chromosomal content: in the male, four sperm cells; in the female, one egg cell with three polar bodies (see fig.352).

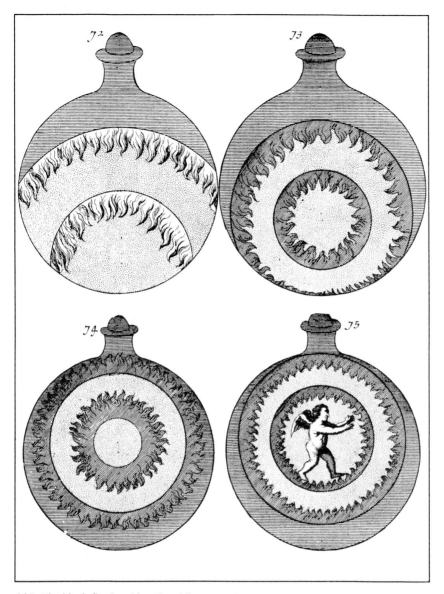

335. The black fire hatching the philosophers' son in the germinating world-egg.

white tincture: When my beloved parents have tasted of life, have been nourished with pure milk and become drunk with my white substance, and have embraced each other in my bed, they shall bring forth the son of the moon, who will excel all his kindred. And when my beloved has drunk from the red rock sepulchre and tasted the maternal fount in matrimony, and has drunk with me of my red wine and lain with me in my bed in friendship, then I, loving him and receiving his seed into my cell, shall conceive and become pregnant and when my time is come shall bring forth a most mighty son, who shall rule over and govern all kings and princes of the earth, crowned with the golden crown of victory by the supreme God who liveth and reigneth ever more.' (1)

Final Sublimation of Soul and Spirit

This passage and its accompanying woodcut identify the Assumption of the Virgin with the ascension of Luna, or the soul, soaring toward the heavenly and incestuous marriage with the Son *or* the Father, identified, in turn, with Sol, or the extracted spirit. The ultimate goal of this movement of sublimation is the Immaculate Conception of the philosophers' son, identified in his fully grown shape with Christ Resurrected (fig.354).

Fig.337 shows a variant of the 'Rosarium' woodcut which, like its model, combines the Virgin's Assumption and Coronation with the ascension of Sol and Luna, preparing in heaven for the Immaculate Conception and Resurrection of the philosophers' son: 'Truly, the moon is the mother; and by the father the son was created; whose father is the sun.' Walking on the waves with ethereal bodies, Sol and Luna adore the Virgin Mother with whom they are raised from earth to heaven.

Heavenly Extraction of Soul and Spirit

Fig.336 shows the nineteenth woodcut of the 'Rosarium' in which the departure of the soul is depicted as the Assumption and Coronation of Mary uniting with the Holy Trinity *(tria unum)*, the latter representing the departed spirit and its espousals to the soul 'in heaven.' Left on earth is the dead body, putrefying in the tomb of Christ and awaiting there its Easter morning. The inscriptions of the flying scrolls bear out the mortifying implications of the scenery while identifying its Christian figures with the Hermetic protagonists: 'Truly, the moon is the mother; and by the father the son was created; whose father is the sun.' 'The dragon dieth not except with his brother and sister; and not with one alone, but with both of them.'

In the engraved variant (fig.338) the philosophers' son standing between his royal parents is crowned with a crown much too big for his small head. The son separated from his father and mother symbolizes the departure of his soul (queen) and spirit (king), which must be returned to his dwindled body in the act of resurrection. This implies his growth into parental stature and his conquest of the hermaphroditic crown, identical with his final reunion with the king and queen in one parental, hermaphroditic figure.

Preparations for the Heavenly Marriage

The text accompanying the 'Rosarium' woodcut expresses the soaring mood of the 'red' putrefaction and presents an ecstatic rebirth fantasy in which the voices of the philosophers' son and his parents blend in a 'triunity' *(tria unum)* of confused identities: 'Unless the soul goes forth from its body, and rise up into heaven, thou makest no progress in this art. The parable of Senior concerning the

336. Soul and spirit united in heaven.

A Germinating World-Egg

Fig.335 shows Barchusen's variation upon the nineteenth woodcut of the 'Rosarium.' The reversal of the flow of fire in plate 72 and the blackening of the reversed flames in plate 73 are followed by the flames' pulsating movement in plates 74-75. The black, cremating fire finally hatches the philosophers' son in plate 75. Subsequently growing into cosmic man and universal ruler, the *infans philosophorum* at present exists only as an unfledged homunculus, or would-be hermaphrodite, in his immature world-egg. The fire maturing this egg is that of the fourth degree, sometimes compared to the sun's heat.

An alchemical author describes this stage of the work as follows: '[The alchemist] is beset by anxiety because the tincture, still suffering from defects, has not yet been brought to its complete birth. For although God in the qualities of nature has become man, man in the qualities of nature has not yet become God or divine. The tincture of life still lacks the spirit of the Holy Ghost. In order that it may win this, it labours in itself toward fixation in the qualities of the sun. For the sun gives spirit, colour, fixation and perfection to the tincture. The colour added to it by the sun is a crimson purple colour, a deep pomegranate red: this being the immutable and permanent colour.' (2)

The Birth of the 'Macrocosmic Son'

The philosophers' child hatched at this stage of the work is sometimes called the *filius macrocosmi*, the 'son of the macrocosmos.' (3) Fig.339 shows his birth in the world-egg, two angels attending his delivery. Like his counterpart in figs.335 and 338, he represents the germinating 'red' coniunctio—the great stone, universal hermaphrodite, or cosmic man *in statu nascendi*. The 'macrocosmic son' is surrounded by the inscription: 'It is the great honour of faithful souls that from their very birth an angel is appointed to preserve and keep each of them.'

The *filius macrocosmi* embodies the idea that man is a microcosm which reflects the macrocosm, or 'God.' Thus, the egg of the 'macrocosmic son' contains the whole universe since it holds its point of reflection in the son's human intellect, capable of grasping its laws. Therefore, *sicut superius, sicut inferius*, 'as above, so below' ('Tabula smaragdina'). This unity of divine and human 'correspondences' in the 'son of the macrocosmos' explains the spiritual ecstasy of the text, from the 'Janitor pansophus.' It reveals the *filius macrocosmi* in the 'yolk' of his cosmic egg as an emblem of omniscient mind resting in the uncreated stage:

'1. God is an eternal being, an infinite unity, the radical principle of all things.

337. The last sublimation of the soul and spirit, ascending with the heavenly Virgin.

His essence is infinite light. His power—omnipotence; His will—perfect goodness; His wish—absolute reality. As we strive to think of Him, we plunge into the abyss of silence, of infinite glory. 2. Many sages have held that an archetypal world existed long before the world of sense, when the archetypal light began to unfold Itself, and set forth in an ideal world a counterpart of the divine mind. This belief is borne out by the words of Hermes Trismegistus, who says that when God changed His form, the universe was suddenly revealed and put forth in the light of actuality—this world being nothing but a visible image of a hidden god. This is what the ancients meant when they said that Pallas leapt forth in divine perfection from the forehead of Jupiter, with the aid of Vulcan (or divine light).

338. The philosophers' son yearning for the parental double-crown and its empire.

173

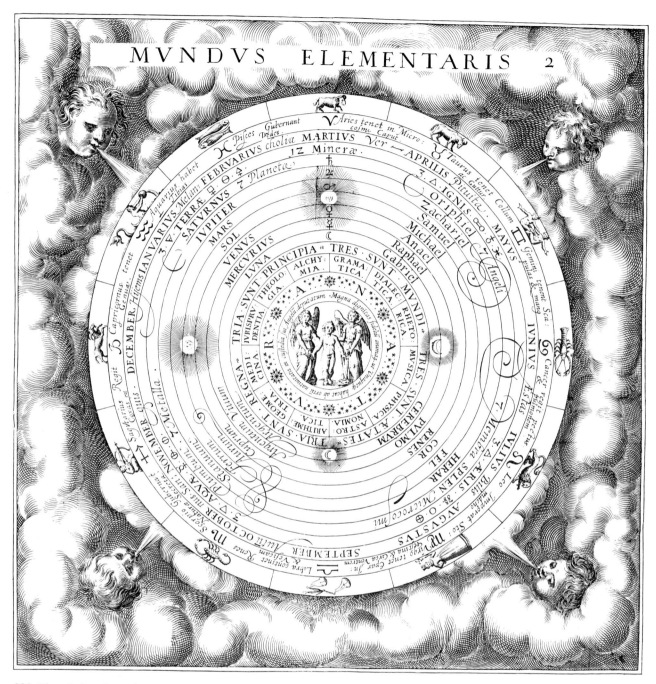

339. The whole universe in an egg shell: the cosmic design packed in the DNA-code of the ovum humanum, the germinating stone.

3. The eternal Father of all things, being not less wise in the ordering, than powerful in the creation, of the world, has made the whole universe to cohere by means of secret influences and mutual subjection and obedience, things below being analogous to things above, and vice versa; so that both ends of the world are nevertheless united by a real bond of natural cohesion. Thus Hermes tells us that things below are the same as things above, and that things above are analogous to things below. 4. He who looks upon nature as anything but the constant expression of God's will is an atheist; every smallest part of the great universe is constantly vitalized and conserved by

Lapidis multiplicativa Auri.

	I.	1000
	II.	10000
	III.	100000
	IV.	1000000
	V.	10000000
	VI.	100000000
Projectio	VII.	1000000000
	VIII.	10000000000
	IX.	100000000000
	X.	1000000000000
	XI.	10000000000000
	XII.	100000000000000

340. Centum milliones millionum tingunt.

the spirit of the divine master, and there is no life or existence apart from His consciously exerted will. It was He that in the beginning moved upon the face of the waters, and brought forth the actual out of the chaos of potentiality.' (1)

The Primary Oocyte or Spermatocyte

If the 'red' mortification symbolizes the reversed course of the first maturation division (meiosis), its figure of germinating rebirth symbolizes the primary oocyte (or spermatocyte), i.e., the attainment of the reproductive cell's condition *prior* to its first maturation division. The

174

remarkable qualities of this cell are its powers of 'multiplication' by means of a 'projection' of itself. These are the very qualities developed by the philosophers' egg or stone when maturing in the hot fire of the rubedo (fig.340).

Projection and Multiplication

Fig.341 shows the queen of the rubedo seated on the red lion of 'multiplication.' In a triumphant gesture she presents the philosophers' egg dyed with the pelican's blood. An emblem of the red tincture, the pelican's blood is duplicated by the lion offering its blood and flesh as food for its hungry cubs. These dual images of 'multiplication' refer to the two concluding operations of the opus alchymicum known as the *multiplicatio* and *proiectio* (fig.340).

The first term has been met with in connection with the citrine multiplication performed in the fifteenth woodcut of the 'Rosarium' (fig.292). Its text explained: 'By reiteration of this [solar] medicine and administration of its goodness with cautionary industry you may arrive at the preparation of the stone [which is not completed] until the mercury transmutes itself into the infinite sun-making and the true moon-making substance, everything depending on its multiplication.'

In order to understand this passage one must bear in mind the alchemical implications of projection and multiplication. These operations refer to the goldmakers' 'projection' of the solar medicine, or golden tincture, upon the white silver, thereby dyeing or gilding it by means of the tincture's 'multiplication' of itself. This work has two stages, a yellow and a red one. We have studied the citrine work of multiplication in which the silvery stone was gilded by the multiplying tincture, i.e., covered only with gold leaf or gold-coloured paint. In the rubedic work of multiplication the tincture is improved to the point where it reaches the powers of infinite multiplication. Not until the attainment of this stage will it be possible for the adept to transmute the stone's mercury entirely into gold. Hence his raising of the fire to its highest degree, by which the tincture will mature and produce its truly dyeing qualities.

The alchemical table reproduced in fig. 340 gives a graphic demonstration of the two last operations of the opus: 1) the 'multiplication of the golden stone . . . dyeing 100,000,000,000,000'; 2) the original act of 'projection' from which results the endless multiplication of the stone in I-XII. The 'Philosophia reformata' lays down the following rule: 'Project on any body as much of it as you please, since its tincture shall be multiplied twofold. And if one part of it in the first place converts with its bodies a hundred

341. The philosophers' egg or stone dyed with the red tincture of multiplication.

parts: in the second it converts a thousand, in the third ten thousand, in the fourth a hundred thousand, in the fifth a million, into the true sun-making and moon-making [substance].' (2)

The Eleventh Key of Basil Valentine

Fig.342 shows Basil Valentine's Eleventh Key whose subject is the multiplication of the stone. The Key opens with the sacrifice of the heavenly stone pro-duced in the previous Key (fig.321). Mars prepares to mow the sun and moon flowers sprouting from two hearts held by a couple of lion tamers or twin-sisters. Simultaneously, the two lions bite each other to shed their blood and mix it. These animals symbolize the Key's Orpheus and Euridice figures, who engage in this very act in order to produce the red tincture or the 'elixir of life.' This is symbolized by the lion cubs multiplying in the footsteps of the right lion. The text explains:

342. Sacrificial preparation of the red tincture of multiplication, or the elixir of life.

343. *At the source of the longest river: the rose garden regained in its permanence.*

Producing the Elixir of Life

'The Eleventh Key to the knowledge of the multiplication of our stone I will put before you in the form of a parable. There lived in the East a wonderful knight named Orpheus, who was possessed of immense wealth, and had everything that heart can wish. He had taken to wife his own carnal and natural sister, Euridice, who did not, however, bear him any children. This he regarded as the punish-ment of his sin in having wedded his own sister, and was instant in prayer to God both by day and by night that He might give him His blessing and grant his prayer.

'One night when he was buried in a deep sleep, there came to him in a dream a winged messenger, named Phoebus, who touched his feet, which were very hot, and said: 'Thou noble knight, since thou hast wandered through many cities and kingdoms and suffered many things at sea, in battle, and in the lists and re-ceived praise from the honourable ladies, the heavenly Father has bidden me make known to thee the following means of obtaining thy prayer: Take blood from thy right side and from the left side of thy spouse. For this blood is the heart's blood of your parents, and though it may seem to be of two kinds, yet, in reality, it is only one. Mix the two kinds of blood and keep the mixture tightly enclosed in the globe of the seven wise masters. There that which is generated will be nourished with its own flesh and blood, and if you do it rightly you will inherit much and leave an innumerable multitude born of your own body. But you must know that the last seed or the first seed from which you were originally made will complete its course of development when the moon has changed for the eighth time. If thou repeat this process again and again thou shalt see children's children, and the off-spring of thy body shall fill the world in order that the Creator may fully possess his heavenly kingdom.'

'When Phoebus had thus spoken, he winged his flight heavenward and the knight awoke. In the morning he arose and did the bidding of the celestial mes-senger, and God gave to him and to his wife many children, who inherited their father's name, glory, wealth, and knightly honours from generation to generation.

'If you are wise, my son, you will find the interpretation of my parable. If you do not understand it, ascribe the blame not to me, but to your own ignorance. I am forbidden to unlock further doors in the castle and must stop here according to my obedience. To whom the Almighty will grant it, it will appear clearly, indeed so clearly that almost nobody will believe it. For I have revealed the matter in a more plain and straightforward manner than any of my predecessors. I have con-cealed nothing; and if you will but re-move the veil of ignorance from your eyes, you will behold that which many have sought and few found. The matter is named all things, and its beginning, middle and end have here been shown to you.' (1)

The red tincture extracted from the wounded Orpheus and Euridice and from the bleeding lions may be amplified by another alchemical description of the 'elixir of life': 'In the human body there is concealed a certain substance of heav-enly nature, known to very few, which needeth no medicament, being itself the

344. *A heavenly queen squandering the riches of her endlessly multiplying gold.*

incorruptible medicament . . . It is a certain ethereal substance which preserves the other elemental parts of the body and causes them to continue . . . In this fortress is the true and indubitable treasure, which is not eaten into by moths, nor dug out by thieves, but remaineth for ever, and is taken hence after death.' (2)

Multiplying Riches of the Rose Garden

Fig.343 shows the alchemist arriving at the philosophers' rose garden after having followed the Hermetic river to its spring. The distance covered is expressed by the solar hill in the background with its nine muses singing and playing on the Parnassus of the arts. The motto explains: 'He who wants to enter the philosophers' rose garden without a key is like unto a man who wants to walk without feet.' (3) The entrance to the garden is heavily bolted and may be opened only by the Twelfth Key of the royal art, which gives access to the rose garden in its revived or *permanent* state.

The text accompanying the engraving indicates that the magic key for opening the garden and 'collecting there the white and the red roses' (4) is buried in the place 'where the bones of Orestes are to be found, namely where the winds, the manslaughter, the reflection, and the ruin of men are found together.' (5) These are symbols for the 'death' suffered during the opening stage of the rubedo.

The magic of the revived rose garden is its endless coining of the philosophical gold and infinite multiplication of the philosophers' stone; its profusion of heavenly children or roses; its shooting fields of corn; its soil of infinite increase. Fig. 344 shows the 'mysteries of the queen' *(reginae mysteria)* (6) in the philosophers' garden. Seated at a table, the queen squanders the multiplying gold on three beggars approaching her with bowls. Fig.346 shows the alchemist at his furnace of multiplication, coining from a stick of gold innumerable money.

The Multiplying Stone of Nature

Fig.345 shows the philosophers' stone multiplying universally while assuming the function of the building stone of nature. The motto explains: 'This stone is projected onto the earth and lifted onto the mountains, it lives in the air and feeds in the rivers, that is, Mercurius.' (7) The text further elucidates the motif:

'Nearly everyone who has just once heard about the philosophers' stone and its power (apart from those who are wholly incredulous) asks where it can be found . . . The philosophers answer this in two ways. Firstly, they say that Adam took the philosophers' stone with him when he left Paradise, and that it is now

345. Philosophers marvelling at the multiplying building stones of nature—the cells.

in you, in me and in everybody, and that birds from far regions took it with them. Secondly, the philosophers answer that it is to be found in the earth, in the mountains, in the air and in the river. Now, which of the two ways is to be followed? In my opinion both ways; but each way in its own manner.' (8)

346. An alchemist coining innumerable amounts of pounds, shilling and pence, L.S.D.

347. States of a 'reddened' soul: children multiplying and playing in the sunlight.

Discovering the Multiplying Stone

In man and nature the alchemist searches for his magical stone, which according to the source of the motto—the 'Rosinus ad Saratantam Episcopum'—is a stone, yet not a stone: 'This stone, which is not a stone, is thrown into the things and exalted in the mountains; it lives in the air and feeds in the river, the mercury, which has many names, and it rests on top of the mountains.' (9) The 'Turba' describes the marvellous powers of the multiplying stone as follows: 'The said one thing enters into every regimen and is found everywhere, being a stone and also not a stone; common and precious; hidden and concealed, yet known by everyone; of

one name and of many names, which is the spume of the moon. This stone, therefore, is not a stone because it is more precious. Without it nature never operates anything. Its name is one, yet we have called it by many names on account of the excellence of its nature.' (10)

A Garden of Death and Multiplication

The twentieth painting of the 'Splendor solis' (fig.347) renders the 'coagulation' which follows upon the 'dissolution.' In the former state mercury is passive, sulphur active, while it is the other way round in the latter state. 'And for this reason the art is compared to the

play of children, in which the one that is on top of the other lies underneath the next moment,' concludes the lapidary text. (1) The stage of 'coagulation' now attained is symbolized by the *ludus puerorum* or 'play of children,' a popular alchemical motif of the work when becoming as easy as 'child's play.' (2) The abundance of children relates the motif to the fertility symbolism of the *multiplicatio* and also to its sense of rejuvenation and rebirth.

Fig.348 shows the hardening of the stone in the 'violent heat' *(aestus graves)* now reigning in the alchemist's furnace. The text compares the process to the way Triptolemus and Achilles were hardened in the fire by their mothers, Ceres (Demeter) and Thetis, who in such manner attempted to endow their sons with invulnerability. The epigram explains:

*Look how Triptolemus and Achilles,
    strong in battle,
Learnt to suffer violent heat, at the
    instruction of their mother.
Divine Ceres hardened the former, Thetis
    the latter, in the fire by night,
While offering by day her breasts,
    rich with milk;
Let the philosophers' beatific medicine
    become accustomed in the same way
As the boy at the breast, so that it
    may enjoy the fire. (3)*

The 'violent heat' alluded to by the text is shown in fig.348 as a cremating fire. Achilles appears as a warrior slain in battle, his body being dragged to the fire by his mother to undergo cremation. The mortal implications of the raging fire are emphasized by the old man behind the rock, probably depicting Saturn, the god of death. With a dramatic gesture Thetis reappears in the background to draw attention to the action in the left half of the picture. Here Achilles' counterpart, Triptolemus, emerges as a sucking infant held by his mother in a field of corn. The goddess of the vegetation is crowned with ears of corn symbolizing multiplication and increase. The engraving's female figures of cremation and nursing, annihilation and multiplication, thus personify the chief motif of the rubedo—*l'amour et la mort.*

Fig.349 shows the transformation of Saturn in the promised land of the alchemists—the philosophers' garden—now revived in its permanent and indestructible form and illuminated by the multiplying sun and moon flowers. The motto reads: 'Saturn waters the earth which carries the flowers of the sun and moon.' (4) The rich soil of the philosophers' garden—its powers of endless germination, growth and fertility—is described by Nicolas Flamel in his treatise 'Summarium philosophicum.' The French alchemist gives a vivid account of the transplantation of the philosophers' tree to the magical dream garden of Hermetic art, a happy empire on which the sun never sets:

'The living fruit—the real living gold and silver—we must seek on the tree; for only there can it grow and increase in size, according to the possibilities of its nature. Without gathering its fruit, we must transplant this tree to a better and richer soil, and to a sunnier spot. Then its fruit will receive more nourishment in a single day than it was wont to receive in a hundred years while it was still in its former sterile soil. I wish you to understand that Mercurius, which is a most excellent tree and contains silver and gold in an indissoluble form, must be taken and transplanted to a soil that is nearer to the sun, that is, in this case gold, where it may flourish exceedingly and be abundantly watered. Where it was planted before it was so shaken and weakened by the wind and the frost that but little fruit could be expected from it. So there it remained a long time and bore no fruit. But in the garden of the philosophers the sun sheds its genial influence both morning and evening, day and night, unceasingly. There our tree is watered with the rarest dew, and the fruit which hangs upon the trees swells and ripens and expands from day to day. It never withers but makes more progress in one year than it did in a thousand years in its former sterile situation.' (5)

A similar description of the wonders of multiplication is found in the 'Aurora consurgens' in which the Hermetic queen of the golden fields says of herself: 'I am that land of the holy promise which floweth with milk and honey and bringeth forth sweetest fruit in due season; wherefore have all the philosophers commended me and sowed in me their gold and silver and incombustible grain. And unless that grain falling into me die, itself shall remain alone, but if it die, it bringeth forth threefold fruit: for the first it shall bring forth shall be good because it was sown in good earth, namely of pearls; the second likewise good because it was sown in better earth, namely of leaves [silver]; the third shall bring forth a thousandfold because it was sown in the best earth, namely of gold.' (6) (Fig.344).

The Final Operation of the Work

In the 'Gloria mundi' instructions are given to the adept as to the 'mode of opening the garden and catching a glimpse of the glorious roses, of the way in which they multiply and bear fruit a thousandfold; also how you may cause the dead body to re-appear, and to be raised again to immortal life, by the power of which it may be able to enter imperfect bodies, purify them, and bring them to perfection and to a state of immutable permanence.' (7) The last operation described in this passage refers to the *proiectio,* the final work of the opus alchymicum.

348. A cremating fire giving birth to the philosophers' son in a shooting field of corn.

The *proiectio* represents the original act which starts the wondrous *multiplicatio* (fig.340): 'Project on any body as much of it as you please, since its tincture shall be multiplied twofold' and from hence on *ad infinitum.* In tracing back the multiplication to its source, the adept gradually forces his way through multiplicity to oneness; ascending the pyramid of the multiplying stone, he finally happens upon the splitting of the One when 'projecting' itself. The proiectio thus becomes the instrument by which the alchemist recovers the primordial stone, the goal of his work. The event is depicted in fig.350, which gives the birth of the stone, or the red king, by means of projection.

349. Saturn watering the multiplying sun and moon flowers in the garden of love.

350. A split-body becoming one body in the mysteries of the final coniunctio.

ber of death 'projects' its inmate as the red king, the universal emperor, or the risen Christ. This figure is the aim of the apprentice alchemist below the tree, who also appears as an agent of wounding and death. The keys of the completed work are held by the newly-married couple, united in death by life eternal.

Tracing the Primordial Germ Cell

Arranged in symmetrical halves, the diagram reproduced in fig.352 shows the crucial stages in oogenesis and spermatogenesis which are analogous processes taking place in homologous organs, i.e., in ovaries and testicles. The evolution of the male and female sex cells is traced from below upward showing: 1) the new individual as produced by 2) the act of fertilization fusing an egg cell and a sperm cell; 3) the second maturation division dividing each sex cell into four replicas of itself (mitosis). While the four sperm cells remain equally big and functional, the four egg cells develop into a big egg cell and three minor polar bodies which eventually disappear. An egg cell is now able to fuse with a sperm cell. 4) The first maturation division 'halving' by meiosis the germ cells through reducing their chromosomal numbers by 50%. The full-chromosomed primary spermatocyte or oocyte is hereby transformed into a sex cell proper.*

5) The primary spermatocytes and oocytes embedded in the germinal epithelium of the testicles and ovaries (fig. 351). Even if these surroundings prove them germ cells, the spermatocytes and oocytes prior to meiosis correspond to normal body cells since they share their full number of chromosomes. Consequently, they multiply in a normal way, i.e., they 'project' themselves into exact replicas of themselves by means of mitotic cell-division (*multiplicatio*, top of diagram).

6) If the individual's sperm and egg cell are traced to their ultimate cell of origin, their multiplication as spermatocytes and oocytes finally contracts and narrows down to the splitting of the primordial germ cell (top of diagram). This crucial process by which the primordial germ cell 'projects' the first exact copy of itself is known in biology as the *primeval mitosis*.

The actual 'birth' of the primordial germ cell is effected in the fetal organism of the individual's mother and father (enclosed, in turn, in the pregnant womb of the individual's grandmothers). The segregation of the primordial germ cells from the body cells is realized by a migration of cells from the wall of the yolk

Recovering the Great Stone by Projection

In the coffin's 'greening' darkness (above), the adept's 'dead body is caused to re-appear and to be raised again to immortal life' by means of a split-process releasing from the corpse its immortal double. Ascending toward heaven, the 'spirit body' is met, at its gate, by a celestial duplicate of itself, or the One. This is the strangest process of the whole work: *in the mysteries of the last coniunctio, the One is recovered by division, a split-body becoming one body in the final act of projection.*

The sexual implications of the event are shown at the bottom of the picture where the alchemist and his sister are united as Sol and Luna by the red tincture or the elixir of life spouting from four pipes in the sarcophagus. The medicine is extracted from the wounded alchemist, bleeding to death in his bridal coffin. A parallel emblem of the rubedic death marriage is the Marriage of the Lamb in New Jerusalem, symbolized by the animal accompanying Luna (see further p.186). The red lion belongs to Sol and represents the rubedo.

The tree of life rising out of the cham-

* The chromosomes in each cell are similar in pairs, or homologous *(indicated by 2 n)*. By contrast, the sex cells only contain half of the number of chromosomes *(indicated by n)*.

sac to the genital ridge of the embryo, identical with the germinal epithelium of the ovaries and testicles. In performing this transition, which represents the individual's primal birth, the cell goes 'from death to eternal life,' i.e., from the 'death' of the normal body cell to the 'eternal life' of the primordial germ cell with its possibilities of continuing the endless and unbroken thread of life.

Since the primordial germ cell is a full-chromosomatic cell, the skein-formed unity of its 46 paternal and maternal chromosomes contains sexual reproduction only as a possibility, not as an urge. *The libido is in a sexually indifferent position.*

The cell's primeval mitosis signifies its first step on the path toward creation (top of diagram). The biological revolution of the 1960s revealed the inner mechanism of this process. In the cell's nucleus the spiral ladders of DNA molecules split in two, thus duplicating the original spiral ladder with its genetic code. The basic genetic secret of (primeval) mitosis proved to be the unique feat of the DNA helix: *it splits in two to duplicate self.*

The Rose Garden of the Ovary

Fig.351 shows a micro-photograph of the primary oocytes embedded in their primary follicles in the ovary's germinal epithelium. The soil of this 'rose garden' is extremely fertile since it contains more than half a million immature eggs (primary oocytes), out of which only some 400 eggs will be ovulated during the active sexual life of the woman. The germinal epithelium of the ovary (and the testes) is also a 'fountain of eternal life' since it forms part of the endless thread of life stretching back to the beginnings of life on this planet (fig.402). In alchemy, the regressive attainment of this libido configuration of the unconscious is symbolized by the 'rosarium philosophorum,' a magical garden of endless germination, teeming with sun and moon flowers and with multiplying roses, egg-stones and angelic children (ludus puerorum motif).

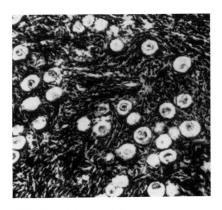

351. The rich soil of the ovary.

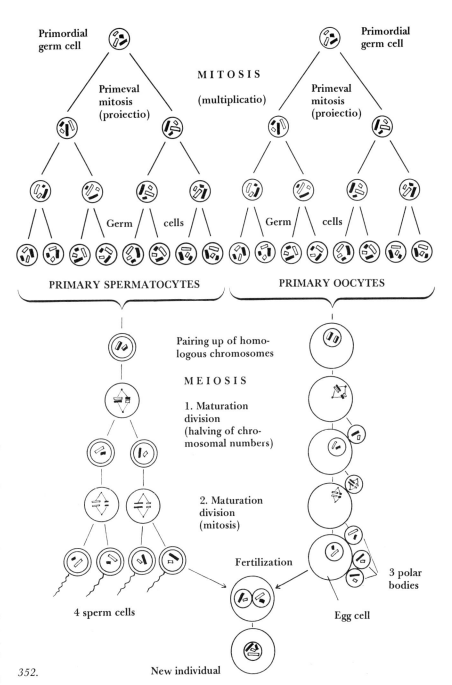

352.

The Coffin of Eternal Life

In tracing the multiplication of his philosophical egg or stone, the alchemist happens upon its ultimate projection, i.e., upon the primal birth of the stone (next pages). In terms of the genetic process, this event symbolizes the regressive revival of the unconscious imprints of primeval mitosis, the 'gateway' of the primordial germ cell. The proiectio reflects this process in that it uncovers the great stone, or ultimate self, by means of division, a split-body becoming one body in the mysteries of the final coniunctio (fig.350 corresponding to top of diagram above).

In terms of the individuation process, the proiectio reflects the *death trauma* which is patterned on the primeval mito-

sis in that it too represents a split-process duplicating self (see pp.182-185). Thus, the proiectio appears as a dual symbol of the reversed course of primeval mitosis and the libido's extinction in the death trauma; *both processes coincide in the final movement of a regressing unconscious terminating the circle of life and individuation.*

This background explains the last transition of the opus which involves the alchemist in a paradoxical and mystical experience of the *ultimate unity of death and primal birth.* As the *opus circulatorium* closes, the end returns to the beginning, the act of death to the act of primal conception. The central Hermetic symbol of this experience is the opened coffin of eternal life (see following pages).

353.

The Trauma of Death: Fourth Coniunctio

Fig.354 shows the twentieth and last woodcut of the 'Rosarium' depicting the resurrection of Christ from his tomb on Easter morning. With the return of the spirit as the Holy Spirit uniting Father and Son, and with the return of the soul as the Queen of Heaven espousing Son and Mother, the hermaphrodite's body is resurrected in its last form as the glorified and incorruptible body of Christ. Waving the banner of victory and making the sign of the Trinity, the haloed Saviour rises with the Easter sun while crying:

*After many sufferings and great martyry
I rise again transfigured, of all blemish
   free. (1)*

The 'transfiguration' refers to the Saviour's 'glorified body' *(corpus glorificatum),* described by the adepts as hard and transparent, clear as crystal and with a fiery, rubeous hue. A product of vitrification, the glassy body of the final rebirth represents the ardently desired body of incorruptibility, capable of surviving death and hence in possession of immortality. The text describes the event in terms of the rubedo, that is, as the fiery birth of the red stone, the red tincture, the red king, the *roi soleil:*

'Hermes: The colour of the soul is [now turned] red. The same: The whiteness wants to be reddened. The same: The albedo is [now] our rubedo. The same: This our stone is fire, created of fire, and turns into fire; its soul dwells in fire. A Hermetic enigma concerning the red tincture: I am crowned and adorned with a diadem and clothed with kingly garments; for I cause joy to enter into bodies. Hermes in his third treatise: Come hither, ye sons of wisdom, let us be glad and rejoice, for the dominion of death is over and the son reigns; he is clothed with the red garment, and the purple is put on. Our son of royal birth takes his tincture from the fire, and death, darkness and the waters flee. The dragon, who watches the crevices, shuns the sunbeams, and our dead son shall live. The king comes forth from the fire and rejoices in the marriage. The hidden treasures will be laid open, and our son, already vivified, is become a warrior of the fire and surpasses the tincture.

'The Metaphors of Bellini, the philosopher, concerning the sun: Know that my father, the sun, has given me power over all the powers and clothed me with the garment of glory. The whole world covets me and runs after me, for I am the Highest; now they have acknowledged my virtue and loftiness. For I am the One and I am compared to my Father who is One, and who gives me power by His grace.' (2)

Enigma of Bologna: Rebirth in a Coffin

Fig.355 shows the engraved variant in which the risen Christ is identified with the hermaphrodite-king presenting his regalia in a coffin turned into the primordial *cella* of rebirth. The famous 'Enigma of Bologna' which, according to an alchemical author, 'was set up by an artificer of old to the honour of God and in praise of the chymic art' (3) describes the final *coniunctio oppositorum* in words matching its ineffable mystery:

'*Aelia Laelia Crispis,* neither man nor woman, nor mongrel, nor maid, nor boy, nor crone, nor chaste, nor whore, nor virtuous, but all. Carried away neither by hunger, nor by sword, nor by poison, but by all. Neither in heaven, nor in earth, nor in water, but everywhere is her resting place.

354. *Resurrection in a glorified body.*

'Lucius Agatho Priscius, neither husband, nor lover, nor kinsman, neither mourning, nor rejoicing, nor weeping, neither mound, nor pyramid, nor tomb, but all. He knows and knows not what he raised up to whom. This is a tomb that has no body in it. This is a body that has no tomb round it. But body and tomb are the same.' (4)

Fig.353 shows Barchusen's variation upon the twentieth woodcut of the 'Rosarium.' The cremating fire blazing in plate 74 and hatching the philosophers' son in plate 75 proves its maturing effects in plate 76, where the child turns into the macrocosmic hermaphrodite. As the fire of conjunction envelops the vessel for the fourth and last time, the philosophers' egg-stone is similarly transmuted into the sun. In the 'Crowne of Nature' the philosophers' child in plate 75 is identified with the 'Thrones' and the hermaphrodite in plate 76 with the 'Cherub' —the angel who, facing God, holds in his hands the crown of the Highest. (5) This figure also represents Mercurius philosophorum, appearing as a fiery spirit surrounded by an aura of pure energy. The event is celebrated in plate 77 by an angel chanting: 'Glory, praise and honour to God on high' (Gloria, laus et honor Dei in excelsis).

Barchusen's very last plate depicts the death trauma: armed with his hour-glass and arrow, Death pierces the alchemist stretched on the ground beside his coffin. Two angels symbolizing his departing soul and spirit ascend with the alchemist's shrine, filled with the treasure of treasures. It is returned to the 'castle [built] to the honour of God' (arx ad honorem Dei). This is seen as a luminous cloud inscribed with the Name of the Highest. Assimilated to the Divine Master in life, the alchemist's purified body, soul and spirit unite at death with the source of light, like to like.

Reviving the Dead Body and Self

Fig.356 shows the operation by which the alchemist raises his dead body to immortal life, i.e., the proiectio. As the adept unlocks the door of the last chamber of the castle, he turns the lid of a coffin containing himself. The eerie moment is reflected in the facial expression of the alchemist who, assuming a double part, perceives the figure of himself in the coffin's darkness. Significantly, his own projected and crowned self gazes back at him with his own air of mystery and surprise. The death trauma is repeated in the background, which shows Typhon (=Set) cutting up Osiris, and Isis gathering his members. The Osirian body of immortality conquered by the projecting alchemist represents a variant of Christ's 'glorified body.' The picture relates to the 'reddened' king's sermon in the 'Rosarium':

355. The risen king opening his cella, or 'narrow chamber,' of death and primal birth.

'I am excellent, I who exalt and depress all, and none of my servants are above me, except one whom it is given to be opposed to me. And he destroys me, yet he does not destroy my nature. And he is Saturn [=Typhon=Death] who separated me from all my limbs. But afterwards I go to my mother [=Isis] who gathers together all my divided and scattered limbs. I am the light of all things that are mine, causing the light to appear openly from within my father Saturn.' (6)

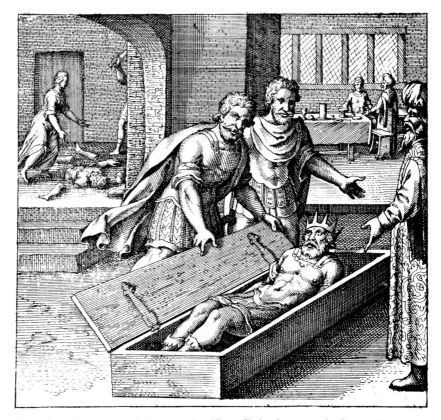

356. The eerie mystery of the opened coffin: splitting in two to duplicate self.

357. The Hermetic quest for Mercurius philosophorum revealed as a quest for the self.

Raising the Ghostly Body of the Self

Fig.357 shows the proiectio and its conquest of dual identity (ego and self). In the deserted streets of a dreamlike city the walking alchemist suddenly confronts his projected image or *doppelganger*. The numinous expression in the alchemist reflects the incarnative implications of the event: the holy ghost perceived is Mercurius philosophorum into whose figure the alchemist has changed himself. 'This spirit becomes corporeal again, after having become spirit from a body,' (1) as the Hermetic philosophers put it.

The hallowed ghost is seated beside a blazing fire attended by a third figure who enacts the engraving's motto: 'Give fire to fire, and Mercurius to Mercurius, and it will suffice thee.' (2) The meaning of this strange advice is evidently that the alchemist when performing the proiectio should join a thing to that which is like the thing itself. In the case of the adept, himself to himself, like to like.*

Fig.358 renders another case of projection: at the end of his labours, the adept leaves his laboratory to take a walk in the garden. As he enters, he suddenly encounters his own grave opened by a

* The picture may be viewed as rendering the primordial image of schizophrenia (meaning 'frenzy of schism'). A rapid and malign individuation process, schizophrenia leads to the final 'integration' of the ego by the self. In its normal form, as represented by the opus alchymicum, the individuation process leads to the final integration of the self by the ego.

dead man appearing to be himself. Rising to meet the alchemist at the intersecting point of life and death, the ghostly body points toward the background landscape illuminated from within by mystical imagery. A ladder reaching from heaven to earth vertically spans a memorial cross. The Latin inscription on the tomb-stone renders the words spoken by the alchemist's projected image: *Et moriendo docebo* – 'I will teach thee how to die.'

Fig.359 shows the alchemical hermaphrodite in the Roman guise of a double-sexed Janus projecting himself at the end of the work. The *doppelganger* carries the staff of universal dominion and the key of the concluded opus. The latter is further indicated by the tail-eater in the foreground performing its last revolution by joining the end to the beginning. The scenery is illuminated by the blinding rays of the projected sun.

The Out-of-the-Body Experience

The alchemical proiectio covers the occult phenomenon which is known as the *out-of-the-body experience*. The term derives from the Second Epistle of St. Paul to the Corinthians in which the apostle describes a mystical experience of a particular nature: 'I will come to visions and revelations of the Lord. I know a man in Christ, fourteen years ago (whether in the body, I know not; or whether out of the body, I know not; God knoweth), such a one caught up even to the third heaven. And I know

such a man (whether in the body, or out of the body, I know not, God knoweth), how that he was caught up into Paradise, and heard unspeakable words, which it is not lawful for a man to utter' (2 Corinthians: 1-4).

Other terms descriptive of the phenomenon as it varies in specific instances are travelling clairvoyance, E.S.P. projection, self-projection, bilocation and extrasensory travel. Occult writers almost always use the terms astral or etheric projection or astral travel. Jung only once described the out-of-the-body experience clinically: in 'Synchronicity: an acausal connecting principle' (1952).

As a technical term, the out-of-the-body experience appears for the first time in Oliver Fox, who described the phenomenon in his book 'Astral Projection: A Record of Out-of-the-Body Experiences' (1920). In 1929 the same occult phenomenon was treated by Sylvan Muldoon in his book 'The Projection of the Astral Body.' The experience is of seeing one's physical body from a viewpoint outside that body, such as standing beside the bed and looking at oneself lying in bed, or floating in the air near one's body. The out-of-the-body experience involves mystical sensations of being able to travel in one's 'astral body' in an ultra-physical realm outside the laws of man's normal space-time-continuum. By way of illustration, the subject may feel his 'astral body' floating through walls or other solid objects or flying around the earth in movements transcending the laws of gravitation and the speed of light.

There is an obvious connection between out-of-the-body experiences and mystical ones. Many of the subjects analyzed by Celia Green in her book 'Out-of-

358. Ghostly meeting in the rose garden.

the-Body Experiences' (1968) make assertions which are similar to those made by mystics. They emphasize the joyful character of their out-of-the-body experience and its sense of 'liberation' and 'completeness.' Moreover, some of them claim to have had a feeling of 'all-knowing and understanding' and a conviction that any question they cared to ask would be answered. Mystics often make similar statements. Celia Green quotes the following, typical examples:

'Reality was my 'floating self' and the objects below seemed as shadows against my floating self.' (3) 'The 'life' was in the body which was floating about 15 ft. above the scene; both were dressed alike and were identical in appearance, but the body on the ground had no life-force, and was simply a Petrushka-like doll with a life-like appearance.' (4) 'Just a disembodied consciousness with a feeling of 'all-knowing and understanding.'' (5) 'I felt mentally free, as if I could go anywhere . . . Now I can go everywhere I wish.' (6) 'Not see or hear anything. But a feeling that by a mere split second thought I could travel millions of *miles.*' (7) 'I experienced much delight at the weightlessness and freedom of the 'spiritual body' in which I found my consciousness located.' (8) 'Everything seemed easy and possible.' (9) 'Then I suddenly felt filled with the utmost joy and happiness. I felt such great freedom, like a bird just being let out of cage for first time in life.' (10)

Multiplication and Projection under LSD

There is a remarkable similarity between out-of-the-body experiences and LSD-experiences of the 'final high,' the latter exemplifying the Hermetic *multiplicatio* and *proiectio* in an unsurpassed manner. Masters and Houston report:

'Some psychedelic subjects 'see' their own body by spontaneously or intentionally employing means other than direct observation and looking into reflecting surfaces. Some are able to project an image of their own body on a wall or into a crystal; or they may close their eyes and envision their own body image. The image projected on a wall is usually perceived as 'flat,' as in a painting; the image in the crystal is seen as dimensional, having depth; the image seen with the eyes closed may be perceived as either flat or dimensional, the subject often expressing uncertainty as to which. A few subjects spontaneously see, or claim to be able to project, an image in space—for example, an image that stands next to them or confronts them and may or may not possess some degree of solidity. One subject claimed to be able to 'multiply' himself several times, simultaneously perceiving several images, replicas or doubles of himself that could occupy any position within his field of vision.

359. 'Nature conquers nature' assert the alchemists. (12) During the last and most traumatic transition in life, nature applies the medicine to alleviate the primal anxiety of death. Connecting the end with the beginning, nature structures the death trauma on the pattern of the primeval mitosis, the individual's 'immaculate conception,' the split-birth of his first cella. Cleft in a mortal body and an immortal 'astral body,' the dying person is thus led by the unconscious to experience his last journey as his first, burial as a heavenly marriage, death as the beginning of reproduction. All ideas of death and rebirth originate in this final point of the unconscious, where the rising and setting sun are identified with each other in a common, blinding reflection.*

'There is also a fairly common experience where the subject seems to himself to project his consciousness away from his body and then is able to see his body as if he were standing off to one side of it or looking down on it from above. A few subjects feel that they are able to leave the 'material body' and move about in something like the 'astral body' familiar to occultists. This astral body is described as being diaphanous and almost, but not quite, immaterial. It may be composed of 'energy,' 'electrical impulses,' and so on. Some identify this astral body with an 'aura' they earlier had perceived as radiating from them, an 'energy force field' surrounding the body. The perception of the aura by psychedelic subjects is very common . . . The experience of observing the body as if from a distance is [also] common in the drug-state . . . The experience may involve a whole series of self-images, the subject looking at his body looking at his body, and so on. It is the familiar picture within a picture within a picture effect, sometimes achieved by employing a series of mirrors.' (11)

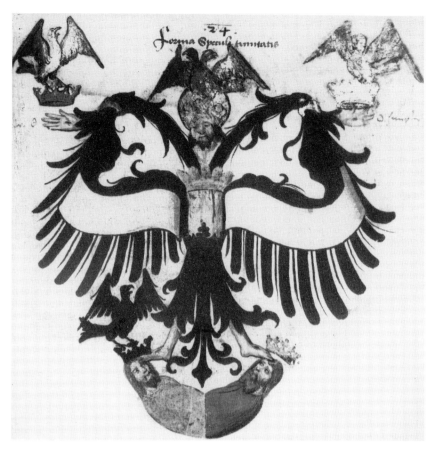

360. A bleeding Christ splitting in the sign of the double eagle on the cross of death.

The 'Red' Death Marriage of Christ

In the 'Book of the Holy Trinity' the lapis is presented as follows: 'When a man holds the red stone in his hand he becomes invisible. When, in order to warm him, one binds the stone with a kerchief to his body, he rises into the air and travels wherever he wishes. If he wants to go down to earth again, he removes the stone from his body and lands softly.' (1)

In the same treatise the red stone is depicted in its Christian garb, as shown in figs.360 and 363. Examples of the famous lapis-Christus parallel, the paintings present the opus as an imitation of the divine work of redemption. The red king reborn in his coffin is identified with the crucified Saviour bleeding to death while uniting in heaven with Mary and the Holy Trinity. A split-body becoming one body, the Saviour in fig.360 emerges as a product of projection: his feet rest on two split-images of himself representing the Father and the Holy Ghost. These figures and their dual unity in the One reappear in the two-headed eagle forming the Saviour's garments.

A classical emblem of the proiectio, the two-headed eagle carries the imperial crown, or the sign of universal dominion. In fig.362 the imperial bird cries out: 'I grant the empire without end.' Fig.361 shows the two-headed eagle identified with 'our Mercurius' and the 'tree of the

philosophers,' both forming part of the final conjunction of the planets. The tail-eater makes up the 'crown' of the philosophical tree, the animal performing its last revolution in which the 'raven's head: the beginning of the art' coincides with the 'lamb's head [which] is the end.'

The latter refers to the Marriage of the Lamb, another popular motif of the last *coniunctio solis et lunae.* The event is depicted in fig.363, also from the 'Book of the Holy Trinity.' In a bold manner the painting fuses the highest Christian figures with the royal figures of the rubedo, Christ, the Lamb, or Sol uniting with Mary, the Woman of the Revelation, or Luna. The biblical passages fused by this theological alchemy read as follows:

'Now there stood by the cross of Jesus his mother, and . . . When Jesus had received the vinegar, he said, It is finished: *and he bowed his head, and gave up the ghost* (John 19:25-30) . . . And there appeared a great wonder in heaven: *a woman clothed with the sun, and the moon under her feet, and upon her head a crown of twelve stars:* And she being with child cried, travailing in birth, and pained to be delivered . . . *And she brought forth a man child, who was to rule all nations with a rod of iron: and her child was caught up unto God, and to his throne* . . . Alleluia: for the Lord God omnipotent reigneth. Let us be glad and rejoice, and give honour to him: *for*

the marriage of the Lamb is come, and his wife hath made herself ready' (Revelation 12:1-5 and 19:6-7).

The Lapis-Christus Parallel

The oldest lapis-Christus parallel occurs in the treatise 'Margarita pretiosa,' written by the alchemist Petrus Bonus of Ferrara around 1330. It reads:

'This art is partly natural and partly divine or supernatural. At the end of the sublimation there germinates, through the mediation of the spirit, a shining white soul which flies up to heaven with the spirit. This is clearly and manifestly the stone. So far the procedure is indeed somewhat marvellous, yet still within the framework of nature. But as regards the fixation and permanence of the soul and spirit at the end of the sublimation, this takes place when the secret stone is added, which cannot be grasped by the senses, but only by the intellect, through inspiration or divine revelation, or else through the teaching of an initiate. Alexander says that there are two categories: seeing through the eye and understanding through the heart. This secret stone is a gift of God. There could be no alchemy without this stone. It is the heart and tincture of the gold, regarding which Hermes says: 'It is needful that at the end of the world heaven and earth be united: which is the philosophic word.' Pythagoras also said in the 'Turba': 'God concealed this from Apollon, so that the world should not be destroyed.'

'Thus alchemy stands above nature and is divine. The whole difficulty of the art lies in the stone. The intellect cannot comprehend it, so must believe it, like the divine miracles and the foundation of the Christian creed. Therefore God alone is the operator, while nature remains passive. It was through the knowledge of their art that the old philosophers knew

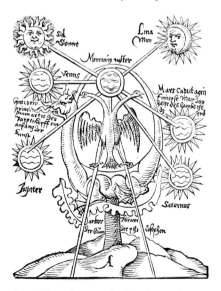

361. The tail-eater closing the work.

362. The bird of universal dominion.

Hence God unlock'd the Gates of
  Paradise,
Rais'd him like Luna to th'Imperiall
  Place,
Sublim'd him to the Heavens, and that
  being done,
Crown'd him in Glory, aequall with
  the Sun.

Four Elements, Brave Armes, and
  Polish'd well
God gave him, in the midst whereof
  did dwell
The Crowned Maid, ordained for to be
In the Fifth Circle of the Mysterie.

With all delicious Unguent flowed she
When Purg'd from Bloody Menstruosity:
On every side her Count'nance
  Brightly shone,
She being Adorn'd with every
  Precious Stone.

A Lyon Greene did in her Lapp reside
(The which an Eagle fed), and from
  his side
The Blood gush'd out: The Virgin
  drunck it upp,
While Mercuries Hand did th'Office
  of a Cupp.

364. The fountain of eternal life.

The wondrous Milk she hasten'd from
  her Breast,
Bestow'd it frankly on the Hungry Beast,
And with a Sponge his Furry Face
  she dry'd
Which her own Milk had often Madefy'd.

Upon her Head a Diadem she did weare,
With fiery Feet sh'Advanced into
  the Aire;
And glittering Bravely in her Golden
  Robes
She took her Place amidst the Starry
  Globes.

The Dark Clouds being Dispers'd, so sate
  she there,
And woven to a Network in her Haire
Were Planets, Times, and Signes, the
  while the King
With his Glad Eyes was her Beleagering.

Thus He of all Triumphant Kings is
  Chiefe,
Of Bodies sicke the only Grand Reliefe:
Such a Reformist of Defects, that hee
Is worshipp'd both by King and
  Commonalty.

To Princes, Priests he yields an Ornament,
The Sicke and Needy Sort he doth
  content:
What man is there this Potion will
  not bless,
As banishes all thought of Neediness?

Wherefore, O God, graunt us a Peece
  of This,
That through the Encrease of its own
  Species
The Art may be Renew'd, and Mortal
  Men
Enjoy for aye its Thrice-Sweet Fruits.
  AMEN. (3)

of the coming of the end of the world and of the resurrection of the dead. Then the soul will be united with its original body for ever and ever. The body will become wholly transfigured, incorruptible, and almost unbelievably subtilized, and it will penetrate all solids. Its nature will be as much spiritual as corporeal. When the stone decomposes to a powder like a man in his grave, God restores to it soul and spirit, and takes away all imperfection; then is that substance strengthened and improved, as after the resurrection man becomes stronger and younger than he was before.

'The old philosophers discerned the Last Judgement in this art, namely in the germination and birth of this stone, for in it the soul to be beatified unites with its original body, to eternal glory. So also the ancients knew that a virgin must conceive and bring forth, for in their art the stone begets, conceives, and brings itself forth. Such a thing can happen only by the grace of God. Therefore Alphidius says of the stone that its mother was a virgin and that its father had never known woman. They knew besides that God would become man on the Last Day of this art, when the work is accomplished; and that begetter and begotten, the old man and the boy, father and son, all become one. Now, since no creature except man can unite with God, on account of their dissimilarity, God must needs become one with man. And this came to pass in Christ Jesus and His virgin mother.' (2)

Grand Finale of Ripley's Cantilena

The finishing stanzas of Ripley's 'Cantilena' effect a similar fusion of Christian and Hermetic figures as that carried out by the 'Book of the Holy Trinity.' The king's apotheosis is presented within the framework of the Virgin's Coronation and Heavenly Marriage:

363. The red death marriage in heaven.

365. The 'red' mystery: the alchemist's incarnation in the Easter sun of resurrection.

take one part of the best and finest gold, poured by means of antimony, and purge three parts thereof. Beat it into plates of the greatest possible thinness, put the whole into a smelting pot, and subject it to the action of a gentle fire for twelve hours. Then let it be melted for three days and three nights more. In this manner the purged gold and stone have been transformed into the purest medicine of subtle spiritual and penetrating qualities.

'For without the ferment of gold no one can compose the stone or develop the tingeing virtue. For the same is very subtle and penetrating if it be fermented and joined with a ferment like unto itself: then the prepared tincture has the power of entering into other bodies and operating therein. Take then one part of the prepared ferment for the tingeing of a thousand parts of molten metal, and then you will learn in all faith and truth that it shall be changed into the only good and fixed gold. For one body takes possession of the other; even if it be unlike to it, nevertheless, through the strength and potency added to it, it is compelled to be assimilated to the same, since like derives origin from like.

'Whoever uses this as a medium shall find whither the vestibules of the palace lead, and there is nothing comparable to the subtlety thereof. He shall possess all in all, performing all things whatsoever which are possible under the sun. O principle of the prime principle, consider the end! O end of the final end, consider the beginning! And be this medium commended unto your faithful care, wherein also God the Father, Son, and Holy Ghost shall give unto you whatsoever you need both in soul and body.' (1)

Final Glory of the 'Splendor Solis'

Fig.365 shows the last painting of the 'Splendor solis' in which the stone is developed as the sun. (The preceding painting, reproduced on p.243, fig.21, depicts nine washerwomen cooking and drying clothes; according to text, they symbolize the final sublimation of the earthly elements into the 'spirit of the quintessence, called the tincture, fermentum, anima, or oil, which is the very next matter to the philosophers' stone.') (2) The 'completion of the stone' is explained by the text of fig.365 as the result of the synthetic procedures of the final operation: 'The reason why all natural things are put together in one body is that there may be a united composition.' (3)

The pictorial motif relates to the twentieth woodcut of the 'Rosarium' in which the resurrected king says: 'I illuminate the air with my light and warm the earth with my heat. I bring forth and nourish the things of nature, plants and stones; with my power I take away the darkness of night, and cause day to endure in the world.' (4)

The Twelfth Key of Basil Valentine

Fig.367 renders the Twelfth Key of Basil Valentine in which the last chamber of the castle is unlocked. Illuminated by the sun and moon, the alchemist watches the roaring furnace ablaze with the fire of the fourth degree. Below the open window the golden flowers sprout from the pot of the lapis, unfolding their petals in the sign of Mercurius philosophorum. At his side the red lion devours the wriggling snake, thus confirming the victory of the fixed principle over the volatile, or the final termination of the law *coagula et dissolve.* Any further attempts

of the snake to dissolve the coagulated stone will be in vain: after four acts of rebirth preceded by four traumas of rebirth, the opus alchymicum and its series of transformations have at length come to an end. The text describes the proiectio and the wonders of the final work:

'The Twelfth and last Key concludes my book. In dealing with this part of the subject I will drop my parabolic and figurative style and plainly set forth all that is to be known. Therefore listen to my following message. When the medicine and stone of the sages has been perfectly prepared out of the true virgin's milk,

A Hermetic-Biblical Symbol of the Stone

'I lead the ships over the sea and build great cities,' (5) sings the solified, omnipotent adept on the last pages of the 'Rosarium.' Fig.366 shows a famous dream city visited by the alchemist in his *corpus coeleste*: the Heavenly City or New Jerusalem described in the Revelation of St.John. The popularity of the motif in alchemy is explained by the biblical vision's incorporation of all the symbols of the rubedo: the sparkling stone, or holy city; the heavenly marriage (of the Lamb); the mysteries of paternal Incarnation; the conquest of death; the water of life and its fountain (fig.364); the tree of life and its fruits; the God of the end and the beginning:

'Come hither, I will shew thee the bride, the Lamb's wife. And he carried me away in the spirit to a great and high mountain, and shewed me that great city, the holy Jerusalem, descending out of heaven from God, having the glory of God [fig.366]: and her light was like unto a stone most precious, even like a jasper stone, clear as crystal; and had a wall great and high, and had twelve gates, and at the gates twelve angels; and . . . the city had no need of the sun, neither of the moon, to shine in it: for the glory of God did lighten it, and the Lamb is the light thereof . . . And he shewed me a pure river of water of life, clear as crystal, proceeding out of the throne of God and of the Lamb. In the midst of the street of it, and on either side of the river, was there the tree of life, which bare twelve manner of fruits, and yielded her fruit every month; and . . . there shall be no more death, neither sorrow, nor crying, neither shall there be any more pain: for the former things are passed away. And he that sat upon the throne said, Behold, I make all things new. And he said unto me, Write: for these words are true and faithful. And he said unto me, It is done. I am Alpha and Omega, the beginning and the end. I will give unto him that is athirst of the fountain of the water of life freely. He that overcometh shall inherit all things; and I will be his God, and he shall be my son' (Rev.21:4-23 and 22:1-2).

Divine Powers of the Spirit Body

The Twelfth Key's statement that the artifex 'shall perform all things whatsoever which are possible under the sun' may be illuminated by a number of features relating to the out-of-the-body state. As demonstrated by Celia Green, the state is characterized by 1) 'solar vision': the subject is able to see through solid obstacles which appear 'transparent' to him. 2) Magical powers of movement: the subject's duplicate body is able to walk through doors and walls. 3) Extra-

366. The Heavenly City, or Great Stone, recreated in its biblical splendour.

sensory perception such as telepathic communication: the subject is able to convey a message, apparently by paranormal means, to another person. Information obtained or transmitted is instrumental in bringing about effective action, for instance in cases of accident or illness. 4) Precognition: the subject may see events which are subsequently reproduced in real life; or he may enact future events in the dream body. 5) Travelling clairvoyance: the subject appears to travel through space to distant places and to obtain information about state of affairs at those places which he could not have

acquired by normal means. 6) Astral travel or complete adaptation to a space-time continuum relativized in a magical way. Subjects describe their ability to leave the Earth, visit other planets, travel into space, into the galaxy, into the cosmos. 7) Mediumistic phenomena, such as automatic writing, spirit possession, or communication with the dead (see pp.202-205). 8) Encountering 'entities'; these appear to be supra-human spiritual beings who may either be demons or protectors and guides (figs.339, 366, 378, 384). (6) Significantly, they seem to be closely related to the experience of dying. (7)

367. Gilded by the fire of the last conjunction in the last room of the Hermetic castle.

368. Astrological symbols of projection: the Fishes of the end and the beginning.

Pisces the Fishes: Fusion with the Ocean

The two fishes above belong to the astrological sign of Pisces, the Fishes, which is the twelfth and last sign of the zodiacal cycle. In alchemy, Pisces is associated with the *proiectio*: reflections of each other, one fish stands for death, or the end, the other for primal birth, or the beginning. The verse accompanying the engraving, from the 'Book of Lambspring,' explains:

All the sages tell you
That two fishes are in our sea
Without any flesh or bones.
Cook them in their own water,
And they will become a vast sea
Which no man will be able to describe.
This is what the sages say:
The two fishes are only one, not two;
They are two, and nevertheless they
* are one,*
And all three things are in it,
Body, soul and spirit.
Now, I tell you most truly,
Cook these three together
That there may be a vast sea. (1)

A mutable, watery sign ruled by Jupiter, Pisces extends from February 20 to March 20, or the wintry period in which the old cycle comes to an end at the same time as the new cycle is prepared, the seeds of spring mysteriously growing out of the ashes of winter. Pisces is composed of two identical fishes arranged parallel to one another but facing in opposite directions. The lower, inverted fish symbolizes involution, or the termination of the world cycle (death). The upper fish symbolizes evolution, or the beginning of a new world cycle (birth). The *identity* of these universal principles in Pisces incorporates the mystery of the beginning as the end, and vice versa. The sign brings together the opposites in their strangest and most sublime form, namely as opposite forces *identified with each other in a point of 'oppositelessness' (nirvana)*.

Even more strongly than the Water Carrier, the Fishes signifies aquatic forces of dissolution, solution and release. Pisces represents the great liberation achieved by the return of creation to the universal solvent. Plumbing the depths of the celestial ocean, Pisces brings about the complete dissolution of the old cycle and the total destruction of its created forms. The energy stored up in these forms is thereby released as pure cosmic force, like water released from a melting iceberg.

Piscean psychology is governed by the 'oceanic feeling' and by a pantheistic view of nature. Sensitive, intuitive and 'psychic,' the Piscean is unconsciously absorbed in a transcendental world, the unfathomable depths of which are reflected in his 'Indian' look. There is a certain melancholy and a sense of tragedy ingrained in the Piscean psyche, which reflects the sign's blend of love and death, Eros and Thanatos, spring and winter. The yogi in nirvana embodies the 'oceanic feeling' of the Fishes and the total *coniunctio* of its design: a drop of water merging with the sea.

The Final Delivery and Rebirth

Fig.371 shows the alchemist-as-astrologer seated at his celestial globe and pointing to the Fishes. In this sign the old philosopher beholds the splendour of the last *coniunctio solis et lunae* bursting to illuminate the heavens at the end of his opus.

Fig.370 presents the mystical sister of Hermetic science, engaged in boiling water to dissolve the astrological fishes swimming in her tub. The picture relates to Lambspring's motif and to a famous dictum: 'The stone . . . is called a pregnant woman because the whiteness has in it the redness which is extracted by the final cooking process.' (2) At the delivery of this woman the alchemists break out in panegyrics such as this one:

'Now is the stone shaped, the elixir of life prepared, the love-child or the child of love born, the new birth completed, and the work made whole and perfect: O wonder of wonders! You have the tincturing tincture, the pearl of the virgin, which has three essences or qualities in one; it has body, soul and spirit, it has fire, light and joy, it has the Father's quality, it has the Son's quality, and has also the Holy Ghost's quality, even all these three, in one fixed and eternal essence and being. This is the Son of the Virgin, this is her first-born, this is the noble hero, the trampler of the serpent, and he who casts the dragon [of death] under his feet and tramples upon him . . . For now the man of paradise is become clear as transparent glass, in which the divine sun shines through and through, like gold that is wholly bright, pure and clear, without blemish or spot. The soul

369. The royal eagles of projection.

is henceforth a most substantial seraphic angel, she can make herself doctor, theologian, astrologer, divine magician, she can make herself whatsoever she will, and do and have whatsoever she will: for all qualities have but one will in agreement and harmony. And this same one will is God's eternal infallible will; and from henceforth the divine man is in his own nature become one with God.' (3)

The Supreme Sublimation of Incest

The grand Hermetic symbol of the final, incestuous coniunctio is the Virgin's Coronation by the Holy Trinity, her Heavenly Marriage and Immaculate Conception. The union of the Three and the One forms part of the alchemist's squaring of the circle (fig.382), the four figures fusing under the *crown* of the Heavenly Marriage *(quadratura circuli)*. In the last Hermetic operation a remarkable Christian Quaternity is thus produced on the basis of the traditional Trinity. (The modernism of this operation is borne out by the fact that the Assumption of Mary was not promulgated as a dogma until 1950 A.D.) With the Immaculate Conception, the incestuous coniunctio is relieved of its last remnants of earth and spiritualized to the extent that the alchemists can say of their stone 'that its mother is a virgin and that its father has never known woman.'* Says the philosopher Penotus of the same operation:

'As to how the son of man is generated by the philosopher and the fruit of the virgin is produced, it is necessary that he be exalted from the earth and cleansed of all earthliness; then he rises as a whole into the air and is changed into spirit. Thus the word of the philosopher is fulfilled: He ascends from earth to heaven and puts on the power of Above and Below, and lays aside his earthly and uncleanly nature.' (4)

The Royal Eagles of Birth and Death

Fig.369 shows the king's eagles descending on his hands after having completed their orbital flight in opposite directions. The event proves to the king that Delfi, his island, is the navel of the earth. According to the motto, the 'two eagles come together: one from the place of the rising sun, the other from the

---

* In the light of the opus alchymicum we may assume that the regressive psychodynamics of the Oedipus complex are the 'fuel' of the individuation process; further, that this process is concerned with a growing sublimation of the Oedipus complex, which through a series of conjunctions is gradually 'purged,' 'abluted' and 'sublimated' into its final form in which the Son incarnated in the Father by means of the Holy Spirit (of projective identification) is married to the Virgin Mother and reborn in her womb.

370. The Piscean mystery of rebirth: dissolution in the vast sea of the virgin's womb.

place of the setting sun.' (5) The opposites brought together by the royal birds are those of east and west, rising and setting, birth and death. This relationship makes them a variant of the Fishes and of the towering symbol of Hermetic projection: the two-headed eagle with the imperial crown (figs.360-363).

371. Final conjunction of the sun and moon in the final sign of the zodiacal cycle.

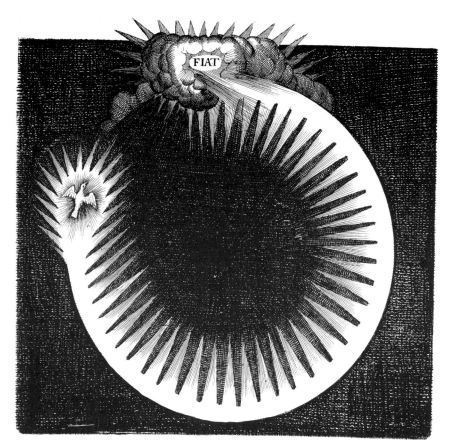

372. *The dove of the Holy Ghost brings the circular work to a close by bending the end toward the 'fiat,' or beginning of Creation. The tail-eater is another variant.*

Reviving the Death Trauma

The 'final end' of the Twelfth Key, the Fish terminating the world-cycle, the eagle of the 'setting sun,' Saturn, Typhon and the dragon, the tomb of the 'Enigma of Bologna,' the red king's coffin and the crucified Saviour dyeing the stone with his blood are all symbolic expressions of the *death trauma*. By this term we mean the archetypal event of the final transition and the primal anxiety attending the suffering of death. Normally this is a deeply unconscious, one-way experience; no one has returned from the dead and given an account of his experience. Yet reports of individuals who have nearly died are available from which something can be learned about life's final moments and the unconscious patterns of dying.

In a recent article in 'Psychiatry' termed 'The Experience of Dying' (1972) Dr. Russell Noyes Jr. has investigated the phenomenon on the basis of a long-neglected 1892 report by the Swiss Geologist Albert Heim. Probably the best collection of sudden-death experiences available, the report details interviews that Heim had with some 30 survivors of Alpine falls after he himself nearly died in a similar accident. Dr. Noyes also analyzes other accounts of 19th and 20th century near-fatal accidents.

Noyes finds that the experience of al-most dying, and presumably of dying itself, often includes three phases, which he calls resistance, life review and transcendence. In the first phase, a person faced with the apparent certainty of sudden death struggles frantically against both the external danger (for instance, a current that threatens to sweep him away as he swims) and a strange longing to surrender to the danger and let himself die.

Meanwhile there is a 'life review' remarkable not only for its vividness but also for the unique perspective upon life that it brings. Heim compares it to 'images from a film sprung loose in a projector or to the rapid sequence of dream images.' (1) As the life review continues, the individual may, from an increasingly distant perspective, view his life in its entirety and in every detail simultaneously. Here he may be impressed with his good and bad characteristics. But as he enters the final phase he relinquishes this view and experiences himself in a new manner. In so doing, he enters a region or dimension which Noyes calls 'a mystical state of consciousness':

'Immediately, as fear is replaced by calm and as active mastery is replaced by surrender, a curious splitting of the self from its bodily representation may occur. Commonly referred to as 'out-of-the-body' phenomena by students of parapsychology, examples of this splitting represent an interesting negation of death. The subject may correctly view his body as near death, but, being outside of it, he witnesses the scene with detached interest.' (2)

Splitting in the Jaws of Death

An example in case is the out-of-the-body experience of a very fit mountaineer struggling to climb back to safety after having shot over the edge of a precipice: 'I found myself hanging on the rope a few feet below the crest of the ridge. I turned, snatched at the rocks and clawed my way back. I had fallen altogether about 20 feet and the rope . . . had held . . . During the time I was doing this a curious rigidity or tension gripped my whole being, mental and physical . . . It was an overwhelming sensation and quite outside my experience. It was as though all life's forces were in a process of undergoing some fundamental evolutionary change, the change called death . . . I know now that death is not to be feared, it is a supreme experience, the climax, not the anti-climax of life.

'For how long I experienced this crescendo of power I cannot say. Time no longer existed as time . . . Then suddenly this feeling was superseded by a feeling of complete indifference and detachment, detachment as to what was happening or likely to happen to that body. I was not falling for the reason that I was not in a dimension where it was possible to fall. I, that is, my consciousness, was apart from my body and not in the least concerned with what was befalling it . . . It is not within my province to discuss that which only death can prove; yet to me this experience was a convincing one; it convinced me that consciousness survives beyond the grave.' (3)

According to Noyes, that kind of experience is not unlike the mystical states

373. *The coffin's fire, 'slow but eternal.'*

of consciousness sometimes brought on by LSD. He suggests, therefore, that one way for scientists to learn more about what it is like to die is to study what happens to people when they take drugs.

LSD and the Death Experience

Is the experience of dying reproduced in the LSD-experience and does this conform to a split-process inducing an out-of-the-body experience of transcendental qualities? Masters and Houston confirm the projection of the 'astral body' in the LSD-state and the supernatural qualities of that projected body (p.185). The equation of this split-process with death-traumatic anxiety is found in Richard Alpert's study on 'LSD' (1966). He compares the LSD-experience to a space trip, in which the critical period is that of leaving the earth. Similarly, the critical phase of the LSD-trip is that of leaving the body:

'The difficulties in 'getting out' are often the result of poor preparation, or lack of either trust in one's guide or feelings of safety with one's surroundings. The difficulty usually occurs during the first hour or two of a session and usually has attendant symptoms of anxiety, nausea, extreme fear or panic . . . *It is the period of psychological death.'* (4)

In his book on 'LSD Psychotherapy' (1968) W.V.Caldwell confirms this statement in a passage comparing psychedelic therapy to psychoanalysis: 'Although most of the material can be covered by a long course of psychoanalysis, there are areas which even psychoanalysis cannot reveal. For instance, death experiences are common in psychedelic therapy; they are rare in psychoanalysis. When a psychedelic patient experiences death, it is a total and very disturbing experience. Only if the therapist has endured it himself can he have an idea of its significance or the direction it will take.' (5)

Projecting the Double at Death

The conclusions of Russell Noyes Jr., Richard Alpert and W.V.Caldwell may be amplified by some interesting observations advanced by Sylvan Muldoon as a result of his attempts to develop a technique of 'astral projection' making it possible to split the personality at free will:

'Exteriorization of the astral body is, in fact, the first step into that mysterious realm called 'death,' which sooner or later all of us must enter. So, reader, if you are interested in this dark phenomenon, if you have stood o'er the casket and gazed upon the cold corpse, and in silent awe have wondered how that being who only shortly before was animate—possessed of intelligence, moving, thinking, and talking, even as you—could now be but a lifeless clod, the same as you shud-

374. Between the marriage candles of Sol and Luna the tail-eater coils up in his primal cell, thus completing the opus circulatorium in the sign of the imperial eagle and the sevenfold planetary star. The circular work is compared by one alchemical treatise to the course of the year in the Zodiac which 'seizing its tail with its head, like a snake, completes it.' (7) Uroboric symbols of the completed work abound in the rubedo.

der to think you too will become, then you are interested in astral projection, for astral projection and death are not unlike . . . The feeling of being 'split through the centre' of the body describes the agony [of the out-of-the-body experience] better than any other words I can think of. It is a sudden thrust of severe pain, as though a sharp-bladed instrument had passed directly through the entire length of the body.' (6)

The statements and observations quoted above point to the conclusion that the splitting of the personality in the out-of-the-body experience signifies an activa-

tion of the unconscious psychodynamics of the death trauma, which are patterned on the same defence mechanism as that encountered in birth-traumatic anxiety, namely splitting. In death-traumatic anxiety we term this mechanism *primal splitting*. The connection between this and the split-body produced by the alchemical proiectio is confirmed by the fact that the latter occurs in a coffin or tomb and that it leads to a transcendental state conforming to the sense of deathlessness and immortality experienced by the individuals examined by Dr.Noyes.

375.

Recovery of the Great, or Cosmic, Stone

'The sun and its shadow bring the work to perfection' (1) reads the motto of fig.375, which shows the alchemical *proiectio* in its cosmic variation. The sinister and poisonous *umbra solis* motif derives from two sources. One is the classical saying of Hermes: 'Son, extract from the ray its shadow,' (2) the other is an equally famous passage from the 'Turba': 'Know that no body is more precious and pure than the sun, and that no dyeing poison is generated without the sun and its shadow . . . He who hath dyed the poison of the sages with the sun and its shadow hath attained to the greatest secret. And know that our silver when it has become red is termed gold.' (3)

In fig.375 the sun and its shadow are united by a golden ring of stars symbolizing the heavenly marriage of Sol and Luna (fig.381). The blending of the two motifs reveals the *matrimonium coeleste* as a death marriage also. Says the 'Rosarium': 'No dyeing poison is generated without the sun and its shadow, that is, its wife.' (4) The position of the moon in the shadow-region of fig.375 bears out this point. The earth in the middle appears as the great lapis 'dyed with the poison of the sages.'

Fig.376 shows an interesting variant of the same motif. The engraving's motto reads: 'Look, with the heavenly movement—the numinous heavenly shadow.' The illustration shows an old alchemist

departing from the earth; surrounded by the solar aura, the glorified, yet terror-stricken, alchemist perceives his 'numinous heavenly shadow,' standing spectre-like on the earth-globe.

Extracting from the Ray Its Shadow

Fig.377 illustrates the operation by which the alchemist 'extracts from the ray its shadow,' or from the 'sun its shadow.' The sun's ray is represented by C and D, its shadow by B and E. The realms of light and darkness are further elaborated in F and G showing the worlds of 'Apollon' and 'Dionysus.' The sun-god raises the alchemist to eternal life under the motto: 'Jehova is the light, saviour and the tree of life.' Dionysus appears as the sun's shadow killing and dismembering the alchemist in the manner of Typhoon or Saturn.

The lapis produced by the gods of life and death appears in A. 'Dyed with the sun and its shadow,' the engraving's top sphere represents the 'divine will and the divine unwillingness,' being and non-being, birth and death—'one from two' *(duabus ab unum)* as the inscription explains this image of a split-body becoming one. The 'two' refer to sphere B representing the 'divine unwillingness from which the divine power carries out the unwillingness of the Father' and to sphere C representing the 'divine will

from which the divine act of wisdom carries out the will of the Father.' 'Yet God is one' *(Deus tamen unus)* repeats the inscription between G and F.

The biblical quotations printed below the engraving outline the features of the dual One: 'I kill and I make alive; I wound and I heal: neither is there any that can deliver out of my hand' (Deut. 32:39). 'For God maketh sore, and bindeth up; he woundeth and his hands make whole' (Job 5:18). 'You have power over life and death, and you lead down to the portals of Death and up from them again' (Sap.16:13).

Fig.378 presents the solar stone shining in saturnian darkness. The lapis is revealed by Mercurius and Saturn, the latter endowed with wings and appearing as the angel of death.

Aura and Halo of the Glorified Body

The sun united with its shadow, lunar wife, or bride of death presents an eclipse surrounded by a solar halo. The aura or halo adorns all figures of the rubedo (figs.376, 377, 353, 354, 360, 363, 380, 387, 400). There is a long historical tradition for belief in the aura, the halo of the saint, or the aureole of the Buddha, the Illumined One, the Deathless One. The spiritual body which in most cultures is assumed to reside within man and to be immortal is a solar body of light. The Egyptian concept of the *ba*, or the soul image of man, was that of his spiritual double. The *ba* was immortal, and its hieroglyph was a star. The same

376. *The aura of a departing alchemist.*

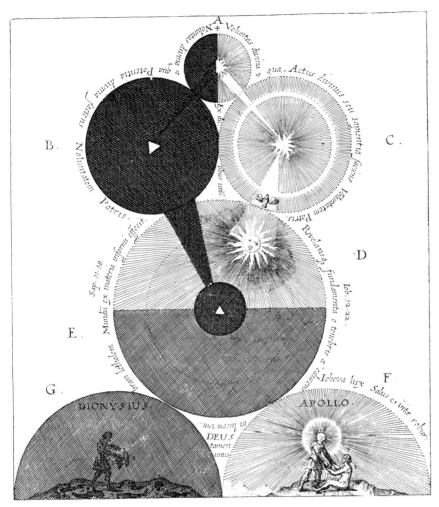

377. Extracting from the ray its shadow: revealing the final unity of life and death.

Perceiving the Clear Light of the Void

The 'sun and its shadow' belong to the obscurest of alchemical themes. Obviously, the 'poison of the sages dyed with the sun and its shadow' refers to the poisoned cup of *death*. Yet this contains simultaneously the elixir of life, a staggering paradox turning the *umbra solis* into the 'greatest secret.' The proiectio brings to the adept the solution: the sun represents the 'glorified body' resurrected from its dead body, or 'shadow,' a split-body becoming one body in the mortal marriage of Sol and Luna 'in heaven.'

If the *umbra solis* signifies the projecting alchemist's experience of ultimate death in its unity with primal birth, the motif also represents this experience in its *cosmic version*, ultimate death being experienced as the Void—the universe in its unmanifested form (fig.377). Incarnated in the body of light, the projecting alchemist is thus tuned into the very process of creation itself and shown the secret connection between non-being and being, the birth of light out of darkness, the conversion of the Void to space, energy, matter, being (fig.377, sphere A).

At this point of ultimate Incarnation, the alchemist spans the mystery and paradox of the dual One: the sameness of Pure Being and Nothing, the Clear Light of the Void, the culmination of consciousness in the cessation of consciousness (nirvana). With the attainment of this transpersonal condition, the alchemist realizes the *coniunctio oppositorum* in its last and supremest form.

---

notion of an inner spiritual body is with the Greeks, the *psyche,* with the Romans, the *genius,* with the Persians, the *fravauli.* Continuing alchemical speculations about the projected double, Paracelsus says that a half-corporeal body, which he calls the 'astral body' *(corpus astrale),* (5) lives beside the body of flesh and is its mirror image.

Aura and Halo of the Dying

It is remarkable that the aura appears as a characteristic of the out-of-the-body experience, the LSD-experience and the death-experience. Celia Green quotes this typical example: 'My 'spirit' appeared to gradually leave my body, and hovered at the foot of the bed. An opaque bright light was shining from my 'spirit' and I saw myself asleep in bed, probably for about twelve seconds.' (6) Masters and Houston state: 'The perception of the aura by psychedelic subjects is very common' (p.185). In his memoirs Jung tells us that his nurse observed his aura as he lay dying in March 1944 (following pages). As witnessed by Joy Snell's 'The Ministry of Angels,' many nurses have had the experience of seeing the halo over the death-bed. (7)

A much-quoted case in occult literature is the so-called 'Monk case' reported by Miss Dorothy Monk in 1922, where eight witnesses saw the halo over a death-bed: 'In our family circle we were witnesses to an extraordinary phenomenon at the death-bed of our beloved mother, and it impressed us deeply . . . After a long illness, aggravated by a case of gastric influenza, our mother died from heart failure . . . We saw that the lower jaw of the dying woman continued to open slowly. For several hours there was no notable change in this phenomenon, with the exception of an aureole of luminous rays of a yellow tint about the head of the sufferer . . . Toward midnight the whole thing disappeared from our vision, although our mother actually did not die until seven o'clock in the morning.' (8)

The aura or halo may be interpreted as an energetic phenomenon related to the *development of the self,* the unconscious, high-powered complex that binds the total personality together.

378. Death revealing the solar stone.

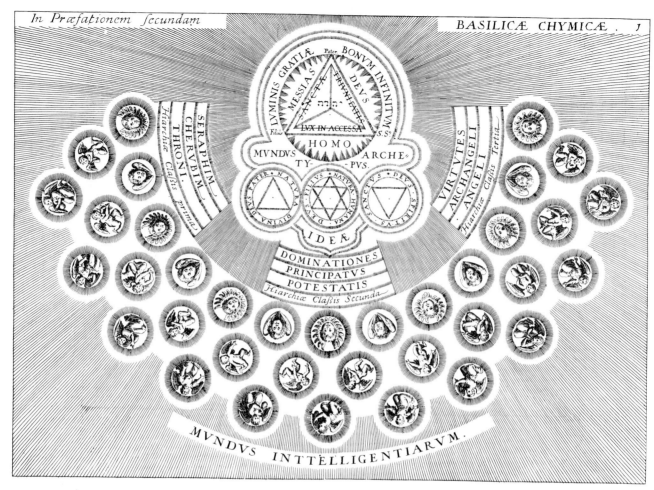

379. *The engraving renders the heavenly stone conquered by the alchemist at the end of the Great Work. The triune Godhead is circumscribed by the crown of the Virgin's coronation, or by the same female circle which surrounds the eggs of the heavenly children. 'The Inaccessible Light of the Holy Trinity' enclosing the 'God Man Messiah' blends with the 'Infinite Good of the Light of Grace' which envelops the 'archetypal world,' or the realm of divine 'ideas.' The small circles inside the solar stone represent 'God the Father, Divine Nature' and 'God the Holy Ghost,' both merging in the Solomonic Seal of 'God the Son, Human Nature.' The celestial throne is surrounded by the 'three classes of the hierarchy,' or the nine choirs of angels—a symbol of the body's growing sublimation on the heavenly ladder climbed by the alchemist. The philosophers' rose garden is represented by the 'Milky Way' of unborn children glimmering as soul-sparks on the firmament. Below stretches the 'world of rational beings,' or created reality.*

C.G. Jung's Experience of Dying in 1944

The Hermetic experience of the proiectio, the great stone 'dyed with the sun and its shadow,' and the celestial marriage may be amplified by Jung's experience of the individuation process in its concluding phase. Significantly, Jung's out-of-the-body experience occurred in connection with his suffering of the death trauma in March 1944. This is his account:

'At the beginning of 1944 I broke my foot, and this misadventure was followed by a heart attack. In a state of unconsciousness I experienced deliriums and visions which must have begun when I hung on the edge of death and was being given oxygen and camphor injections. The images were so tremendous that I myself concluded that I was close to death. My nurse afterward told me, 'It was as if you were surrounded by a bright glow.' This was a phenomenon

which she had sometimes observed in the dying, she added. I had reached the outermost limit, and do not know whether I was in a dream or an ecstasy. At any rate, extremely strange things began to happen to me.

'It seemed to me that I was high up in space. Far below I saw the globe of the earth, bathed in a gloriously blue light. I saw the deep blue sea and the continents. Far below my feet lay Ceylon, and in the distance ahead of me the subcontinent of India. My field of vision did not include the whole earth, but its global shape was plainly distinguishable and its outlines shone with a silvery gleam through that wonderful blue light. In many places the globe seemed coloured, or spooed dark green like oxydized silver. Far away to the left lay a broad expanse—the reddish-yellow desert of Arabia; it was as though the silver of the earth had there assumed a reddish-gold huc. Then came the Red Sea, and far, far

back—as if in the upper left of a map—I could just make out a bit of the Mediterranean. My gaze was directed chiefly toward that. Everything else appeared indistinct. I could also see the snow-covered Himalayas, but in that direction it was foggy or cloudy. I did not look to the right at all. I knew that I was on the point of departing from earth.

'Later I discovered how high in space one would have to be to have so extensive a view—approximately a thousand miles! The sight of the earth from this height was the most glorious thing I had ever seen. After contemplating it for a while, I turned around. I had been standing with my back to the Indian Ocean, as it were, and my face to the north. Then it seemed to me that I made a turn to the south. Something new entered my field of vision. A short distance away I saw in space a tremendous dark block of stone, like a mctcorite. It was about the size of my house, or even bigger. It was floating in space, and I myself was floating in space. I had seen similar stones on the coast of the Gulf of Bengal. They were blocks of tawny granite, and some of them had been hollowed out into temples. My stone was one such gigantic dark block. An entrance led into a small antechamber. To the right of the entrance, a black Hindu sat silently in lotus posture upon a stone bench. He wore a white gown, and I knew that he expected me.* Two steps led up to his antechamber, and inside, on the left, was the gate to the temple. Innumerable tiny niches, each with a saucerlike concavity filled with coconut oil and small burning wicks, surrounded the door with a wreath of bright flames.' (1)

'During those weeks I lived in a strange rhythm. By day I was usually depressed. I felt weak and wretched, and scarcely dared to stir. Gloomily, I thought, 'Now I must go back to this drab world.' Toward evening I would fall asleep, and my sleep would last until about midnight. Then I would come to myself and lie awake for about an hour, but in an utterly transformed state. It was as if I were in an ecstasy. I felt as though I were floating in space, as though I were safe in the universe—in a tremendous void, but filled with the highest possible feeling of happiness. 'This is eternal bliss,' I thought. 'This cannot be described; it is far too wonderful!' Everything around me seemed enchanted.

* The identity of the yogi in the lotus position inside the heavenly stone or floating temple was revealed to Jung in a dream experienced shortly after these visions. The dream clearly expressed the dynamics of the proiectio and so confirmed the out-of-the-body experience of Jung's visions. In the dream Jung entered a small hillside chapel and was surprised to find no image of the Virgin on the altar, but instead a wonderful flower arrangement. In front of the altar sat a yogi in deep meditation, and Jung saw that he had Jung's own face (cf. fig.357). At this he woke up in profound terror, thinking: 'Aha, so he is the one who is meditating me. He has a dream, and I am it.' And Jung adds, 'I knew that when he awakened, I would no longer be.' (2)

380. Red incarnation in the solar stone.

381. The engraving shows the heavenly marriage of Sol and Luna united by a wedding ring of golden stars. Hovering in a state of weightlessness in space, their astral bodies merge with the earth-globe, or the great stone, dyed with the 'sun and its shadow.' Its geometrical design is explained in fig.382, which renders the squaring of the circle.

'At this hour of the night, the nurse brought me some food she had warmed—for only then was I able to take any, and I ate with appetite. For a time it seemed to me that she was an old Jewish woman, much older than she actually was, and that she was preparing ritual kosher dishes for me. When I looked at her, she seemed to have a blue halo around her head. I myself was, so it seemed, in the Pardes Rimmonim, the garden of pomegranates, and the wedding of Tifereth with Malchuth was taking place. Or else I was Rabbi Simon ben Jochai, whose wedding in the afterlife was being celebrated. It was the mystic marriage as it appears in the Cabbalistic tradition. I cannot tell you how wonderful it was. I could only think continually, 'Now this is the garden of pomegranates! Now this is the marriage of Malchuth with Tifereth!' I do not know exactly what part I played in it. At bottom it was I myself: I was the marriage. And my beatitude was that of a blissful wedding.

'Gradually the garden of pomegranates faded away and changed. There followed the Marriage of the Lamb, in a Jerusalem festively bedecked. I cannot describe what it was like in detail. These were ineffable states of joy. Angels were present, and light. I myself was the 'Marriage of the Lamb.' That, too, vanished, and there came a new image, the last vision. I walked up a wide valley to the end, where a gentle chain of hills began. The valley ended in a classical amphi-theatre.

It was magnificently situated in the green landscape. And there, in this theatre, the *hierosgamos* was being celebrated. Men and women dancers came onstage, and upon a flower-decked couch All-father Zeus and Hera consummated the mystic marriage, as it is described in the *Iliad*. All these experiences were glorious. Night after night I floated in a state of purest bliss, 'thronged round with images of all creation' . . . It is impossible to convey the beauty and intensity of emotion during those visions. They were the most tremendous things I have ever experienced.' (3)

'There is something else I quite distinctly remember. At the beginning, when I was having the vision of the garden of the pomegranates, I asked the nurse to forgive me if she were harmed. There was such sanctity in the room, I said, that it might be harmful to her. Of course she did not understand me. For me the presence of sanctity had a magical atmosphere; I feared it might be unendurable to others. I understood then why one speaks of the odour of sanctity, of the 'sweet smell' of the Holy Ghost . . . The visions and experiences were utterly real, not a product of imagination; there was nothing subjective about them; they all had a quality of absolute objectivity. We shy away from the word 'eternal,' but I can describe the experience only as the ecstasy of a non-temporal state in which present, past, and future are one.' (4)

382. Resting unity of the sexes in the 'sexless' nucleus of the great, or primal, stone.

The Alchemical Squaring of the Circle

Above, the alchemist performs the squaring of the circle, thereby turning the two sexes into one. The motto repeats a saying of the 'Rosarium': 'Make a circle out of a man and woman, derive from it a square, and from the square a triangle: make a circle and you will have the philosophers' stone.' (1) As informed by the text, the triangle denotes the unity of body, soul and spirit. Of this operation Petrus Bonus says: 'In this conjunction of resurrection, the body becomes wholly spiritual, like the soul herself, and they are made one as water is mixed with water, and henceforth they are not separated for ever, since there is no diversity in them, but unity and identity of all three, that is, spirit, soul and body, without separation for ever.' (2)
According to the text of fig.382, the quadrangle denotes the synthesis of the four elements, just as the circle signifies the stone's 'transformation into permanent redness; by this action woman turns into man and they become a unity . . . in which there is rest and eternal peace.' (3) This statement reflects the supreme sublimation of sex in the fourth coniunctio: as 'woman turns into man' and vice versa, the lapis blends the sexual opposites

in a 'resting unity and eternal peace' signifying the libido's indifferent position in the great stone, the Hermetic symbol of the primordial germ cell (pp.180-181).

The Indifference of the Great Liberation

Emotional indifference is a hallmark of the out-of-the-body experience. Nearly all Celia Green's subjects stress the importance of an unconflicted emotional state, or a 'blank mind,' as a prerequisite of their experience. (4) Emotional disturbance or conflict normally leads to a termination of the out-of-the-body state. Fear, for instance, will turn the experience into an extremely negative adventure. Subjects emphasize that the experience is a positive one until feelings of fear arise—fear of inability to terminate the state or of 'being unable to get back into the body.' (5) Egotistical desire or erotic emotion also interferes with the state in a negative way. Oliver Fox suggests that the motto for the 'astral projectionist' should be: 'I may look, but I must not get too interested—let alone touch!' (6) Muldoon and Carrington emphasize the same aspect: 'Sex is a 'stress' which works against itself, so far as projection of the astral body is concerned;

for such an intense desire would become emotional . . . consequently the astral body would not project; in fact it would be drawn more closely into the physical body instead of moving outwards from the zone of quietude.' (7)
The change of motivation is in the direction of greater 'detachment,' 'impersonality' and 'objectivity.' (8) The majority of subjects describe themselves as being calm, relaxed, detached or indifferent: 'I cannot stress enough the complete feeling of detachment I had—sorry, to say 'feeling' is wrong. Probably disinterest is the better word.' (9) Indifference is felt above all in relation to the body. A number of Celia Green's subjects remark that although they retained a cognitive awareness of their relationship with their physical body, they were not emotionally identified with it: 'Although I *knew* the person lying on the bed was myself, it was as though I were looking at someone else.' 'Cognitive awareness of being connected with it; no apparent physical or emotional connection.' 'While recognizing it as my own I felt no possessiveness towards it.' 'I was completely calm, in fact disinterested . . . My body could have been any body or any object, come to that, such was my state of disinterest.' (10) Celia Green sums up the out-of-the-body state in this way: 'The common, and crucial, feature is freedom from emotional conflict, or 'unconflictedness.'' (11) Jung's comments on the psychological state in which he experienced his *unio mystica* run along the same lines:
'The objectivity which I experienced in . . . the visions is part of a completed individuation. It signifies detachment from valuations and from what we call emotional ties. In general, emotional ties are very important to human beings. But they still contain projections, and it is essential to withdraw these projections in order to attain to oneself and to objectivity. Emotional relationships are relationships of desire, tainted by coercion and constraint; something is expected from the other person, and that makes him and ourselves unfree. Objective cognition lies hidden behind the attraction of the emotional relationship; it seems to be the central secret. Only through objective cognition is the real *coniunctio* possible.' (12)

Buddha's Concept of Nirvana

Indifference, of course, is a key concept of Buddha's nirvana, the 'oppositelessness' of which signifies man's final liberation from selfish craving and self-centred desire: 'This, monks, is the noble truth of the cessation of pain, the cessation without a remainder of craving, the abandonment, forsaking, release, nonattachment . . . producing insight and knowledge and tending to calm, to higher knowledge, enlightenment, nirvana.' (13)

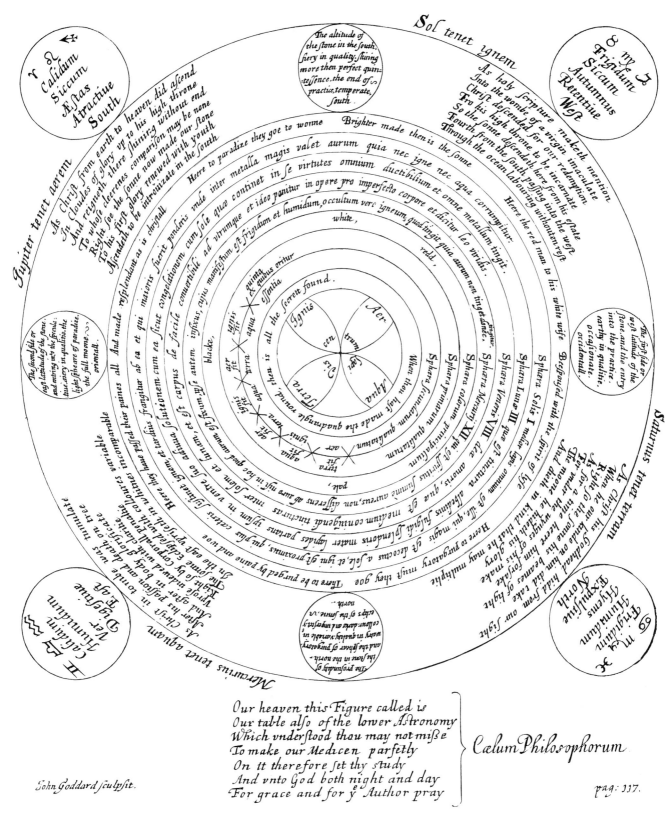

Our heaven this Figure called is
Our table also of the lower Astronomy
Which vnderstood thou may not misse
To make our Medicen parfetly
On it therefore set thy study
And vnto God both night and day
For grace and for ye Author pray

Cælum Philosophorum

pag: 137.

John Goddard sculpsit.

383. The engraving shows George Ripley's Wheel, described by the author as a 'figure containing all the secrets of the treatise both great and small' (headline, fig. 382). The figure appears as a mandala with twelve spheres cross-like divided by four corner circles. They represent the 'tetrameria' or 'quartering' of the process, reflecting in turn the seasonal quartering of the yearly cycle, the model of the circular work. The four small circles inserted give the various positions of the stone during its cyclic course with the sun. The inner spheres describe the most important planets, or metals, and their functions; the 'principal colours: pale, black, white and red'; the 'primary and secondary qualities' participating in the circular distillation of the elements (second and third spheres from the centre) 'from which emerges the quintessence.' The last sphere reads: 'When thou hast made the quadrangle round, then is all the secret found.' The operation is performed in the innermost circle, whose quintessential flower-mandala merges the four elements in the 'centre of the stone.'

199

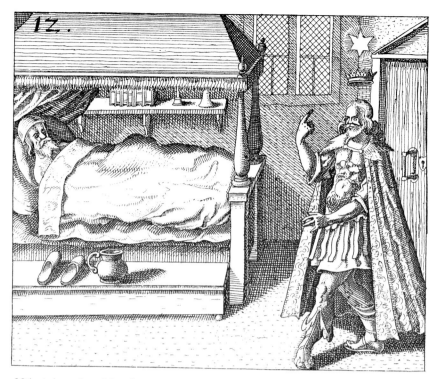

384. A dreaming alchemist projecting his astral body in the shape of the red king.

The Circular Distillation of the Elements

The circular distillation of the elements presented by the inner circles of Ripley's Wheel forms another motif of the concluding work. By this operation the 'quintessence' is produced—the 'fifth element' in which the elements are contained in their original unity and synthetic form. The quintessence is a synonym for the etheric body or *corpus subtile*, a relationship demonstrated by figs.384-385, which render an alchemist's experience of the *corpus glorificatum* and *circulatio distillare*. Moving in the time between sleep and waking, the old philosopher 'in violent terror' (1) beholds the vision of himself in the lucid dream (fig. 384). This is his account of the ghostly experience:

'I saw in the far distance a faint light becoming clearer and clearer and coming ever nearer toward me. All my strength being sapped and still looking down before me, I beheld a luminous, transparent figure of the same substance as the air. He had a crown on his head full of stars and I saw wondrous things, for all his interior organs could be discerned. His brain was like a crystalline water moving all the time like a cloud. In his chest, his heart appeared like a ruby . . . He also carried a mantle of white linen studded with flowers of all colours, being green on the inside. But from heart to head and from head to heart I saw an ever-moving vapour. With its hand the ghostly figure knocked on the wall with great noise and afterward disappeared.' (2)

The holy ghost leaves behind him 'a little leaden box full of rust' (placed in fig.384 in the philosopher's lap). 'Inside it was an open book with pages made of bark from beeches, for it was an old book. In it was a parabolic figure and an old poem about the old Adam. I studied many days and nights in that book until it was suddenly opened to me. As I read it, I soon understood many things, for I saw at noon, as if in Africa, the fiery lion, and again, at midnight, under the pole star, the bear. And I thanked God in all eternity for his wondrous work, and [so] I reached the goal of the sealed Book of Nature.' (3)

Fig.385 shows the alchemist's vision of the cross-like conjunction of nature's opposites (pole star–Africa–midnight–midday–fiery lion–icebear), which the engraving identifies with the circular distillation of the elements at the hands of the mystical sister. Says an alchemical author of this operation: 'Through circumrotation, or a circular philosophical revolving of the quaternarius, it is brought back to the highest and purest simplicity of the monad . . . Out of the gross and impure One there cometh an exceeding pure and subtle One.' (4)

The Red Mass of Alchemy

Another image of the *corpus glorificatum* is presented with fig.386, which reproduces the fourth and last illustration of Stefan Michelspacher's 'Cabala' (previous engravings in figs.5, 81, 167). Entitled '4. The End: Multiplication,' the picture shows the five planetary gods gathered on top of the Mountain of the Adepts, their puffers raised to signify the

concluded work. Above them, two crossed fire-swords pierce the roof of heaven while releasing a flood of light. They represent the two remaining planets, Sol and Luna, and their ascent into heaven, or the philosophers' garden. A huge rainbow uniting heaven and earth rises above the thunder clouds while illuminating the transcendent scenery.

Encircled by the five planetary crowns, the royal couple pray in front of a Christian communion-table in the *rosarium philosophorum*. The table also represents the 'well of life,' just as it forms the base of the mercurial, planetary fountain. Its throning figure is the red king, or risen Christ, performing the Red Mass of alchemy, described thus by the 'Theatrum chemicum': 'And now the king gives his red and bleeding flesh to be eaten by us all.' (5) The Saviour's body forms the lower angle of the Trinity; two of its sides are composed of light-beams drawn by haloed doves, one symbolizing the Holy Ghost given up by the crucified Son (upper corner, right), the other the Holy Ghost emanating from the solar Father (upper corner, left). The third side is formed by a river of blood flowing from a wine press enclosing Christ with his cross. Squeezed by an angel turning the spindle's fastener and plate, the Saviour's body emits a stream of blood continuing in the jet of blood gushing from the king's right side wound. An emblem of the red tincture, the blood is offered by Christ to Sol and Luna in two chalices.

The red king, or resurrected Christ, is frequently compared to the second Adam, 'the Lord from heaven' (1.Cor.15: 35-55). Whereas the original Adam is made of the corruptible four elements, the second Adam is a product of the circular distillation and so consists of the pure and incorruptible quintessence. Says the 'Aurora consurgens': 'The second Adam, who is called the philosophic man, passed from the pure elements into eternity. Therefore, since he consists of a simple and pure essence, he endures forever. As Senior saith: One thing there is that never dieth, for it continueth by perpetual increase, when the body shall be glorified in the final resurrection of the

385. Performing the circular distillation.

386. Kneeling before the communion table of the rubedo: 'And now the king gives his red and bleeding flesh to be eaten by us all.'

dead, wherefore the Creed beareth witness to the resurrection of the flesh and eternal life after death. Then saith the second Adam to the first and to his sons: Come, ye blessed of my Father, possess you the eternal kingdom prepared for you from the beginning of the Work, and eat my bread and drink the wine which I have mingled for you, for all things are made ready for you. He that hath ears to hear, let him hear what the spirit of the doctrine saith to the sons of the discipline concerning the earthly and the heavenly Adam, which the philosophers treat of in these words: When thou hast water from earth, air from water, fire from air, earth from fire, then shalt thou fully and perfectly possess our art.' (6) (Fig.383.)

387. Magic powers of a solified emperor: 'From the dead he makes the living.' (1)

Reviving the Emperor Death

Fig.387, from Thurneisser's 'Quinta essentia,' presents the last chamber of the alchemical castle and its sacred inmate: the great hermaphrodite adorned with the imperial crown and illuminated by the solar halo. The bisexual emperor sits on a chest filled with innumerable riches and protected by a heavy lock, the key of which is held by the owner. The emperor's left arm rests on a large volume entitled 'Herbarium,' thereby showing the close connection between alchemy and the science of herbs, vegetables, roots or drugs.* The remaining volumes deal with the related subjects of 'Mutatio,' 'Quinta Aessentia,' 'Mysterium Aeternitatis' and 'Natura Rerum' ('The Nature

of Things'). The two last volumes show the poles of alchemical learning, the 'Archidoxa' ('The Supreme [Hermetic] Tenets') and the Bible ('Biblia'). Fig.390, also from Thurneisser's 'Quinta essentia,' renders the conjunction of Sol and Luna in the 'fountain of the sun and moon.' The act coincides with the savage whipping of the winged dragon, who is killed by the emperor in his skeletal form. The identity of Death and the great hermaphrodite is proved by the skeleton's whipping instrument: the wedding bouquet of Sol and Luna. Further, the skeleton is gilded by the light of the united sun and moon. The transformation of Death and Dragon into figures of Eternal Life is expressed by the verse thus:

The dragon is dead without fighting,
It swells and grows, emitting a sulphur-
*   ous vapour, and,*
Like a sponge, it produces sap; its
Meat has the power of silver and gold. (2)

* Chemicals are the key of the opus alchymicum, whose recipe for the magic potion—the *elixir vitae*—went into the grave with all the other secrets of alchemical tradition and art.

As the dragon's blood gushes into the fountain of the sun and moon, the red tincture is gathered in two vessels termed *lapis* and *aqua*. The white tincture appears as the 'milk [obtained] by the art' *(lac arte)*, gathered by the Emperor Death as he holds forward a basin to the monster's spouting breasts.

The four medals reproduced in figs. 388-389 paraphrase the ancient alchemical dictum: 'Do not deny resurrection to the dead.' (3) In the first medal of fig.388 the alchemist is raised from his grave by the Almighty proclaiming: 'I resolve abundantly.' The inscription amplifies: 'Through putrefaction dies the corporeal vegetation and a new spiritual one breaks forth.' In the second medal the mystical sister armed with a sword kills the tail-eater as he performs his last revolution. The inscription explains: 'One must kill him in a wise fashion since he will reveal death.'

In the first medal of fig.389 the sun illuminates a trinitarian design of fire-breathing dragons hovering over the celestial ocean of the rubedo. This is the universal sea symbolized by Pisces and known among the adepts as the great arcanum, the 'red sea,' the 'elixir of life,' the 'eternal water.' In Kalid's 'Liber trium verborum' the substance is termed the 'acid of the philosophers and the penetrative spirit, hidden, tincturing, aggregating and reviving: rectifying and enlightening all the dead and causing them to rise again.' (4) The inscription strikes a similar note: 'Now is the time to make the dead living and to heal the sick.'

The last medal copies a 'Pandora' woodcut (not reproduced in this study), in which the tail-eater's last revolution coincides with its presentation of the imperial coronation pillow. 'The man' and 'the woman's' seed flow together in the middle of the pillow from which arises the emperor's crown (adorning the primordial egg in the 'Pandora' original). The inscription states: 'Death is now conquered and our son reigns invested with our silver and flesh.'

A Study of Deathbed Visions

The alchemical pictures on these pages render a strange motif of the rubedo: the work of 'making the dead living,' of 'resurrecting the dead.' Can this motif be explained by the psychology of dying?

388. Revelation of the secrets of death.

In fact, it can. In the beginning of the 1960s the American doctor Karlis Osis carried out researches into the fantasies and visions of dying patients. A questionnaire was sent to 640 doctors and nurses who reported their observations of 884 people. The material was computerized and published in a statistical study termed 'Deathbed Observations by Physicians and Nurses' (1961). These were the main results:

'Surprisingly enough, fear is not the dominant emotion in dying patients according to the opinion of both physicians and nurses in our sample. They indicate discomfort and pain as the most common emotions in the dying. Two of our three groups of respondents also noted that *indifference* is more frequent than fear. Most surprising, of course, is the large number of patients who are said to be elated at the hour of death. This mood is apparently quite frequent among terminal patients. Naturally, there are some variations in our sample, but all three percentage groups indicate substantial proportions of patients elated (1 out of 20, 1 out of 50, and 1 out of 16) at the most dreaded time of life. These findings point to a phenomenon of marked psychological significance which is definitely worth a careful inquiry. What is the cause of the last-hour elation? What is the difference between persons who die in a state of panic and those who are peaceful and tranquil?' (5)

LSD-Like Visions of the Dying

'Visions, or hallucinations of predominantly non-human content connected with transcendental existence, were abundantly reported, observations totaling 884 cases. They are proportionately much more frequent in our sample of deathbed cases than in the normal population of the two surveys discussed in previous chapters. The proportion is about 10:1, which indicates an extremely marked trend. If terminal patients hallucinate, why do they see ten times more visions than persons who hallucinate in normal health? Is this merely an adaption of hallucinations to the death situation, or does it mirror another aspect of reality? Follow-up cases indicated that age, sex, body temperature, medication, and impaired consciousness do not have any marked relationship to the occur-

389. The work of making the dead living.

390. The Hermetic conquest of Death: psychological integration of the death trauma.

rence of visions in terminal patients. The same is true for non-terminal cases except that the majority of these patients were in an impaired state of consciousness, being quite out of touch with reality.' (6)

'It is interesting to note that in the non-terminal group 5 out of 9 patients had clouded consciousness during the visions; in the terminal group only 2 out of 15 patients had clouded consciousness. Apparently this difference in the pattern of consciousness is closely connected with whether the patient is about to die or will recover. As a rule, *the dying see visions with clear consciousness.*' (7)

'Our follow-up studies elicited a number of descriptions of visions. Some are quite in line with traditional religious imagery concerning heaven, as in this report of a general practitioner: 'Woman patient had had thyroidectomy and was unconscious for several hours. When she came to she said she had been on a high hill

like a divide and could look down into the Promised Land. Could not describe it well but said it was beautiful, and she was not afraid to cross over because it was so beautiful.' The traditional image of the Heavenly City was also described. For instance one observer quoted a patient as saying that he went to 'a beautiful city—the beauty was indescribable,' and that he would have been 'very happy but could not find me.'

'The other type of vision is not traditional but very much in line with imagery associated with hallucinogenic drugs such as LSD/25 or mescaline. Illustrating a type of imagery bordering on both types, a nurse reported: 'A six-year-old boy dying of polio described heaven, stating he saw beautiful flowers, heard birds singing, stated he was going to this beautiful land.' Another example was that reported by a patient who 'told about seeing birds with brightly-lighted eyes or tails flying in a jumbled circle.' (8)

TOM · I   P · 238   14

VI   II   X

Ora
Lege Lege Lege Relege labora
et Invenies.

391. *The adept and his sister making the gesture of the secret at the end of the work.*

Heavenly Visions of the Last Transition

'The emotional quality of the visionary experiences is expressed predominantly as indescribable beauty and peace. However, subjects taking hallucinatory drugs sometimes find themselves confronted with a very disagreeable kind of imagery which Aldous Huxley calls 'Hell.' In our sample we find something similar along traditional lines in this case: 'The patient had a horrified expression, turned his head in all directions and said, 'Hell, Hell, all I see is Hell.'' Another had the terrifying feeling of being buried alive. These were the only two cases in our collection to strike a distressing emotional note—a small minority indeed when compared with the number reporting peace and beauty . . . If anything, there seemed to be only increased intensity of beauty and happiness, i.e., differences of degree, not of quality. Characteristic responses are: 'Why did you bring me back, Doc? It was so nice there,' or 'I want to go back, let me go back.' Apparently the visionary experiences can be so gratifying that after them the patients have a strong wish to die.' (1)

The Resurrection of the Dead

'The abundant amount of data obtained for comparison between hallucinations of deathbed patients and those of persons in normal health revealed the following marked differences: healthy persons hallucinate predominantly the living; terminal patients hallucinate predominantly the dead; visions and hallucinations of religious figures are much more frequent in our sample of the dying than in the samples of healthy individuals. These are findings of major importance, although they relate only to broad classifications . . . The predominance of the dead in deathbed apparitions was previously found in studies by Barret, Hyslop and Hart who claimed that deathbed apparitions are comprised 100% of dead hallucinatory persons. Although our study shows a predominance of the dead in deathbed hallucinations, the proportions were as follows: 52.3% dead; 28.1% living; and 19.6% religious figures. The respective percentages were approximately the same in our follow-up sample. The British samples of hallucinations of persons in normal health show precisely the opposite trend: twice as many hallucinations of living as of dead persons. Therefore the predominance of hallucinations of the dead seems to be a real characteristic of terminal cases and those non-terminal cases involving a very narrow escape from death . . . A number of physicians and nurses reported that patients died immediately after the hallucinations [of the dead], e.g., saying, 'Now, Ann, I am coming,' and expired instantly. In other words, the process of death and the actions of the [dead] hallucinatory figures appear closely integrated . . . The hallucinations heralded death within a day in the majority of cases.' (2)

In summing up the main results of his statistical study on 'Deathbed Observations,' Karlis Osis concludes: 'We have certainty on only two essential points: Our study verified the impression of Barret, Hyslop and others that deathbed hallucinations of persons 1) predominantly represent the dead and 2) are of an apparitional quality.' (3)

Dr. Osis' conclusions are supported by many similar statements from priests and doctors. In his book 'A Case Book for Survival' A.T. Baird quotes the Rev. Dr. Worcester as saying that on several occasions he had seen dying persons brighten up as they appeared to see friends who had 'gone before.' He added: 'In every instance within my experience this has proved the immediate precursor to death.' Dr. Worcester further said that this was the experience of 'the old doctors' (who remained with patients until the end). The old doctors expected death soon after the patients appeared to see friends who had pre-deceased them. (4) As may be seen from Joy Snell's book 'The Ministry of Angels' (1950), nurses make the same statements.

'And what the dead had no speech for,
when living,
They can tell you, being dead: the
communication
Of the dead is tongued with fire beyond
the language of the living.'
        T.S. Eliot: *Little Gidding.*

Grand Conclusion of the 'Mutus liber'

Fig.391 shows the penultimate plate of the 'Mutus liber.' The departing curtains of the laboratory reveal three furnaces with burning oil-lamps; below, three persons cut down the smoking wicks of their lamps while supplying them with fresh oil. In the 'Splendor solis' oil appears as a synonym for the tincture or quintessence 'which is the very next matter to the philosophers' stone' (p.188). Probably the substance also contains a reference to the last oil used by the Church for anointment of the dying. Both interpretations agree with the symbolism of the last 'Mutus liber' plates.

The middle figure shows the philosophers' son, presented as a dwarf with his playthings, a rack and a ball (*ludus puerorum* motif). He is flanked on his left by a paternal figure of indeterminate sex (hermaphrodite), on his right by a maternal figure representing the soror mystica. The parental figures (who correspond to the alchemist and his sister in the bottom row) carry a mop or unlighted torch stuck under their right arms.

The birth of the philosophers' son in the second row is followed by the operations of multiplication and projection performed in the two bottom rows. Heated by the fire of the fourth degree, the two furnaces develop the multiplying replicas of the sun and moon, the 'infinite sun-making and the true moon-making substance.' The proiectio is symbolized by the scales of equilibrium inserted between the sun and moon furnaces and by the mirror-like symmetry reigning in the bottom half of the engraving. All objects and persons are arranged in a perfect symmetrical pattern: 1) the sun and moon furnaces 2) the circular measuring instruments with three stalks, each stalk representing 24 hours 3) the two boxes with weights under the scales 4) the mortar's ornamental snakes 5) the dishes of the sun and moon furnaces flanking the mercurial vessel of conjunction 6) the alchemist and his sister. The Hermetic couple makes the gesture of the secret at the end of the work while whispering: 'Pray, read, re-read and toil—and thou shalt find.'

The magic symmetry or *projective identity* of the alchemist and his soul sister may be amplified by one of the last passages of the 'Rosarium.' Sol is speaking: 'When I shall be united with my white wife, pure and humid and pure to the touch, I add to the beauty of her face [my own] and also to her goodness and virtue, for she obeys me. Therefore, when I shall be united with her, nothing shall be better in the whole world and nothing equal to it, for she shall conceive and grow and become like me in substance and colour, since the semen is multiplied by this magistery. And so, out of me will be born one similar to me . . . In this will be fulfilled the great gift of

392. The bridal couple ascending with the dying hero-god in the final resurrection.

God, which is above every secret belonging to the sciences of this world and is the treasure of all treasures.' (5)

Redemption from Fire by Fire

The last 'Mutus liber' engraving, reproduced in fig.392, illustrates the end of the opus. Kneeling as Sol and Luna, the alchemist and his sister join hands in the hour of their celestial marriage, celebrated under the red sun. The threefold rope held by their free hands connects them with Mercurius Ascending or Christ Resurrected, crowned with the wreath of victory by two angels. Below lies the abandoned ladder of ascent, now made superfluous by the union of heaven and earth. Another symbol of the concluded opus is found on the ground with the Hercules figure writhing in agony under the scorching fire of the sun and moon united. The motif alludes to Hercules' fate at the end of his *opera*. According to legend, Deiraneira, his bride, invested Hercules with a shirt of flame soaked in the poisonous blood of Nessus, the Centaur. With the Nessus-shirt of his death/marriage clinging to his body and burning its way into his flesh, Hercules struggled to the top of Mount Oite to unite there with the gods. Fulfilling his destiny, Hercules mounted a funeral pyre, thus escaping fire by fire while ascending in a transfigured form to the Olympus. A second allusion to Sol and Luna's death marriage is contained in the inscription on their wedding band: *Oculatus abis*—'Provided with eyes thou departest.'

393. The alchemist's mystical sister refined to the purity of the Queen of Heaven.

Fig.393 shows the alchemical anima, or soul-bride, in her highest incarnation as Sapientia, or goddess of Wisdom. At her side the tree of life blossoms in a spring outside time, neither budding nor fading, transcending the scheme of gene-ration. The Queen of Heaven presents two flying scrolls, the inscriptions of which reproduce a celebrated passage in the 'Aurora consurgens': 'Her fruit is more precious than all the riches of this world, and all the things that are desired are not to be compared with her. In her right hand are length of days and health *(longitudo dierum et sanitas)*, in her left, glory and infinite riches *(gloria ac divitiae infinitae)*. Her ways are beautiful operations and praiseworthy, not unsightly nor ill-favoured, and her paths are measured and not hasty, but are bound up with stubborn and day-long toil. She is a tree of life to them that lay hold on her, and an unfailing light. Blessed shall they be who retain her, for the science of God shall never perish.' (1)

Later, the alchemical Queen of Heaven presents herself as the dual One: 'I am the flower of the field and the lily of the valleys, I am the mother of fair love and of fear and of knowledge and of holy hope (2) . . . I am the mediator of the elements, making one to agree with another; that which is warm I make cold, and the reverse, and that which is dry I make moist, and the reverse, and that which is hard I soften, and the reverse. I am the end and my beloved is the beginning, I am the whole work and all science is hidden in me. I am the law in the priest and the word in the prophet and the counsel in the wise. I will kill and I will make to live and there is none that can deliver out of my hand.' (3)

The Four Stages of the Anima

Sapientia expresses the adept's subli-mation of his soror mystica into her high-est degree of perfection. In alchemy, the anima passes through four stages of de-velopment corresponding, in turn, to the four stages of conjunction. Untransform-ed and primitive, the anima of the first conjunction appears as Eve, or earth-wo-man—an animal object of *sexual love*. As Jung says of the anima at her lowest lev-el: 'Woman is here equated with the mother and only represents something to be fertilized.' (4)

Sublimated and idealized, the anima of the second conjunction appears as Lu-na, or moon-woman—an object of *roman-tic love,* the goal of Eros, not of sex. The classical expression is Helen of Troy, the romantic love object of the kings and princes of Greece, the 'face that launched a thousand ships.'

Elevated and spiritualized, the anima of the third conjunction appears as the Divine Virgin, or heavenly woman—the object of *spiritual love.* Transcending sex and Eros, the anima here becomes the emblem of uncontaminated love and pure devotion. The classical expression is Dan-te's Beatrice who leads the poet on to the spheres of paradise and the marvels of heavenly love.

394. Raising the balls of fire to the heat of the phoenix's pyre and the sun's orb.

Transcendentalized and etherized, the anima of the fourth conjunction appears as the Mother of God, or the Consort of God—the object of *mystic love*. Transcending sex, Eros and Holy Love, the anima at this stage is so filled with spirit that she acquires hermaphroditic features—those of Athena and Mona Lisa, the Greek and Western goddesses of Wisdom. Other classical incarnations are Isis, Kwan-Yin and Mary, the Woman of the Immaculate Conception.*

Conquest of the Magical Elixir of Youth

Fig.395 presents a famous motif of the concluded work, immortalized in Goethe's 'Faust': the old alchemist's restoration to a state of eternal youth. The motto reads: 'Enclose the tree and the old man in a house with dew; as he eats of the fruit, the old man will turn into a youth.' (6) The source is the 58th sermon of the 'Turba': 'Take that white tree surrounded by dew, build around it a round, dark house, put in it a man stricken in years, a hundred years old, and lock the house, so that no wind or dust may penetrate to them. After that leave them in their house for eighty days: I say to you in truth, that that old man will not stop eating the fruit of that tree, till he becomes a youth. O, how wonderful is nature, which transforms the soul of an old man into the body of a youth, and the father is become the son. Blessed be God, the supreme creator.' (7)

The 'white tree' refers to the lunar tree maturing in the closed vessel and finally producing the solar fruit, the red apples of immortality. The engraving's text compares the fruit-tree to the old man's daughter, thus following Hermetic doc-

395. *An old alchemist eating the apples of immortality in the arbour of Wisdom.*

trine which ranges the elixir of life with the 'mysteries of the queen.' Says the 'Aurora consurgens': 'Wisdom standing at the door saith: Behold, I stand at the gate and knock: if any man shall hear my voice and open the door, I will come in to him and he to me, and I will be satisfied with him and he with me . . . Whosoever by his science shall open this house shall find therein an unfailing living fount that maketh young, wherein whoever is baptized, he shall be saved and can no more grow old.' (8) The death marriage in the arms of the Queen of Heaven is

hinted at by the concluding text of fig. 395: 'Man can only be rejuvenated by death itself and the beginning of the following eternal life.' (9)

Fig.394 shows the 'four fire-balls governing the work.' (10) In the 'Scala philosophorum' they are defined as follows: 'The first [degree], slow and mild, as of the flesh or embryo; the second, moderate and temperate, as of the sun in June; the third, great and strong, as of calcining fire; the fourth, burning and vehement, as of fusion.' (11) A famous alchemical symbol of the last ball of fire is the phoenix's pyre, a classical emblem of the rubedo.

Created by a dying Roman civilization, the phoenix myth is closely related to the sun and the mystery of death and resurrection. Legend has it that the phoenix, when it saw death drawing near, made a nest of sweet-smelling wood and resins, which it exposed to the full force of the sun's rays. As the nest caught fire, the phoenix was burnt to ashes, but out of the ashes arose another phoenix—the bird's projected and immortal double. Along with the resurrected phoenix rose its infinitely multiplying offspring, flying out of its ashes and testifying to the bird's powers of endless reproduction (fig.399). Merging the flames of love and death, the phoenix symbolizes the adept's self-cremating passion, which in death sees the highest manifestation of love. The tail-eater is another symbol of this fusion of the existential opposites.

* The corresponding four stages of the animus may be outlined as follows: 1) Untransformed and primitive, the animus appears as sexual muscleman—Tarzan, boxer, athletic champion, etc. 2) Sublimated and idealized, the animus appears as romantic hero—poet, filmstar, explorer, political liberator, etc. 3) Elevated and spiritualized, the animus appears as spiritual guide—professor, clergyman, prophet, guru, etc. 4) Transcendentalized and etherized, the animus appears as the Illumined One—Christ, Buddha, Saint, etc. LSD-experiences confirm this ultimate transformation of soul. Masters and Houston report: 'The female guide may be seen as a goddess, as a priestess, or as the personification of wisdom or truth or beauty. Descriptions of some of these 'archetypal' perceptions have included seeing the guide's features as 'glowing with a luminous pallor' and her gestures as being 'cosmic, yet classical.' The clothing has been seen by subjects to change and 'flow,' from the vestments of an Egyptian Isis figure to the robes of an Athena. As a final metamorphosis she has sometimes become some variation of a sort of future space deity, hovering between stars and clad in garments of star dust, glacial ice, and so on . . . [Similarly,] the male guide may be seen as a Buddha or Buddha-like figure.' (5)

396. *The fire of self-cremating passion.*

The text within the woodcut reads:
Tracht fleisich disem Zael nach. Daru er ist gestellet auch.
Die Erd ist der Eleme uhrsprüng von dir Erd komen sie her und werden wider da zu bracht.
Visita
Interiora Terra Rer
Prudentia
Occultu
Simplicitas
ABC 123

397. *Final conquest of the heavenly stone: identification with All That There Is.*

Transformation into Cosmic Man

Figs. 397-398 show a last motif of the rubedo: the alchemist's incarnation as Anthropos, or 'cosmic man,' also identified with the second or heavenly Adam. Fig. 397 presents Basil Valentine's vision of the great stone, the Benedictine superman supporting as Atlas the cosmic globe with its multitude of stars, the earth occupying the centre. The sun is in Pisces, the moon in Aquarius, the circular work at its end. The inscription reads: 'Seek this poster with diligence: therefore it has been shown to you. The earth is the source of the elements; they come forth from the earth and return to it again.' The flying scroll is inscribed: 'Visit the interior parts of the earth; by rectifying thou shalt find the hidden stone.'

The three-headed bust of an antique philosopher conveys 'prudence,' the *infans philosophorum* with his ABC 'simplicity.' The union of these modes testifies to the Benedictine's attainment of the highest lucidity of which the human intellect is capable. The state of mind is that of child and genius. Says an alchemical treatise: 'The work is not brought to perfection unless it ends in the simple . . . for man is the most worthy of living things and nearest to the simple, and this because of his intelligence.' (1)

The woodcut reproduced in fig. 397 is accompanied by the verse:

*I am the one who carries heaven
    and earth,
While studying both with the
    utmost diligence.
First I display prudence,
    then simplicity,
That my day's wages may follow soon.*
    (2)

Fig. 398 renders another variant of the 'cosmic man' produced at the end of the opus. The corner emblems show the various alchemical tools: the Hermetic vase, the scales, the square, the ruler and the compasses. In the middle of the woodcut the alchemist's Christ-like figure conforms to a cross formed by the black dots that also run in a circle, thus symbolizing his union of two geometrical figures related to the squaring of the circle.

The central circle shows the alchemist's body as a union of the four elements, while the ring surrounding him demonstrates a parallel union of sun and moon, above and below, light and darkness, male and female. The reappearance of the alchemist's head at the top of the picture is a *proiectio* symbol, while the numbers represent the 'denarius,' anoth-

er symbol of wholeness and perfection (1 + 2 + 3 + 4).

The stone produced in fig. 397 may be amplified by a passage in the 'Rosinus ad Sarratantam Episcopum,' one of the oldest alchemical texts in Arabian style: 'This stone is below thee, as to obedience; above thee, as to dominion; therefore from thee, as to knowledge; about thee, as to equals . . . This stone is something which is fixed more in thee [than elsewhere], created of God, and thou art its ore, and it is extracted from thee, and wheresoever thou art it remains inseparably with thee . . . And as man is made up of the four elements, so also is the stone, and so it is [dug] out of man, and thou art its ore, namely by working; and from thee it is extracted, that is, by division; and in thee it remains inseparably, namely by knowledge. [To express it] otherwise, fixed in thee: namely in the Mercurius of the wise; thou art its ore: that is, it is enclosed in thee and thou holdest it secretly; and from thee it is extracted when it is reduced [to its essence] by thee and dissolved; for without thee it cannot be fulfilled, and without it canst thou not live, and so the end looks to the beginning, and contrariwise.' (3)

Frightening Experience of the One

The psychological implications of Basil Valentine's cosmic man may be amplified by a psychedelic experience of the same figure. Unexperienced and poorly guided, a young American journalist was hurled by 490 milligrams of mescaline to the same top of the mountain which Basil Valentine had conquered after a lifelong *opus circulatorium:*

'I didn't like what was happening. I was starting to remember something, and it seemed to have some connection with

398. *Cross and circle finally united.*

sunlight and a cradle. But what could it be? Then it came to me that I was gradually remembering my own identity, like an amnesia victim who slowly recovers his past. Finally it all fell together, and I remembered who I was. And it was so simple, really. I was life. I was Being. I was the vibrant force that filled the room, and was the room. I was the world, the universe. I was everything. I was that which always was and always would be. I was Jim [the guide], and Jim was me, and we were everybody else; and everybody else was us, and all of us put together were the same thing, and that same thing was the only thing there was. We were not God. We were simply all that there was, and all that there wasn't God. It was us, alone. And we were each other, and nowhere anywhere was there anything else but us, and we were always the same, the one and only truth.

'Jim,' I said, 'can you get me out of this?'

"Uh-huh. You want to try it another half-hour?'

'Yes,' I said. 'Let us try it another half-hour.'

'Having been reunited with the Ground of my Being, I wanted urgently to be estranged from it as quickly as possible. But I tried to hold on, at least for a while, and I tried to laugh at the terrifying idea that was building up in my mind. 'I don't want to be God,' I said. 'I don't even want to be city editor.' But it did no good to laugh, and I stopped trying. Of course I wasn't God, I knew that. But I was All That There Was, and I didn't want to be that, either. It was dark now, and I could hear children playing somewhere outside the hospital—under a street lamp, no doubt—and their lonely voices filled me with sadness. *The children*, I thought. The children, and Jim, and me: we were all the God there was. And it was sad and awful, because I wanted there to be a God. For the children at least, if not for me. But the loss of God was not the worst of it; there was something far worse even than that. The loss of my little self was not the worst of it; nor indeed did I regret that at all. It was what I had gained. I had gained the whole universe, it seemed, and that was more than I could cope with—more than I could bear.

'I didn't want it.

'But who was I, who didn't want it? I was Everybody, the Self. And now I knew what the little selves were for, I thought. They were a fiction designed to protect the Self from the knowledge of its own Being—to keep the Self from going mad. For surely, without them, the Self might be driven to insanity by the thought of its own audacity, and the thought of its loneliness, and the thought as well of the danger it was in. And it *was* in danger, I knew that perfectly well. Since it was All That There Was, there

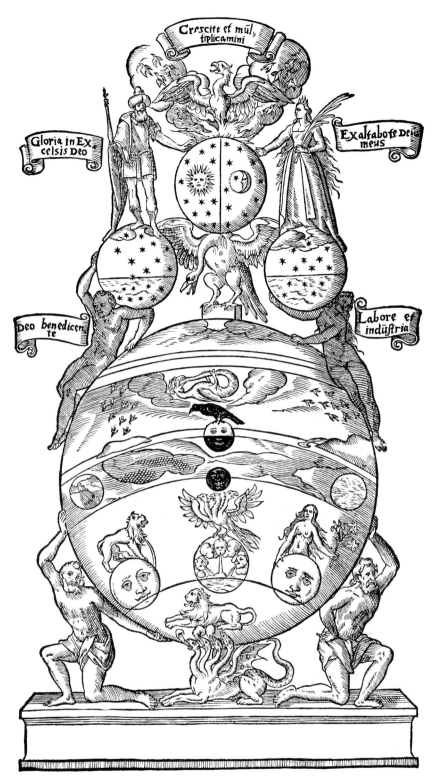

399. *Libavius' monument of the opus shows two giants supporting the sphere of the Little Work. The dragon and lion guard its entrance and the room of its first conjunction of the sun and moon. The blackening and whitening of their bodies in the nigredo and albedo finally lead to their second reunion in the full moon rising out of the silvery sea (top of sphere). Flights of birds ascending and descending frame 'a vision of heaven, where a dragon lies on his back devouring his tail, an image of the second coagulation.' (4) The completion of the Little Work 'by labour and industry' and 'by the grace of God' is followed by Sol and Luna's ascent on the Swan's wings. Their heavenly marriage in the Phoenix's sphere completes the Great Work. 'Increase and multiply' cries the bird of death and birth, accompanied by the thanksgivings of the Arab king and his white wife: 'Glory to God on High,' 'I exalt thee my God.'*

was nothing to assure it of its own immortality. And in fact, I could sense, there was that which resisted both its Being and Becoming. And this something was nothing more than Nothingness itself, against which the Self had exerted its ontic will to Become [fig.377]. Thus the ontic anxiety, as Tillich expressed it: the ultimate fear of ultimate non-Being . . .

'Oh God, we're not supposed to look at this. Not now. Maybe in a million years, or a billion years, or ten billion years. But not now, not yet. It was wrong to do this. The drug . . . not right . . . we shouldn't be fooling with . . .' My voice trailed off, and I thought about Freud. I thought that Freud didn't know what he was talking about, and the unconscious was very simple, really: the unconscious was this knowledge I now had of ultimate Being, and our repressions of it had their roots in an existential terror, not neurosis. It was real, and it was horrifying. It was more than most of us could accept, and thus we took refuge in smaller identities and well-defined roles, creating a limited world we could comfortably live in, pretending all the time there was Something Else. But there was nothing else, and deep down inside us we knew it, and we suffered. It took courage to Be, just as Tillich said, and most of us didn't have that courage. So we rejected our Being—and not by killing ourselves, because death was impossible, but by denying our real identity. By refusing to face what we actually were.

"Jim,' I said, 'we're all there is' . . . All That There Is. But even this—*even this*—was not the worst of it. I said that I was frightened by what I had gained, and this was true. But I had lost something, too, and it was more important to me than my wretched self, and more important even than God. For along with my own self I had lost all the other selves as well. I had lost other people. And I missed them very much. I wanted there to be someone else. Anyone else. And if there had been just two of us—really two of us—and we two were All That There Was, that would not have been so hard. But there was no one else; there was only the One . . .

"Jim,' I said, 'get me out of this.' So he got the Thorazine, and he got me out of it. And the doctors let me go home, where there was someone to meet me. 'I'm not going to hurt anybody,' I said. 'I'm just going to hurt.' I did, too, for several days. Then the mood wore off, and I went back to the world I knew, and I worked in it.

'Sometimes I would catch glimpses of that different world I had seen in the hospital room, and I would wonder if the experience was going to start all over again. But it never did . . . I include this epilogue simply as an item of interest, if it is, and certainly not as a testament. Obviously there were too many unknown factors involved to draw any conclusions.

Nevertheless, and just the same, it is something to think about. I shall think about it for the rest of my life.' (1)

Incarnation in the Source of Light

Fig.400 shows the 'reddened' alchemist incarnated in the midday sun. He is depicted as the 'fireplace of triple nature,' the 'vegetable, animal and mineral' realms symbolized by the golden flower, the philosophers' son and the planetary mountain. The big circle represents the 'globe of earth, water and air,' a gravid womb involving the alchemist in the 'fiat' of his own conception (centre of circle).

The fourth element is represented by the sun which forms the head of the meditating alchemist, thus symbolizing his 'solar' state of consciousness. Pregnant with the four elements in their ultimate state of unity, the transfigured alchemist appears as a full-breasted woman or hermaphrodite.

Illumination by the Lucid Dream

The solar state of the 'reddened' alchemist may be translated into psychodynamic terms. As we have seen, the final illumination of the opus is closely connected with the proiectio which we have equated with the out-of-the-body experience. A remarkable psychological feature is yet to be mentioned in this connection; although there is clear evidence that the out-of-the-body experience takes place at an unconscious level so deep that it fathoms the trauma of death, the experience is one of *full consciousness*. Jung observed that his 'visions and experiences were utterly real, not a product of imagination; there was nothing subjective about them; they all had a quality of absolute objectivity' (p.197). Karlis Osis noted about the deathbed hallucinations: 'The dying see visions with clear consciousness' (p.203).

All extant accounts of the out-of-the-body experience emphasize the same psychological feature: *the deep unconsciousness of the state is fully conscious!* This remarkable condition has been termed a 'lucid dream' by the Dutch doctor F.van Eeden who was one of the first to describe the out-of-the-body experience. (2) A modern authority on the subject, Celia Green, in her study on 'Lucid Dreams' (1968), defines the state as a dream in which the subject knows that he is dreaming; although asleep he is able to reflect rationally just as he has voluntary control over the course of his dream. 'Lucid dreams raise very important questions for philosophers and psychologists,' she goes on. 'If someone can critically examine his environment, asking himself whether he is dreaming, and concluding that he is not—although he is—what criterion can we use at any time to decide

whether we are awake or asleep? Are we to say that a person having a lucid dream is conscious or unconscious?' (3)

This question may be answered with the paradoxical statement that he is both. Applied to the alchemical symbolism of the rubedo, the above observations result in the conclusion that the lucid dream state of the out-of-the-body experience gives the psychological aspect of the last conjunction of the opus alchymicum. In the marvels of the proiectio conscious and unconscious, ego and self, earth and heaven are fused into a unity. Weightless in a pure body of light, the alchemist wakes up to a universe having no opposite, perceiving here the supreme illumination of the work: the Clear Light of the Void.

An alchemical treatise expresses the dynamic interplay and final assimilation of conscious and unconscious in the following way: 'So many times must the heaven above the earth be reproduced, until the earth becomes heavenly and spiritual, and heaven becomes earthly, and is joined to the earth; then the work will be finished.' (4) Another expression is the circular distillation of the elements: 'The circulation of spirits or circular distillation means the outside to the inside, the inside to the outside, likewise the lower and the upper; and when they meet together in one circle, you could no longer recognize what was outside or inside, or lower or upper; but all would be one thing in one circle or vessel. For this vessel is the true philosophical Pelican, and no other is to be sought for in all the universe.' (5)

In his last major work on alchemy Jung attempted to define the completed individuation process in terms of an 'approximation' and 'modification' of the conscious and unconscious positions within the psyche: '[The relations between the ego and the unconscious] are for the layman . . . a *terra incognita* which is not made any more accessible by broad generalizations. Even the imagination of the alchemists, otherwise so fertile, fails us completely here. Only a thorough investigation of the texts could shed a little light on this question. The same task challenges our endeavours in the field of psychotherapy. Here too are thousands of images, symbols, dreams, fantasies and visions that still await comparative research. The only thing that can be said with some certainty at present is that there is a gradual process of approximation whereby the two positions, the conscious and unconscious, are both modified.' (6)

Jung's cautious formulation is dwarfed by the actual dynamics of the individuation process in its final transition where the out-of-the-body experience leads to the lucid dream state in which man's conscious and unconscious minds are finally made one.

J. J.
BECHERI
Spirensis
Med: D:
S.Cæs. Maj:
Consiliarij.
Mille
HYPOTHESES
Chymicæ
De
SVBTERRANEIS
M.D.C.LXVIII
TRIPLEX NATVRÆ OFFICINA
AER
Vegetabilis
Animalis
Mineralis
AQVA
TERRA

400. The alchemical engraving of the solified adept at the end of the Great Work forms the frontispiece of a book by J. J. Becher 'Spirensis Med. D. Caes. Maj. Consilarij.' entitled 'One Thousand Chemical Hypotheses Concerning the Subterranean Realms, 1668.'

401.

Psychedelic Psychology: the 'New Alchemy'

Figs.401-402 render the concluding stage of the alchemical work in two modern, psychedelic versions. Fig.401 shows Michael Green's LSD-vision of the Buddha in nirvana: 'Gautama centred his mind and body. He spun through the thousand past reincarnations. Tumbled down his DNA code and died, merging in the centre of the solar, lunar, diamond, peacock eye of fire that men call God. Illumination.' (1)

The right half of the Buddha's face forms a skull, or a symbol of death, extinction, the Void. The left half of the Indian's face renders the nirvana state of the Illumined One, enclosed in his primordial germ cell and sharing its libidinal indifference. The LSD-Buddha is surrounded by the fantastic vegetation of the 'philosophers' garden,' appearing as a teeming realm of oocytes, follicles, body cells, DNA molecules and dividing cells. (One cell-division is depicted at the bottom of the drawing, the other in the

space outside the Buddha's dark jaw.)

An equally interesting cell-division and primal yin-yang cell appear in the LSD-inspired 'Evolution Mandala' by Dion Wright reproduced on the opposite page. The primordial germ cell of all creation is depicted in the centre of the mandala, where a chain of DNA molecules encircles the protoplasma underlying all cellular creation. Appropriately, this centre is inscribed 'We are all one.' The bottom half of the mandala shows the primeval mitosis of the primordial germ cell, or the first act of generation from which the rest of creation has resulted, man included.

The protoplasma, or 'primal matter,' of the first cell is constituted by the four elements of organic life—hydrogen (H), oxygen (O), carbon (C), and nitrogen (N)—which in a 'circular distillation' with solar energy are supposed to have formed the first living molecules on earth.

The Phylogenetic Unconscious

The drawing suggests the possibility of an LSD-induced re-experience of the whole course of evolution. This, indeed, is possible in a subtle way; the fact is that the individual's biological development from primordial germ cell to nine-month-old fetus describes the entire evolution in a kind of concentrated summary. This idea was formulated by the German biologist Ernst Haeckel, whose biogenetic law states that the individual's biological evolution, or ontogenesis, represents a summary of the biological evolution of the race, or phylogenesis. During fetal development the individual experiences in an analogous way all the stages that earth's living creatures have gone through in their billion-year-old evolution.

Man has once been through the stages corresponding to those of one-celled organisms, worms, fishes, reptiles, and mammals. *Man as primordial germ cell corresponds to the creation of the first cell on earth. Man's primeval mitosis corresponds to the first cell's division or generation of itself, the crucial beginning of all evolution.*

The ego's experience of phylogenesis through ontogenesis, that is, its analogous recapitulation of the whole evolutionary sequence of life on this planet, is graphically rendered by fig.402, which reveals the cosmic dimension of the regressive process described in this study. Timothy Leary has given us a vivid, if characteristically extravagant, account of the ego's experience of the *phylogenetic unconscious* in LSD-induced regressions:

'The Psychedelic Correlates of these evolutionary and genetic concepts are to be found in the reports of almost every LSD tripper. The experience of being a one-celled creature tenaciously flailing, the singing, humming sound of life exfoliating; you are the DNA code spinning out multicellular aesthetic solutions. You directly and immediately experience invertebrate joy; you feel your backbone forming; gills form. You are a fish with glistening gills, the sound of ancient foetal tides murmuring the rhythm of life. You stretch and wriggle in mammalian muscular strength, loping, powerful, big muscles; you sense hair growing on your body as you leave the warm broth of water and take over the earth.' (2)

'Is it entirely inconceivable that our cortical cells or the machinery inside the cellular nucleus 'remember' back along the unbroken chain of electrical transformations that connects every one of us back to that original thunderbolt in the Precambrian mud? Impossible, you say? Read a genetics text. Read and reflect about the DNA chain of complex protein molecules that took you as a uni-celled organism at the moment of your

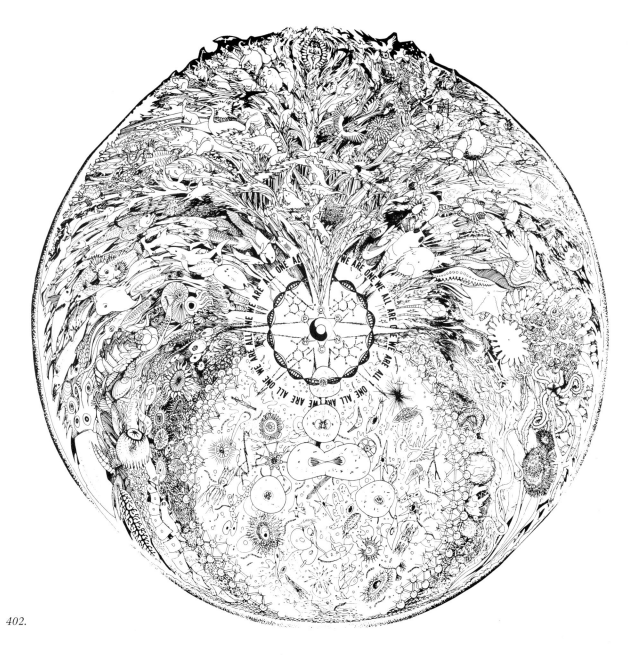

402.

The Cosmic Unconscious

conception and planned every stage of your natural development. Half of that genetic blueprint was handed to you intact by your mother and half by your father, and then slammed together in that incredible welding process we call conception.

"You,' your ego, your good old American social self, have been trained to remember certain crucial secular-game landmarks: your senior prom, your wedding day. But is it not possible that others of your 10 billion brain cells 'remember' other critical survival cross-roads, like conception, intra-uterine events, birth? Events for which our language has few or no descriptive terms? Every cell in your body is the current carrier of an energy torch which traces back through millions of generation transformations. Remember that genetic code?' (3)

Masters and Houston and many other researchers have confirmed Leary's contention that this kind of evolutionary 'trip' is experienced by a sizeable proportion of subjects taking LSD. Stanislav Grof, who appears to be as careful and methodical a researcher as Leary is a flamboyant one, has also independently arrived at conclusions which are nearly identical:

'In this type of [phylogenetic or evolutionary] experience the subject identifies with his animal ancestors on various levels of development; this is accompanied by a realistic feeling that the subject is exploring his own evolutionary pedigree. The identification is rather complex, complete and authentic; it involves the body image, a variety of physical feelings and physiological sensations, specific emotions, and a new perception of the environment. Occasionally the subjects report insight into zoological or ethological facts that by far exceed the level of their education in natural sciences. In addition, the experiences involved appear to be qualitatively different from human experiences and frequently even seem to transcend the scope of human fantasy and imagination. The subject can have, for example, an illuminating insight into what it feels like when a snake is hungry, when a turtle is sexually excited, or when a salmon breathes through its gills. Identification is most frequent with other mammals, with birds, reptiles, amphibians and various species of fish. Occasionally, the subjects report identification with much less differentiated forms of life, such as coelenterates or even unicellular organisms. Evolutionary experiences are sometimes accompanied by changes in neurological reflexes and certain abnormal motor phenomena that appear to be related to the activation of archaic neuronal pathways.' (4)

Another noted LSD-scientist, W.V. Caldwell, describes the 'unicellular' experience as 'a return to an almost protoplasmic state of organization, to the very lowest level of vital organization that can support awareness.' (5) Timothy Leary has termed this phase of the psychedelic regression the 'solar (soul) stage' and described it as the ego's 'awareness of energy transactions among molecular structures inside the cell—triggered off by large doses (300 gammas) of LSD.' (6) Leary goes on to define 'molecular psychology' or 'psychophysics' as the 'study of the interactions between the nervous system and the molecular events inside the body.' (7)

At this ultimate level of consciousness centred on structures within the body, the ego is involved in what Leary calls 'soletics' or 'atomic-nuclear dramas.' (8) This is so because molecules are made up of *atoms* and because atoms participate in the most fundamental process of universal creation—the creative mystery of *light*.

In this final, stupendous transition the ego is involved in an experience of what might be termed the 'extra-terrestrial unconscious' or 'cosmic unconscious.' The transition is realized in the out-of-the-body experience which gives the *ego's incarnation in the body of light*. The event signifies the involvement of consciousness in the ultimate force in the universe, in the mysteries of Creation and the Void, being and non-being, the nature of Universal Mind, the essence of the Cosmic Self.

This is the goal of the opus alchymicum, which with the attainment of the 'solar' condition comes to an end. States the 'Tabula smaragdina,' or 'Emerald Table of Hermes,' the *Magna Charta* of alchemy:

'1. True, without deceit, certain and most true.

2. What is below, is like what is above, and what is above is like that which is below, for the performing of the marvels of the One.

3. And as all things proceed from the One, through the meditation of the One: so all things proceed from this one thing, by adaptation.

4. Its father is the sun, its mother is the moon; the wind hath carried it in its belly; its nurse is the earth.

5. This is the father of all the perfection of the whole world.

6. Its power is complete when it is turned towards the earth.

7. You shall separate the earth from the fire, the subtle from the gross, smoothly and with great cleverness.

8. It ascends from the earth to heaven, and descends again to the earth, and receives the power of the higher and the lower things. So shall you have the glory of the whole world. So shall all obscurity yield before thee.

9. This is the strong fortitude of all fortitude: because it will overcome every subtle thing and penetrate every solid.

10. Thus was the world created.

11. Hence will there be marvellous adaptations, of which this is the means.

12. And so I am called Hermes Trismegistus, as having three parts of the philosophy of the whole world.

13. What I have said concerning the operation of the sun is finished.' (9)

Acknowledgements

I am deeply indebted to cand. med. et pharm. Svend Aage Damgaard Nielsen for help and inspiration during the initial stages of this book. Seminarielektor, dr. phil. Vagn Lundgaard Simonsen and universitetslektor, cand. mag. Andreas Simonsen generously assisted with the Latin translations. The librarians Bernt Løppenthin, Eilert Corvinius, Martha Weis Clausen, Poul Aagaard Christiansen, and Else Weise from the University Library, Department II, Copenhagen, helped me in numerous ways in the course of my work with the library's alchemical collection, one of the finest in the world. Ellen Bick Meier patiently corrected the English manuscript, and Vilhelm Jensen carefully photographed the old engravings at Robert W. Peyraths Klicheanstalt. For personal help during the preparation of this book I wish to express my sincere thanks to Vera and Carl Johan Michaelsen, Grethe and Robert W. Peyrath, Mogens Bang, Kirsten Fabricius, Erik Langhoff, and Finn Jacobsen. The book is dedicated to my aunt, Gertrud Nielsen.

Bibliography

Italics indicate the references used in the notes.

Anatomiae auri: Mylius, Johann Daniel: Anatomiae auri sive tyrocinium medico-chymicum. Frankfort, 1628.

Ars chemica: Ars chemica, quod sit licita recte exercentibus, probationes doctissimorum iurisconsultorum . . . Strasbourg, 1566.

Artis aurif.: Artis auriferae quam chemiam vocant . . . Basel, 1610. 3 vols. The edition quoted in this study.

Artis aurif. (1593): The edition quoted by Jung.

Artis aurif. (1572): The edition quoted by Jong.

At. fugiens: Maier, Michael: Atalanta fugiens. Frankfort, 1617.

Aureum vellus: Aureum vellus, oder Güldin Schatz und Kunstkammer . . . von dem . . . bewehrten Philosopho Salomone Trismosino . . . disponiert. Hamburg, 1708.

Aurora consurgens: Aurora consurgens. Edited, with a commentary, by Marie-Louise von Franz. London, 1966.

Barchusen: Barchusen, Johann Conrad: Elementa chemiae. Leiden, 1718.

Berthelot: Berthelot, Marcellin: Collection des anciens alchimistes Grecs. Paris, 1887-88. 3 vols.

Berthelot: Chimie: Berthelot, M.: La chimie au moyen âge. Paris, 1893. 3 vols.

Bibl. chem.: Mangetus, Joannes Jacobus (ed): Bibliotheca chemica curiosa. Geneva, 1702. 2 vols.

Blos: Blos, Peter: On Adolescence, A Psychoanalytic Interpretation. New York, 1967.

Boschius: Boschius, Jacobus: Symbolographia. Augsburg, 1702.

Buntz: Buntz, Herwig: Deutsche alchimistische Traktate des 15. und 16. Jahrhunderts. Munich, 1969.

Caldwell: Caldwell, W. V.: LSD Psychotherapy. New York, 1968.

Cameron: Cameron, Norman: Personality Development and Psychopathology. Yale, 1963.

Cohen: Cohen, Sidney: The Beyond Within: the LSD Story. New York, 1967.

Deutsches Theatr. chem.: Roth-Scholz, Friedrich (ed.): Deutsches Theatrum chemicum. Nuremberg, 1728-32. 3 vols.

Dyas chymica: H. C. D.: Dyas chymica tripartita. Frankfort, 1625.

Eleazar: Eleazar, Abraham: Uraltes chymisches Werk. Leipzig, 1760.

Franz: Aurora consurgens. Edited, with a commentary, by Marie-Louise von Franz. London, 1966.

Freud GW 2/3: Freud, Sigmund: Die Traumdeutung. Über den Traum. London, 1942. Gesammelte Werke, vol.2/3.

Freud GW 8: Werke aus den Jahren 1909-1913. London, 1943. Ges. Werke, vol.8.

Freud GW 9: Totem und Tabu. London, 1944. Ges. Werke, vol.9

Freud GW 11: Vorlesungen zur Einführung in die Psychoanalyse. London, 1944. Ges. Werke, vol.11.

Freud GW 12: Werke aus den Jahren 1917-1920. London, 1947. Ges. Werke, vol.12.

Freud GW 13: Jenseits des Lustprinzips. Massen-Psychologie und Ich-Analyse. Das Ich und das Es. London, 1940. Ges. Werke, vol.13.

Freud GW 14: Werke aus den Jahren 1925-1931. London, 1948. Ges. Werke, vol.14.

Freud GW 15: Neue Folge der Vorlesungen zur Einführung in die Psychoanalyse. London, 1944. Ges. Werke, vol.15.

Freud GW 16: Werke aus den Jahren 1932-1939. London, 1950. Ges. Werke, vol.16.

Freud GW 17: Schriften aus dem Nachlass. London, 1941. Ges. Werke, vol.17.

Geber: Darmstaedter, Ernst: Die Alchemie des Geber. Berlin, 1922.

Gray: Gray, Ronald D.: Goethe the Alchemist. Cambridge, 1952.

Grossen Stein: Basilius Valentinus: Ein kurtzer summarischer Tractat von dem grossen Stein der Uhralten. Zerbst, 1602.

Hartmann: Essays: Hartmann, Heinz: Essays on Ego Psychology. New York, 1964.

Holmeyard: Holmeyard, E. J.: Alchemy. London, 1957.

Hyginus: Hyginus, C. J.: Fabularum liber. Paris, 1578.

Jacobson: Self and Object World: Jacobson, Edith: The Self and the Object World. London, 1965.

Jong: Jong, H. M. E. de: Michael Maier's Atalanta fugiens. Leiden, 1969.

Jung CW 5: Jung, Carl Gustav: Symbols of Transformation. London, 1956. Coll. Wks., vol.5.

Jung CW 6: Psychological Types. London, 1960. Coll. Wks., vol.6.

Jung CW 7: Two Essays on Analytical Psychology. London, 1953. Coll. Wks., vol.7.

Jung CW 8: The Structures and Dynamics of the Psyche. London, 1960. Coll. Wks., vol.8.

Jung CW 9.1: The Archetypes and the Collective Unconscious. London, 1959. Coll. Wks., vol.9.1.

Jung CW 9.2: Aion. London, 1959. Coll. Wks., vol.9.2.

Jung CW 10: Civilization in Transition. London, 1964. Coll. Wks., vol.10.

Jung CW 11: Psychology and Religion. East and West. London, 1958. Coll. Wks., vol.11.

Jung CW 12: Psychology and Alchemy. London, 1953. Coll. Wks., vol.12.

Jung CW 13: Alchemical Studies. London, 1967. Coll. Wks., vol.13.

Jung CW 14: Mysterium Coniunctionis. London, 1963. Coll. Wks., vol.14.

Jung CW 15: The Spirit in Man, Art, and Literature. London, 1966. Coll. Wks., vol.15.

Jung CW 16: The Practice of Psychotherapy. London, 1954. Coll. Wks., vol.16.

Jung: Memories: Jung, C. G.: Memories, Dreams, Reflections. New York, 1963.

Kessler: Psychopathology: Kessler, Jane W.: Psychopathology of Childhood. Englewood Cliffs, 1966.

Klein: Contributions: Klein, Melanie: Contributions to Psycho-Analysis 1921-1945. New York, 1964.

Klein: Developments: Klein, M. and others: Developments in Psycho-Analysis. London, 1952.

Klein: Envy and Gratitude: Klein, M.: Envy and Gratitude. London, 1957.

Klein: New Directions: Klein, M. and others: New Directions in Psychoanalysis. London, 1955.

Klein: Psa. of Children: Klein, M.: The Psycho-Analysis of Children. London, 1969.

Kopp: Kopp, Hermann: Die Alchemie in älterer und neuerer Zeit. Heidelberg, 1886. 2 vols.

Mahler: Child Psychosis: Mahler, Margaret: On Child Psychosis and Schizophrenia. The Psychoanalytic Study of the Child, vol.7, pp.286-303.

Mahler: On Symbiotic Child Psychosis: Mahler, Margaret and Gosliner, Bertram J.: On Symbiotic Child Psychosis. The Psychoanalytic Study of the Child, vol.10, pp.195-211.

Mahler: Sadness: Mahler, Margaret: On Sadness and Grief in Infancy and Childhood. The Psychoanalytic Study of the Child, vol.16, pp. 332-349.

Masters and Houston: Masters, R. E. L. and Houston, Jean: The Varieties of Psychedelic Experience. New York, 1966.

Medicina catholica: Fludd, Robert: Medicina catholica. Frankfort, 1629.

Michelspacher: Michelspacher, Steffan: Cabala, speculum artis et naturae, in alchymia. Augsburg, 1654.

Mus. herm.: Musaeum hermeticum reformatum et amplificatum . . . Frankfort, 1678.

Occulta philosophia: Basilius Valentinus: De occulta philosophia. Von den vorborgenen Philosophischen Geheimnussen der heimlichen Goldblumen und Lapidis Philosophorum. Frankfort, 1603.

Pandora: Reusner, Hieronymus: Pandora: Das ist, die edelst Gab Gottes, oder der Werde und heilsame Stein der Weysen. Basel, 1582.

Phil. ref.: Mylius, Johann Daniel: Philosophia reformata. Frankfort, 1622.

Pret. marg.: Bonus, Petrus: The New Pearl of Great Price. London, 1963. English translation by Waite, Arthur Edward after Bonus, Petrus: Pretiosa margarita novella. Edited by Janus Lacinius Calabrus. Venice, 1546.

Psa. St. of Child: The Psychoanalytic Study of the Child, edited by Ruth S. Eissler, Anna Freud, Heinz Hartmann, Marianne Kris. New York, 1945-76.

Quinta essentia: Thurneisser zum Thurn, Leonhard: Quinta essentia. Leipzig, 1574.

Rank: Inzest: Rank, Otto: Das Inzest-Motif in Dichtung und Sage. Leipzig, 1926.

Rank: Trauma: Rank, O.: Das Trauma der Geburt und ihre Bedeutung für die Psychoanalyse. Leipzig, 1924.

Rosarium: Rosarium philosophorum. Printed as second part of De alchimia opuscula. Frankfort, 1550. No pagination. Reprinted in Artis auriferae, q. v.

Ruland: Ruland, Martin: Lexicon alchemiae, sive Dictionarium alchemisticum. Frankfort, 1612.

Silberer: Silberer, Herbert: Probleme der Mystik und ihrer Symbolik. Vienna, 1914.

Splendor solis: Trismosin, Salomon: Splendor solis . . . With explanatory notes by J. K. London, 1920. See also Aureum vellus.

Summum bonum: Fludd, Robert: Summum bonum. Frankfort, 1629.

Symbola aureae: Maier, Michael: Symbola aureae mensae duodecim nationum. Frankfort, 1617.

Theatr. chem.: Theatrum chemicum, praecipuos selectorum auctorum tractatus . . . Ursel, 1602, vols.I-III. Strasbourg, 1613, vol.IV. Strasbourg, 1622, vol.V. Strasbourg, 1661, vol.VI. The edition quoted by Jung CW 12, CW 14 and CW 16.

Theatr. chem. (1659, 1660, 1661): Theatrum chemicum. Strasbourg, 1659, vols.I-IV; 1660, vol.V; 1661, vol.VI. The edition quoted by Jung CW 13.

Theatr. chem. britannicum: Theatrum chemicum britannicum . . . collected with annotations by Elias Ashmole. London, 1652.

Turba: Ruska, Julius Ferdinand (ed.): Turba philosophorum. Berlin, 1931.

Utriusque cosmi: Fludd, Robert: Utriusque cosmi maioris scilicet et minoris metaphysica, physica atque technica historia. Oppenheim, 1617. 2 vols.

Viridarium: Stolcius de Stolcenberg, Daniel: Viridarium chymicum figuris cupro incisis adornatum et poeticis picturis illustratum. Frankfort, 1624.

Waite: The Hermetic Museum Restored and Enlarged. London, 1893. 2 vols. A translation of *Musaeum hermeticum* by Arthur E. Waite.

Notes

A name in parenthesis refers to the engraver.

6-7

Figs.1-2. Petrarcha, Francesco: Das Glückbuch Beydes des Guten und Bösen. Augsburg, 1539, pp.CVI and LV (the Petrarcha Master).
Fig.3. Khunrath, Heinrich Conrad: Amphitheatrum sapientiae aeternae. Hanau, 1604 (Paul van der Doort).

8-9

Fig.4. Sabor, C. F. von: Practica naturae vera. N. p. o. p. o. o., 1721, frontispiece.
Fig.5. Michelspacher, emblema I (Rafael Custodis after a drawing by S. Michelspacher). The picture series of the opus printed in this treatise consists of 4 large engravings reproduced in figs.5, 81, 167, 386.

10-11

Fig.6. Geber: De alchimia libri tres. Argentoratum, 1531, p.VII.
Fig.7. Ulstad, Phillip: Celum philosophorum. Strasbourg, 1527, p.LXI.
Fig.8a. Porta, Giambattista della: De distillationibus. Strasbourg, 1609, p.43.
Fig.8b. Libavius, Andreas: Syntagmatis selectorum. Frankfort, 1615, p.413.
Figs.9-13. Porta, Giambattista della: op. cit., pp.40, 43, 40, 42, 41.
1. Theatr. chem., I, p.164. CW 12 § 349.
2. Bibl. chem., I, p.875. CW 12 § 351.
3. Mus. herm., p.693. Waite, II, p.193.
4. Quoted after Jung, C. G. and others: Man and his Symbols. London, 1964, p.27.
5. Hoghelande: Liber de alchimiae difficultatibus. Theatr. chem., I, p.199. CW 12 § 350.
6. Ruland, under *imaginatio.* CW 12 § 394.
7. Artis aurif., II, p.139. CW 12 § 218, 360.
8. Ruland, p.327. CW 12 § 390. CW 14 § 707.
9. Cf. Jung CW 14 § 157-159.

12-13

Fig.14. Theatr. chem. britannicum, p.12.

14-15

Fig.17. Phil. ref., p.117 (B. Schwan).
Fig.18. Ibid., p.96 (B. Schwan).
Fig.19. Utriusque cosmi, II, p.219 (M. Merian). Robert Fludd (1574-1637) was an English physician, interested in natural sciences, alchemy, astronomy and occult sciences. His unfinished work *Utriusque cosmi maioris* appeared in the same year as the *Atalanta fugiens*, in 1617 at Oppenheim, with the same publisher and engraver. Both Robert Fludd and Michael Maier were prominent defenders of the Fraternity of the Rosicrucians and probably knew each other.
1. The Ordinal of Alchemy is printed in Theatr. chem. britannicum, pp.13-106 and in Mus. herm., pp.434-532. Waite, II, pp.1-67.
2. Mus. herm., p.444. Waite, II, p.12.
3. Theatr. chem., V, p.252. CW 16 § 414 n.7. Cf. Mus. herm., p.341. Waite, I, p.275. Senior was an Arabian alchemist by the name of Muhammad ibn Umail at-Tamimi (c. 900-960), whose *Book of the Silvery Water and Starry Earth* was edited by E. Stapleton and M. Hidayat Husain in vol.12 of the *Memoirs of the Asiatic Society of Bengal* (1933). The Latin translation of this treatise was printed in Strasbourg 1566 under the title *De Chemia Senioris antiquissimi philosophi libellus.* Reprints in Bibl. chem., II, and Theatr. chem., V.
4. Agrippa von Nettesheim: De incertitudine et vanitate omnium scientiarum. The Hague, 1653, ch.XC. CW 16 § 414.
5. See Jung CW 12 § 333 and Read, John: Prelude to Chemistry. London, 1936, p.146. One of the earliest testimonies of a definite structure of the alchemical work is presented by the *Turba philosophorum* (ed. Ruska, pp.137-138). The treatise consists of 70 sermons and was composed between 850 and 950 by an Arabian author adapting the tenets and ideas of Pre-Socratic natural philosophy. The *Turba* was regarded as a kind of Bible by the alchemists.
6. Dorn: Speculativae philosophiae. Theatr. chem., I, p.308. CW 14 § 118.
7. Phil. ref., p.117.
8. Artis aurif., II, p.233. CW 16 § 531. CW 12 § 142.

16-17

Fig.20. Barchusen, p.503.
Fig.21a and b. Dyas chymica, plates 5 and 7.
Fig.22a and b. Ibid., plate 2 (M. Merian).
Fig.23. Splendor solis, plate 1.
1. Johann Conrad Barchusen tells us that his engraved picture series was copied from 'a handwritten book in a Benedictine monastery in Swabia' (op. cit., p.503). After ten years of search, the author of this study finally, in 1968, succeeded in discovering this 'handwritten book' in the Sidney M. Edelstein Foundation Library, New York. The manuscript, which consists of 67 water-colours, is entitled *The Crowne of Nature or the doctrine of the souereigne medecene declared in 67 Hierogliphycall fugurs by a namlese Author.* As the manuscript refers to the *Rosarium philosophorum* (1550), and as its first water-colour probably copies a woodcut in Giovanni Battista Nazari's *Della transmutatione metallica sogni tre* (1599), we may date *The Crowne of Nature* to the early part of the 17th century. Barchusen's engraved version of the illuminated manuscript contains 78 pictures as compared to the 67 pictures of the original; however, the two versions are identical, and Barchusen's added pictures (plates 1-6, 9, 16-17, 74, 77-78) merely amplify the symbolic-pictorial action of the original. *The Crowne of Nature* builds heavily on the *Rosarium* and may be described as a paraphrase of this treatise, its amplifications, however, being of a highly original quality. The *Barchusen/Crowne of Nature* series of the opus is reproduced in figs.20, 24, 46, 70, 105, 135, 154, 179, 198, 206, 210, 217, 228, 240, 262, 271, 283, 287, 291, 306, 329, 335, 353.
2. The 1582 version in the British Museum (Ms. Harley 3469) of Salomon Trismosin's *Splendor solis* is a copy of the German original, which was produced in the second quarter of the 16th century. The whole opus is here depicted in 22 paintings. The paintings reproduced in this study derive from the 1582 version, faithful to the original but superior in artistic execution. They are reproduced in figs.23, 38, 44, 45, 60, 63, 131, 161, 164, 171, 202, 205, 248-253, 290, 347, 365. The penultimate painting is reproduced on p.243, fig.21. According to Kopp (I, p.243), Salomon Trismosin, the reputed 'preceptor' of Paracelsus, is a fictitious figure. He is stated as the author of some of the treatises in the *Aureum vellus,* a collection of alchemical treatises printed at Rorschach, 1598.
3. Splendor solis, p.17. Hali is a corruption of Kalid ibn Yazid (660-704), the Arabian Omayyad prince who according to legend translated Greek treatises on alchemy into Arabic. His oft-quoted *Liber trium verborum* is generally regarded as a Latin, medieval forgery.
4. Artis aurif., II, p.138.
5. Kirchweger, Anton Joseph: Aurea Catena Homeri. Leipzig, 1728, ch.x and p.180. For accounts of the *putrefactio,* see Jung CW 12 § 334. CW 14 § 114, 494, 714. CW 16 § 375. Silberer, pp.81, 202. Gray, pp.12-17.

18-19

Fig.24. Barchusen, p.503.
Fig.25. Rosarium woodcut 1550. Jung's analysis in CW 16 § 404-409. The secret doctrine of alchemy and the structure of the *opus alchymicum* have been expressed by a number of picture series, the most important of which is the *Rosarium philosophorum.* The medieval treatise was first printed 1550 in Frankfort as part II of the collection *De alchimia opuscula* and accompanied by 20 woodcuts based on original draw-

14-15

Fig.15. Basil Valentine: Revelation des mysteres des teintures essentielles des sept metaux. Paris, 1668 (engraving on title-page). The picture shows the mythical Benedictine 'Brother Basilius Valentine, the Philosopher of the West' at the end of the Great Work, his right hand holding the elixir of life, his left clutching the Twelfth Key. Behind him, the masculine and feminine principles merge in the Solomonic Seal, gilded by the united sun and moon. Alchemical books and bottles fill the monk's laboratory, illustrating the two aspects of alchemy, those of 'Theoria' and 'Practica.' Opposite, 'Hermes Trismegistus, the Philosopher of the East' watches a reflector exploiting the sun's energies in his laboratory. The viola da gamba and the organ express the harmony of the spheres and the heavenly music perceived at the end of the Great Work. The inscription reads: 'Sing for the Lord on strings and instruments'; 'Holy harmony drives away the evil spirits; Saturn is the medicine against intemperance.'
Fig.16. Mus. herm., p.373. Waite, I, p.307 (M. Merian). The three figures to the left depict Basil Valentine, Thomas Norton and Cremer, Abbot of Westminster, all famous figures of alchemy.
1. Jung CW 14, pp.xiii-xiv.
2. Jung CW 16 § 497.
3. Artis aurif., II, p.138. CW 16 § 411, 413.

ings now lost together with the manuscript. The *Rosarium* is a compilation whose historical components have not yet been sorted out. The author is anonymous but the treatise has been ascribed to Petrus Toletanus or his alleged brother, Arnold of Villanova, both living in the second half of the 13th century. The dating of the *Rosarium* is much disputed: Berthelot assigns it to the middle of the 14th century (Berthelot: Chimie, I, p.234), Ruska to the middle of the 15th century (Turba, p.342). Jung speculates along the following lines: 'The present form of the *Rosarium* based on the first printing of 1550 is a compilation and probably does not date back further than the 15th century' (CW 11 § 92 n.31). This conclusion is supported by the fact that at least four woodcuts are derived from *The Book of the Holy Trinity*, written by an anonymous German alchemist at the time of the Council of Constance (1414-1418). See Buntz, p.37.

When in 1622 the German physician and alchemist Johann Daniel Mylius published a condensed version of the *Rosarium* in his *Philosophia reformata*, the Frankfort engraver Balthazar Schwan furnished him with engraved variants of the original 20 woodcuts. Throughout this study both series are printed side by side; a comparison between them reveals the faithfulness of Schwan to his original, even if there are some important variations, notably in figs.12-16 [figs.273, 280, 289, 293, 301] and in fig.19 [fig.338]. (Schwan has endowed each of his engravings with a number in its left upper corner.) The *Rosarium* series of the opus is reproduced in figs.25, 36, 54, 106, 136, 176, 180, 199, 229, 241, 263, 274, 281, 288, 292, 300, 307, 330, 336, 354. Balthazar Schwan's engraved variations of the *Rosarium* woodcuts are reproduced in figs.26, 35, 58, 107, 137, 175, 181, 201, 230, 242, 264, 273, 280, 289, 293, 301, 308, 331, 338, 355.
Fig.26. Phil. ref., p.224 (B. Schwan after fig.25).
Fig.27. Vreeswyck, Goosen van: De Goude Leeuw. Amsterdam, 1672, p.100.
1. Bibl. chem., II, p.656. CW 12 § 476 n.138.
2. As mentioned above, *The Crowne of Nature* depends heavily on the *Rosarium* and may be described as a paraphrase of this treatise.
3. Artis aurif., II, p.137.
4-6. Ibid., pp.137, 138, 139.
7. Viridarium, fig.LXXXI.

20-21
Fig.28. Coenders van Helpen, Barent: Tresor de la philosophie des anciens. Cologne, 1693, p.29.
Fig.29a and b. Dyas chymica, plate 5.
Fig.30a and b. Ibid., plates 3 and 7 (M. Merian).
Fig.31. Marolles, Michel de: Tableaux du temple des muses. Paris, 1655, 1er Tableau.
1. Aurora consurgens, p.51. An alchemical compilation whose components have been sorted out by Marie-Louise von Franz, q. v. She dates the treatise to the middle or second half of the 13th century.
2. Artis aurif.,(1593), I, p.293. CW 13 § 429 n.6.
3. Dee: Monas hieroglyphica. Theatr. chem. (1659), II, p.196. CW 13 § 429 n.6.
4. Ibid., p.258. CW 13 § 429 n.6. For an account of 'The Dangers of the Art,' see Jung CW 13 § 429-435. For a description of the prima materia and a discussion of its meaning, see Jung CW 12 § 425-466 and Silberer, pp.80-102.
5. Theatr. chem. (1659), I, p.160. CW 13 § 429 n.8. Cf. also Artis aurif. (1593), II, p.264. CW

13 § 429 n.1. Alphidius is reported to have been an Arabian alchemist living in the 12th century. His sayings were widely acclaimed in early medieval literature. The dating may be true only of the Lation translations of his works. Probably Alphidius is identical with the Alkides or Assiduus cited by Senior. See Franz, p.15.
6. Artis aurif. (1593), I, p.83. CW 13 § 429 n.1.
7. See Jung CW 12 § 429.
8. Theatr. chem. (1659), I, p.182. CW 13 § 429. For psychedelic experiences of the 'primal matter,' see Cohen, pp.42-43, 131-132, 177-178, 242 and Masters and Houston, pp.63, 98-99, 152.
9. Phil. ref., p.305. CW 14 § 246 n.441.
10. Atwood, M. A.: Hermetic Philosophy and Alchemy. New York, 1960, p.124. CW 12 § 103 n.36. The *Tractatus aureus* is ascribed to Hermes and is of Arabian origin. CW 12 § 454.
11. Berthelot, III, ii, 1 and III, vi, 6. Franz, p.161. Zosimos was a Greek alchemist writing about 300 and combining the worlds of Egyptian magic, Greek philosophy, Gnosticism, Neo-Platonism, Babylonian astrology and Christian theology. His corrupted name in alchemy is Rosinus. See Jung CW § 456-461.
12. Turba, p.122. Franz, p.161.
13. Sendivogius: Novum lumen chemicum. Mus. herm., p.574. CW 12 § 350.
14. Ibid., pp.87-88. Waite, I, pp.79-80.

22-23
Figs.32-33. Symbola aureae, pp.141, 91.
Fig.34. Medicina catholica, preface (no pagination) (M. Merian).
1. Jung CW 12 § 41 and 439. For Jung's concept of the shadow, see CW 7 § 103 and CW 16 § 124-146.
2. Jung CW 8 § 14. See also CW 13 § 335.
3. Symbola aurcae, p.141. CW 12 § 514.
4. Ibid., p.91.
5. Theatr. chem. (1659), I, p.181. CW 13 § 429.
6. Jung CW 13 § 209 and CW 12 § 425-446.
7. Jacobson, Edith: Adolescent Moods and the Remodeling of Psychic Structures in Adolescence. Psa. St. of Child, vol.16, p.166.
8. Spiegel, Leo A.: A Review of Contributions to a Psychoanalytic Theory of Adolescence. Psa. St. of Child, vol.6, p.376.
9. Deutsch, pp.22-23. See further Blos, passim.

24-25
Fig.35. Phil. ref., p.224 (B. Schwan after fig. 36).
Fig.36. Rosarium woodcut 1550. Jung's analysis in CW 16 § 410-452.
Fig.37. At. fugiens, emblema XL (M. Merian). Jong, pp.259-263. The *Atalanta fugiens* was written by Michael Maier (1568-1622), a German physician and alchemist who in 1608 became court physician to the Emperor Rudolph II in Prague. Another important book by Maier is the *Symbola aureae mensae duodecim nationum* (1617). As shown by H. M. E. de Jong, the *Atalanta fugiens* derives all its motifs from the collection of medieval and Arabian treatises printed in the *Artis auriferae* (1572). Another feature is stressed by Jong: 'Maier's work can be considered as a manifesto of the Rosicrucian movement of purification and soul-therapy, which culminates in Mozart's 'Magic Flute,' a masonic manifestation' (op. cit., p.x). Together with Robert Fludd, Michael Maier was a devoted adherent of the ideas of the Rosicrucians and in his *Silentium post clamores* (1617) defended them while stressing that alchemists and Rosicrucians preached the same truth. The

history of the fictitious Fraternity of the Rosicrucians mainly centres on three anonymous publications, namely the *Fama fraternitatis* (Kassel, 1614), the *Confessio fraternitatis* (Kassel, 1615) and the *Chymische Hochzeit* (Strasbourg, 1616), probably written by the Lutheran theologian Johann Valentin Andreae (1586-1654). In the 17th century a wealth of alchemical and Rosicrucian material filtered into the symbols, doctrines and rituals of freemasonry, which began to grow into an esoteric fraternity in that century.
Fig.38. Splendor solis, plate 4.
1. See Jung CW 16 § 410-452.
2. Artis aurif., II, p.143. CW 16 § 411.
3. Ibid., p.161.
4-5. At. fugiens, p.169.
6. For Jung's interpretation of the Sol-Luna symbolism of alchemy, see CW 14 § 117. Jung's concept of the anima and animus complexes appear in CW 6 § 887-890, CW 9.1 § 114-147, CW 7 § 320-340. The development of the anima in LSD-experiences may be studied in Masters and Houston, pp.92-93.

26-27
Fig.39. Bibl. chem., I, p.938. The *Mutus liber,* or 'Mute Book,' was published 1677 at La Rochelle by Pierre Savouret. The author is anonymous and has never been discovered. The Latin inscription of the first engraved plate (fig.39) reads: 'The Wordless Book, in which nevertheless the whole of Hermetic Philosophy is set forth in hieroglyphic figures, sacred to God the merciful, thrice best and greatest, and dedicated to the sons of the art only, the name of the author being Altus.' The engravings printed in this study have been taken from Manget's *Bibliotheca chemica curiosa* (Geneva, 1702), which reproduces the crude original engravings of the *Mutus liber* in a superior artistic variant, executed by an unknown engraver. The copy and the original are identical in form and content except for the background of the first engraving (fig.39), which shows the sea breaking into the land, a detail not contained in the original French engraving.
Fig.40. Boschius, Class.I, Tab.23.
Fig.41. Bibl. chem., I, p.938.
1. The *Mutus liber* series of the opus is reproduced in figs.39, 41, 48, 52, 75, 92, 123, 141, 227, 254, 259, 275, 325, 391, 392.
2. Blos, p.101. See also Jacobson, E.: Adolescent Moods. Psa. St. of Child, vol.16, pp.176-177.

28-29
Fig.42. Mus. herm., p.393. Waite, I, p.324 (engraving after Grossen Stein, p.29).
Fig.43. Vreeswyck, Goosen van: De Goude Leeuw. Amsterdam, 1675, p.125.
Figs.44-45. Splendor solis, plates 2-3.
1. Mus. herm., p.249. Waite, I, p.201.
2. The 'Twelve Keys of Basil Valentine' was published 1599 at Eisleben. Basil Valentine was a Benedictine monk reported to have lived at Erfurt in the second half of the 15th century. The figure, however, is fictitious; the real author of the so-called Valentinus texts is supposed to have been Johann Thölde (c. 1600), the salt manufacturer of Frankenhausen in Thuringia and the reputed secretary of the Rosicrucian Order. The first printed work ascribed to Basilius Valentinus appeared in 1599 at Eisleben under the title *Ein kurtzer summarischer Tractat von dem grossen Stein der Uhralten*. This work contained the 'Twelve Keys of Basil Valentine' and a second edition appeared al-

ready 1602 at Zerbst. It was followed by *Von den natürlichen und übernatürlichen Dingen* (Leipzig, 1603), *De occulta philosophia* (Leipzig, 1603) and the *Triumph Wagen Antimonii* (Leipzig, 1604). There is general agreement on the post-Paracelsian nature of the Valentinus texts concerning which Jung remarks: 'Stylistically, Valentine's writings undoubtedly belong to the end of the sixteenth century at the earliest. The author is strongly influenced by Paracelsus and has taken over his idea of the Archaeus as well as his doctrines about astral and elemental spirits. The author also mentions the *lues Gallica*, which it appears was first described as the *morbus Gallicus* by the Italian doctor Fracastoro in a didactic poem published in 1530' (CW 12 § 508). The 'Twelve Keys of Basil Valentine' are reproduced in figs.42, 115, 153, 169, 226, 256, 272, 285, 296, 321, 342, 367. In addition to the 'Twelve Keys,' this study reproduces a number of pictures and engraved variations derived from Basil Valentine's works mentioned above; in figs.15, 16, 89, 120, 124, 126, 132, 133, 142, 173, 182, 193, 238, 295-297, 326, 384-385, 397.

3. Mus. herm., p.394. Waite, I, p.325.
4. Blos, Peter: Second Individuation in Adolescence. Psa. St. of Child, vol.22, pp.171, 178.
5. Mus. herm., p.394. Waite, I, p.325. Jung interprets the wolf archetype as an equivalent of Ares or Mars in astrological symbolism. See CW 13 § 176-177. For the animal transformations occurring during LSD-experiences, see Masters and Houston, pp.206-207.

30-31

Fig.46. Barchusen, pp.503-504.
Fig.47. Boschius, Class.I, Tab.13.
Fig.48. Bibl. chem., I, p.938.
1. See Jung's interpretation of the engraving in CW 16 § 538.
2. Freud's concept of the superego is presented in GW 13, pp.262 ff. and GW 17, pp.136 ff.

32-33

Fig.49. At. fugiens, emblema XXXIX (M. Merian). Jong, pp.255-259.
Fig.50. Becher, Johann Joachim: Institutiones chimicae prodromae. Frankfort, 1664, frontispiece.
Fig.51. Becher, J. J.: Oedipus chimicus. Amsterdam, 1664, frontispiece.
Fig.52. Bibl. chem., I, p.938.
1. At. fugiens, p.165. The Oedipus legend is told in Sophocles: King Oedipus, V, 955 ff. See Freud's interpretation in GW II/III, p.270, GW 9, p.100 and GW 14, p.412.
2-3. At. fugiens, pp.166-167.
4. Jung CW 9,1 § 52-56.
5. Masters and Houston, p.147.
6. Caldwell, p.264.
In the present, revised edition of 'Alchemy' the author has given a new interpretation of the fourth, ninth and twelfth engravings of the 'Mutus liber' (figs.52, 227, 275).

34-35

Fig.53. Artis aurif., II, p.148 (woodcut after fig.54).
Fig.54. Rosarium woodcut 1550. Jung's analysis in CW 16 § 450-452.
Fig.55. At. fugiens, emblema XXX (M. Merian). Jong, pp.217-221.
Fig.56. Drawing of unknown origin.
1. Mus. herm., p.219. Waite, I, p.178.
2. At. fugiens, p.130.
3. Artis aurif., II, p.148.

4. For an account of Hartmann's theory of drive neutralization, see Hartmann: Essays, pp.170-176 and 227-240.
5. Jung CW 16 § 452. The king's 'move in the direction of wholeness' is further emphasized.

36-37

Fig.57. Quinta essentia, Second Book.
Fig.58. Phil. ref., p.224 (B. Schwan after fig. 54).
Fig.59. Quinta essentia, Second Book.
1. Ibid., Second Book.
2. Phil. ref., pp.61 ff. CW 14 § 138.
3. CW 14 § 140. For Jung's account of the role of sulphur and mercury in alchemical symbolism, see CW 14 § 110-173.
4. Mus. herm., p.24. Waite, I, p.26. CW 14 § 134.
5. Theatr. chem., I, p.423. CW 14 § 137.
6. Ibid., p.482.
7. Jung: Memories, p.167.
8. Rank as quoted by Mullahy, Patrick: Oedipus, Myth and Complex. New York, 1948, pp. 168-169. See also Rank: Trauma, passim.
9. See Klein: Psa of Children.

38-39

Fig.60. Splendor solis, plate 5.
Fig.61. Boschius, Class.I, Tab.32.
Fig.62. Ibidem, engraving on title-page.
Fig.63. Splendor solis, plate 6. The accompanying text describes the 'tree of life.' See Aureum vellus, p.177.
1. Freud GW 11, p.167; further interpretations of the same motif in GW 2/3, pp.291 ff and pp.331, 360, 366-370, 372-376. GW 8, p.106.
2. Jung CW 5 § 659.
3. Jacobson, Edith: The Self and the Object World. Psa. Study of Child, vol.9, p.113.
4. Morienus: Sermo de transmutatione metallica. Artis aurif. (1593), II, p.21. CW 16 § 484 n.
8. Morienus (Morienes or Marianus) is reputed to have been a Christian scholar and alchemist from Alexandria, who became the teacher of the Omayyad prince, Kalid ibn Yazid (660-704).
5. Artis aurif. (1593), II, p.352. CW 16 § 484 n.8.
6. Ibid., pp.22-23. CW 12 § 386.

40-41

Fig.64. At. fugiens, emblema IV (M. Merian). Jong, pp.71-75.
Fig.65. Ibid., emblema XLVII (M. Merian). Jong, pp.285-289.
Fig.66. Iconum Biblicarum. Frankfort, 1626, pars II, p.83 (M. Merian).
Fig.67. Mus. herm., p.351. Waite, I, p.285 (M. Merian after Buntz, p.121).
1. At. fugiens, p.25. The source is Pseudo-Aristotle: Tractulus Aristotelis. See Jong, p.72.
2. Artis aurif., II, pp.161-162. CW 14 § 174. Hali is a corruption of Kalid.
3. At. fugiens, p.197.
4. Mus. herm., p.351. Waite, I, p.285. Buntz, p.121.
5. Ibid., p.350. Waite, I, p.284. Lambspring's verse is reproduced in Buntz, p.122. His original treatise, written in German in the 15th century, carries the title *Tractatus de lapide philosophorum*. Its origins are all of Arabian provenance, see Buntz, pp.101-105.
6. Theatr. chem. (1660), V, p.633. Jong, p.288. Rhazes is the Latin form of Al-Razi, a famous Arabian physician and alchemist from the 9th and beginning of the 10th century. His chief work was translated into Latin under the title *De Aluminibus et Salibus*.

7. Freud's description and interpretation of 'primal scene fantasies' in GW 2/3, pp.461 f. and 590 f. GW 5, p.127. GW 11, pp.384-389. GW 12, pp.54-75, 101, 120, GW 15, p.94.
8. Freud, Anna: Aggression: Normal and Pathological. Psa. St. of Child, vol.3/4, p.40.
9. Despert, J. Louise: Dreams in Children of Preschool Age. Psa. St. of Child, vol.3/4, pp. 176-177. Relevant literature concerning the motif described on these pages may be found in Klein: Psa. of Children, pp.275-281; Niederland, William G.: Early Auditory Experiences, Beating Fantasies, and Primal Scene. Psa. St. of Child, vol.13, p.496; Klein: Developments, p. 276; Klein: New Directions, p.504. See also Cameron, p.661.
1o. The magic love-hate object of earliest infancy is the mother with the penis, or the *phallic mother*. This deeper level of the Oedipus complex was uncovered by post-Freudian and Kleinian psychoanalysis, which demonstrated the Oedipal conflict as the *end-product* of a long previous development. When the boy between his fourth and sixth years experiences his sexual drive in the form of a phallic love for his mother, she is divested of the killing and castrating features of the 'phallic mother' of the earlier period. As the figure of the combined parents is fully and consciously divided into *father and mother* concomitantly with the child's discovery of the sexual difference, the growing boy relinquishes his bisexual identification with the hermaphroditic mother figure. In so doing, he detaches the killing and castrating features from her imago and instead projects them on to the father as the anatomical representative of his own discovered sex. Thus, in the mature, phallic or classical phase of the Oedipus complex, the father alone assumes the role of the murderous castrator in the boy's imagination. This relieves the mother of her earlier, tainted features: as the boy's aggressive impulses are deflected on to the father, who is envied for the possession of the mother, the mother herself remains the idealized object who may retain the features of a libido uncontaminated by cruel aggression.

42-43

Fig.68. Coenders van Helpen, Barent: Trésor de la philosophie des ancients. Cologne, 1693, p.189.
Fig.69. Vreeswyck, Goosen van: Verfolg van't Cabinet der Mineralen. Amsterdam, 1674, p. 185.
1. See Jung CW 14 § 181.
2. Vreeswyck, G. van: op. cit., p.185.
3. See Jung CW 14 § 179-180.
4. Klein: Psa. of Children, p.45, cf. also pp. 78-79, 205-206, 230.
5. Aurora consurgens, p.107. CW 12 § 382.
6. Norton: Crede mihi, seu Ordinale. Mus. herm., pp.453-454. Waite, II, p.18.

44-45

Fig.70. Barchusen, p.504.
Fig.71. Anatomiae auri, part V, p.6 (M. Merian after Pandora, p.22).
1. Mahler, M., Pine, Fred, and Bergman, Anni: The Psychological Birth of the Human Infant. London, 1975, pp.41-120. See also Mahler: Child Psychosis, pp.286-301. Mahler: On Symbiotic Child Psychosis, pp.195-211. Mahler: Sadness, pp.332-349.
2. Mahler: On Symbiotic Child Psychosis, p. 196.
3. For the regressive formation of the *'phallic mother,'* see notes for pp.40-41.
4. Mahler: Child Psychosis, pp.292-293.

46-47

Fig.72. Utriusque cosmi, I, pp.4-5 (M. Merian).
Fig.73. Hyginus, p.88.
Fig.74. Denstonius, Arnold Bachimius: Pan-Sophia enchiretica. Nuremberg, 1682, frontispiece (W. P. Kilian).
1. Mahler: Sadness, p.334.
2. Piaget, Jean: Play, Dreams and Imitation in Childhood. London, 1967, pp.72-73, 160-161, 170, 211, 242, 285, 290. For Piaget's concept of egocentrism, see further Flavell, John H.: The The Developmental Psychology of Jean Piaget. New York, 1965, pp.60-64, 156-157, 256, 271-279, 332, 399. Cf. Kessler: Psychopathology, p. 31. Jung CW 10 § 69-70. Masters and Houston, pp. 23, 30-31, 78-79, 217.

48-49

Fig.75. Bibl. chem., I, p.938.
Fig.76. At. fugiens, emblema XVI (M. Merian). Jong, pp.141-145.
Fig.77. Phil. ref., p.190 (B. Schwan).
1. At. fugiens, pp.74-75. The motif of the wingless male and the winged female derives from Senior: Theatr. chem., V, p.229. The same motif appears in Arnold of Villanova who, speaking of the two stones, says: 'The one has wings and the other has none.' Speculum alchymiae. Theatr. chem. (1659), IV, p.537. For the same motif in Lambspring, see Mus. herm., p.348. Waite, I, p.282. Buntz, p.120.
2. Mus. herm., p.349. Waite, I, p.283.
3. Ibid., p.349. Waite, I, p.283.
4. At. fugiens, pp.74-75.
5. Klein: Psa. of Children, p.283 and Klein: Developments, pp.122-168.
6. Klein: Developments, pp.16, 58, 132, 134-135, 140, 145, 166, 168, 207, 211, 283. For the concept of drive diffusion, see Hartmann: Essays, pp.186-206 and 227-228. Relevant studies for the symbolism described on these pages may be found in Cohen, pp.44, 70, 73, 121, 141, Kessler: Psychopathology, pp.52, 274-276 and Blos, p.242.
7. Klein: Psa. of Children, pp.187-188.
8. Mahler: Child Psychosis, pp.294-298.

50-51

Fig.78. Morley, Christopher Love: Collectanea chymica leydensia. Lugduni Batavorum, 1693, frontispiece (J. Mulder).
Fig.79. Saint-Phalle, Niki de: Rosy Birth, 1964. Moderna Museum, Stockholm.
1. Klein: Developments, pp.203-221, 232-236, 257-269, 282-285.
2. For a description of projection, see Klein: Psa. of Children, pp.200-208.
3. Klein: Envy and Gratitude, passim.
4. Lantos, B.: The Two Genetic Derivations of Aggression with Reference to Sublimation and Neutralization. International Journal of Psychoanalysis, vol.39, pp.116-120.
5. Spock, Benjamin: Innate Inhibition of Aggressiveness in Infancy. Psa. St. of Child, vol. 20, pp.242-243. Rene Spitz's study of 'anaclitic depression' in Psa. St. of Child, vol.2, pp.313-342.

52-53

Fig.80. Glauber, Rudolph: Teutschlandes Wohlfahrt. Amsterdam, 1660, p.156 (engraving after Grossen Stein. Leipzig, 1612, p.234).
Fig.81. Michelspacher, plate 2. The word Cabala at the bottom of the engraving refers to the famous Bible of Jewish mysticism, which in the 16th century was made accessible to a wider public by the translations of Johann Reuchlin and Pico della Mirandola. Traces of cabalistic

tradition are frequently noticeable in alchemical treatises from the 16th century on. The strange creature of fig.81 probably symbolizes Adam Kadmon—the arcane substance, or the primordial, hermaphroditic being of the Cabala.
1. For a description of the manic-depressive reaction, see Cameron, pp.558-576.
2. Glauber, Rudolph: op. cit., p.156.

54-55

Fig.82. Hierne, Urbani: Actorum chymicorum holmiensium. Stockholm, 1712, frontispiece. The psychological world of the picture is described in Klein: New Directions, p.419.
Fig.83. Utriusque cosmi, I, tractatus II, p.323 (M. Merian).
Fig.84. At. fugiens, emblema XLII (M. Merian). Jong, pp.266-268.
Fig.85. Symbola aureae, p.192.
1. See Jung's description of the anima mundi in CW 14 § 13-14.
2. At. fugiens, p.177.
3. Ars chemica, p.21. CW 13 § 184.
4. Berthelot, II, iv, 24. CW 14 § 23. See also CW 12, figs.10-12 and 157.
5. Jung CW 12 § 84.
6. Eisler, Robert: Der Fisch als Sexualsymbol. Imago, vol.3, pp.165-193.
7. At. fugiens, p.178.
8. Jung CW 6 § 888, CW 13 § 146, 162-163 and 356. Cf. Blos, pp.105, 137. For Melanie Klein's theories on the infantile origins of homosexuality, see her Psa. of Children, pp. 102-104, 111, 157, 188-190, 309-315, 333.
9. Symbola aureae, p.192. Avicenna is the Latin form of Abu Ali ibn Sina (980-1037), a famous Arabian physician and alchemist whose 'Book of the Remedy' was translated into Latin under the title De mineralibus.

56-57

Fig.86. At. fugiens, emblema II (M. Merian). Jong, pp.63-66. The source is the Tabula smaragdina: 'Its nurse is the earth' (see p.214).
Fig.87. Vreeswyck, Goosen van: De Groene Leeuw. Amsterdam, 1674, p.135.
Fig.88. At. fugiens, emblema V (M. Merian). Jong, pp.75-80.
Fig.89. Ibid., emblema XXIV (M. Merian). Jong, pp.186-190. The source is The First Key of Basil Valentine. The picture's wolfish imagery gives an interesting confirmation of Bertram Lewin's 'oral triad'—the wish to eat, to be eaten (to be reborn), and to sleep (to die). Lewin, Bertram D.: The Psychoanalysis of Elation. New York, 1950, pp.102-126, 129-165.
1. See Jung CW 14 § 13-14.
2-3. At. fugiens, pp.17, 29.
4. Tractatulus aristotelis. Artis aurif., I, pp.236-237. CW 14 § 30. Jong, pp.75-80. For a psychoanalytical examination of the motif, see Klein: Developments, pp.254-256, 300.
5. Vreeswyck, G. van: op. cit., p.135.
6. Kanner, Leo: Autistic Disturbance in Affective Contact. The Nervous Child, vol.2, pp.217-250. See also Kanner, L.: Early Infantile Autism. Journal of Pediatrics, vol.25, pp.211-217.
7. See Mahler: Child Psychosis, passim.
8. See Mittelmann, Bela: Intrauterine and Early Infantile Motility. Psa. St. of Child, vol.15, pp. 104-109.
9. Klein: Developments, pp.292-320. For relevant observations concerning the motifs described on these pages, see Jacobson, E.: The Self and the Object World. Psa. St. of Child, vol. vol.9, pp.98-99, 101, 106 and Freud, Anna: Discussion of Dr. Bowlby's Paper. Psa. St. of Child, vol.1, p.56.

58-59

Fig.90. Mus. herm., p.365. Waite, I, p.299 (M. Merian after Buntz, p.135). Lambspring's series of the king's son is reproduced in figs.90, 91, 125, 150, 151. The origin of the story is the Arabian Allegory of Alphidius. See Buntz, pp. 103 and 160-161.
Fig.91. Mus. herm., p.363. Waite, I, p.297 (M. Merian after Buntz, p.133).
Fig.92. Bibl. chem., I, p.938.
1. Cf. Klein: Envy and Gratitude, passim.
2. Mus. herm., p.363. Waite, I, p.297.
3. Ibid., pp.362-364. Waite, I, pp.296-298. Buntz, pp.133-136.
4. Ibid., p.365. Waite, I, p.299.

60-61

Fig.93. Locques, Nicolas de: Les Rudiments de la Philosophie Naturelle. Paris, 1665, frontispiece (N. Bonnart).
Fig.94. Symbola aureae, p.5.
Fig.95. Phil. ref., p.107 (B. Schwan).
1. Bettelheim, Bruno: The Empty Fortress. London, 1967, p.325.
2. Symbola aureae, p.5.

62-63

Fig.96. At. fugiens, emblema XXXVII (M. Merian). Jong, pp.247-251.
Fig.97. Hyginus, p.88.
Figs.98-104. Pret. marg., pp.38-41. The Pretiosa margarita novella is a compilatory work written about 1330 by the Italian alchemist Petrus Bonus of Ferrara. It was first published at Venice, 1546, by Janus Lacinus in an abridged and paraphrased form. Appearing in the preface as 'a Minorite from Calabria,' Lacinius in the same section presents his picture series of the opus under the title 'Typicarum imaginum expositio' ('Exposition of the figures and images').
1. Theatr. chem., II, p.289. For the significance of the lion, see Jung CW 14 § 404-414.
2-3. At. fugiens, pp.157, 159.
4. Artis aurif. (1572), II, p.55.
5. The Pretiosa series of the work is reproduced in figs.98-104, 212-216, 245-246.
6. Cf. Ferenczi, Sandor: Thalassa, A Theory of Genitality. Vienna, 1924, p.5.
7-8. Theatr. chem., V, pp.240-241. Jung CW 14 § 386 and 409.
9. Pret. marg., pp.38-41.

64-65

Fig.105. Barchusen, p.505.
Fig.106. Rosarium woodcut 1550. Jung's analysis in CW 16 § 453-456.
Fig.107. Phil. ref., p.224 (B. Schwan after fig. 106).
Fig.108. At. fugiens, emblema XXXIV (M. Merian). Jong, pp.234-239.
1. The relationship is demonstrated above, under the notes for pp.16-17.
2. The Crowne of Nature, p.8.
3. Artis aurif., II, p.158. CW 12 § 360.
4. Ibid., p.157.
5. At. fugiens, p.145. From Senior: Theatr. chem., V, pp.246-247. CW 14 § 77.

66-67

Fig.109. Pandora, p.213.
Fig.110. Vreeswyck, Goosen van: De Groene Leeuw. Amsterdam, 1674, p.206.
Fig.111. Photo by Will McBride.
1. Artis aurif., II, p.153.
2. See Jung CW 9.1 § 533-535 and CW 12 § 140 n.17. Cf. also Viridarium, fig.XXVIII and

Occulta philosophia, pp.2-3. The symbolic value of thunder and lightning as projections of the birth trauma is confirmed by LSD-experiences of rebirth. See Masters and Houston, pp. 226-228.
3. Theatr. chem., V, p.241.
4. Pandora, p.212.
5. Rank: Trauma, passim.
6. Freud, S.: Hemmung, Symptom und Angst. GW 14, pp.111-207.
7. Dr. H. M. I. Liley, an expert obstetrician, advances the following observations: 'It has long been argued that the newborn baby's brain and memory are not developed, or he would be able to recall the agony of his birth. Memory, however, depends upon association. Birth is an unprecedented experience for the baby, unrelated to anything that he has known before, or probably will ever know in the future. He remembers it well enough that he does not want it to happen again. If you tried to put the baby through the same experience the day after he was born, he would resist violently. This time he would know enough to relate the experience to a previous unpleasant one, and he would fight with all his power. Of course, nobody could be so lacking in compassion as to make the baby go through his birth again. If you merely pull a tight garment over the head of a newborn baby he will fight, flaying out with his arms, wriggling his whole body, and crying loudly with distress, just as he did at his birth. He wants no more restricting orifices to navigate.' Liley, H. M. I. and Day, Beth: Modern Motherhood. London, 1968, pp.77-78.
8. Flanagan, G. Lux: The First Nine Months of Life. London, 1963, pp.85-86.

68-69
Figs.112-113. Theatr. chem. britannicum, pp. 213, 350.
Fig.114. Phil. ref., p.96 (B. Schwan).
Fig.115. Mus. herm., p.398. Waite, I, p.329 (engraving after Grossen Stein, p.41).
1. Artis aurif., II, p.249.
2. The Apollon identification of fig.114 is presented by the Viridarium, fig.XXXVI and its accompanying text. For an account of the Apollon myth, see Kerenyi, Carl: The Gods of the Greeks. London, 1958, pp.119-121.
3. Artis aurif., II, p.249. CW 14 § 164.
4. Mus. herm., pp.399-400. Waite, I, pp.329-330.
5. Jung CW 5 § 654.
6. Masters and Houston, pp.275-276.

70-71
Fig.116. At. fugiens, emblema XIX (M. Merian). Jong, pp.158-162.
Figs.117-118. Pandora, pp.25,27.
Fig.119. Mus. herm., p.345. Waite, I, p.279 (M. Merian after Buntz, p.115).
1. Pandora, p.26. Hieronymus Reusner's *Pandora* series of the work was published 1582 at Basel and based on the *Rosarium* series. An engraved version of the *Pandora* woodcuts was made by Matthaeus Merian and published in Johann Daniel Mylius' *Anatomiae auri* (1628). The engravings are reproduced in figs.71, 122, 157, 191, 224.
2. Pandora, pp.29-30.
3. At. fugiens, p.85.
4. Mus. herm., p.345. Waite, I, p.279.
5-6. At. fugiens, pp.86, 87.
7. Mus. herm., pp.344-345. Waite, I, pp.278-279.
8. Klein, Melanie: Our Adult World. London, 1960, pp.2, 55, 9.

9. Klein: Developments, p.296.
10. Ibid., pp.300-307.

72-73
Fig.120. Chevalier, Sabine Stuart de: Discours philosophique. Paris, 1781, vol.1, p.1. ('Designed by Sabine Stuart de Chevalier, drawn by Hostoul, engraved by Jacques le Roy.') The engraving is clearly modelled on fig.122 by M. Merian, whose split image of the philosopher's head reappears as the split image of Basil Valentine. The text rationalizes this feature by explaining the second monk as 'another Benedictine . . . weeping at the loss of a clergyman, that is, Basil Valentine' (op. cit., p.ii).
Fig.121. Pandora, p.229.
Fig.122. Anatomiae auri, part V, p.8 (M. Merian after figs.117-118).
1. Artis aurif., II, p.161.
2. Mus. herm., pp.396-397. Waite, I, pp.327-328. LSD-experiences of rebirth confirm the psychodynamic patterns described on these pages. Masters and Houston report: 'Occasionally, body shrinkage is encountered as an aspect of regression to an infantile or even fetal state. With fetalization, there then may occur an experience of rebirth' (op. cit., p.73).

74-75
Fig.123. Bibl. chem., I, p.938.
Fig.124. Viridarium, fig.XCVII (engraving after Occulta philosophia, p.54).
Fig.125. Mus. herm., p.367. Waite, I, p.301 (M. Merian after Buntz, p.137).
Fig.126. Phil. ref., p.354 (B. Schwan after Occulta philosophia, p.54).
1. Mus. herm., pp.364-366. Waite, I, pp.298-300.
2. Rosarium-version. De alchimia opuscula. Frankfort, 1550, II, p.133. Reprinted in Bibl. chem., II, pp.87 ff. CW 13 § 161.
3. Protrepticus, II, 16. CW 5 § 530.
4. Cashman, John: The LSD Story. Greenwich, 1966, pp.83-84.
5. Rank: Trauma, pp.22, 26. See also Rank: Inzest, pp.277-278 and Rank, Otto: Eine Neuroseanalyse in Träumen. Leipzig, 1924, p.137. Cf. Klein: Contributions, p.92.
6. Allegoria sapientum. Theatr. chem. (1660), V, p.59. CW 13 § 426.

76-77
Fig.127. At. fugiens, emblema XX (M. Merian). Jong, pp.162-166.
Fig.128. Ibid., emblema XXIX (M. Merian). Jong, pp.214-217.
Fig.129. Ibid., emblema I (M. Merian). Jong, pp.55-63.
Fig.130. Ibid., emblema XXV (M. Merian). Jong, pp.191-195.
1-2. Ibid., pp.89, 91.
3. The Works of Geber. Englished by Richard Russell, 1678. New edition with introduction by E. J. Holmyard. London, 1928, p.135. CW 14 § 632 n.279. Geber is the Latin rendering of Jabir ibn Hayyan, the famous Arabian alchemist who worked at the court of Harun al-Raschid (764-809). By many alchemists he was regarded as the founder of the art, but recent researches have shown that a number of his works are foreign attributions. His popular *Summa perfectionis* is a medieval, Latin forgery conjectured by E. Darmstaedter to have been written in the 12th or 13th century in southern Italy or Spain.
4-5. At. fugiens, pp.89, 125.
6. Artis aurif., I, p.272. Jong, p.216.
7. Robert Plank's conclusion of the meaning of

the salamander archetype. On 'Seeing the Salamander.' Psa. St. of Child, vol.12, p.382.
8-9. At. fugiens, pp.14, 109.
10. Artis aurif. (1572), II, p.270. Jong, p.224.
11. Aurora consurgens, p.133. CW 14 § 468.

78-79
Fig.131. Splendor solis, plate 7.
Fig.132. Occulta philosophia, p.53.
Fig.133. Phil. ref., p.354 (B. Schwan after fig. 132).
Fig.134. At. fugiens, emblema XXXI (M. Merian). Jong, pp.221-224.
1. Occulta philosophia, pp.53-54.
2. Ibid., pp.53-54. See also Mus. herm., p.803. Waite, I, p.263. CW 12 § 338 n.19.
3. Artis aurif., I, p.108. CW 12 § 336.
4. Rosarium phil. Artis aurif., II, p.157. CW 16 § 454 n.2.
5. Consilium coniugii. Ars chemica, p.64. CW 16 § 454 n.2.
6. Rosarium phil. Artis aurif., II, p.139. CW 16 § 454 n.3.
7-8. At. fugiens, p.133.
9. Aureum vellus, p.179. CW 14 § 465-473 and CW 12 § 434-436.
10. Freud GW 11, p.162. See also GW 2/3, pp. 404-408, GW 8, p.76 and GW 13, pp.181-183. Klein: Contributions, p.92.

80-81
Fig.135. Barchusen, p.506.
Fig.136. Rosarium woodcut 1550. Jung's analysis in CW 16 § 457-466.
Fig.137. Phil. ref., p.243 (B. Schwan after fig. 136).
Fig.138. Symbola aureae, p.319.
1. Artis aurif., II, p.175. CW 14 § 64 n.147.
2. Ibid., p.159. A quotation from Senior: Theatr. chem., V, p.217.
3. A quotation from Senior: Theatr. chem., V, p.221. CW 14 § 3 n.12.
4. Artis aurif., II, p.161.
5. The Crowne of Nature, p.10.
6-8. Ibid., pp.10, 11, 12.
9. Artis aurif., II, pp.160-161. CW 12 § 477. The *Rosarium's* conjunction is modelled on the 'Vision of Arisleus,' which forms the headline of the chapter describing the *coniunctio sive coitus (Arisleus in visione)*. The vision is described on p.113 of this study.
10. Symbola aureae, p.319.
11. See Fennichel, Otto: The Psychoanalytical Theory of Neuroses. London, 1946, p.209.

82-83
Fig.139. Engraving on fly leaf by Matthaeus Merian. Schweizerisches pharmaziehistorisches Museum, Basel.
Fig.140. Photo by Anatomisk Institut, Copenhagen.
Fig.141. Bibl. chem., I, p.938.
1. Masters and Houston, p.322.
2. Jung CW 11 § 240.
3. For an account of the Eleusinian Mysteries, see Schmitt, Paul: Ancient Mysteries and their Transformation. The Mysteries: Papers from the Eranos Yearbooks. New York, 1955, pp.93-118.
4. Artis aurif., I, p.116. CW 16 § 454. See also Jacobson: Self and Object World, p.52.

84-85
Fig.142. Mus. herm., p.201. Waite, I, p.166 (M. Merian after Occulta philosophia, frontispiece and p.70).
Fig.143. Codex Medicus Graecus 1. Dioscorides. 'Livres des plantes.' 16th century. Nationalbibliothek. Vienna.

Fig.144. At. fugiens, emblema XXXII (M. Merian). Jong, pp.226-229.
Fig.145. Photo by Eugen Ludwig. Anatomisches Institut der Universität Basel.
1. Masters and Houston, pp.224-225.
2. The Crowne of Nature, p.14.
3. Artis aurif., I, pp.297-298. CW 14 § 630 n.271.
4-5. At. fugiens, pp.137, 139.
6. Dorn: De genealogia mineralium. Theatr. chem. (1659), I, p.574. CW 13 § 409 n.29.
7. Khunrath, H.: Von hylealischen Chaos. Magdeburg, 1597, p.270. CW 13 § 406.
8. Artis aurif., I, pp.90-91. CW 14 § 157. The classical study of the *arbor philosophica* is Jung's 'The Philosophical Tree,' CW 13 § 304-482.

86-87
Fig.146. Bentz; Adolph Christoph: Philosophische Schaubühne. Nuremberg, 1706, frontispiece.
Fig.147. Miscellanea d'alchimia. 14th century MS. (Ashburnham 1166). Bibliotheca Medica-Laurenziana. Florence.
Fig.148. Urbigerus, Baro: Aphorismi urbigerani. London, 1690, frontispiece.
Fig.149. Photographic reconstruction by Johannes Fabricius.
1. Masters and Houston, pp.88-89.
2. Figulus, Benedictus: Paradisus aureolus hermeticus. Frankfort, 1608. CW 13 § 404.
3. Theatr. chem. (1659), V, p.790. CW 13 § 403.
4. Phil. ref., p.260. CW 13 § 422.
5. Ibid., p.314. CW 13 § 403.
6. Jung CW 13 § 376.
7. Turba, p.324. CW 13 § 403.
8. Ars chemica, p.160. CW 13 § 423.
9. Khunrath, H.: Von hylealischen Chaos, p.20. CW 13 § 423.
10. Theatr. chem. (1659), I, pp.513 ff. CW 13 § 380-381.
11. See Jung CW 13 § 460 and 410.
12. Ventura: De ratione conficiendi lapidis. Theatr. chem. (1659), II, p.226. CW 13 § 410.
13. Mus. herm., pp.240, 270. CW 13 § 410.
14. Jung CW 13 § 410.
15. The Upanishads (ed. by Swami Prabhavananda and Frederick Manchester). New York, 1960, p.23.

88-89
Fig.150. Mus. herm., p.369. Waite, I, p.303 (M. Merian after Buntz, p.139).
Fig.151. Ibid., p.371. Waite, I, p.305 (M. Merian after Buntz, p.141).
Fig.152. Ibid., p.359. Waite, I, p.293 (M. Merian after Buntz, p.129).
Fig.153. Ibid., p.396. Waite, I, p.327 (engraving after Grossen Stein, p.35).
1. Ibid., p.371. Waite, I, p.305. Buntz, p.141.
2. Ibid., p.368. Waite, I, p.302. Buntz, p.140.
3. Aurora consurgens, p.83.
4. Mus. herm., p.371. Waite, I, p.305. Buntz, p.141.
5. Ibid., p.370. Waite, I, p.304. Buntz, p.142.
6. Ibid., p.358. Waite, I, p.292. Buntz, p.130.
7. Ibid., p.397. Waite, I, p.328.
8. Kerenyi, Carl: The Gods of the Greek, p.100.

90-91
Fig.154. Barchusen, p.507.
Fig.155. Caneparius, Petrus Maria: De atramentis cuiuscunque generis. Venice, 1619, title-page.
Fig.156. Phil. ref., p.354 (B. Schwan after Occulta philosophia, p.56).

Fig.157. Anatomiae auri, part V, p.8 (M. Merian after Pandora, pp.29 and 32).
1. The *stella perfectionis* is reproduced in Kieser, Franciscus: Cabala chymica. Mühlhausen, 1606, p.128.
2. The Crowne of Nature, p.15.
3. Adams, Evangeline: Astrology. New York, 1970, p.77.
4. Occulta philosophia, pp.56-58. CW 13 § 267.

92-93
Fig.158. Becher, Johann Joachim: Physica subterranea. Leipzig, 1703, frontispiece.
Figs.159-160. Symbola aureae, pp.450, 238.
1. Holmyard, E. J. (ed. and trans.): Kitab al-'ilm al-muktasab. Paris, 1923, p.37. CW 14 § 6.
2-3. Symbola aureae, pp.450, 238.
4. Artis auriferae, I, p.391. CW 11 § 47 n.21.
5. Bibl. chem., I, p.401 ff. CW 11 § 47 n.22.
6. Cohen, pp.156-157.

94-95
Fig.161. Splendor solis, plate 8.
Fig.162. Dyas chymica, plates 4 and 8.
Fig.163. Ibid., plates 10 and 2 (M. Merian).
Fig.164. Splendor solis, plate 9. For a discussion of modern projections of the hermaphrodite, see Deutsch, pp.79-81.
1. Senior as quoted by the Rosarium. Artis aurif., II, p.162. The motif of the red slave and the white woman is described in Jung CW 14 § 2 and 188, CW 12 § 84 and 187, CW 16 § 458.
2. Aureum vellus, pp.181-182.
3. Artis aurif., I, p.230. CW 12 § 477.
4. Jacobson, Edith: Contribution to the Metapsychology of Psychotic Identifications. Journal of the American Psychoanalytical Association, vol.2, pp.239-262. The passage quoted on pp.251-252.

96-97
Fig.165. At. fugiens, emblema XXXVIII (M. Merian). Jong, pp.251-255.
Fig.166. Quinta essentia, p.clxii.
Fig.167. Michelspacher, plate 3.
1. Rosinus ad Sarratantam. Artis aurif., I, p.199.
2. Cf. Jung CW 11 § 755-757.

98-99
Fig.168. Utriusque cosmi, I, p.26 (M. Merian).
Fig.169. Mus. herm., p.400. Waite, I, p.331 (engraving after Grossen Stein, p.46).
Fig.170. Vreeswyck, Goosen van: Verfolg van't Cabinet der Mineralen. Amsterdam, 1675, p. 4.
1. Phil. ref., p.116. CW 16 § 376.
2. Ibid., p.118.
3. See Jung CW 16 § 376 n.26.
4. Mus. herm., p.400. Waite, I, p.331.
5. Raymund Lully: Ultimum Testamentum. Artis aurif., III, p.1. Cf. also Symbola aureae, pp.379 f. CW 12 § 433.
6. Artis aurif., II, p.172. CW 14 § 733.
7. Hoghelande: Liber de alchemiae difficultatibus. Theatr. chem., I, p.166. CW 14 § 729 n.183.
8. Aurora consurgens, p.352.
9. Mus. herm., p.688. Waite, II, p.189.
10. Jung CW 17 § 331 a.
11. Caldwell, p.181.
12. The Order for the Burial of the Dead in the Book of Common Prayer of the Episcopalian Church of England.

100-101
Fig.171. Splendor solis, plate 10.
Fig.172. At. fugiens, emblema XLI (M.Merian).

Jong, pp.263-266.
Fig.173. Phil. ref., p.359 (B. Schwan after Occulta philosophia, p.61).
Fig.174. At. fugiens, emblema XLVIII (M. Merian). Jong, pp.289-304.
1. Aureum vellus, p.186.
2. See Jung CW 11 § 345.
3. At. fugiens, p.173.
4. Ibid., pp.174-175. Jong, pp.264-265.
5. Summary of the *Allegoria Merlini*, printed in Artis aurif., I, pp.252-254 and Theatr. chem., I, pp.705-709. CW 14 § 357-367.
6. Ripley's *Cantilena* gives a good example of these ailments, as does the *Visio Arislei* and the *Allegoria Merlini*.
7. At. fugiens, p.201.

102-103
Fig.175. Phil. ref., p.243 (B. Schwan after fig.176).
Fig.176. Rosarium woodcut 1550. Jung's analysis in CW 16 § 467-474.
Fig.177. Phil. ref., p.117 (B. Schwan).
Fig.178. Ibid., p.359 (B.Schwan after Occulta philosophia, p.63).
1. Artis aurif., II, p.165.
2. Ibid., p.166. CW 16 § 467.
3. Ibid., p.168. CW 14 § 729 n.182.
4. Mus. herm., p.48. Waite, I, pp.46-47.
5. Lorichius, Johannes: Aenigmatum Libri III, fol. 23 r. Frankfort, 1545. CW 14 § 89.
6-7. Arieti, Silvano (ed.): American Handbook of Psychiatry. New York, 1959, p.940.
8. Eliot, T. S.: The Family Reunion. London, 1960, p.31. Significantly, the crime of Eliot's chief figure is the same as that committed by the alchemical king in the oceanic waters of the *coniunctio sive coitus*. See Eliot: op. cit., pp. 30, 62, 93, 104-105. Also Fabricius, Johannes: The Unconscious and Mr. Eliot. Copenhagen, 1967, pp.125-126.
9. Landis, Carney: Varicties of Psychopathological Experience. New York, 1964, p.276.
10. Cf. Jacobson, Edith: Depression. Psychoanalytical Quaterly, vol.12, pp.555-560.
11. Cameron, p.521.

104-105
Fig.179. Barchusen, p.508.
Fig.180. Rosarium woodcut 1550. Jung's analysis in CW 16 § 475-482.
Fig.181. Phil. ref., p.243 (B. Schwan after fig.180).
Fig.182. Ibid., p.359 (B. Schwan after fig.193).
1. Artis aurif., II, p.171.
2. Ibid., p.172.
3. Ibid., pp.171-172. CW 16 § 478.
4. The Crowne of Nature, p.18.
5. Artis aurif., I, p.204. CW 14 § 417.
6. Ars chemica, pp.141 f. CW 18 § 21.
7. Redlich, Fredrick C. and Freedman, Daniel X.: The Theory and Practice of Psychiatry. New York, 1966, p.542.

106-107
Fig.183. At. fugiens, emblema L (M. Merian). Jong, pp.310-313.
Fig.184. Hyginus, p.89.
Figs.185-190. Photos by Department of Embryology, Carnegie Institution of Washington.
1. Ventura: De ratione conficiendi lapidis. Theatr. chem., II, p.291. CW 16 § 657, n.25.
2. At. fugiens, p.209.
3. Turba, p.162. CW 14 § 15.
4. Artis aurif., II, p.123. CW 14 § 65 n.159.
5. Mus. herm., p.332. Waite, I, p.267. CW 14 § 65.
6. Theatr. chem., IV, p.991. Franz, p.247.

7-11. Artis aurif., II, pp.169, 157, 149, 176, 181.
12. Barbault as quoted by MacNeice, Louis: Astrology. London, 1964, p.95.

108-109
Fig.191. Anatomiae auri, pars V, p.15 (M. Merian after Pandora, pp.35, 37, 39, 40).
Fig.192. Mus. herm., p.361. Waite, I, p.295 (M. Merian after Buntz, p.131).
Fig.193. Viridarium, fig.XCIX (engraving after Occulta philosophia, p.59).
1-3. Pandora, pp.35, 38, 39.
4-5. Artis aurif., II, pp.172, 168.
6. Occulta philosophia, pp.59-60. CW 13 § 276.
7. Mus. herm., p.360. Waite, I, p.294. Buntz, p.132.
8. Cephalus Arioponus (Copus Martinus): Mercurius triumphans. Magdeburg, 1600, p.144.
9. Jung CW 8 § 800.

110-111
Fig.194. At. fugiens, emblema XXXIII (M. Merian). Jong, pp.229-234.
Fig.195. Phil. ref., p.190 (B. Schwan).
Fig.196. At. fugiens, emblema XIII (M. Merian). Jong, pp.124-129.
Fig.197. Ibid., emblema III (M. Merian). Jong, pp.66-71.
1. Ibid., p.141.
2. Turba, p.139. CW 16 § 468.
3-4. Artis aurif., II, pp.177, 175.
5. At. fugiens, p.62.
6. Phil. ref., p.201.
7-8. At. fugiens, pp.21, 22.
9. Artis aurif., II, p.177.
10. Artis aurif., I, p.322.
11. Artis aurif, I, p.179. CW 14 § 316 n.595.
12. Aurora consurgens, pp.97-98.

112-113
Fig.198. Barchusen, p.508.
Fig.199. Rosarium woodcut 1550. Jung's analysis in CW 16 § 483-493.
Fig.200. At. fugiens, emblema XXVIII (M. Merian). Jong, pp.206-213.
Fig.201. Phil. ref., p.243 (B. Schwan after fig.199).
1-2. Artis aurif., II, pp.179, 181.
3. Theatr. chem., V, p.222. CW 16 § 483.
4. Artis aurif., II, pp.179-180.
5. At. fugiens, p.123.
6. Consilium coniugii. Ars chemica, p.167. CW 14 § 34 n.229.
7. Theatr. chem., V, p.894. CW 14 § 34 n.229.
8. Turba, p.161.
9. Artis aurif., I, p.95. The Rosarium version of the Visio Arislei appears in Artis aurif., II, pp.159-161. See also Jung CW 12 § 435-436, 496-498 and Ruska, J. F.: Die Vision des Arisleus. Historische Studien und Skizzen zur Natur und Heilwissenschaft. Berlin, 1930, pp.22-26.

114-115
Fig.202. Splendor solis, plate 11.
Figs.203-204. Dyas chymica, plate 10 (M. Merian).
Fig.205. Splendor solis, plate 12.
1. At. fugiens, p.97.
2-3. Aureum vellus, pp.187, 189.
4. Mus. herm., pp.129-131. Waite, I, pp.110-111. CW 14 § 494.
5-6. Turba, pp.152, 127-128. CW 13 § 439.

116-117
Fig.206. Barchusen, p.509.
Fig.207. Dyas chymica, plate 3 (M. Merian).

Fig.208. At. fugiens, emblema XI (M. Merian). Jong, pp.115-119.
Fig.209. Photo by Department of Embryology, Carnegie Institution of Washington.
1. The Crowne of Nature, p.28.
2. Artis aurif., II, p.182.
3. Turba, p.158.
4. Artis aurif., II, p.180. CW 16 § 484.
5. See Franz, p.199. Jung CW 9.2 § 195.
6. Artis aurif., II, pp.180-181. CW 16 § 484.
7. Masters and Houston, pp.31-32.

118-119
Fig.210. Barchusen, p.509.
Fig.211. Mus. herm., p.337. Waite, I, p.281 (M. Merian after Buntz, p.117).
Figs.212-216. Pret. marg., pp.42-45.
1. Artis aurif., II, p.177.
2. Geber, p.53.
3. Artis aurif., II, p.177.
4-5. The Crowne of Nature, p.31.
6. Artis aurif., II, p.183.
7. Pret. marg., pp.42-46.
8. Mus. herm., p.336. Waite, I, p.280. Buntz, p.118.
9. See Jung CW 12 § 523.
10. Parzival, Book IX, lines 1494-1501. CW 12 § 552.
11. Shephard, Odell: The Lore of the Unicorn. London, 1930, p.244.

120-121
Fig.217. Barchusen, p.509.
Figs.218-219 and 221-223. Nilsson, Lennart and others: Et Barn bliver til. Copenhagen, 1966, pp.44-48.
Fig.220. Hyginus, p.90.
1. Ruland, p.276.
2. Holmyard, p.45.
3. Paracelsus: De vita longa, Lib.IV, Ch.VI. CW 13 § 173 n.17.
4. Artis aurif., II, p.180.
5. The Crowne of Nature, p.35.
6. Turba, pp.122-123.

122-123
Fig.224. Anatomiae auri, pars V, p.20 (M. Merian after Pandora, pp.42, 45, 48).
Fig.225. Fludd, R.: Integrum morborum mysterium . . . Frankfort, 1631. Engraving on title-page by M. Merian.
Fig.226. Mus. herm., p.402. Waite, I, p.333 (engraving after Grossen Stein, p.51).
Fig.227. Bibl. chem., I, p.938.
1. Pandora, p.44.
2. Mus. herm., p.403. Waite, I, p.334.
3. Ibid., p.4o4. Ibid., p.335.

124-125
Fig.228. Barchusen, plates 44-47, pp.509-510.
Fig.229. Rosarium woodcut 1550. Jung's analysis in CW 16 § 494-524.
Fig.230. Phil. ref., p.262 (B. Schwan after fig.229).
Fig.231. Photo by Department of Embryology, Carnegie Institution of Washington.
1. Artis aurif., II, p.184.
2-4. Ibid., p.185.
5. Ibid., p.186.
6. Ibid., pp.184-185.

126-127
Fig.232. Phil. ref., p.190 (B. Schwan).
Fig.233. At. fugiens, emblema VII (M. Merian). Jong, pp.88-94.
Fig.234. Mus. herm., p.355. Waite, I, p.289 (M. Merian after Buntz, p.125).

Fig.235. Ibid., p.357. Ibid., p.291 (M. Merian after Buntz, p.127).
1. Ibid., p.354. Ibid., p.290. Buntz, p.126.
2. Ibid., p.356. Ibid., p.290. Buntz, p.128.
3. Pret. marg., pp.256-257, 262.
4. Theatr. chem., V, p.219.
5. Ibid., p.229. CW 14 § 372.
6. Berthelot, III, p.xxviii. Franz, p.365.
7. Grasseus: Arca arcani. Theatr. chem., V, p.314. CW 12 § 518 n.6.
8. Aurora consurgens, pp.63-65.
9. Mus. herm., p.357. Waite, I, p.291. Buntz, p.127.

128-129
Fig.236. Phil. ref., p.216 (B. Schwan).
Fig.237. Symbola aureae, p.57. Jung's analysis of Maria Prophetissa in CW 12 § 209.
Fig.238. Phil. ref., p.361 (B. Schwan after Occulta philosophia, p.65).
Fig.239. At. fugiens, emblema VIII (M. Merian). Jong, pp.95-100.
1. Barnaud: Commentarium. Theatr. chem., III, pp.847 ff. CW 14 § 66.
2. Ventura: De ratione conficiendi lapidis. Theatr. chem., II, pp.292 f. CW 14 § 179-180.
3. Symbola aureae, p.57.
4. Theatr. chem., V, p.257.
5. Ibid., p.258. Franz, p.348.
6. Viridarium, fig.XC.
7-8. At. fugiens, pp.41, 42-43.

130-131
Fig.240. Barchusen, p.510.
Fig.241. Rosarium woodcut 1550. Jung's analysis in CW 16 § 525-537.
Fig.242. Phil. ref., p.262 (B. Schwan after fig.241).
Fig.243. Photo by Department of Embryology, Carnegie Institution of Washington.
1. Artis aurif., II, p.192.
2. Phil. ref., p.20. CW 14 § 320.
3. Artis aurif., II, pp.190-192.

132-133
Fig.244. Pandora, p.215.
Figs.245-246. Pret. marg., pp.46-47.
Fig.247. Pandora, p.211.
1. Kaplan, Bert: The Inner World of Mental Ilness. New York, 1964, p.88.
2-3. Theatr. chem., V, pp.219, 229.
4-6. Pandora, p.214.
7-8. Ibid., p.210.
9. Pret. marg., pp.46-47.
10. Ripley's Cantilena is printed and analyzed in CW 14 § 368-463.

134-135
Figs.248-253. Splendor solis, plates 13-18.
1-6. Aureum vellus, pp.190-195.

136-137
Fig.254. Bibl. chem., I, p.938.
Fig.255. Boschius, Class. III, Tab. 36.
Fig.256. Mus. herm., p.405. Waite, I, p.335 (engraving after Grossen Stein, p.57).
Fig.257. At. fugiens, emblema XII (M.Merian). Jong, pp.119-124.
1. Turba, pp.303-304.
2. Berthelot, VI,v, 6. CW 12 § 209.
3. See Jung CW 16 § 526.
4. Artis aurif., II, p.185.
5. Mus. herm., pp.405-406. Waite, I, pp.336-337.
6. At. fugiens, pp.58-59.
7. Pordage, John: Philosophisches Send-Schreiben vom Stein der Weisen. Deutsches Theatr. chem., I, p.583. CW 16 § 515.

138-139

Fig.258. Symbola aureae, p.509.
Fig.259. Bibl. chem., I, p.938.
Fig.26o. Phil. ref., p.96 (B. Schwan).
Fig.261. Ibid., p.117 (B. Schwan).
1. Song of Songs 6:10. This passage is frequently quoted by the treatises and provides the title for the *Aurora consurgens*.
2. [Melchior:] Addam et processum sub forma missae, a Nicolao [Melchiori] Cibenensi. Theatr. chem., III, p.853. CW 12 § 480.
3. Ibid., p.853. In CW 11 § 414 Jung interprets the Mass as the rite of the individuation process.
4. Symbola aureae, p.509.
5. Jung CW 11 § 290.
6. Theatr. chem., V, p.228. CW 14 § 319, 630.
7. Ibid., V, p.231.
8. Artis aurif., II, p.221. CW 14 § 154 n.181.

140-141

Fig.262. Barchusen, plates 48-51, pp.510-512.
Fig.263. Rosarium woodcut 1550.
Fig.264. Phil. ref., p.262 (B. Schwan after fig.263).
Fig.265. Ibid., p.107 (B. Schwan).
1. Penotus: De medicamentis chemicis. Theatr. chem. (1659), I, p.601. CW 13 § 279.
2. Artis aurif., II, p.198.
3-5. Ibid., pp.199-200.
6. Theatr. chem., V, pp.232-233. CW 16 § 403.

142-143

Fig.266. At. fugiens, emblema VI (M. Merian). Jong, pp.81-87.
Fig.267. Phil. ref., p.126 (B. Schwan).
Figs.268-270. Photos by Department of Embryology, Carnegie Institution of Washington.
1. Artis aurif., II, p.200.
2-3. At. fugiens, p.33.
4. Theatr. chem., V, p.224. CW 14 § 630.
5. Ibid., p.231. CW 14 § 319 and 630.
6. Mus. herm., p.694. Waite, II, pp.194-195.
7. Quoted after George Seferis in March, R. and Tambimuttu: A Symposium for T. S. Eliot. London, 1948, p.134.

144-145

Fig.271. Barchusen, p.512.
Fig.272. Mus. herm., p.407. Waite, I, p.337 (engraving after Grossen Stein, p.62).
Fig.273. Phil. ref., p.262 (B. Schwan after fig.274).
Fig.274. Rosarium woodcut 1550.
1-2. Artis aurif., II, p.206.
3. Ibid., p.207.
4. Ibid., I, p.188. CW 14 § 23 n.161.
5. Ibid., II, pp.207-208.
6. Mus. herm., pp.408-409. Waite, I, pp.338-339.
7. At. fugiens, p.51.

146-147

Fig.275. Bibl. chem., I, p.938.
Fig.276. Dyas chymica, plates 9 and 4 (M. Merian).
Fig.277. Zadith Senior: De chemia Senioris . . . Strasbourg, 1566, verso of frontispiece.
Fig.278. At. fugiens, emblema XLIII (M. Merian). Jong, pp.268-272.
Fig.279. Libavius, Andreas: Alchymia . . . recognita, emendata et aucta. Frankfort, 1606. Woodcut on title-page.
1. Ibid., Commentarium, part II, pp.55 f.
2. Symbola aureae, p.200. CW 14 § 2.
3-9. Theatr. chem., V, p.219. CW 14 § 560.

148-149

Fig.280. Phil. ref., p.281 (B. Schwan after fig.281).
Fig.281. Rosarium woodcut 1550.
Fig.282. Dürer; Albrecht: Melancholia.
1. Artis aurif., II, p.212.
2. Ibid., pp.212-213.
3. Viridarium, fig.LXXIII.

150-151

Fig.283. Barchusen, p.512.
Fig.284. Hyginus, p.90.
Fig.285. Mus. herm., p.409. Waite, I, p.339 (engraving after Grossen Stein, p.66).
Fig.286. Barth, L. G.: Embryology. New York, 1953. Photo on cover of book.
1. Mus. herm., pp.409-410 and 414. Waite, I, pp.339-340 and 343.
2. Morrish, Furze: Outline of Astro-Psychology. London, 1952, pp.264-265.
3. Havemann, Ernest and the Editors of Life: Birth Control. New York, 1967, p.83.

152-153

Fig.287. Barchusen, p.512.
Fig.288. Rosarium woodcut 1550.
Fig.289. Phil. ref., p.281 (B. Schwan after fig. 288).
Fig.290. Splendor solis, plate 19.
1-2. Artis aurif., II, pp.215-216.
3. Gray, p.78.
4. Dante: Purgatory IX:20-49.
5. Artis aurif., II, p.222. CW 13 § 272.
6. Aureum vellus, p.196.
7. Aurora consurgens, p.51.

154-155

Fig.291. Barchusen, p.512.
Fig.292. Rosarium woodcut 1550.
Fig.293. Phil. ref., p.281 (B. Schwan after fig.292).
Fig.294. Photo by Dr. Daniele Petrucci. University of Bologna.
1. Artis aurif., II, p.223.
2. Geber, pp.166-167.
3. Artis aurif., II, pp.223-224.
4. Mus. herm., p.352. Waite, I, p.286. Buntz, p.124.
5. Eleazar, p.63.

156-157

Fig.295. Chevalier, Sabine Stuart de: Discours philosophique. Paris, 1781. No pagination.
Fig.296. Mus. herm., p.415. Waite, I, p.344 (engraving after Grossen Stein, p.70).
Fig.297. Phil. ref., p.96 (B. Schwan after Grossen Stein, p.70).
1. Mus. herm., pp.415-416. Waite, I, pp.344-345.
2. Chevalier, Sabine Stuart de: op. cit., p.203.
3. Berthelot, III, vi, 18.
4. Jung CW 13 § 270.

158-159

Fig.298. At. fugiens, emblema XXIII (M. Merian). Jong, pp.181-186.
Fig.299. Ibid., emblema XLIX (M. Merian). Jong, pp.304-309.
Fig.300. Rosarium woodcut 1550.
Fig.301. Phil. ref., p.281 (B. Schwan after fig. 300).
Fig.302. Eleazar, engraving No.7 inserted after the index. The *Uraltes Chymisches Werck* by Abraham Eleazar, or Abraham the Jew, was published in 1735 at Erfurt. It is a forgery which purports to be the secret Book of Abra-

ham the Jew, mentioned by Nicolas Flamel (see notes for pp.166-167).
1. At. fugiens, p.205.
2. Ibid., pp.206-207.
3-4. Artis aurif., II, pp.229, 230.
5-6. Ibid., p.234.
7. German inscription in the left upper corner of fig.302.
8-9. Eleazar, pp.108, 110.
10. At. fugiens, p.103.

160-161

Fig.303. Balduinus, Christianus Adolphus: Aurum . . . hermeticum. Amsterdam, 1675, frontispiece.
Fig.304. Vreeswyck, Goosen van: De Roode Leeuw. Amsterdam, 1672, p.169.
Fig.305. Janitor pansophus, fig.IV. Mus. herm., final page (M. Merian's signature in the right bottom corner). Waite, II, p.309.

162-163

Fig.306. Barchusen, p.512.
Fig.307. Rosarium woodcut 1550.
Fig.308. Phil. ref., p.300 (B. Schwan after fig. 307).
Fig.309. Shettles, Landrum B.: Ovum humanum. Munich and Berlin, 1960, fig.9.
1. For the lunar and solar mountains, see Rosinus ad Euticiam. Artis aurif., I, p.163.
2. Artis aurif., II, p.237.
3. Ibid., pp.237-238.
4. Ibid., pp.235-236.

164-165

Figs.310-319. Janitor pansophus, fig.III. Mus. herm., final leaf but one in book. Waite, II, p. 307 (M. Merian).
Fig.320. Summum bonum. Engraving on title-page (M. Merian).
Fig.321. Mus. herm., p.418. Waite, I, p.346 (engraving after Grossen Stein, p.76).
1. Jurain, Abtala: Hyle und Coahyl. Translated from Ethiopian into Latin and from Latin into German by Johannes Elias Müller. Hamburg, 1732, ch.VIII, pp.52 ff. CW 12 § 347.
2. Hippolytus: Elenchos, VIII, 17, 1. CW 14 § 32 n.221.
3. Mus. herm., pp.418-419. Waite, I, pp.347-348.
4. Inscription in Janitor pansophus under fig. 319.
5. Dante: Paradiso XXXI:27.

166-167

Fig.322. Aureus tractatus de philosophorum lapide, frontispiece. Mus. herm., opposite p.1. Waite, I, p.4 (M.Merian).
Fig.323. Hyginus, p.91.
Fig.324. I. M. D. R.: Bibliotheque des philosophes chimiques. Paris, 1741, II, p.195.
1. Verse printed under fig.322.
2. According to Flamel's autobiography, the *Figures of Abraham the Jew* 'fell into my hands for the sum of two florins, a gilded book, very old and large. It was not of paper or parchment, as other books be, but was only made of delicate rinds (as it seemed unto me) of tender young trees. The cover of it was of brass, well bound, all engraven with letters and strange figures.' (Taylor, F. Sherwood: The Alchemists. New York, 1962, p.127.) The *Figures of Abraham the Jew* show the influence of Cabbalistic symbolism on medieval alchemy.
3-6. Taylor, F. Sherwood: op. cit., pp.129, 127, 129.

168-169

Fig.325. Bibl. chem., I, p.938.
Fig.326. Phil. ref., p.361 (B. Schwan after Occulta philosophia, p.67).
Fig.327. Ibid., p.167 (B. Schwan).
Fig.328. Ibid., p.126 (B. Schwan).
7-9. Taylor, F. Sherwood: op. cit., pp.128-129, 127.
1. Occulta philosophia, pp.67-68. CW 14 § 296. CW 13 § 280.

170-171

Fig.329. Barchusen, p.512.
Fig.330. Rosarium woodcut 1550.
Fig.331. Phil. ref., p.300 (B. Schwan after fig. 330).
Figs.332-334. Photos by Dr. R. G. Edwards. Scientific American, August 1966, pp.76-77.
1-3. Artis aurif., II, pp.240-241.

172-173

Fig.335. Barchusen, plates 72-75, p.512.
Fig.336. Rosarium woodcut 1550.
Fig.337. Phil. ref., p.167 (B. Schwan).
Fig.338. Ibid., p.300 (B. Schwan after fig.336).
1. Artis aurif., II, pp.247-248. CW 16 § 495.
2. Pordage, John: Philosophisches Send-Schreiben. Deutsches Theatr. chem., I, p.585. CW 16 § 516-517.
3. See Jung CW 14 § 15, 163, 238, 355, 373, 419. CW 12 § 26, 335, 420.

174-175

Fig.339. Janitor pansophus, fig.II. Mus. herm., leaf inserted at the end of book. Waite, II, p. 305 (M. Merian).
Fig.340. Bibl. chem., I, p.69.
Fig.341. Phil. ref., p.126 (B. Schwan).
Fig.342. Mus. herm., p.420. Waite, I, p.348 (engraving after Grossen Stein, p.92).
1. Janitor pansophus. Text accompanying fig. II. Waite, II, p.315.
2. Phil. ref., p.92. CW 14 § 462 n.272.

176-177

Fig.343. At. fugiens, emblema XXVII (M. Merian). Jong, pp.201-206.
Fig.344. Phil. ref., p.216 (B. Schwan).
Fig.345. At. fugiens, emblema XXXVI (M. Merian). Jong, pp.243-247.
Fig.346. Ibid., emblema XVIII (M. Merian). Jong, pp.152-154.
1. Mus. herm., pp.420-422. Waite, I, pp.348-349.
2. Dorn: Philosophia meditativa. Theatr. chem., I, pp.456-458. CW 14 § 114.
3. At. fugiens, p.117.
4. Rosarium. Artis aurif. (1572), II, p.307. This is the source of the engraving. See Jong, p.203.
5. At. fugiens, p.118.
6. Symbola aureae, p.336. CW 14 § 536. CW 12 § 421.
7-8. At. fugiens, pp.153, 154.

178-179

Fig.347. Splendor solis, plate 20.
Fig.348. At. fugiens, emblema XXXV (M. Merian). Jong, pp.239-242.
Fig.349. Symbola aureae, p.555.
9. Artis aurif., I, p.198. Jong, p.245.
10. Turba, p.122.
1-2. Aureum vellus, p.198; also Jung CW § 302.
3. At. fugiens, p.149.
4. Symbola aureae, p.555.
5. Mus. herm., pp.176-177. Waite, I, pp.144-145. For an account of the philosophers' garden under LSD, see Cohen, pp.168-169. A pictorial statement of the celestial garden of LSD may be found in Martin Carey's *Celebration: the Rose*, reproduced in Masters, R. E. L. and Houston, Jean: Psychedelic Art. London, 1968, p.65.
6. Aurora consurgens, pp.141-143.
7. Mus. herm., pp.218-219. Waite, I, pp.177-178.

180-181

Fig.350. Thomas Aquinas: De Alchimia, fol. 99. Leyden. Rijksuniversiteit Beibliotheek. Codex Vossianus 29.
Fig.351. Shettles, Landrum B.: Ovum humanum, fig.1.
Fig.352. Diagram by Johannes Fabricius.

182-183

Fig.353. Barchusen, p.512.
Fig.354. Rosarium woodcut 1550.
Fig.355. Phil. ref., p.300 (B. Schwan after fig. 354).
Fig.356. At. fugiens, emblema XLIV (M. Merian). Jong, pp.273-278.
1-2. Artis aurif., II, pp.252, 248.
3. Symbola aureae, p.169.
4. The *Enigma of Bologna* is reproduced in Jung CW 14 § 51. Jung offers an interpretation in § 52-103.
5. The Crowne of Nature, pp.66-67.
6. Artis aurif., II, p.249. CW 14 § 15 and 216.

184-185

Fig.357. At. fugiens, emblema X (M. Merian). Jong, pp.107-112.
Fig.358. Henkel, J. F.: Unterricht von der Mineralogie. Dresden, 1747, frontispiece.
Fig.359. Cartari, Vincenzo: Le imagini de gli dei. Padua, 1608, p.38.
1. Dorn: Physica Trismegisti. Theatr. chem., I, p.431. CW 14 § 293.
2. At. fugiens, p.49.
3-4. Green, Celia: Out-of-the-Body Experiences. London, 1968, p.39.
5-7. Ibid., p.119.
8-10. Ibid., pp.86, 119, 86.
11. Masters and Houston, pp.86-87.
12. The axiom of Pseudo-Democritus, quoted in many variants, reads in its original form: 'Nature rejoices in nature, nature subdues nature, nature rules over nature.' Berthelot, II, i, 3. CW 14 § 21 n.152.

186-187

Fig.360. Das Buch der Heiligen Dreifaltigkeit. Munich. Staatsbibliothek. Codex Germanicus 598, fol.24 r.
Fig.361. Pandora, p.241.
Fig.362. Boschius, Class.III, Tab.44.
Fig.363. Das Buch der Heiligen Dreifaltigkeit. Codex Germanicus 598, fol.81 r.
Fig.364. Boschius, Class.III, Tab.7.
1. Das Buch der Heiligen Dreifaltigkeit. Codex Guelf. 468 f. 169 ra f.
2. Bibl. chem., II, ch.VI, pp.29 ff. CW 12 § 462.

188-189

Fig.365. Splendor solis, plate 22.
Fig.366. Iconum Biblicarum. Strasbourg, 1630, pars III, p.159 (M. Merian).
Fig.367. Mus. herm., p.422. Waite, I, p.350 (engraving after Grossen Stein, p.97).
1. Ibid., pp.422-423. Waite, I, pp.350-351.
2. Aureum vellus, p.200.
3. Ibid., p.202.

4. Artis aurif., II, p.250. CW 13 § 283 n.11.
5. Ibid., p.249.
6. See Lilly, J. C.: The Center of the Cyclone. New York, 1972.
7. Ibid., pp.25-27.

190-191

Fig.368. Mus. herm., p.343. Waite, I, p.277 (M. Merian after Buntz, p.113).
Fig.369. At. fugiens, emblema XLVI (M. Merian). Jong, pp.282-285.
Fig.370. Ibid., emblema XXII (M. Merian). The engraving is the only instance in which Merian departs from the text, which here deals with the 'whitening' process of the albedo. As indicated by the two fishes swimming in the tub, the engraving's motif belongs to the final stage of the opus. This relationship is also emphasized by Jong (p.179), who further points out that the concluding line of the epigram—'Make the trout [or fish] dissolve in its own fluid'—alludes to the belief that gold was to be found in the belly of the trout (p.180).
Fig.371. Utriusque cosmi, II, tractatus primus, p.71 (M. Merian).
1. Mus. herm., p.342. Waite, I, p.276. Buntz, p.114. Cf. Senior: Theatr. chem., V, p.222. CW 14 § 164.
2. Lagneus: Harmonia chemica. Theatr. chem. (1659), IV, p.726. Jong, p.181.
3. Pordage, John: Philosophisches Send-Schreiben. Deutsches Theatr. chem., I, pp.585-588. CW 16 § 516-517.
4. Theatr. chem., I, p.681. CW 14 § 295.
5. At. fugiens, p.193.

192-193

Fig.372. Utriusque cosmi, I, p.49 (M. Merian).
Fig.373. Boschius, Class.III, Tab.10.
Fig.374. Anatomiae auri, pars V, p.26 (M. Merian after Pandora, p.243).
1. Psychiatry, vol.35, May 1972, p.175.
2. Ibid., p.178.
3. Quoted after Toynbee, Arnold and others: Man's Concern with Death. London, 1968, p. 197.
4. Alpert, Richard and Cohen, Sidney: LSD. New York, 1966, p.27.
5. Caldwell, p.87.
6. Muldoon, Sylvan J. and Carrington, Hereward: The Projection of the Astral Body. London, 1971, pp.45 and 84.
7. At. fugiens, p.191.

194-195

Fig.375. At. fugiens, emblema XLV (M. Merian). Jong, pp.278-282.
Fig.376. Schulz, Godfred: Scrutinium cinnabarium seu triga cinnabriorum. Halle, 1680, frontispiece.
Fig.377. Medicina catholica, preface (no pagination) (M. Merian).
Fig.378. Respurs, P. M. von: Besondere Versuche vom Mineral-Geist. Leipzig, 1772, frontispiece.
1. At. fugiens, p.189.
2. Tractatus aureus, ch.II. Ars chemica, p.15. CW 14 § 117.
3. Turba, p.130.
4. Artis aurif., II, p.186. See also p.151: 'The foundation of the art is the sun and its shadow.'
5. See Jung CW 13 § 160, 188, 205-207.
6. Green, C.: Out-of-the-Body Experiences, p. 78.
7. Muldoon, S. and Carrington, H.: The Phenomena of Astral Projection. London, 1969, pp.105-107.
8. Ibid., pp.107-108.

196-197
Fig.379. Mylius, J. D.: Opus medico-chymicum. Frankfort, 1618. Tractatus II, pars secunda huius praefationis (no pagination) (M Merian).
Fig.380. Utriusque cosmi, I, p.19 (M. Merian).
Fig.381. Phil. ref., p.167 (B. Schwan).
1. Jung: Memories, pp.289-290.
2. Ibid., p.299.
3. Ibid., pp.293-295.
4. Ibid., pp.295-296.

198-199
Fig.382. At. fugiens, emblema XXI (M. Merian). Jong, pp.166-176.
Fig.383. Theatr. chem. britannicum, p.117 (John Goddard after George Ripley's original design).
1. Artis aurif., II, pp.169-170. CW 12 § 167.
2. Bonus, Petrus: Pretiosa margarita novella. Edited by Janus Lacinius. Venice, 1546, pp. 119 ff. Franz, p.366.
3. At. fugiens, p.95.
4-5. Green, C.: Out-of-the-Body Experiences, pp.111, 89-90.
6. Fox, Oliver: Astral Projection. N. p. o. p. o. o., p.44.
7. Muldoon, S. and Carrington, H.: The Projection of the Astral Body, p.181.
8-11. Green, C.: op. cit., pp.98, 94, 101-103, 112.
12. Jung: Memories, pp.296-297.
13. The Teachings of the Compassionate Buddha (ed. E. A. Burtt). New York, 1955, p.30.

200-201
Fig.384. Phil. ref., p.361 (B. Schwan).
Fig.385. Ibid., p.361 (B. Schwan after Occulta philosophia, p.75).
Fig.386. Michelspacher, emblema IV. The Red Mass depicted by the engraving is saturated with Grail symbolism. The royal Christ closely resembles the bleeding king of the Grail myth, King Amfortas, whose chief task was the service of the Grail. The hallowed vessel, which contained the blood of the pierced Saviour, was brought by Joseph of Arimathea to a foreign country where a knightly order formed around the Grail and its service. The medieval quest of the Holy Grail attempted to discover its castle and to heal its sick king. As evidenced by Wolfram von Eschenbach (c. 1200), the quest was identified with that of the philosophers' stone, the Grail in *Parzival* appearing as a stone of magical and divine qualities. See Jung, Emma and Franz, Marie-Louise von: Die Graalslegende in psychologischer Sicht. Zurich, 1960, p.154.
1. Occulta philosophia, p.73.
2-3. Ibid., pp.72-74. CW 13 § 106.
4. Khunrath, Heinrich Conrad: Von hylealischen . . . Chaos. Magdeburg, 1597, p.204. CW 12 § 165.
5. Trevisanus: De chemico miraculo. Theatr. chem., I, p.802. CW 14 § 181 n.315.
6. Aurora consurgens, pp.129-131.

202-203
Fig.387. Quinta essentia, First Book.
Fig.388. Dyas chymica, plates 5 and 9.
Fig.389. Ibid., plate 8 (M. Merian).
Fig.390. Quinta essentia, Eleventh Book.
1. An oft-repeated saying. Phil. ref., p.191. CW 14 § 4 n.21.
2. Quinta essentia, Eleventh Book.
3. Berthelot, III, viii, 2. Zosimos quotation. Franz, p.369.
4. Kalid: Liber trium verborum. Artis aurif., I, p.227. Franz, p.370.

204-205
Figs.391-392. Bibl. chem., I, p.938.
1. Osis, Karlis: op. cit., pp.29-30.
2. Ibid., pp.39-40, 85-86 and 55.
3. Ibid., p.89.
4. Quoted after Crookall, Robert: The Supreme Adventure. London, 1961, p.124.
5. Artis aurif., II, pp.249-250.

206-207
Fig.393. At. fugiens, emblema XXVI (M. Merian). Jong, pp.195-201.
Fig.394. Ibid., emblema XVII (M. Merian). Jong, pp.146-152.
Fig.395. Ibid., emblema IX (M. Merian). Jong, pp.100-107.
Fig.396. Boschius, Class.I, Tab.34.
1-3. Aurora consurgens, pp.35-37, 139, 143.
4. Jung CW 16 § 362.
5. Masters and Houston, pp.92-93.
6. At. fugiens, p.45.
7. Turba, p.161. Jong, p.102. CW 14 § 181.
8. Aurora consurgens, pp.101-103.
9-10. At. fugiens, pp.46, 77.
11. Artis aurif. (1572), II, p.135.

208-209
Fig.397. Occulta philosophia, p.47.
Fig.398. Albertus Magnus: Philosophia naturalis, 1524, title-page.
Fig.399. Libavius, A.: Alchymica. Frankfort, 1606. Commentarium, part II, p.51.
1. Liber Platonis quartorum. Theatr. chem., V, pp.139 and 189. CW 14 § 493 n.361.
2. Occulta philosophia, p.47.
3. Artis aurif., I, pp.198-200. CW 9.2 § 257.
4. Libavius, A.: op. cit., p.54. CW 12 § 400.

210-211
Fig.400. Becher, Johann Joachim: Actorum Laboratorii chymici Monacensis, seu Physicae Subterraneae. Frankfort, 1669, p.1.
1. Braden, William: The Private Sea LSD and the Search for God. Chicago, 1968, pp.195-200.
2. Eeden, F. van: A Study of Dreams. Proceedings of the Society for Psychical Research, vol. 26, pt.47.
3. Green, C.: Lucid Dreams. Oxford, 1968. Statement on the jacket, also quoted in Man, Myth, and Magic, No.41, London, 1970.
4. Philosophia chemica. Theatr. chem., I, p. 492. CW 12 § 469 n.113.
5. Hermes Trismegistus: Tractatus vere aureus. Leipzig, 1610, pp.262 f. CW 12 § 167 n.44.
6. Jung CW 14 § 275.

212-213
Fig.401. Leary, Timothy: High Priest. New York, 1968, p.337. Pen and ink by Michael Green.
Fig.402. Psychedelic Review, No.10, 1969. First page. Evolution Mandala by Dion Wright.
1. Leary, Timothy: The Politics of Ecstasy. London, 1970, p.249.
2-3. Ibid., pp.24-25.

214
4. Grof, Stanislav: Varieties of transpersonal experiences: observations from LSD psychotherapy. Journal of Transpersonal Psychology, 1973, vol.5, pp.62-63.
5. Caldwell, p.142.

5. Osis, Karlis: Deathbed Observations by Physicians and Nurses. New York, 1961, p.23.
6. Ibid., pp.84-85.
7. Ibid., pp.30-31.
8. Ibid., pp.28-29.

6. Leary, T.: The Politics of Ecstasy, p.279.
7-8. Ibid., pp.280-281.
9. The *Tabula smaragdina* is one of the oldest of Hermetic documents. The earliest known form is in Arabic (9th century), probably a translation from a Syrian source (4th century) that may ultimately have been based on a Greek original. See Ruska, J. F.: Tabula Smaragdina: ein Beitrag zur Geschichte der hermetischen Literatur. Heidelberg, 1926.
Tailpiece from Sincerus, Aletophilus: Via ad transmutationem metallorum fideliter aperta. Nuremberg, 1742, title-page.

The Individuation Process Reflected in the Poetical Work of T. S. Eliot (1888-1965)

Prima Materia: the Opening of the Work:
Prufrock and Other Observations (1910-1916).
The First, or Earthly, Trauma of Rebirth:
Poems (1917-1920).
The First Coniunctio: Earthly Rebirth:
The Waste Land (1921-1922).
Nigredo: 'Black' Death and Putrefaction:
The Hollow Men (1924-1925).
Sweeney Agonistes (1926-1927).
Albedo: the 'Whitening' Work of Ablution:
Journey of the Magi (1927).
Salutation (Ash-Wednesday II) (1927).
The Second, or Lunar, Trauma of Rebirth:
A Song for Simeon (1928).
'Perch'io non spero' (Ash-Wednesday I) (1928).
Animula (1929).
'Som de l'escalina' (Ash-Wednesday III) (1929).
The Second Coniunctio: Lunar Rebirth:
Ash-Wednesday IV-VI (1930).
Marina (1930).
Citrinitas: 'Yellow' Death and Putrefaction:
Triumphal March (1931).
Five-Finger Exercises (1933).
The Third, or Solar, Trauma of Rebirth:
Landscapes (1934-1935).
The Rock (1934).
Murder in the Cathedral (1935).
The Third Coniunctio: Solar Rebirth:
Difficulties of a Statesman (1936).
Burnt Norton (Four Quartets I) (1936).
The Family Reunion (1939).
Rubedo: 'Red' Death and Putrefaction:
The Family Reunion (1939).
East Coker (Four Quartets II) (1940).
The Dry Salvages (Four Quartets III) (1941).
The Trauma of Death: Fourth Coniunctio:
Little Gidding (Four Quartets IV) (1942).
To Walter de la Mare (1948).
The Cocktail Party (1949).
The Confidential Clerk (1954).
The Elder Statesman (1959).

In 'The Unconscious and Mr. Eliot: a Study in Expressionism' (1967) the author of this study has shown the unconscious background of Eliot's poetry to be explicit in his critical concepts.

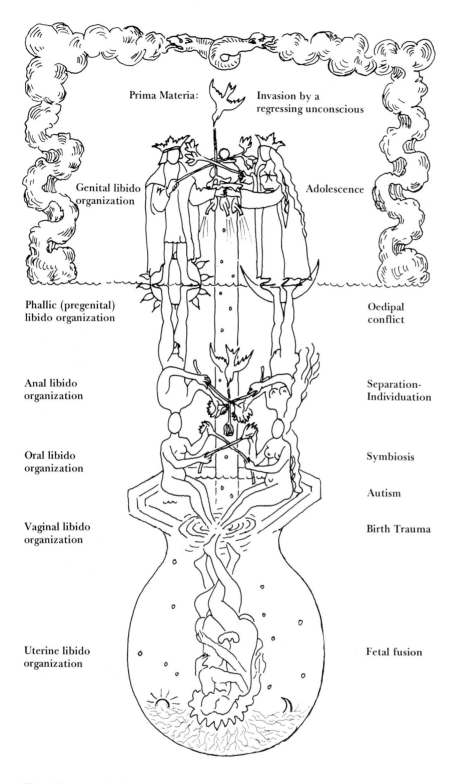

Prima Materia:
Invasion by a regressing unconscious

Genital libido organization

Adolescence

Phallic (pregenital) libido organization

Oedipal conflict

Anal libido organization

Separation-Individuation

Oral libido organization

Symbiosis

Autism

Vaginal libido organization

Birth Trauma

Uterine libido organization

Fetal fusion

'naked' Oedipal conflict of childhood, coinciding with the establishment of the phallic (pregenital) libido organization. The king's *separation* from his queen (along the anal libido organization) is undone by his descent into the *symbiotic* water of the queen's well, filled with the 'virgin's milk' (oral libido organization), the 'fountain's vinegar' (vaginal libido organization), and the 'water of life' (uterine libido organization).

After penetrating the reflecting and *autistic* surface of his queen's well, the king changes from Narcissus into King Oedipus, gradually activating the *birth trauma* as he attempts to penetrate the royal well and its vaginal libido organization. At the bottom of the well the king reaches the mercurial ocean and its uterine libido organization, thereby fusing into hermaphroditic unity with his queen in the 'water of life.' Transformed into the father and copulating with the queen-mother while being enclosed in her womb as her son, the king finally realizes the Oedipus complex at its primal, archetypal level, where the *foetus in utero* condition effects the conjunction of the opposites in the primal act.

In terms of the individuation process, the action of the first five woodcuts of the 'Rosarium' symbolizes the unconscious maturation processes underlying *adulthood*. The chaotic experience of the prima materia renders the ego's experience of a regressing unconscious uncovering repressed conflict and reviving the 'archaeological' layers of the libido. In terms of age, this process takes place in the first half of the twenties, *a highly critical period in the life of every individual.* Birth trauma and rebirth are psychodynamic processes of the unconscious operating in the second half of the twenties, *a crowning period in the life of every individual.*

The diagram opposite illustrates the same process and summarizes the first 24 plates of the 'Barchusen/Crowne of Nature' series of the opus. The prima materia is represented by the sea, or the *unconscious* (the *id*), which is at one and the same time the primary source of psychic energy and the seat of the instinctual drives. The moon represents the unconscious *anima*, the sun, *ego-consciousness.* Constantly aware of itself, the ego is the adapting, integrating and synthetic part of the personality which mediates between *inner reality* (=the unconscious) and *outer reality* (=the object world). The ego performs this task by modifying, selecting, controlling and coordinating the drives of the unconscious and so adapting them to the demands of the environment. The sun's *shadow* represents the repressed drives of the unconscious which are not compatible with the ego's social mask, or *persona*, the latter embodying the ideal ego, or *ego-ideal.* This is originally represented by the father, just as the *woman-ideal* (anima) is repre-

Three Diagrams of the Individuation Process

The above diagram summarizes the symbolic action of the first five woodcuts of the 'Rosarium.' The fogs and vapours spewed out by the two-headed mercurial serpent and the waters gushing from the mercurial fountain symbolize the invasion of consciousness by a regressing unconscious, an event accompanied by feelings of anxiety and 'me-

lancholy' and by a sense of ego-loss. The emergence of the king and queen out of the 'primal matter' of the opening work signifies the regressive revival of *adolescence*—the last formative phase of the individual—in which the birth of love, or the establishment of the genital libido organization, is accompanied by the resuscitation of the infantile *Oedipus complex.*

The stripping of the king and queen symbolizes the regressive revival of the

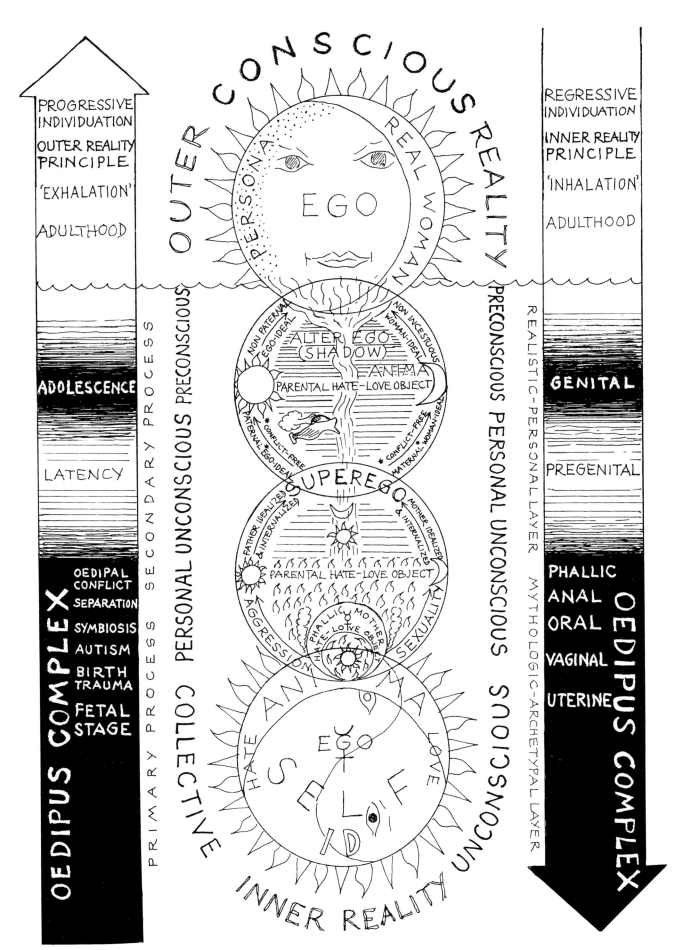

CONSCIOUS REALITY

OUTER

PROGRESSIVE INDIVIDUATION

OUTER REALITY PRINCIPLE

'EXHALATION'

ADULTHOOD

REGRESSIVE INDIVIDUATION

INNER REALITY PRINCIPLE

'INHALATION'

ADULTHOOD

PERSONA

EGO

REAL WOMAN

NON PATERNAL EGO-IDEAL

NON INCESTUOUS WOMAN-IDEAL

ALTER EGO (SHADOW)

ANIMA

PARENTAL HATE-LOVE OBJECT

PATERNAL EGO-IDEAL

CONFLICT-FREE

CONFLICT-FREE

MATERNAL WOMAN-IDEAL

ADOLESCENCE

GENITAL

LATENCY

PREGENITAL

SUPEREGO

FATHER IDEALIZED & INTERNALIZED

MOTHER IDEALIZED & INTERNALIZED

PARENTAL HATE-LOVE OBJECT

AGGRESSION

SEXUALITY

PHALLIC MOTHER HATE-LOVE OBJECT

OEDIPAL CONFLICT

SEPARATION

SYMBIOSIS

AUTISM

BIRTH TRAUMA

FETAL STAGE

PHALLIC

ANAL

ORAL

VAGINAL

UTERINE

HATE

ANIMA

LOVE

EGO

SELF

L ID

OEDIPUS COMPLEX

OEDIPUS COMPLEX

PRIMARY PROCESS   SECONDARY PROCESS

PERSONAL UNCONSCIOUS   PRECONSCIOUS

COLLECTIVE   PERSONAL UNCONSCIOUS

REALISTIC-PERSONAL LAYER

MYTHOLOGIC-ARCHETYPAL LAYER

PRECONSCIOUS   PERSONAL UNCONSCIOUS

INNER REALITY

sented by the mother. However, since adolescence signifies a revival of the Oedipus complex (repressed by the superego during latency), the ego must outgrow its attachment to the parental love-hate object for the second time. This is the 'work' of adolescence, implying a successful transformation of the *paternal ego-ideal* into a *non-paternal ego-ideal,* and a corresponding transformation of the *maternal woman-ideal,* or anima, into a *non-incestuous woman-ideal.* If the ego is successful in these tasks, it will achieve independence and maturity and may marry a *real woman.* If not, it remains dependent and immature and 'marries' a dream woman of autoerotic qualities.

A similar but different 'work' is to be performed during the *latency* period, where the *superego* helps the growing ego to identify positively with the father as the representative of a *conflict-free ego-ideal* and to love the mother as the representative of a *conflict-free woman-ideal* (anima).

The Two Universal Drives

The instinctual drives modified, selected and controlled by the ego during the above growth-processes are those of *aggression* and *sexuality.* Together they form the *id,* or the primal nucleus of the libido. The sexual drive serves the purpose of individual, and thus racial, propagation in the struggle for life; it asserts itself in the urge to protect, nourish, and merge with life *(love).* The aggressive drive (including hunger) serves the purpose of individual, and thus racial, preservation in the struggle for life; it asserts itself in the urge to conquer, subdue, or destroy life *(hate).*

If consciousness is what the ego is actually aware of at any given moment, this rather narrow field extends into the *preconscious,* or foreconscious, which contains those unconscious elements which are latently conscious, that is, capable of becoming conscious with relative ease. A vital part of the continuum from unconscious to conscious, the preconscious includes the host of immediate perceptions and memories available to us if our attention requires them. The preconscious is governed, in the main, by *secondary process,* so that, structurally, the preconscious falls under the domain of the ego and its synthetic function.

The preconscious gradually extends into the unconscious part of the psyche, the 'upper' layer of which belongs to the individual and is therefore termed the *personal unconscious.* This layer reflects the ego's entire history since infancy and early childhood; it contains the records of the ego's developmental 'ascent' through the *vaginal, oral, anal, phallic, pregenital and genital libido organizations;* its handling of the appropriate defence mechanisms against externally and internally generated anxiety; its host of personal memories and forgotten experiences, etc. The deepest layer of the unconscious is termed the transpersonal, universal, or *collective unconscious.* Structured along the *uterine libido organization,* the collective unconscious contains the prenatal memories of the ego, or the archetypal imprints of the total course of evolution, stored up in the neurological memory bank of the brain and ranging from primordial germ cell to fully developed fetus. This deepest layer of the mind and its transformative processes represent the supreme principle, the supreme oneness of being, the *self.*

The third diagram of the individuation process reproduced on this page shows the process in its entire course. The diagram is purely schematic, based on an average life-span of seventy years, and following the traditional division of life into periods of seven years. The phantom sun to the left represents the biological completion of the individual around the age of eighteen after four major periods of prenatal change and four major periods of postnatal change. These include: 1) gametogenesis; 2) ovulation, fertilization, morula-blastocyst formation and implantation; 3) embryonic development; 4) fetal development and birth; 5) infancy and early childhood; 6) middle childhood; 7) prepuberty; and 8) adolescence. This entire development we subsume under the title *progressive individuation.*

The diagram shows the other half of the individuation process, that which we term *regressive individuation.* Together the two aspects of the individuation process express the cosmic principle of 'exhalation' and 'inhalation,' the rhythm of the universe itself. The second half of the individuation process comprises four major periods of psychobiological change: 1) adulthood; 2) middle age; 3) late middle age; and 4) death.

Each of these maturational stages is preceded by a critical period involving a process of profound psychobiological transformation. These critical periods are shown by the hatched troughs of the sun, in which the individual has to make fundamental psychic as well as physiological adjustments. During these transitional stages, unconscious symbols found in dreams will conform to the alchemical patterns of mortification and putrefaction—later to change into symbols of death and rebirth as the individuation process moves out of its chrysalis stages, into its butterfly stages.

Future Avenues of Research

We have interpreted the complicated structure of the *opus alchymicum* as the symbolic expression of an inner transformation process at work in man's unconscious psyche. By means of the alchemical work we have uncovered the subtle pattern of this cosmic process reverberating in the depths of the unconscious and aiming at establishing the unity of man and nature, conscious and unconscious, ego and self. Four avenues are open in the future for a confirmation of our thesis: 1) LSD-research; 2) a systematic study of the symbolic transformation processes occurring in dreams during an individual's whole life; 3) a systematic study of the symbolic transformation processes discernible in the *opus* of a great artist (e.g., T. S. Eliot, p.225); 4) a systematic study of the symbolic transformation processes occurring during the entire course of *schizophrenia,* a rapid and malign individuation process, or the pathological expression of the individuation process.

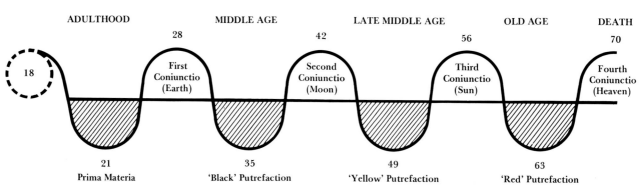

ADULTHOOD		MIDDLE AGE		LATE MIDDLE AGE		OLD AGE		DEATH
	28		42		56			70
18	First Coniunctio (Earth)		Second Coniunctio (Moon)		Third Coniunctio (Sun)			Fourth Coniunctio (Heaven)
	21 Prima Materia		35 'Black' Putrefaction		49 'Yellow' Putrefaction		63 'Red' Putrefaction	

APPENDIX
SURVEY OF PICTURE SERIES

The 'Rosarium Philosophorum' Series

1a   2a

3a   4a

The series of woodcuts reproduced in figs.1a-20a derive from the first Frank-

5a   6a

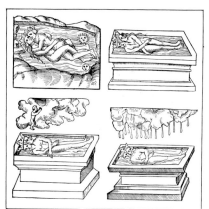

7a   8a

fort edition of the *Rosarium philosophorum* published in 1550 (see pp.216-17). When in 1622 the German physician and alchemist Johann Daniel Mylius published a condensed version of the 'Rosarium philosophorum' in his *Philosophia reformata*, the Frankfort engraver Balthazar Schwan furnished him with engraved variants of the original woodcuts. The series of engravings is reproduced on pp.232-233 (figs.1-20), each of the engravings having been endowed by Schwan with a number in its left upper corner. A comparison between the two picture series reveals the faithfulness of Schwan to his original, even if there are some important variations, notably in figs.12-16 and in fig.19.

Fig.1a renders the dramatic opening of the opus with the overflowing of the mercurial fountain, of whose water a party of alchemists drink in the engraved

variant (fig.1). Fig.2a gives the meeting of the solar king and lunar queen, who in the engraved variant (fig.2) stand on the backs of two lions, classical emblems of incest in alchemical symbolism. In fig.3a the brother and sister strip naked in order to engage in the 'conjunction or intercourse' shown in figs.4a-5a. In the engraved variant of the fifth woodcut of the 'Rosarium' (fig.5) the king and queen fuse into unity in a bed formed as a mussel, thus expressing the submarine nature of the royal intercourse. Behind the curtain of the bed the united sun and moon are about to be devoured by two ravens, symbols of the nigredo ('blackness') which follows upon the union of the king and queen.

The Black Stage of the Work

In fig.6a the royal hermaphrodite lies dead in a marriage-bed turned sarcophagus and tomb. In the engraved variant (fig.6) Devil and Death stand guard at the royal coffin which contains the putrefying bodies of the king and queen. The 'extraction of the soul' is rendered by fig.7a, whose engraved variant (fig.7) shows the departure of both the 'soul' and the 'spirit', leaving the entombed brother and sister in the shape of two angels. In fig.8a the heavenly dew falls to ablute the impure 'body' that has remained in the sarcophagus as the tangible product of the incestuous, hermaphroditic union. The pregnant womb of the hermaphrodite in the engraved variant (fig.8) reveals the approaching rebirth which is realized in the subsequent pictures.

In fig.9a the soul returns from heaven as a homunculus in order to quicken the corpse abluted and purified by the foregoing 'operation.' The union of the king and queen in the manner of two copulating birds devouring each other produces the winged hermaphrodite on the full

9a   10a

11a   12a

Basic Structure of the Alchemical Work

13a   14a

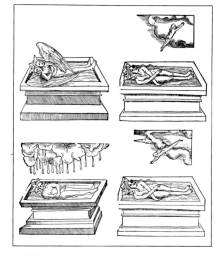

15a   16a

moon in fig.10a. The 'white' rebirth is followed by a new bout of death and putrefaction described in figs.11a-16a.

17a   18a

19a   20a

As the royal intercourse comes to an end, the queen forces the king to withdraw from her womb—a 'fermentation' of their love which the engraved variant shows in explicit detail (fig.11). In fig. 12a the winged and 'fermenting' king sinks into a sarcophagus, his solar body being cleft by an arrow from his queen's bow in the engraved variant (fig.12).

Fig.13a shows the hermaphrodite expiring in its heart-shaped wings of love, an act varied by the engraving by showing the hermaphrodite leaning against a gravestone during its flight with Mercurius (fig.13). In fig.14a the 'lunar life is terminated as the spirit deftly ascends to heaven,' as the 'Rosarium' says—an act which the engraved variant presents as

The ten medals of the title-page of Mylius' 'Philosophia reformata' (1622) present a number of classical motifs of the opus alchymicum. The medal top left depicts the Queen of Heaven (p.206), while, clockwise, the other medals render: the Great Stone dyed by the sun and its shadow (p.194); the orbital flight of the king's eagles (pp.190-91); the fermentation of Sol and Luna in the white foliated earth (pp.140-43); the intercourse of the winged and wingless lions (pp.48-49); the gushing waters of the mercurial fountain (pp.18-25); the quadrature of the circle and the unity of the sexes in the Great Stone (pp.197-98); the 'conjunction or intercourse' of Sol and Luna (pp.80-81); the rejuvenation of the alchemist by the fruits of the tree of immortality (p.207); the slaying of the dragon by Sol and Luna (p.77).

1. A party of alchemists drink of the inimical wine from the spouting mercurial fountain, an act opening the work.

2. King and queen fall in love on the backs of two lions, emblems of their sulphurous and incestuous passion.

3. The royal partners strip themselves to initiate the alchemical water-marriage with its fusion of the sexes.

4. King and queen descend into the mercurial well to attain to hermaphroditic oneness at its bottom.

5. The royal partners perform their submarine coitus in a wedding-bed shaped as a mussel.

6. The bridal bed is turned into sarcophagus and tomb, Devil and Death guarding the damned couple.

7. Soul and spirit leave the mummified brother and sister to ascend in the shape of two angels.

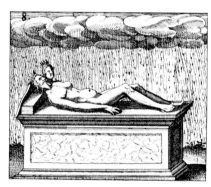

8. The royal hermaphrodite quickens with the heavenly dew, promising a new pregnancy and a new birth.

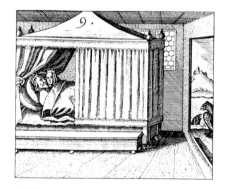

9. King and queen engage in a birdlike intercourse, the partners pecking each other to death while fusing into one.

10. Sol and Luna fuse into one on top of the moon, surrounded by symbols of the 'white' conjunction.

11. The winged partners are buried in the earth like grains of corn, dying to bring forth much fruit.

12. Luna pierces her winged husband in the neck of a solar vessel spelling both 'fermentation' and 'illumination.'

the abduction of Ganymede by the eagle of Zeus (fig.14). In fig.15a the heavenly dew ablutes the body of the putrefying hermaphrodite, whose approaching rebirth is elaborated by the engraved variant (fig.15). It shows Sol and Luna being led by their Great Mother and fertilized by their Heavenly Father. In fig.16a the soul and spirit return from heaven as a mature woman to quicken the royal corpse awaiting its resurrection and new birth. In the engraved variant (fig.16) Sol and Luna terminate their winged ascent (or descent) inside the tubelike well entered in fig.12. As they climb out of the well they tread on the soil of the gory pelican, an alchemical symbol of death and rebirth. The resurrection of the royal couple takes place in fig.17a, which gives the third conjunction of the opus alchymicum or its 'heavenly marriage.'

Endowed with bat-wings, the hermaphrodite triumphs on the solar hill at whose foot the three-headed mercurial snake expires. The gory pelican and the red lion are seen in the background, while the shining fruits of the sun tree appear left. The mortification of the heavenly marriage is shown in fig.18a where the 'green and golden lion' devours the sun and moon, who separate and cruelly expire in the belly of the cosmic beast—studded with stars in the engraved variant (fig.18).

The Glorious End of the Work

In fig.19a the departure of the soul appears as the assumption of Mary and her coronation 'in heaven.' Meanwhile the dead body lies in the tomb of Christ awaiting its Easter morning. In the engraved variant (fig.19) the philosophers' son between his royal parents is crowned with a crown which is much too big for his small head. The son separated from his father and mother symbolizes the departure of his soul (queen) and spirit (king) which must be returned to his dwindled body in the act of resurrection. This implies his growth into parental stature and his conquest of the hermaphroditic crown, identical with his final reunion with the king and queen in one parental, hermaphroditic figure.

This is the drama shown in fig.20a, which gives the resurrection of Christ from his tomb on Easter morning. In the engraved variant (fig.20) the hermaphroditic king rises from his primordial *cella*, chamber or coffin, which symbolizes the final rebirth experienced in connection with the fourth and final conjunction of the opus alchymicum. Its entire structure is thus seen to form a long process of transformation including four stages of conjunction preceded by four traumatic acts of rebirth.

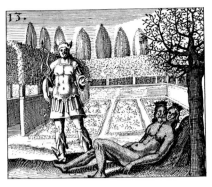

13. The hermaphrodite leans against a gravestone while winging its way to the sun with Mercurius philosophorum.

15. Sol and Luna are guided by their heavenly mother and fertilized by their heavenly father.

17. King and queen fuse into one on top of the sun, surrounded by symbols of the 'yellow' conjunction.

19. King and queen escape from the lion's belly with a little heir growing up to wear the supreme crown.

14. The eagle of Zeus snatches the hermaphrodite, like Ganymede carried to heaven on powerful wings of ascension.

16. Sol and Luna leave the tubelike well entered in fig.12 and set foot on the pelican's soil of death and rebirth.

18. Their heavenly marriage is mortified by the 'green and golden lion,' initiating the final act of death and rebirth.

20. Grown to full stature, the heir of heaven and earth rises from his grave to grasp the sceptre of cosmic dominion.

1. King and queen meet to produce the philosophers' stone in the company of Saturn and his howling wolf, both *malefici* of the opening work.

2. King and queen unite in the figure of the Boy Mercurius, endowed with wings and presenting the staff of Hermes to two astonished alchemists.

3. The traumatic aspect of the king's conjunction with his queen is expressed by animal symbols of death and devouring.

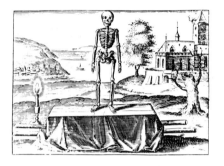

4. Death and putrefaction terminate the Hermetic marriage, its figure of rebirth entering the 'black' stage of the alchemical work.

5. The parents of the philosophers' son come together for a new conjunction in a vessel of ashes and death, germinating love and resurrection.

6. King and queen unite for the second time, married by the white bishop in the sign of the snowy swan and under the multi-coloured rainbow.

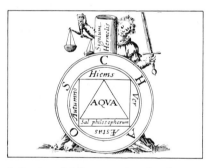

7. Justice with her sword and scales executes judgement over the 'white' stone in the vessel. The double-lined circles denote the philosophers' egg.

8. Alchemists in a germinating churchyard aim at a difficult goal and at a key promising resurrection from death and corruption.

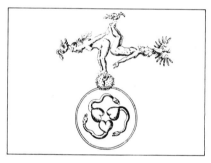

9. King and queen rotate on top of the philosophers' egg while winging their way into heaven. Mercurial serpents fertilize the egg's interior.

10. The heavenly stone of the third conjunction merges Sol and Luna in the trinitarian sign of Mercurius philosophorum, or God.

11. Death and putrefaction inaugurate the final phase of the work, in which the adept sets out to produce the stone of multiplication and eternal life.

12. The alchemist arrives at the end of his work, illuminated by the fire of the last conjunction and the light of the united sun and moon.

The Twelve Keys of Basil Valentine

One of the strangest figures of alchemy is the Benedictine monk Basilius Valentinus, reported to have lived at Erfurt in the second half of the fifteenth century. There is no contemporary evidence for any of the circumstances relating to Basil Valentine; in fact, the works attributed to him refer to events that occurred after his death. Thus, for instance, he mentions the discovery of America and the 'new disease among soldiers' termed 'Franzosen,' a name used in this sense only from about 1493 with the syphilitic epidemic. Basil Valentine also mentions metal printer's type, not used before the fifteenth century, and tobacco, introduced into Europe by Nicot in 1560. The Benedictine monk is also heavily influenced by Paracelsian ideas, just as he himself appears as an important contributor to the iatrochemical literature of the time.

Although a number of different individuals have been suggested, the authorship of the Valentinus texts is most commonly attributed to Johann Thölde, a councillor and salt boiler of Frankenhausen in Thuringia. At the end of the sixteenth century he began his edition of the first Valentinus texts with 'Ein kurtzer summarischer Tractat von dem grossen Stein der Uhralten' (Eisleben, 1599). This work contained the 'Twelve Keys of Basil Valentine' but without illustrations. A second edition appeared already in 1602 at Zerbst, and this was furnished with crude woodcuts of the 'Twelve Keys.' An engraved variant *(left)* was published in 1618 with Michael Maier's 'Tripus aureus' accompanied by a Latin translation of the *Zwölff Schlussel.* Later works by Basilius Valentinus included 'Von dem naturlichen und ubernaturlichen Dingen' (Leipzig, 1603), 'De occulta philosophia' (Leipzig, 1603), the 'Triumph Wagen Antimonii' (Leipzig, 1604), and 'Letztes Testament' (Jena, 1626).

The language of the Valentinus texts is an Upper Saxony dialect, and the style is a mixture of verbosity, pious mysticism, and sharp invective against the orthodox physicians of the day. The most important alchemical work of Basil Valentine is undoubtedly his 'Twelve Keys,' which became one of the most frequently reprinted treatises of the seventeenth and eighteenth centuries.

'The Crowne of Nature'

Besides the 'Rosarium' series and 'The Twelve Keys of Basil Valentine,' the alchemical secret of transmutation is revealed by the 'Crowne of Nature' series, printed in Johann Conrad Barchusen's *Elementa chemiae* (Leiden, 1718). Barchusen (1666-1723) was a famous chemist teaching at the University of Utrecht, and his various books reflect his personal development from practising pharmacist

LABORE ET COELI FAVORE

to professor of a new academic discipline, chemistry. Barchusen tells us in the preface of his book that its engraved picture series was copied from 'a handwritten book in a Benedictine monastery in Swabia,' and that 'these pictures at first sight appeared to me to refer to the production of the philosophers' stone' (p.503). After ten years of search, the author of this study finally, in 1968, succeeded in discovering this 'handwritten book' in the Sidney M. Edelstein Foundation Library, New York. The manuscript, which consists of 67 water-colours, is entitled 'The Crowne of Nature or the doctrine of the souereigne medecene declared in 67 Hierogliphycall fugurs by a namlesse Author.' As the manuscript refers to the 'Rosarium philosophorum' (1550), and as its first water-colour probably copies a woodcut in Giovanni Battista Nazari's 'Della transmutatione metallica sogni tre' (1599), we may date 'The Crowne of Nature' to the early part of the seventeenth century. Barchusen's engraved version of the illustrated manuscript contains 78 pictures as compared to the 67 pictures of the original; however, the two versions are identical, and Barchusen's added pictures (plates 1-6, 9, 16-17, 74, 77-78) merely amplify the symbolic-pictorial action of the original. 'The Crowne of Nature' builds heavily on the 'Rosarium' and may be described as a paraphrase of this treatise, its amplifications, however, being of a highly original quality.

'By labour and the aid of heaven,' reads the inscription of the engraving which adorns Barchusen's title-page.

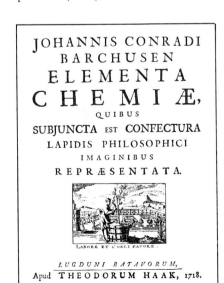

JOHANNIS CONRADI
BARCHUSEN
ELEMENTA
CHEMIÆ,
QUIBUS
SUBJUNCTA EST CONFECTURA
LAPIDIS PHILOSOPHICI
IMAGINIBUS
REPRÆSENTATA.

LABORE ET COELI FAVORE.

LUGDUNI BATAVORUM,
Apud THEODORUM HAAK, 1718.

Barchusen's 'Elementa chemiae,' 1718.

1-5. Opening stage of the alchemical work.

235

6-9. Initial meeting of sun and moon.

10-13. Growing love of sun and moon.

14-17. Opening of the vessel of rebirth.

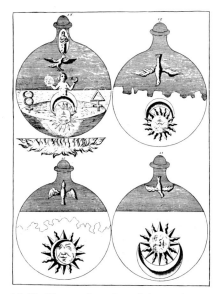

18-21. First conjunction of the work.

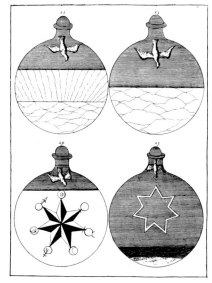

22-25. The 'star of perfection' developed.

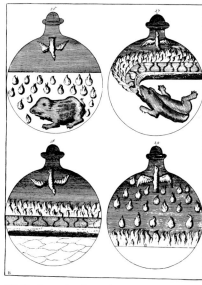

26-29. Putrefaction of the homunculus.

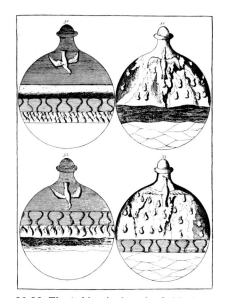

30-33. The 'whitening' work of ablution.

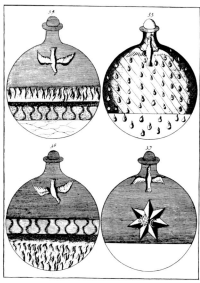

34-37. Circular distillation of elements.

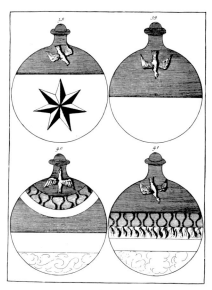

38-41. The calcination of the elements.

236

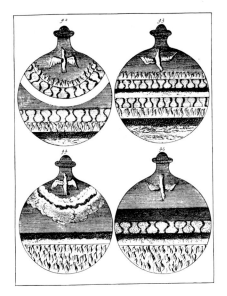

42-45. Calcining fire of 'reverberation.'

46-49. The second or 'white' conjunction.

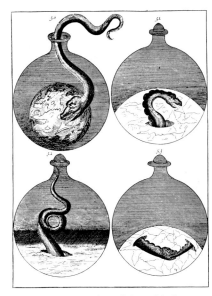

50-53. Fermentation of the 'white' stone.

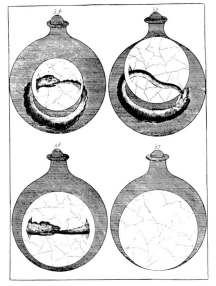

54-57. Cleavage division of the lunar egg.

58-61. Solar transformation of lunar egg.

62-65. Conquest of the mercurial serpent.

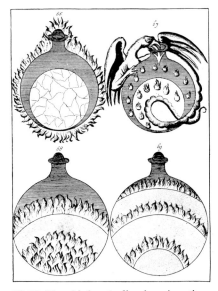

66-69. The third or 'yellow' conjunction.

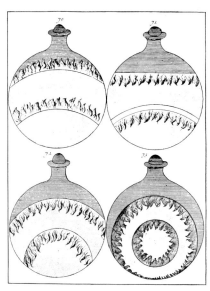

70-73. Putrefaction of the 'yellow' stone.

74-78. The fourth or 'red' conjunction.

237

'The Mute Book'

One of the most interesting representations of the symbolic structure of the alchemical work is given by the *Mutus liber,* or 'Mute Book,' published 1677 at La Rochelle by Pierre Savouret. The author is anonymous and has never been identified. The Latin inscription of the first engraved plate (fig.39) reads: 'The Wordless Book, in which nevertheless the whole of Hermetic Philosophy is set forth in hieroglyphic figures, sacred to God the merciful, thrice best and greatest, and dedicated to the sons of the art only, the name of the author being Altus.' The engravings printed in this study have been taken from Manget's 'Biblotheca chemica curiosa' (Geneva, 1702), which reproduces the crude original engravings of the 'Mutus liber' in a superior artistic variant, executed by an unknown engraver. The copy and the original are identical in form and content except for the background of the first engraving, which shows the sea breaking into the land, a detail not contained in the original French engraving. Two angels with trumpets awaken the dreaming adept for the ascension of the ladder of Jacob, finally abandoned in the last engraving with the conjunction of heaven and earth.

The intervening pictures render the development of the alchemical process of transmutation under the aegis of Neptune, Jupiter, Venus, Luna, Sol, Saturn, and Mercurius. In plate 3 the alchemical couple experiments with symbolic figures of submarine love, while in plate 4 they collect the 'May-dew' of spring and generation — the prima materia from which they finally manage to produce silver and gold in plates 5-6, and the philosophers' son in plates 7-8.

In plate 9 the 'May-dew' is turned black and the prima materia exposed to renewed processes of sublimation and purification. These are seen to produc the second conjunction of Sol and Luna in the sign of ten, and the child of their union in plates 10-11.

A new bout of mortification and putrefaction ensues in plate 12 where the alchemist and his sister renew their refining processes of the primal matter. The success of their operations appears with plate 13, in which Sol and Luna unite for the third time in the sign of endless multiplication.

In plate 14 the smoking wicks of the oil lamps in the laboratory are cut down by the philosophers' son in his dwarfish state and by two parental figures with unlighted torches. The heated sun and moon furnaces of the bottom row produce the multiplying replicas of Sol and Luna, who finally unite in plate 15. The alchemist and his sister ascend with the composite figure of their union, who symbolizes Mercurius philosophorum, or the risen Christ.

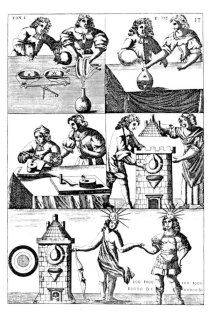

The 'Splendor Solis' Series

1. Two philosophers debate in front of the alchemical temple, the portal and doorstep of which lead to a green meadow with flowers and a running brook. On the dais of the sanctuary is erected the 'coat of arms of the art,' which shows the sun and moon as rulers of the temple.

2. An adept points to the Hermetic vessel while exclaiming: 'Let us go and seek the nature of the four elements.' The separation of the elements for examination is one of the means of producing the prima materia. Another is the putrefaction and decoction of the elements 'in the way of our secret art.' By means of these procedures the fearful opening of the work is initiated.

3. The work begins with the overflowing of the mercurial fountain, spouting the waters of the prima materia and the urine of children while developing the seven planets in evil disorder. 'Make one water out of two waters,' reads the inscription on the martial alchemist's shield. 'You who seek to create the sun and moon, give them to drink of the inimical wine.'

4. Sol and Luna, or king and queen, develop out of the planetary chaos of the prima materia. The queen's scroll is inscribed 'the heroine's milk,' the king's scroll 'coagulate the masculine.' The union of the sexual opposites epitomizes the alchemist's attempt at uniting all the opposites of nature in the 'coniunctio sive coitus,' one of the synonyms for the stone.

5. The alchemists' exploration of the foundations of nature takes them into the depths of the mountain and the earth. In the darkness they encounter the biblical figures of Mordecai, Esther, Ahasuerus, Bigthan and Teresh. The atmosphere is one of secretive sex and suppressed regicide. Mermaids, sea-horses and small children reveal the regressive current of symbolic action.

6. An alchemist climbs the Hermetic tree to pluck its fruits and plant its branches in the meadow. The surrounding scenery shows a king with his sons and courtiers spying on a group of naked bathing women. The picture's symbolic action renders the awakening of sexual curiosity, an event which is followed by the king's descent into the bath in the following picture.

7. The old king drowns in the sea but is miraculously saved and reborn in his son and successor. The 'king's son' carries a sceptre with the seven planetary stars in an ordered circle, and a golden apple with the dove of paternal incarnation. The figure of rebirth is described as wearing 'three costly crowns, the one of iron, the other of silver, and the third of pure gold.'

8. Another variant of the king's descent into the bath shows the 'negro' or Ethiopian rising from the 'black, dirty and foul-smelling slime' to embrace his heavenly queen. 'She clothed the man with a purple robe, lifted him up to his brightest clearness, and took him with herself to heaven,' reads the text. The subsequent picture shows the man and woman's strange reunion in heaven.

9. The whitened Ethiopian and his feathered queen embrace and fuse into the angelic figure of the hermaphrodite, the goal of the alchemical work. Surrounded with a halo, the winged figure holds a target in its right hand and an egg in its left, symbols of the philosophers' stone or egg. The target shows a circle composed of the four united elements of the quintessence.

10. The glory of the Hermetic marriage is followed by the cruel sacrifice of its body of rebirth. 'I have killed thee,' says the henchman, 'that thou mayest receive a superabundant life, but thy head I will carefully hide . . . and . . . the body I will bury, that it may putrefy and grow and bear innumerable fruit.' This action signifies the onset of the nigredo.

11. The foul body of rebirth is cooked and cleansed in a cauldron. A fellow alchemist applies the bellows to the fire while a dove descends on the alchemist's head, proof that the whitening work has been initiated and the nigredo brought to an end.

12. The vessel develops a little boy fighting the dragon with his bellows and phial, the medicine of which he pours into the dragon's throat. 'A wondrous light shall be seen in the darkness,' says the text of the 'whitening' work, which unfolds on a background of scenes from country and city.

13. The white dove is delivered from the nest of its copulating parents while a pope crowns a king in his palace, and two alchemists engage in processes of sublimation and distillation. 'A heavy body cannot be made light without the help of a light body,' explains the text, which crystallizes yet another image of winged rebirth in fig.14.

14. On a background of war and violence the vessel presents the precarious formation of the 'trinitarian' bird of promise. 'The heat cleanses that which is unclean,' explains the text. 'It throws off the mineral impurities and bad odours and renews the elixir.' The subsequent picture shows the bird's monstrous transformation in the vessel.

15. On a background of sports exercises the vessel presents the traumatic transformation of its bird of promise. The text explains the event as symbolizing the return of the soul: 'The philosophers say that whosoever can bring to light a hidden thing is a master of the art . . . he who can revive the soul will have the experience.'

16. Set in a landscape of love, dancing and music, the vessel presents the many colours of the peacock's tail, which herald the dawn and the return of the soul. The dark night of the soul is at an end and the vessel prepared for the silver wedding of the king and queen. This event is shown in the two following pictures.

17. The vessel of rebirth is presented on the background of a city in which men pursue the study of the seven liberal arts. The lunar queen is merged with the face of the sun and is shown in a pregnant condition. 'Distil seven times and you will have removed the destructive moisture,' explains the text, which shows the male coniunctio in fig.18.

18. The solar king merges with the face of the moon on a background of hunting and fishing scenes. The lunar fire illuminating the king is defined by the text as that of the Archer, where the fire 'is not burning hot but under the rule of air, or in a state of rest and peace.' The final pictures of the series render the end of the work.

The 'Splendour of the Sun'

The twenty-two paintings reproduced in this study derive from the 1582 version of Salomon Trismosin's *Splendor solis,* now in the British Museum (Ms. Harley 3469). The Harley-manuscript is a copy of the German original, which was produced in the second quarter of the sixteenth century. The paintings are faithful to the original, but they are superior in artistic execution.

The 'Splendor solis' was published for the first time in a collection of alchemical treatises appearing at Rorschach, 1598, under the title: 'Aureum vellus, oder Guldin Schatz und Kunstkammer . . . von dem . . . bewehrten Philosopho Salomone Trismosino . . . in sonderbare unterschiedliche Tractätlein disponiert, und in das Teutsch gebracht.' Other editions of the 'Aureum vellus' appeared at Basel, 1604, and at Hamburg, 1708, and the 'Splendour of the Sun' soon became as popular as the 'Twelve Keys of Basil Valentine.'

According to Hermann Kopp (I, p.243), Salomon Trismosin, the reputed 'preceptor' of Paracelsus, is a fictitious figure. He is stated as the author of some of the treatises in the 'Aureum vellus,' in which the first treatise deals with his *Wanderschafft* after 1473. In Germany and Italy he learned the art of alchemy, and, as he tells the reader, 'when I from Venice came to a still better place, I was acquainted with Cabbalistic and magic books in the Egyptian language. These I translated into Greek and again into Latin, and so I found and collected the whole treasure of the Egyptians' (p.4).

According to his own testimony, Salomon Trismosin late in life managed to prepare the philosophers' stone, which enabled him to conquer his decrepit state and to rejuvenate himself by means of only half a grain of the *lapis.* His wrinkled and yellow skin again became smooth and white, his cheeks turned red and his grey hair black, and he once more perceived the motions of youthful desire.

At the time of writing, Salomon Trismosin looks back at a span of 150 years since the miraculous event, and still he feels himself in the heyday of youth and full of professional vigour. 'I, Trismosin, have completely rejuvenated myself and other brave people by means of this secret, and if one wished for it, one might keep oneself alive with this *Arcano* until the advent of Doomsday—except that this would be against the eternal wisdom of God' (p.36). Among those that Salomon Trismosin boasts of having helped and rejuvenated with his art are a number of seventy-to-ninety-year-old women whom he has enabled once more to give birth to many children.

19. After the conjunction of the solar and lunar bodies in figs.17-18 the alchemical process of transformation enters upon a stage of putrefaction and fermentation which 'turns the matter black.' According to the text, this is due to the lunar body's conjunction with the solar sulphur or golden ferment.

20. The play of children in the nursery chamber is compared by the text to the stage of coagulation which follows upon the stage of dissolution. The abundance of children relates the motif to the fertility symbolism of the multiplicatio and to its sense of rejuvenation. The picture probably describes the third conjunction of the opus.

21. Nine washerwomen cooking and drying clothes are explained by the text as symbolizing the final sublimation of the earthly elements into the 'spirit of the quintessence, called the tincture, fermentum, anima, or oil, which is the very next matter to the philosophers' stone.' The stone is produced in fig.22.

22. The 'splendour of the sun' illuminates a morning landscape and inaugurates the 'red' stage. The text explains the solar stone as a result of the synthetic procedures of the final operation: 'The reason why all natural things are put together in one body is that there may be a united composition.'

243

Mordecai, 38, 240
Morienus (Morienes) Romanus, 22, 39, 62, 104, 112, 116, 125, 130, 135, 218
Morley, Christopher Love, 219
Morrish, Furze, 151, 223
mortificatio, 98, 100, 104, 228, 239; *see also* putrefactio
morula, 125, 143
Moses, 84
mother, identification with, 34; love of, 31, 100, 115; phallic mother, 41, 45, 50-51, 55, 59, 75
mountain, 58-59; solar, 161-63, 166-67, 169, 240
Mozart, Wolfgang Amadeus, 217
Muldoon, Sylvan, 184, 193, 198, 224-25
multiplicatio, 136, 154, 174-79, 200, 205, 209, 239, 243
Mundus, 115
mussel, 81, 230-32
Mutus liber, 26-27, 30-31, 33, 48, 59, 74, 82-83, 123, 136, 138-39, 146, 168, 204-5, 238-39
Mylius, Johann Daniel, 36, 86, 98, 215, 217, 219-20, 225, 230-31
Myrrha, 100

Naaman, 110-11
narcissism, 55, 60
Nazari, Giovanni Battista, 216, 235
Nebuchadnezzar, 85
negro (moor, Ethiopian), 94, 241
Neptune, 27, 30, 137, 239
Nicholas Cusanus, 93
Nicodemus, 65
Niederland, William G., 218
nigredo, 14, 81, 98-109, 230, 234, 241
nirvana, 195, 198, 212
Noah, 18, 24
Norton, Thomas, 14, 43, 216, 218
Noyes Jr., Russel, 192-93

Oboel, 147
objective cognition, 198
Oedipus, 32, 37, 100, 218
Oedipus chimicus, 32-33
Oedipus complex, 12, 23; pregenital or phallic elaboration of, 34-39; anal- and oral-sadistic elaboration of, 40-59; vaginal-uterine elaboration of, 60-97; primal Oedipus complex of rebirth, 60-97, 226; adolescent revival of, 27, 29-30, 226-28; discovery of, 37; putrefaction of, 98-109; purification of, 110-23; sublimation of, 124-39; spiritualization of, 140-69; etherization of, 170-211; fuel of the individuation process, 191
Olympiodorus, 55
ontogenesis, 107, 212
opus alchymicum, 12; coloured sequence of, 146-47; pictorial rendering of, 230-43; concealment of, 14, 24, 186, 204
opus circulatorium, 15, 17, 143, 192-93, 199, 208
opus contra naturam, 16-17, 22
oral stage, 34, 226
Orestes, 177
Orion, 158
Orpheus, 175-76
Ortulanus, 130

Osiris, 6, 100, 183
Osis, Karlis, 203-4, 210, 225
out-of-the-body experience, 184-85, 189, 190-93, 195-98, 210, 214
ovarian follicle, 161; follicular hill, 163
ovary, 161, 163, 181

Pandora, 66, 70, 72-73, 90-91, 108, 122, 132-33, 202; *see also* Reusner, Hieronymus
Paracelsus, 120, 195, 222, 243
paranoid-schizoid libido position, 57, 70
parricide, 12, 31-33, 35, 40, 62, 89, 103
participation mystique, 47
Parzival, 225
Paul, St., 59, 184, 200
peacock, 30, 33-35, 94, 143, 153, 156; tail of, 242
pelican, 10-11, 16, 66, 125, 159-63, 175, 210, 233, 237
Penotus, Bernardus Georgius (Bernardus á Portu), 191, 223
Perenelle, 166-67
Persephone, 89
Perseus, 159
persona ('mask'), 50, 226-27
Peter, St., 167
Petrarcha, Francesco, 216, 225
Petrarcha Master, 6, 20
Petrus Toletanus, 217
phallic stage, 34, 226
phallus, 60, 64-65, 73, 75, 87, 89, 157
phoenix, 207, 209
phylogenesis, 107, 212-13
Piaget, Jean, 47, 219
Pine, Fred, 218
Pisces the Fishes, 15, 52, 190-91, 208
placenta, 85, 87
planet(s), seven, 18, 28, 61, 241
planetary metals, 50, 84, 87, 92
planetary spheres, 15
Plank, Robert, 220
Plato, 130
poison, 106, 108, 134, 155, 170, 182
Pordage, John, 222, 224
Porta, Giambattista della, 216
precognition, 189
preconscious, 227-28
Pretiosa margarita novella, see Bonus, Petrus
prima materia, 8-11, 18-23, 26, 28, 30, 54, 226
primal act (scene), 34, 40-41, 226
primary identification, 57-60, 65, 71, 74, 77
primary identity, 86, 89, 94
primary process thinking, 33
primordial germ cell, 156, 180-81, 212
proiectio, 174-75, 179-87, 190-95, 197, 205
projection, 10-11, 43, 51, 53, 57, 71, 198
projective identification, 71
projective identity, 205
psychedelic psychology, 212
putrefactio, 16-17, 21, 239-40, 243; black, 98-109, 228, 236; yellow, 140-51, 228, 237; red, 170-79, 228, 234, 237
Pyrrhus, 76
Pythagoras, 136, 186
Python, 68

queen and king, *passim*
Queen of Heaven, 206-7, 231
Quinta essentia, see Thurneisser zum Thurn, Leonhart
quintessence, 19, 188, 199-200, 202, 241, 243

Rabbi Simon ben Jochai, 197
rainbow, 153, 234
Rank, Otto, 12, 37, 66-67, 69, 75, 81, 215, 218, 220
raven, 102, 146-47; raven's head, 98, 105, 108-9, 114-15, 186
Raymundus, 144, 152
reaction formation, 43
Read, John 216
rebirth, 12; earthly (first coniunctio), 80-97; lunar (second coniunctio), 130-39; solar (third coniunctio), 162-69; heavenly (fourth coniunctio), 182-211; in adulthood, 96, 228; in middle age, 131-32, 228; in late middle age, 169, 228; in old age, 196-98, 207, 228; trauma of (first), 64-79; trauma of (second), 124-29; trauma of (third), 152-61; trauma of (fourth), 182-93
rebis, see hermaphrodite
Redlich, Frederick C., 221
regicide, 38, 54, 63, 66, 240
regression, 12, 21, 23, 27-29, 45, 57-58, 66, 69, 82, 96-97, 171, 181
REM-sleep, 83
repression, 43, 51, 53; primal, 67, 70, 96; removal of, 22-23
Respurs, P. M. von, 224
resurrection of the dead, 187
Reuchlin, Johann, 219
Reusner, Hieronymus, 44, 215, 220
Rhazes (or Rhasis), 40, 112, 218
Rhea, 89
ring, 81, 197
Ripley, George, 87, 109, 133-35, 142, 187, 199-200, 221-22
Robert of Chester, 6
Romulus and Remus, 56
Rorschach test, 10
Rosarium philosophorum, 13, 15, 19, 24, 34, 40, 64, 66, 69, 72, 77, 80-81, 98, 102, 104, 106, 108, 110-12, 116-18, 120, 122, 124-25, 128-31, 133, 136, 139-40, 142, 144-45, 148, 152-54, 158, 162-63, 170, 172, 175, 182-83, 188-89, 194, 198, 205, 230, 232-33
Rosarius, 24, 130
rose, 24, 26, 34, 64, 100; garden, 72, 160-61, 176-79, 196, 201-2; *rosa mystica*, 12, 34, 165
Rosinus, 100, 124, 178, 208, 217; *see also* Zosimos
Roth-Scholz, Friedrich, 215
Roy, Jacques le, 220
rubedo, 14, 170-214, 243
Ruland(us), Martin, 11, 120, 125-26, 222
Ruska, Julius Ferdinand, 216-17, 222, 225

Sabor, C. F. von, 216
sadism, 33, 40-41, 51, 73
Sagittarius the Archer, 52, 121, 135, 157, 242
Saint-Phalle, Niki de, 51, 219

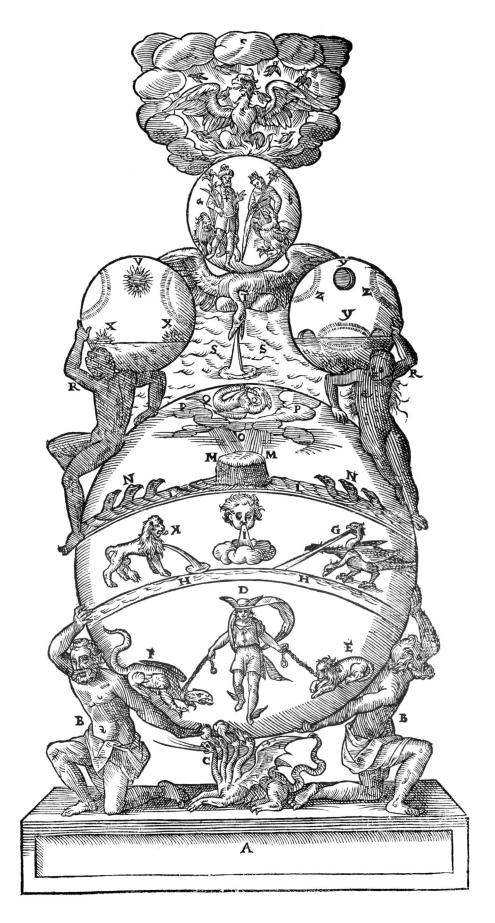

A. Libavius: Alchymia, 1606, Commentarium, part II, p.55.